Chaucer's Biblical Poetics

Chaucer's Biblical Poetics

Lawrence Besserman

UNIVERSITY OF OKLAHOMA PRESS
NORMAN

Also by Lawrence Besserman

The Legend of Job in the Middle Ages (Cambridge, Mass., and London, 1979)
Chaucer and the Bible: A Critical Review of Research, Indexes, and Bibliography (New York and London, 1988)
(gen. ed.) *An Anthology of Medieval Literature* (Tel Aviv, 1991) (in Hebrew)
(ed.) *The Challenge of Periodization: Old Paradigms and New Perspectives* (New York and London, 1996)

Library of Congress Cataloging-in-Publication Data

Besserman, Lawrence L., 1945–
  Chaucer's biblical poetics / by Lawrence Besserman.
    p.   cm.
  Includes bibliographical references and index.
  1. Chaucer, Geoffrey, d. 1400—Religion.   2. Bible—Criticism, interpretation, etc.—History—Middle Ages, 600–1500.
  3. Chaucer, Geoffrey, d. 1400.   Canterbury tales.   4. Bible— In literature.   5. Rhetoric, Medieval.   I. Title.
  PR1933.R4B48   1998
  821'.1—dc21   98-13350
  ISBN 0-8061-3067-9 (cloth   CIP
  ISBN 0-8061-3068-7 (paper)

1 2 3 4 5 6 7 8 9 10

For Judy

Contents

Illustrations

Acknowledgments

This book is the fruit of almost twenty years of research on an intriguingly controversial aspect of Chaucer's poetry. I first began to think seriously about the special role of the Bible in Chaucer's poetry in 1977, when, as a visiting lecturer at the Hebrew University of Jerusalem, I taught a course on the *Canterbury Tales* to students whose ability to recognize Chaucer's biblical allusions (from at least one half of the Bible) was remarkably detailed. In the years that followed, I published several articles on individual works in which Chaucer's artistic goals in using the Bible seemed to be especially elusive and complex, but I decided that a full critical treatment of this aspect of his poetry would first require a comprehensive account of the biblical elements in all his extant works. In *Chaucer and the Bible* (Garland, 1988), I provided a bibliographic survey and review-essay on the study of Chaucer's uses of the Bible and an index of the biblical quotations and allusions in all of Chaucer's works. The present book, drawing to a large extent on the data compiled in the latter study, interprets the significance of the pervasive biblical diction, imagery, and themes in Chaucer's works in relation to the literary, social, and political contexts of late medieval biblical poetics.

Some of the material in this book originally appeared in essays that have been extensively revised for use in the present context. A collective word of thanks is due to the editors and publishers of the journals and books in which the original essays appeared (for details, see "Works Cited"). In chapter 2 and the conclusion, I draw on several paragraphs from *Chaucer and the Bible* and repeat part of the argument from "Augustine, Chaucer, and the Translation of Biblical Poetics." In chapters 4 and 5 I draw on "Chaucer and the Bible: The Case of the *Merchant's Tale*"; "Chaucer and the Bible: Parody and Authority in the *Pardoner's Tale*"; and "*Glosynge Is a*

Glorious Thyng: Chaucer's Biblical Exegesis." In chapter 6 I draw on "Biblical Exegesis, Typology, and the Imagination of Chaucer." Some of the material in chapters 2 and 6 was presented in lectures at the State University of New York at Buffalo, the Graduate Center of the City University of New York, Harvard University, New York University, the University of Nebraska at Lincoln, and the University of Notre Dame. For their invitations and or helpful comments on those lectures I want to thank Howard Adelson, Larry Benson, Gerald Bruns, Mary Carruthers, Margaret Cullinane, Alfred David, Robert Edwards, Dolores Frese, Robert Haller, Gerhart Joseph, Paul Olson, and Derek Pearsall. The comparison between Chaucer's and Gower's uses of the Bible in chapter 5 was presented as part of a paper on "Chaucer, Gower, and the Bible" delivered at the Modern Language Association of America convention in San Francisco, December 1991. My thanks to Robert Yeager for inviting me to participate in that session.

I am also pleased to thank the following scholars for answering specific bibliographical queries and providing other kinds of advice and assistance: Piero Boitani, Emily Budick, Susan Cavanaugh, Rémi Gounelle, Ralph Hanna, Anne Hudson, Richard Kieckhefer, Robert Lerner, Richard Newhauser, Lee Patterson, Robert Raymo, and Julian Wasserman. I owe thanks to Sanford Budick and Wolfgang Iser for inviting me to participate in a workshop on "Institutions of Interpretation" (1988–91) under the auspices of the Hebrew University's Center for Literary Studies. I am grateful to the two readers for the University of Oklahoma Press (one anonymous, the other Professor George Economou) who suggested a number of revisions that have improved the book. I want to thank two people on the staff of the University of Oklahoma Press, Kimberly Wiar, Senior Editor, and Alice K. Stanton, Associate Editor, for faithfully and skillfully shepherding the book from manuscript to print; I also wish to acknowledge the unfailingly scrupulous and sharp-eyed work of Larry Hamberlin, who copyedited the manuscript. My wife, Judith Besserman, read several drafts of the entire manuscript and helped improve and shorten the final one.

A collective word of thanks is also due to the librarians of the British Library, Bobst Library at New York University, Butler Library at Columbia University, the New York Public Library, the

Pierpont Morgan Library, and the Mount Scopus and Jewish National and Hebrew University libraries, where the research for this book was carried out. I would especially like to acknowledge the assistance provided by Ms. Aurelia Tambour, Interlibrary Loans Librarian at the Mount Scopus Library, Hebrew University. My grateful thanks also go to Leoni Mandel and Tirza Heidingsfeld, my research assistants, who hunted down articles or books in different libraries and efficiently handled related administrative tasks. The late Morton W. Bloomfield, my beloved teacher and friend, encouraged me to pursue the project and expressed his belief in its significance. I am deeply indebted to Morton for his interest and support of this and all my other academic undertakings; I only wish that I had worked more expeditiously, so that he could have seen the present book. I believe that it would please Morton to know that Caroline, his widow, has maintained an interest in my work. For me, as for many of Morton's students and colleagues, Caroline Bloomfield's cordial friendship and gracious hospitality are valued not only for themselves but as memorials of Morton's rich legacy.

My research during the period 1993–96 was supported by a grant from the Israel Science Foundation, administered by the Israel Academy of Sciences and Humanities.

Chaucer's Biblical Poetics

Introduction

I believe that the Bible alone is the answer to all our questions, and that we need only to ask repeatedly and a little humbly, in order to receive this answer. . . . Only if we will venture to enter into the words of the Bible, as though in them this God were speaking to us who loves us and does not will to leave us alone with our questions, only so shall we learn to rejoice in the Bible.

Dietrich Bonhoeffer, in a letter to Rüdiger Schleicher[1]

For most of Chaucer's English contemporaries—men and women, members of the religious establishment and secular people, commoners and aristocrats—the Bible was presumed to be the preeminent authority on all matters of human endeavor and concern. This presumption was, of course, a familiar feature of European culture throughout the Middle Ages.[2] In late fourteenth-century England, however, there were also vexed attempts by various factions to redefine the claims of biblical authority and to wield that authority in ways that the Church and other institutional powers considered contentious, if not heretical. A central argument of this book is that Chaucer's biblically suffused poetry reflects his response both to long-standing medieval truisms about the preeminence of biblical authority and to the late medieval and specifically English problematization of those truisms.

There are hundreds of diverse biblical allusions and quotations throughout Chaucer's works, especially in the *Canterbury Tales*.[3] Yet Chaucer's innovative literary uses of the Bible and the concomitant delight that he evinces in his poetic responses to the "literariness" of biblical narratives are aspects of his art that have not been generally acknowledged or adequately explored.[4] By analyzing and interpreting many of Chaucer's key biblical quotations and allusions,

I hope to validate my claim that Chaucer's poetry is engaged with a set of literary and philosophical themes and motifs that can be comprehended under the rubric of "medieval biblical poetics."

Chaucer's contribution to the shaping of late medieval biblical poetics is especially evident in those of his works that display a growing interest in what one critic has called "the largest questions of interpretation, in the reliability of text and textual tradition, and in the recovery of truth from the written word."[5] As I hope to demonstrate in this study, the complex and sometimes shockingly self-reflexive literary uses of the Bible in Chaucer's works constitute his creative response to what he and many of his contemporaries had come to regard as the diverse and correspondingly complex poetics of the Bible. Paying close attention to what Chaucer *does* with the Bible and biblical interpretation in his poetry, as well as to what he *says* about the Bible, not only enhances our understanding of his originality as a literary artist but also enables us to appreciate the important shift that his uses of the Bible mark within the broader context of fourteenth-century English culture.

In chapter 1, "The Bible and Late Medieval Literary Culture," I situate Chaucer's use of the Bible in the context of late medieval vernacular biblical poetics. I begin with a survey of the material resources for knowledge of the Bible in Chaucer's day: glossed and unglossed biblical manuscript formats; aids to Bible reading (gospel harmonies, concordances, *distinctiones*); biblical transla- tions and paraphrases; and works like the *Biblia pauperum, Bible moralisée*, and *Speculum humanae salvationis*, which blended selected portions of the sacred text with visual images. Finally, I consider Chaucer's literary appropriations of the Bible in relation to the biblically influenced writing of his contemporaries or near- contemporaries: European poets such as Dante, Petrarch, and Boccaccio; Chaucer's fellow Ricardian poets, Langland, Gower, and the *Gawain* poet; the contemporary vernacular biblical dramatists; and the school of late medieval English authors of works of biblically focused religious meditation and affective spirituality. Thinking about Chaucer's biblically suffused writing in relation to that of his European and English contemporaries highlights the importance of biblical poetics as a common if hitherto undervalued element in various domains of Ricardian culture; it also better enables us to appreciate Chaucer's surprisingly diverse appropriations of the Bible for secular literary purposes, discussed in subsequent chapters.

Chapter 2, "The Bible as Book, Metaphor, and Model for Secular Literature," treats the significance of Chaucer's many references to the Bible's existence as a book. I begin with a discussion of those passages in which Chaucer either speaks explicitly about the Bible as a book or in which he describes or imagines the Bible's physical presence. Next I consider Chaucer's metaphoric extrapolations of the image of the Bible as an authoritative book and their application to other books. I conclude by analyzing three crucial passages in the *Canterbury Tales* in which Chaucer explicitly links his own poetic practice to the Bible and biblical poetics. In these passages Chaucer defines his own secular poetics in terms that he derives from biblical precedents and from an aspect of Augustinian biblical poetics often neglected by modern critics.

Chapter 3, "Biblical Translation, Quotation, and Paraphrase," examines a number of passages, mainly in the *Tale of Melibee* and the *Parson's Tale*, in which Chaucer translated or closely paraphrased biblical verses. By comparing these passages with both their proximate intermediate and ultimate biblical sources, we find considerable evidence of Chaucer's extensive range of biblical knowledge. We also see how Chaucer went beyond his proximate intermediate sources, filling in their partial quotations and occasionally turning their thinnest allusions into substantial passages of paraphrase, translation, and sometimes even into miniature biblical narratives. In several instances, Chaucer's systematic changes and modifications of the biblical materials in his proximate sources are seen to reflect his views on controversial political and religious topics.

In Chapter 4, "Partial or Oblique Quotations and Allusions," I concentrate on Chaucer's frequent assignment of purposefully partial, oblique, or distorted biblical paraphrases and translations to his narrators and characters. The passages discussed in this chapter, all from the *Canterbury Tales*, show Chaucer's narrators and his characters as argumentative exegetes who use and often abuse biblical texts more or less explicitly, quoting from, alluding to, or interpreting the Bible more or less extensively in ways that provide a gloss to the fictional situations at hand. After treating selected passages from the *Summoner's* and *Pardoner's Tales*, I focus on the Wife of Bath's extensive use in her *Prologue* of partial quotations and oblique allusions from 1 Corinthians 7, Proverbs, and other biblical books. The chapter concludes with a discussion of the partial quotations and oblique allusions in the *Merchant's Tale.*

Chapter 5, "Biblical 'Glossing' and Poetic Meaning," focuses on the thematization in Chaucer's works of the widespread but contentious late medieval practice of biblical glossing. Glossing as a mode of biblical interpretation—what Chaucer calls *glosing*—is considered in the context of Chaucer's other frequent engagements with problems of interpretation, especially in the *Canterbury Tales.* Understanding the cultural context and assessing the various functions that *glosing* serves in Chaucer's poetics also entails a brief preliminary discussion of the origins and growth of biblical glossing and a brief look at the literary uses of biblical glossing among Chaucer's fellow Ricardian poets, Langland and Gower.

In chapter 6, "'Figura' and the Making of Vernacular Poetry," I assess the place of *figura* in Chaucer's poetics in two ways: first, by considering those explicit biblical or exegetical motifs ("types" or "figures") that Chaucer actually deploys in his works; and second, by looking at the frequently contentious figural interpretations of characters and motifs that critics have proposed. The survey in this chapter of explicit or putatively oblique figural allusions is focused on four of Chaucer's early dream visions, the *Book of the Duchess*, the *House of Fame*, the *Parliament of Fowls*, and the *Legend of Good Women*, and on two of the *Canterbury Tales*, the *Nun's Priest's Tale* and the *Pardoner's Tale.*

In my conclusion, I consider Chaucer's biblical poetics in relation to an earlier and generally discredited tradition of Chaucer criticism, a criticism that asserted the poet's putative links to the Reformation and assigned him two roles, the "Father of English Poetry" and the "Father of Modern Standard English." Here I argue on the basis of the evidence adduced in the preceding chapters that if Wyclif is undisputed claimant of the title "Father of the English Bible," then Chaucer may equally be considered one of the godparents. Surprisingly, a tendency to overlook the extent and significance of Chaucer's biblical poetics is already evident in the assertions of the poet's putative links to

Protestantism by writers in the Reformation. Looking in the wrong places, Reformation writers took little or no notice of Chaucer's substantial role in the vernacularization of scripture. Similarly, as a survey of recent feminist, new historicist, and other postmodern critical approaches to Chaucer shows, the tendency to overlook the massive presence of the Bible and biblical poetics in Chaucer's poetry continues.

The quote from Dietrich Bonhoeffer that serves as the epigraph to this introduction declares its author's faith in the Bible as a sufficient source of divine guidance. Of course Chaucer and his contemporaries also assumed that the Bible was divinely inspired, an expression of God's will for humankind to follow. And yet, as the various inscriptions of biblical diction, imagery, and narrative in Chaucer's works seem strongly to imply, Chaucer could not possibly have shared Bonhoeffer's strong Protestant faith—it was Wyclif's faith, and would be Luther's, too—in the Bible's ability to convey all that a Christian must know and do for his or her salvation. On the other hand, Chaucer also seems to have been troubled by the opposing view, which held that laymen were not competent to interpret the Bible for themselves—a view espoused as orthodoxy by leading fourteenth-century English and European churchmen. As we shall see, it was by depicting the clash of these views that Chaucer created some of his most intriguingly complex and profoundly engaging poetry.

CHAPTER 1

The Bible and Late Medieval Literary Culture

We tell them to each other in the evening, and they take place in Norway, Italy, Algeria, the Ukraine, and are simple and incomprehensible like the stories in the Bible. But are they not themselves stories of a new Bible?

Primo Levi, *Survival in Auschwitz*

It is often said that Saint Jerome's Latin translation of the Bible (c. 380–420), which would later come to be known as the "Vulgate," was the most popular book of the European Middle Ages.[1] But "popular" in what sense? Ample evidence suggests that the vast majority of people in the Middle Ages rarely if ever had access to either the Vulgate or any other Latin Bible; and furthermore—as Chaucer's Wycliffite contemporaries never ceased from acrimoniously protesting—only a small number of those who could read in the vernacular had access to translations of the Bible in any language, let alone English.[2] At the same time, however, in the cultural milieu of the sophisticated and highly literate original audience of Chaucer's poetry, the situation was entirely different. For Chaucer and the majority of his well-educated primary audience, Latin Bibles and Latin and vernacular aids to Bible reading (gospel harmonies, *distinctiones*, and concordances), works excerpted or otherwise closely derived from the Bible (the *Bible moralisée, Biblia pauperum,* and *Speculum humanae salvationis*), various complete or partial English and French translations and paraphrases of the Bible, and—most significantly for our present purposes—biblically inspired but original works of literature in the vernacular were all readily available and readily usable.[3]

I

Throughout the English Middle Ages, richly illuminated one-volume Latin Bibles ("pandects") and one-volume Gospel books were produced at the cost of extraordinary effort and enormous expense. Though they may have been intended for regular ceremonial or liturgical use, these masterpieces of manuscript and bookmaking art were clearly not made for sustained and repeated reading by individuals; rather, as George Henderson observes, they seem to have been perceived primarily as latter-day versions "of the divine sanctuary on earth"—books fittingly constructed and decorated to serve as habitations for the Word of God.[4] It is indeed a biblical manuscript of the latter type, a "book with lettre of gold" and with its "wordes al with gold ywriten," which Chaucer introduces in the *Second Nun's Tale* (VIII 202, 210)—that is, an illuminated Bible of the kind that was still being produced in Chaucer's time both for church use and private aristocratic ownership.[5]

At the same time, the need for what we might call more "user-friendly" Bibles was also being met. The catalogues of monastic and cathedral libraries frequently list complete multivolume Vulgate Bibles under the title *bibliotheca* or *bibliotheca sacra*, so named not only because of their size but also because they were felt to constitute in themselves, as Walter Cahn puts it, "a vast repository of wisdom, a library, a world."[6] Typically, a complete early twelfth-century *bibliotheca* was a set of four, five, or six volumes that might include, in addition to the text of the Old and New Testaments, various lists of liturgical readings and tables or calendars of festivals, Jerome's and other prefaces to the Bible (sixty-four in all!), brief prefatory summaries of individual books, Jerome's *Index nominorum hebraeorum*, and the "Eusebian Canons."[7]

From the latter part of the twelfth century and on into Chaucer's day, multivolume Latin Bibles came to include the composite commentary of the *Glossa ordinaria* (placed in the margins and also intercalated between the lines of the sacred text); and from the latter part of the fourteenth century, the commentary of Nicholas de Lyra became another standard feature.[8] It is important to bear in mind that despite the help that these reference tools afforded the learned medieval reader, the chapter divisions in these and other medieval Bibles were frequently erratic, and there were no typographically distinct and numbered verse divisions (an innovation that would come only in the mid-sixteenth century); looking something up in the Bible, and then finding it again later on, was therefore not as simple a procedure as it is today.[9] Still, Bibles with easily legible citations of standard patristic interpretations placed so conveniently close to the *verba Dei* themselves would have been an invaluable tool for those preachers, teachers, and serious students of Holy Writ who wanted to prepare a disputation or a sermon on a biblical text. These annotated Bibles provide physical evidence of how a scholarly late medieval reader and secular author like Chaucer would have encountered the orthodox and convenient but potentially dangerous proximity of the biblical text and its gloss—a proximity that sometimes resulted in a man-made gloss being incorporated into the divinely revealed text.[10] Though only a few biblical allusions in Chaucer's poetry reflect the direct influence of the *Glossa ordinaria*, and even fewer show his use of de Lyra's commentaries, there are nevertheless many passages throughout his works, and especially in the *Canterbury Tales*, in which the issue of proper and improper glossing provided Chaucer with poetic capital.[11]

In the first half of the thirteenth century, as the multivolume glossed Bible was becoming more widely distributed, so was an extremely compact one-volume unglossed Bible. As Laura Light explains, the creation of this compact Bible was made possible by two revolutionary innovations in book production at the University of Paris: the development of an "extremely thin, almost translucent parchment" and the adoption of "a minute, very compact gothic book hand," derived from the script used for the gloss in twelfth-century Bibles, for transcribing the text of the Bible itself.[12] Bibles in this new, thirteenth-century "pocket book" format were popular not solely on account of their portability. They were also sought after because of their "searchability," facilitated by the appended reference tools that miniaturization had made possible. These reference tools might include an *Index nominorum hebraeorum*, a gospel harmony, summaries of individual biblical books, a list of the Epistles and Gospels for the Mass, a list of sermon themes arranged according to the liturgical year, a topical concordance, and a list of some sixty topics to help prevent heresy.[13]

A one-volume pocket Bible, conveniently formatted and equipped with all of the latter accessories, would have been especially useful for Dominican or Franciscan preachers.[14] Whether the pocket Bible was originally developed to serve the preaching needs of the friars or the study and research needs of the university community, its use for these and other purposes (liturgical, devotional, professional or amateur reading and study) spread rapidly among preachers, students, professors, and "upper levels of the laity and clergy" alike.[15] Its immediate uses notwithstanding, as Light points out, this new biblical format "marks the beginning of a new era in the history of the medieval Vulgate"; for it was only with the appearance of the pocket Bible, from around the year 1230 and thereafter, "that the Bible which we so take for granted today, the individually owned volume containing the complete Old and New Testaments in a modest format, appears in significant numbers."[16] Multivolume large Bibles and more compact standard-size single- or two-volume Bibles were still being copied in the thirteenth century, but the newly developed one-volume "pocket" Bible rapidly gained wide popularity.[17]

Only a relatively small number of people owned Latin pocket Bibles.[18] And even though the format was new, pocket Bibles continued to have the same wide variations of chapter division found in older and larger biblical formats.[19] Similarly, the new miniaturized biblical manuscripts also shared the frequent textual variations so common among earlier and larger Vulgate Bibles.[20] Indeed, as the pocket Bible caught on and spread, so did the problem of textual variants. Approximately a century after the pocket Bible came into use, Nicholas de Lyra could still lament that "the literal sense" of the Bible, "which is the foundation, seems in these modern times to be much obscured; partly through the fault of scribes"; and some sixty-five years later, the author of the General Prologue to the Wycliffite Bible (writing around 1395) could still point to the existence of "ful many bibles in Latyn ful false" as a justification for the Wycliffite project of translating "the bible out of Latyn into English."[21]

In addition to pocket Bibles, other Latin Bibles produced in the thirteenth and fourteenth centuries were generally more compact and also more readily available than in previous periods. Chaucer might well have owned a Latin Bible in the popular "pocket" format. In the late 1380s and 1390s, however, when he was in his forties and fifties and at work on *Troilus* and the most thoroughly biblical among his *Canterbury Tales*, a slightly larger format—an octavo Bible like Harley 2807 or Harley 2814, for example—would have been easier on his eyesight.[22] If we assume for the moment that Chaucer did own such a Bible, and if we imagine him reading it regularly to reinforce and expand his knowledge of what the liturgy, sermons, proverbs, and other intermediate sources had taught him about the Bible and its diction, imagery, and narrative content, then the extensive and varied biblical references in his poetry are easier to explain.[23]

Chaucer's biblical references are even easier to account for if we assume that in addition to the convenience of a compact one-volume Vulgate Bible, he made use of any or all of three invaluable Bible-reading aids that were spreading throughout Europe in the thirteenth and fourteenth centuries: gospel harmonies, *distinctiones*, and concordances. Gospel harmonies in Latin, French, and English were "second-order" biblical works in which details from the story of Jesus' birth, ministry, and death in the four Gospels were woven together into a single and coherent "masterplot."[24] Located both theoretically and sometimes also physically on the borders of the canonical books of the Bible,[25] gospel harmonies presented a significant portion of the New Testament in a form with which Chaucer and his literate contemporaries would have been familiar. Indeed, when Chaucer adverts to the problem of discrepancies between various gospel accounts of the Passion in the link between his tales of *Sir Thopas* and *Melibee* (VII 936–52), he relates that problem to what he claims is the parallel one of possible discrepancies between his own *Tale of Melibee* and its source. Though the brief but significant observations in the *Thopas-Melibee* link do not tell us whether or not Chaucer owned either a separate manuscript of a gospel harmony or a Bible that included one among its supplementary materials, the passage does reflect Chaucer's keen critical awareness of how works like Clement of Llanthony's *Unum ex quattuor* inevitably problematized the claim of univocal biblical authority that they were trying to support.

Another auxiliary and second-order source of biblical knowledge available to Chaucer was the *distinctio*. A product of late twelfth-century Parisian university culture, the *distinctio* is a list of citations from all the passages in the Bible in which a specific thing or concept is mentioned. Alphabetized compilations of a number of such lists, *distinctiones*, were reference works of variable length and complexity that students of theology and preachers found especially useful; but their usefulness for any close reader of the Bible is also apparent.[26] Indeed, even if *distinctiones* were primarily intended for the use of preachers, university professors, and students, they also could provide a poet like Chaucer with a handy tool for integrating an array of biblical terms, motifs, and themes culled at a glance from a diversity of biblical texts.[27]

Like *distinctiones*, the alphabetical concordance was another new biblical finding tool that emanated from the Dominican School of Saint Jacques in thirteenth-century Paris and spread quickly throughout Europe and England.[28] As Mary and Richard Rouse point out: "By the 1340s, Thomas Waleys in his *Ars predicandi* takes it for granted that a preacher would have access to a concordance for preparing his sermons; the same is true of the later *Ars predicandi* of John of Chalons (ca. 1376[?])."[29] Like the Parisian pocket Bibles, biblical concordances dating from the latter half of the thirteenth century were also often small and portable volumes.[30] But whatever the format, for the medieval preacher or scholar—or scholarly poet—who needed to track down a biblical quotation, the biblical concordance was a revolutionary labor-saving invention.

Chaucer's conception of biblical narrative was also influenced by the illustrated compendia known as the *Bible moralisée*, the *Biblia pauperum*, and the *Speculum humanae salvationis*.[31] In the *Bible moralisée* the Latin text of the historical books in the Old Testament is accompanied by luxurious illustrations of allegorically matched Old and New Testament scenes and a marginal commentary in French. As both the prohibitive cost of its sumptuously produced manuscripts and its focus on moralized interpretations of biblical historical narratives suggest, the *Bible moralisée* was an art form skillfully crafted both to educate and to flatter those warfaring noblemen who were able and willing to pay an astronomical price.[32] In the far more widely distributed *Biblia pauperum*, full-page illustrations of biblical scenes are juxtaposed from across the Old Testament–New Testament divide, accompanied by a medley of biblical verses cited in Latin from the Old and New Testaments, with occasional apocryphal or legendary visual motifs—all arranged according to well-established patristic and later ecclesiastical patterns of typological biblical exegesis.[33]

In the *Speculum humanae salvationis*, produced in 1324, Latin biblical passages and illustrations of Old and New Testament events are juxtaposed in a narrative sequence that interlaces canonical and apocryphal story matter according to the same figural understanding of the Bible that motivated the creators of the *Biblia pauperum*. However, the *Speculum humanae salvationis* (which was translated into Dutch, French, German, and Czech, as well as Middle English) provides its audience with less visual imagery and a good deal more of the biblical text. Though the title *Biblia pauperum* ("Bible for the poor") might seem to suggest otherwise, the use of heavily abbreviated Latin in the latter work and in the *Speculum humanae salvationis* indicates that these compendia of typologically matched canonical and apocryphal biblical stories were initially meant for the use of learned friars or other clerics who were intending to instruct laymen who knew little or no Latin.[34] The *Biblia pauperum* and *Speculum humanae salvationis* begin from the Annunciation and conclude with the Apocalypse and Last Judgment, but they constantly dip back throughout the earlier stages of biblical history. Though their coverage of the Old and New Testaments is chronologically extensive, the *Biblia pauperum* and *Speculum humanae salvationis* present an allegorical understanding of selected highlights of the Bible—an ideologically driven reordering of selected texts with illustrations, not the text of the Bible itself. Despite their titles, works like the *Bible moralisée*, the *Biblia pauperum*, and the *Speculum humanae salvationis* were not really meant to be taken for actual "Bibles"; nor would it be likely for anyone to have regarded them as such. They were the equivalent of our modern-day editions of "selected highlights," or perhaps more like our illustrated "users' guides"—works that connected some of the better-known with the more recondite facts of biblical and apocryphal history in order to instruct the medieval reader or listener in the structure and meaning of the arc of salvation history that had been partially realized but whose full unfolding was still to come.

Though Chaucer often used biblical materials in sophisticated and highly original ways that went well beyond the allegorical and typological methods of interpretation employed in the *Bible moralisée*, the *Biblia pauperum*, and the *Speculum humanae salvationis*, we must be mindful that works like these informed a good deal of what might be called the "biblical thinking" of his age. Reading the Bible in Latin, French, or English would have prepared Chaucer's audience to perceive the poet's wide-ranging allusions to Old Testament subjects—to the binding of Isaac and the trials of Job in his depiction of the suffering of Griselda in the *Clerk's Tale*, to Genesis in his depiction of the anti-Paradise of January's garden and to the Song of Songs in his depiction of January's grotesque wooing of May in the *Merchant's Tale*, and to scores of other biblical scenes and images. But it was the audience's experience of the words and pictures in biblically derived compendia like the *Biblia pauperum* and *Speculum humanae salvationis* that would have conditioned their interpretation of these and other biblical allusions by Chaucer, just as it would have conditioned their interpretation of the biblical texts themselves.

II

In addition to direct knowledge of Latin and vernacular Bibles and the various aids to Bible reading, Chaucer and his audience would also have experienced the authoritative weight of the Bible through its pervasive presence in sermons, the liturgy, and ecclesiastically sponsored art.[35] Late medieval English people would have encountered the authoritative diction and imagery of the Bible—and the seemingly incontestable paradigms of religious and social practice that biblical diction and imagery conveyed—through various other cultural forms. We can safely assume, for example, that Chaucer and most members of his contemporary audience were familiar with some version of the idea that God had given mankind two revelations, in two "books," the Book of Nature and the Book of Scripture.[36] Though no character in Chaucer ever uses the expression "Book of Nature," his Criseyde does obliquely evoke the topos when she addresses an apostrophe to Jove, "auctour of nature" (*Troilus and Criseyde* 3.1016); similarly, in the *Franklin's Tale* the pagan Dorigen alludes to the same topos, even as she impiously questions it by doubting that there can possibly be a place within the natural order of "Eterne God" for "grisly feendly rokkes blake" (V 865–93). These two oblique evocations of the "Book of Nature," one of two poles in a fundamental dyad of medieval Christian metaphysics, occur in pagan settings and in the words of pagan heroines who are unable to claim full philosophical possession of the truth to which their words are pointing.

In comparison with the latter indirect and frustrated evocations of the "Book of Nature," Chaucer's allusions to the parallel topos of the "Book of Scripture" are unvexed. This is the case when his narrators or characters within his narratives introduce explicit appeals to the authority of biblical revelation with phrases like "the book seith" and "our book seith," or "the gospel seith" and "Cristes gospel seith," or simply "Christ seith," "book seith," or "gospel seith."[37] By contrast, Chaucer never uses the word *scripture* to refer to the Bible.[38] Rather, he uses *scripture* to refer to miscellaneous authoritative writings, documents, or inscriptions: unspecified books of astrological lore (*Knight's Tale* I 2044), an elided passage from Virgil's *Aeneid* (*Legend of Good Women* 1144–45), and either the written authority for a scene in the story of Troilus and Criseyde or the mottoes inscribed on the rings that Troilus and Criseyde exchange in that scene (*Troilus* 3.1366–69).[39]

III

The imbricated pagan and biblical texture of Chaucer's poetry begins to seem less puzzling when we consider that important thirteenth- and fourteenth-century ecclesiastical and secular authors alike had begun to employ biblical texts in highly original ways and to make audacious claims about the common literary norms and procedures that pagan, secular, and religious works were now held to have in common with the Bible and with one another.[40] In Italy this new view of the status of the Bible in relation to secular literature is evident in the writings of lesser Italian literary lights such as Giovanni del Virgilio and Albertino Mussato, as well as in the works of Dante, Petrarch, and Boccaccio.[41] Though scholars have repaid Chaucer's largely unacknowledged debt to Dante, Petrarch, and (especially) Boccaccio for helping to shape his ideas about poetry, they have yet to take into full account just how much those ideas about poetry were shaped by what Chaucer and his Italian predecessors all perceived to be the affinities between biblical and secular poetry and biblical and secular poetics.[42]

Of all the major European writers of the Middle Ages whose works Chaucer knew and frequently borrowed from or alluded to, there was none who had explored the intertextual relations of secular and sacred writing more fully than Dante. For example, in the early *Vita nuova* (1292–95) Dante employs a scribal metaphor that links him implicitly to Saint John the Evangelist, a biblical author-as-scribe, and he links his secular book of personal revelations to the sacred revelations of the Apocalypse.[43] Drawing on various biblical sources "to resolve a 'courtly' question of love," Dante also portrays Beatrice in the *Vita nuova*—as he would again in the *Commedia*—as "a Christ-like presence" (if not actually a "type" of Christ) who enables him to work out his conception of worldly love and its affiliations to Aristotelian, Stoic, and biblically derived ideas of Christian mystical truth.[44] In the *Convivio* (c. 1304–7) Dante drew an apparently clear distinction between what he as a poet was engaged in doing and what divinely inspired biblical authors and later writers on sacred subjects were doing—a distinction between the "allegory of the poets" and "the allegory of the theologians."[45] And yet, in a frequently quoted and much-discussed passage from his *Letter to Can Grande* (1317), Dante elides the difference between secular and biblical literature and explains the "polysemous" nature of his *Commedia* by comparing it point for point with the fourfold exegesis of Psalm 113(114):1–2.[46] After his audacious recommendation of fourfold biblical exegesis as a suitable hermeneutic for the *Commedia*, Dante returns to secular literary canons when he further explains the nature of his ambitious poem in terms of what Seneca, Terence, and Horace said about the differences between "comedy" and "tragedy."[47] But when it comes to defining the end or "final cause" of his fictional *Commedia*, Dante once again speaks about his poem in a manner that aligns it unmistakably with the Bible:

> The end of the whole and of the part could be multiple, that is, both immediate and ultimate. But, without going into details, it can be briefly stated that the end of the whole as of the part is to

remove those living in this life from the state of misery and to lead them to the state of happiness.[48]

In this explanation of the "end" or purpose of the *Commedia*, Dante in fact implies the absolute congruence of his secular narrative with the Bible, at least with respect to the "end" that each work seeks to achieve.[49]

Petrarch's response to the literary authority of the Bible was not as bold in theoretical conception or as poetically vivid and original in application as Dante's, but in one instance, at least, its importance for Chaucer was equally great. As I have argued elsewhere, Chaucer's *Clerk's Tale* can be read as a subtly textured and biblically suffused revisionary response to Petrarch's biblically underwritten but conventionally allegorical revision of Boccaccio's tale of Griselda in the *Decameron*.[50] Like Dante, Petrarch offered Chaucer yet another model for sounding out the affiliations of secular and biblical literary domains, and a model for exploring the relevance of the Bible for his career as a serious secular author.[51] In the *De otio religioso* (1347), as Hans Baron demonstrates, Petrarch gives "exhaustive testimony . . . about the gradual growth of his biblical interests."[52] At first, as Petrarch explains, because in his earlier education he had been under the tutelage of teachers "who ridiculed the Psalter of David and all the other books of sacred Scripture for being nothing but foolish fables" ["qui psalterium daviticum . . . et omnem divine textum pagine non aliter quam aniles fabulas irriderent"], he found that he was repelled by the "simplicity" and "insignificance" of the outward surface of the Bible.[53] But then he read Augustine's *Confessions*: "Thus, in the joyful company of the Holy Scriptures, I now move with awe in an area which I had previously despised, and everything, I find, is different from what I had presumed" ["Ita hoc pulcerrimo comitatu Scripturarum sacrarum fines quos ante despexeram venerabundus ingredior et invenio cuncta se aliter habere quam credideram"].[54] This change in Petrarch's attitude to the Bible induced him to add a number of biblical *Vitae* to the original Roman plan of the *De viris illustribus* and then to include all of the patriarchs and other biblical figures depicted in the *De viris* in a revised version of the *Trionfo della fama*.[55]

In a famous letter to his brother Gherardo, Petrarch is even more explicit in asserting the deep affinity between secular literature and the Bible.[56] He draws his brother's attention to the Bible's use of figurative language ("To call Christ now a lion, now a lamb, now a worm, what pray is that if not poetical?"), its use of allegory (exemplified in Christ's parables), of different poetic genres (such as the "heroic songs and other kinds" composed by Moses, Job, David, Solomon, and Jeremiah), and of meter (found in the Psalms)—all of which, Petrarch asserts, will support the conclusion that "one may almost say that theology actually is poetry, poetry concerning God"—a conclusion justifying the further inference that the Bible in fact provides a mandate, if not a model, for the creation of secular poetry.[57] Further evidence of Petrarch's view of the central importance of the Bible in mandating secular writing is found in his letter of 1341 to Giovanni Colonna (*Familiares* 6.2). Though Petrarch's main topic is pagan Roman history, and especially the history of the Republic, he begins the letter by singing the praises of "Christ's gospel . . . without which the more we have learnt, the more ignorant and wretched we shall be; to which as the highest citadel of truth all things must be referred; on which alone, as the firm foundation of sound learning, all human toil is built."[58]

Following in the footsteps of both Dante and Petrarch, Boccaccio cautiously observes in his *Life of Dante* (1351/1360) that even though the Bible is the product of the Holy Spirit and pagan poetry is the work of mere pre-Christian mortals, both sacred and secular writing use allegory (i.e., "veiled language") in ways that are essentially identical:

> the ancient poets have really followed, as far as possible for the human mind, in the steps of the Holy Spirit, who as we see in Holy Writ, revealed to future generations his deepest secrets through many mouths, causing them to speak in veiled language what he purposed to show unveiled, through works in due time.[59]

But in another well-known passage Boccaccio had already pressed the analogy between sacred and secular literature much further than either Dante or Petrarch had been willing to do, when he used it to defend the bawdiness of the stories in his *Decameron* (1349–51):

What books, what words, what letters, are more holy, more worthy, and more revered than those of the Holy Scriptures? And yet there are many who have perversely interpreted them and have dragged themselves and others down to eternal damnation because of this. Everything is, in itself, good for some determined goal, but badly used it can cause a good deal of harm; and I can say the same of my stories.[60]

And if Boccaccio says this when he is defending the bawdy stories included in the *Decameron*, later he will use virtually the same defense against possible detractors of his loftiest secular literary endeavor, the compendious Latin treatise on pagan myth entitled *De genealogia deorum* (c. 1350–71?):

There are the words of Holy Writ, clear, definite, charged with unalterable truth, though often thinly veiled in figurative language. Yet they are frequently distorted into as many meanings as there are readers. This makes me approach my own task with less misgiving.[61]

Boccaccio is apparently being ironic when he claims that his authorial misgivings are diminished when he observes that readers frequently distort the words of the Bible and come up with their own private and incorrect understanding of the "unalterable truth" of the Word of God. The observation might be just as likely to strike both authors and readers of secular literature as disabling rather than reassuring. But Boccaccio's link between the vulnerability of the Bible to misinterpretation and the similar vulnerability of his own compositions is crucial. For even if there was irony in Boccaccio's linkage of biblical and bawdy or pagan secular writing, the cumulative evidence of a perceived connection between secular and sacred writing in the literary culture of Boccaccio and other early Italian humanists is still overwhelming.

IV

Closer to home, Chaucer was surrounded by biblically focused modes of vernacular writing. In works like the Middle English *Ormulum* (c. 1200) and *Cursor mundi* (c. 1300), and in the three outstanding biblically based works known as *Pearl, Cleanness,* and *Patience* (all c. 1375?), English authors had striven to convey biblically defined lessons of right and wrong action in secular literary forms that they felt to be more trustworthy than those derived from the *Aeneid* or French Arthurian romances.[62] The lesson was the thing, and the Bible was the surest and most impressive source of edifying lessons to be found. Yet the imaginative appeal of secular literature was not to be entirely forsworn. Though both the *Ormulum* and *Cursor mundi* survey biblical history from Creation to Doomsday, neither is a close translation of the Bible; they both omit much narrative and nonnarrative biblical material, and they both include apocryphal and exegetical interpolations.[63] Similarly, Old Testament paraphrases such as the Middle English *Genesis and Exodus* (c. 1230), *Jacob and Joseph* (c. 1250), and *Joseph and Asenath* (c. 1400) not only elaborate upon their biblical sources with commentary and apocryphal additions but also display the same tendency to "medievalize" biblical settings, events, and characters evident in the treatment of classical subjects by contemporary secular romancers.[64] At the same time, a very thin line separates encyclopedic biblical poems such as the *Ormulum, Cursor mundi,* and other poetic renderings of discrete biblical narratives or linked sequences of biblical narratives from French and English vernacular translations of the Bible (excluding the Wycliffite versions). Indeed, the difference between the two kinds of biblical compositions does not seem always to have been strictly regarded. No conclusive evidence proves that Chaucer was directly influenced by any specific work from the large body of contemporary or near-contemporary vernacular biblical materials. Vernacular biblical paraphrases and translations, however, were prominent features of Chaucer's cultural milieu. When compared with these works, the artistry of Chaucer's most richly biblical works—and the artistry of the biblically centered works by his Ricardian contemporaries, Langland, the *Pearl* (or *Gawain*) poet, and Gower—stands out all the more sharply.[65]

To some extent, the freer literary use of the Bible by Chaucer and his fellow Ricardian poets must have been inspired by the contemporaneous flourishing of vernacular biblical drama. The popularity of vernacular plays on religious themes is hinted at in Chaucer's reference to the "pleyes of myracles" that the Wife of

Bath attends (*Wife of Bath's Prologue* III 558) and in the several references to contemporary biblical drama in the *Miller's Prologue* and *Tale* (I 3124, 3384, 3538–43). This new European literary genre was designed to enable its mass audience to experience the religious history of the world from the Fall of the Angels and Creation of Man to the Passion of Christ and the Last Judgment, following the outline of key events recorded in the Old and New Testaments and their apocryphal elaborations.[66] Vernacular biblical plays had clear and committedly didactic and affective religious purposes, but this did not prevent the authors, actors, and numerous other participants in the staging of the plays from doing their best to entertain as wide an audience as possible. Though fourteenth- and fifteenth-century English vernacular biblical drama was analogous to, and in part had its remote origins in, the institutionally approved liturgical rituals of the church, it had developed in ways that some orthodox and reform-minded critics considered to be dangerously secular, even profane.[67]

One source of the critics' concern was the wide disparity that frequently existed between canonical biblical history and the vernacular playwrights' free recreation of it. The disparity is consistently evident, for example, in the many plays that deal with the life of Christ. Here it is not the gospels but rather apocryphal traditions, and especially works of affective piety like the *Meditationes vitae Christi*, the *Vita Jesu Christi*, and Richard Rolle's mystical writings that shape diction, imagery, and action.[68] In the Towneley play of the *Crucifixion*, for example, in a scene that has only the slenderest biblical basis, the crudely sadistic antics of four *tortores* are set against the uncanny silence of a Christ who speaks for the first time only after the *tortores* have done their best to mortify him.[69] The scene is a far cry from the biblical verses that tell of two false witnesses and bystanders at the trial of Jesus before the High Priest Caiaphas who buffet and spit on Jesus (in Matthew 26:60, 67). The heightened pathos of the Towneley *Crucifixion*, in which Jesus's first speech is uttered from the cross and is addressed to "you pepyll that passe me by," implicates the spectator of the play in the story of Christ's Passion in a powerfully personal way.[70]

V

As we have seen, the vernacular biblical drama was influenced by Latin and English works of affective piety. Because they all took biblical themes as their subject, a clear line separating Ricardian religious poetry and the vernacular biblical drama from fourteenth-century devotional literature is hard to draw. Outstanding among the English authors of devotional works was Richard Rolle. A charismatic and controversial religious teacher, Rolle, as critics of medieval English literature were once fond of observing, became the dominant literary figure of the first half of the fourteenth century (ca. 1300–1349), just as Chaucer was to be the dominant literary figure of the second half of the century.[71] In both his English and his Latin writings, Rolle's quest for God was shaped, and his spiritual identity confirmed, in terms appropriated from the Bible, especially from Psalms and Canticles.[72]

In a study of the European religious milieu of fourteenth-century saints, Richard Kieckhefer observes that the works of Rolle and other fourteenth-century religious writers exemplify an increasing attention to the biblical account of the life of Christ, and especially to the Passion, which these writers treated with unprecedented authorial freedom and affective intensity.[73] Two biblically derived works that devote a disproportionate amount of space to the events of the Passion and that had a wide influence in their original Latin versions and in the many vernacular translations and adaptations they inspired are the pseudo-Bonaventuran *Meditationes vitae Christi* (c. 1300) and Ludolph of Saxony's *Vita Jesu Christi* (c. 1350).[74] Another biblically suffused work that treats various stories from the New Testament with a particular focus on Christ's Passion is Aelred of Rievaulx's *De institutione inclusarum* (c. 1160–62), a guide for anchoresses that achieved wide popularity throughout medieval England in both its Latin and English versions.[75] Like other works in the genre, Aelred's spiritual guide is a kind of Christian midrash, a combination of translation, paraphrase, and invented narrative expansions and homiletical and interpretive commentary on selected passages in the New Testament.[76]

Aelred revised and supplemented the text of the Bible in the *De institutione* so that pious readers and listeners could more easily become imaginatively involved in its biblically derived stories of salvation history, and especially in its stories from the life of Christ.[77] The Middle English version of Aelred's *De institutione* in the Vernon Manuscript is dated between 1382 and 1400—the period in which Chaucer is presumed to have written most of his extant poetry, including *Troilus and Criseyde* and the most abundantly biblical of the *Canterbury Tales*.[78] Two prose works roughly contemporary with Chaucer that display the same imaginative freedom in handling their biblical sources as the Middle English version of Aelred's *De institutione inclusarum* are the anonymous *Middle English Prose Complaint of Our Lady* (c. 1390?) and Nicholas Love's *Mirror of the Blessed Lyf of Jesu Christ* (c. 1410).[79] Focused on the Passion, the *Complaint of Our Lady* is narrated by the Virgin Mary, who speaks with great emotion not only about the crucifixion of her son, but about his trial, flagellation, and other events in the Passion narrative cycle that she says she witnessed—events in which according to the silence of the gospels she did not participate. Nicholas Love's *Mirror of the Blessed Lyf of Jesu Christ* is a somewhat free translation of the fourteenth-century pseudo-Bonaventuran *Speculum meditationis vitae Christi*; it too recounts the Passion narrative, but is embellished with fewer apocryphal additions than either the *De institutione* or the *Complaint of Our Lady*.[80]

Pondering the narrative gaps and filling in the frequently uncanny silences in the canonical Gospels, European dramatists and poets (influenced by long-standing apocryphal traditions) created a devotionally motivated and emotionally affective literature in which the actions and speeches of various characters in the gospel accounts of the Passion were fleshed out.[81] In the wake of a highly emotive and Passion-centered Franciscan spirituality, the Virgin Mary's disturbingly silent suffering became a focal point for literary responses to the Passion narratives. A new subgenre of religious lyric poetry, the "Planctus Mariae," was soon flourishing in Latin and in all the European vernaculars of the later Middle Ages, including Middle English.[82] These Marian laments are perhaps directly reflected in the strain of lyric pathos evident throughout Chaucer's poetry, especially in his frequent depictions of the pathetic careers of women and children: the sufferings of figures like Dido in the *House of Fame*, Criseyde in *Troilus and*

Criseyde, the string of love's martyrs in the *Legend of Good Women*, the martyred "litel clergeoun" of the *Prioress's Tale*, Ugolino's children in the *Monk's Tale*, Virginia in the *Physician's Tale*, Cecilia in the *Second Nun's Tale*, Constance in the *Man of Law's Tale*, Griselda in the *Clerk's Tale*, and Dorigen in the *Franklin's Tale*.

Chaucer's penchant for the "poetry of pathos" has recently become something of a critical commonplace.[83] Critics have observed that Chaucer creates melodramatic scenes that include lengthy and highly emotive speeches or narratorial apostrophes, frequently leading his readers back to the Bible—to the binding of Isaac, the sacrifice of Jephthah's daughter, the suffering of Job, Christ's Passion, and other biblical "type scenes" with archetypically emotive power—in order to induce an emotional state suited to the contemplation of the narrative fiction at hand. If an "An ABC," the *Man of Law's Tale*, the *Prioress's Tale*, and the *Second Nun's Tale* are Chaucer's most obviously affective religious works, they are by no means the only ones with strong affinities to the large body of contemporary biblically inspired Middle English prose, lyric, narrative, and dramatic religious art. Indeed, as Thomas Bestul has shown, even the *Parson's Tale*, an otherwise intellectually rigorous and single-mindedly didactic work that follows its similarly bland didactic sources, seems to have been modified by Chaucer and turned partly into an affective "meditacioun" through the addition of strikingly emotive descriptions of the Passion and Last Judgment.[84]

When Primo Levi asks (in the passage quoted as the epigraph to this chapter) if the "simple and incomprehensible" stories of the Holocaust that he records are "not themselves stories of a new Bible," the question is fraught with a grimly implicit irony. And when Boccaccio juxtaposes sacred and secular texts as he claims that "the ancient poets have really followed, as far as possible for the human mind, in the steps of the Holy Spirit," and then claims (even more audaciously) that miscellaneous misreadings of the Bible are validating precedents for his own bawdy vernacular narratives, the ironies involved may be less bloody than those evoked by his countryman Primo Levi some six hundred years later, but they are no less fraught with radical cultural implications. As we shall see in the following chapters, Chaucer's various uses of the Bible throughout his poetry suggest that he too had complex and radically innovative ideas about the relationship between secular and sacred writing and their alignment within the newly emerging English vernacular literary culture that he was helping to create.

CHAPTER 2

The Bible as Book, Metaphor, and Model
for Secular Literature

> . . . *the Redcrosse Knight him gave*
> *A booke, wherein his Saveours testament*
> *Was writ with golden letters rich and brave,*
> *A work of wondrous grace, and able soules to save.*

Spenser, *The Faerie Queene* 1.9.19.6–9

When Spenser's Redcrosse Knight gave Prince Arthur a soul-saving illuminated New Testament, he was reciprocating and also outdoing Arthur's gift of a "boxe of Diamond" containing a "few drops of liquor pure" to heal any physical wound. When Bibles enter Chaucer's fictional worlds, they sometimes also function as stage properties, either as books physically present and with a potentially soul-saving role to play in the story's action or as books whose offstage existence and powerfully salubrious potential is evoked. However, Bibles sometimes also appear in Chaucer's poetry as the vehicles of various metaphorical tenors, that is, as imaginative extensions of the idea of the Bible as a book. And even more surprisingly, the Bible sometimes serves as an exemplar invoked by the Chaucerian narrator in diverse contexts for guidance in his own literary practice. In all three cases, Chaucer's references to the Bible as a book play a significant role in defining the central concerns of the works in which they occur.

I

Chaucer's narrators and characters within his narratives frequently advert to the Bible's concrete existence in seemingly matter-of-fact ways, but the effect is often anything but matter of fact. At other times, his fictional speakers either assume or seek to throw off the Bible's authoritative figurative "weight." And sometimes they confront the two kinds of biblical "weightiness"— both its actual weighty "bookness" and its figurally unrivaled authoritative "weight"—at one and the same time.[1] Probably the most memorable instance of Chaucer's use of the Bible as a stage property is the "Britoun book, written with Evaungiles" in the *Man of Laws Tale* (II 666). The relevant details of the scene are as follows. An innocent heroine, named Constance, has been accused by a nameless villainous knight of murdering her patroness, the virtuous Hermengyld. The knight is himself guilty of the murder, committed in revenge on Constance for having rejected his advances; but he has planted circumstantial evidence that implicates Constance, and when the murder of Hermengyld is discovered he accuses Constance outright. King Alla of Northumbria, however, is filled with pity for the virtuous Constance, and so he orders an inquest at which the guilty accuser is made to swear an oath on "a book" (II 662–76).[2]

Chaucer's handling of this scene and the manner in which a "Britoun book, written with Evaungiles" functions in its formal legal proceedings can be instructively compared with the parallel scenes in his two known sources. In Nicholas Trevet's Anglo-Norman *Chronicle*, which was Chaucer's principal source for the *Man of Law's Tale*, it is the false knight himself, and not "Elda" (Chaucer's "King Alla"), who unwittingly initiates a trial by ordeal when he seizes a "liure des Euangeiles" (i.e., a Gospel book) from the hands of Lucius, the Bishop of Bangor, and swears a false oath. This act immediately leads to his unmasking as the murderer and his death by divine intervention.[3] Trevet also provides an additional detail from the history of this "liure des Euangeiles" when he tells us that it had been used by Constance and Hermengyld for their nightly religious devotions. In Gower's version, which Chaucer also seems to have consulted when he wrote the *Man of Law's Tale*, the false knight swears his oath on "a bok" at his own initiative, as in Trevet's *Chronicle*; but unlike both Trevet and Chaucer, Gower never explicitly states that the "bok" was a Bible (see *Confessio amantis* 2.868–73).[4]

In Chaucer's rendering of the scene, it is not the false knight who impulsively reaches for a Bible. Rather, it is King Alla—and it is significant that Alla is "*King* Alla" only in the *Man of Law's Tale*—

who initiates a judicial inquest in which the Bible is used in an oath-taking ceremony.[5] A second departure from both Trevet and Gower in Chaucer's version—and one that for our present purposes is especially noteworthy—is the suggestion that the "book" King Alla used was either a Celtic vernacular translation of the Gospels or a locally produced copy of the Gospels in Latin, as Chaucer's historicizing reference to a "Britoun book" implies.[6]

Whether it was a Latin or a vernacular Gospel book, the knight's false oath is immediately punished: a heavenly hand smites him "upon the nekke-boon" and his eyes "broste out of his face." This divine intervention is then followed by a rapid, biblically textured denouement. First, a mysterious voice from heaven, echoing phrases from Psalms 49[50]:19–22, proclaims Constance's innocence:

> . . . "Thou hast desclaundred, giltelees,
> The doghter of hooly chirche in heigh presence;
> Thus hastou doon, and yet I holde my pees!"
>
> (II 674–76)[7]

Then we are briefly told about the sentencing and execution of the perjured and now-eyeless murderer, the conversion of King Alla "and many another in that place" to Christianity, and, climactically, the marriage of Constance to her newly christened savior (III 677–93).

Chaucer's minor departures from his sources for the trial scene in the *Man of Law's Tale* all serve to establish a sense of social and political order different from that depicted in Trevet and Gower. Though the outcome of the story is the same in all three accounts, only Chaucer makes King Alla's active administration of justice and his ready reliance on the miraculous power of (vernacular?) Scripture the means by which the work of God's providential design is accomplished.[8] Chaucer, like the Wycliffites, was deeply concerned with the crucially related question of how the Bible and its authority could be put to use in deciding questions of religious, political, and social policy. Throughout this study we shall see that Chaucer's poetry frequently reflects a serious engagement with contentious contemporary social issues, including the overlapping and sometimes conflicting authorities of royal, baronial, and ecclesiastical forces, a conflict of authorities that Chaucer's Wycliffite contemporaries found to be especially troubling.[9]

More often, however, when Bibles are invoked or are physically present in Chaucer's poetry, the effects that they bring about are less sudden and less dramatically decisive. In the *Wife of Bath's Prologue*, for example, we learn that Jankin, the Wife's fifth husband, "wolde upon his Bible seke" for a certain "proverbe of Ecclesiaste" (III 650–51). Having found the antifeminist verse he was seeking—"Where he [i.e., 'Ecclesiaste'] comandeth and forbedeth faste ['strictly'] / Man shal nat suffre his wyf go roule [roll, wander] aboute" (III 652–53)—Jankin would then infuriate his wife by quoting it to her. As it happens, the verse in question is the antifeminist "wisdom" of Ecclesiasticus 25:34: "Give no issue to thy water, no, not a little; nor to a wicked woman liberty to gad abroad." But "Ecclesiaste" was ambiguous in Middle English. It could refer to either Ecclesiastes or Ecclesiasticus, or to either of the putative authors of those authoritative biblical books (Solomon and Jesus the son of Sirach, respectively), or, more generally, to any church official, ecclesiastic, or divine.[10]

Luckily for him, however, Jankin's Bible remains safely offstage. For when the Wife finally loses all patience with his antifeminist haranguing, she vandalizes one of his books by tearing out a leaf (III 635)—or was it three leaves (III 790)? The damaged book is what the Wife calls Jankin's "book of wikked wyves," an anthology of antifeminist lore that in fact included at least one canonical book of the Bible, "the parables of Salomon" (III 685, 679).[11]

II

Early in his career, when Chaucer read and translated the *Roman de la rose*, he encountered a startlingly vivid portrayal of the Bible as both a physically and metaphorically weighty object.[12] The Bible in question is, along with a "rasour sharp," one of two unusually placed accouterments in Jean de Meun's description of the figure he calls *Faus Semblant* (False Seeming). The relevant passage in the Middle English *Romaunt* reads as follows:

And Fals-Semblant saynt, je vous die, [girded]
Had, as it were for suche mister, [craft, occupation]
Don on the cope of a frer,
With chere symple and ful pytous;

Hys lokyng was not disdeynous,
Ne proude, but meke and ful pesyble.
About his necke he bare a byble.
And squierly forth gan he gon,
And, for to rest his lymmes upon,
He had of Treason a potente; [staff, crutch]
As he were feble, his way he wente.
But in his sleve he gan to thringe [thrust, press]
A rasour sharp and wel bytynge.

(lines 7406–18)[13]

The arch-hypocrite False Seeming, with a Bible on his chest and a razor up his sleeve, served as Chaucer's model for features of at least three characters in the *Canterbury Tales*: Friar Huberd in the *General Prologue*, Friar John in the *Summoner's Tale*, and the Pardoner—both in the *General Prologue* and as we come to know him more intimately in his *Prologue* and *Tale*. Like their French ancestor, all three of these corrupt English ecclesiastics brandish biblical authority as a weapon or tool for carrying out their deceptive practices.[14]

In the *General Prologue* we are told that Friar Huberd utters his "*In principio*" (the opening words of Genesis and the Gospel of John, perhaps recited as a good luck charm) in so "pleasant" a manner that even shoeless widows reward him with a donation of at least a farthing (I 253–55).[15] In the *Summoner's Tale* the despicably mercenary Friar John repeatedly calls attention to an absent and inaccessible Bible as he tries to gull the sickly but skeptical Thomas into giving him a donation. The Bible, he tells Thomas, provides the basis of the sermon he will outline for him, but in deference to Thomas's limited intelligence, he will gloss the biblical verses instead of quoting them (III 1788–92). In contrast to the unabashedly secular Physician of the *General Prologue*, whose "studie was but litel on the Bible" (I 438), Friar John claims to be intimately familiar with Holy Writ. The Bible, he asserts, is the source of his spiritual nourishment: "I am a man of litel sustenaunce; / My spirit hath his fostryng in the Bible" (III 1844–45). But when Friar John's financial interest is at stake, what he offers his auditor is a self-serving gloss in place of the nourishing but absent biblical text.[16]

The Pardoner's exploitation of the Bible is more extensively described. We are told that he carries a pillowcase packed with pseudo-artifacts of religion, including alleged relics from the life and times of Christ (I 685–706). We also learn that he excels at reading from the Bible in church services ("Wel koude he rede a lessoun or a storie" [I 709]). Later on in the pilgrimage, when it is the Pardoner's turn to tell a tale, he applies his whetted tongue to what he knows best. He delivers a masterly sermon peppered with references to specific biblical injunctions and biblical narratives that encourage his listeners to avoid avarice, swearing, gluttony, gambling, and other vices. In addition, he urges his gullible and presumably illiterate audience—an imaginary congregation before whom he pretends to be preaching—to check his references: "The hooly writ take I to my witnesse," "Looketh the Bible, and ther ye may it leere," "Redeth the Bible, and fynde it expresly" (VI 483, 578, 586). Together with their pervasive influence on the rest of his speech, the Pardoner's explicit pointers to the Bible's authority serve to underline the inaccessibility of the book itself, at least for the imaginary audience being addressed.[17] In etching the biblical facets of the Pardoner's portrait, Chaucer has abstracted the detail of the Bible about False Seeming's neck (where it hangs pre-sumably ready for use in preaching, but also suggests a symbolic weight and marker that punishes and betrays its bearer) and has refashioned it into the verbal habits of a speaker who has digested the Bible and compulsively "spits it out," as he says, in the form of "venym under hewe / Of hoolynesse" (VI 421–22).[18]

The ways in which Friar John and the Pardoner direct the eyes and ears of their audiences to a Bible that most presumably cannot read for themselves, and behind whose cover these corrupt eccle-siastical showmen operate by reading with a self-serving selectivity and self-enhancing exegetical bias, are both fascinating and chillingly malevolent to contemplate.[19] Their invocations of an absent Bible resemble the similar but far more benign allusions by Chauntecleer, the rooster in the *Nun's Priest's Tale*. Chauntecleer urges Bible reading when he tries to settle the ruffled feathers of his wife, Pertelote, and to convince her that dreams are truly pro-phetic: "I pray yow, looketh wel / In the olde testament, of Daniel" (VII 3127–28), "Reed eek of Joseph" (VII 3130), and "Looke of Egipte the kyng, daun Pharao" (VII 3133). Similarly, in an aside, the Nun's Priest himself urges Bible reading—"Redeth Ecclesiaste of flaterye" (VII 3329)—as a way for his audience to learn how to avoid succumbing to what the case of Chauntecleer proves may sometimes be the lethal effects of flattery.

III

Chaucer's metaphorical and figurative evocations of the Bible can sometimes be just as thematically charged as those instances in his works when the Bible is actually present, or when a character or narrator points to the Bible's physical presence offstage. Perhaps we should begin by discounting Chaucer's occasional use of the words "scripture" (*Legend of Good Women* 1144, *Boece* 1, pr.4.123 and 170, and *Troilus and Criseyde* 3.1355, 1369) and "scriptures" (*Knight's Tale* 2044) to mean "writing" or "written record," and—by metaphorical extension—"an authoritative text or document."[20] In the *Legend of Good Women* Chaucer uses "scripture" to refer to the *Aeneid* by Virgil, "oure autour" (1139). This use of the term reflects the idea that the Bible and pagan classics are parallel sources of authoritative knowledge, an idea that was shared by John of Salisbury and many other writers in the later Middle Ages. Similarly, "scriptures" in the *Knight's Tale* is a term used to refer to the geomantic signs of the planet Mars, but here the metaphoric extension foregrounds a clash between the competing authorities of a deplored pagan science and the normative, biblically underwritten Christian belief—a clash that the tale as a whole seems to be trying to reconcile.[21]

Occasionally, Chaucer's metaphoric extrapolations from the Bible as a book are more specific, as they involve characters or events that exist within its pages. Consider the metaphorical hyperbole in the following lines from the *Book of the Duchess*, spoken by the Black Knight, who is praising his deceased beloved, Blanche:

> To speke of godnesse, trewly she
> Had as moche debonairte
> As ever had Hester in the Bible,
> And more, yif more were possyble.

(lines 985–88)

Now the primary focus of the metaphor here is of course a biblical heroine, Esther, and not the Bible in which her story is told. Yet when the grieving Black Knight tactfully concedes that Blanche's *godnesse* and *debonairte* (graciousness) would surpass the biblical Esther's only if it were possible for anyone to surpass a biblical paragon, biblical authority is subtly if playfully being affirmed at the same time as it is being called into question.

Elsewhere in Chaucer's works, there are other hyperbolic comparisons of characters to biblical figures. These often display playful authorial irreverence and amusing incongruities that provide a telling contrast to the Black Knight's more delicate reference to Esther. Thus in the *Legend of Good Women* Chaucer once again adduces Esther as a paragon of beauty, but this time the beautiful lady being praised is the pagan Alceste, who is said to surpass Esther, and two male biblical paragons of beauty, Absalom and Jonathan, as well:

> Hyd, Absolon, thy gilte tresses clere;
> Ester, ley thou thy meknesse al adown;
> Hyd, Jonathas, al thy frendly manere.

(F 249–51)

The linking of Alceste to Esther and Absalom will seem a bit less strange (or at least we shall better understand the conventions that underlie the strangeness) if we recall that Peter of Riga's *Aurora*—a work that Chaucer is known to have drawn upon— includes a description of the physical beauty of the Virgin Mary that is largely a revision of an earlier description of the beauty of Absalom. The effeminate beauty of Absalom as he is portrayed in the *Aurora* contributed not only to the *effictio* of Mary in the *Aurora* but also to the stylized portraits of other medieval religious and secular heroines—including, of course, Absalon in the *Miller's Tale*.[22]

The *Clerk's Tale* includes a parallel use of a hyperbolic simile in which biblical and fictional characters are matched, allegedly to the disadvantage of the former. In this case, however, the point of comparison is not physical beauty, and the conclusion drawn from the comparison reaches out beyond the fiction to an alleged truth about the world at large. For the Clerk claims that all women, and not only his heroine Griselda, surpass the patience exemplified by the biblical Job (IV 932–38).[23] In the *House of Fame* (1243–46) Chaucer's placement of the biblical Joab among famous pagan warriors and trumpeters—the Roman Messenus (Misenus, son of Aeolus) from Virgil's *Aeneid,* Thiodamas, the Argive augur from Statius's *Thebaid,* "and other mo"—is a more straightforward though by no means innocuous conjunction of biblical and pagan characters.[24] In the *Merchant's Tale* the Job sound-alike Joab appears once again paired with Thiodamas (IV 1719–20). But this time he is mentioned in a simile that ominously denigrates his and Thiodamas's trumpeting in comparison to the musical accompaniment at the wedding banquet of the ill-fated January and May.

In Book 3 of the *House of Fame* (lines 1320–40), Chaucer the visionary sees a large company of heralds and "pursuivants," each wearing a different heraldic crest. These criers of "ryche folkes laudes" are so numerous that Chaucer can't possibly describe all of their armorial markings. To express the fact of this inexpressibility, he turns the Bible into the massive vehicle of a metaphoric hyperbole:

> But noght nyl I, so mot y thryve,
> Ben aboute to dyscryve
> Alle these armes that ther weren,
> That they thus on her cotes beren,
> For hyt to me were impossible;
> Men myghte make of hem a bible
> Twenty foot thykke, as y trowe.
>
> (lines 1329–35)

Similarly, in the *Canon's Yeoman's Tale* the Bible is once again the vehicle of a metaphoric hyperbole, with the tenor of the metaphor this time being the inexpressibility of an alchemist's lexicon:

> Yet forgat I to maken rehersaille
> Of watres corosif, and of lymaille,
> And of bodies mollificacioun,
> And also of hire induracioun;
> Oilles, ablucions, and metal fusible,—
> To tellen al wolde passen any Bible

That owher is; wherfore, as for the best,
Of alle thise names now wol I me reste.

(VIII 852–59)

The latter two metaphorically "enormous" Bibles should remind
us that even in the age of the pocket Bible, large and heavy
pandects and multivolume Bibles were still to be found.[25] Furthermore, given the frequency of the use of the word "bible" in the
titles of lengthy medieval French works of moralization, the
Middle English term may also have carried an additional aura of
serious and exhaustively thorough social criticism.[26] For Chaucer
and his contemporaries, then, the metaphoric idea of a "Bible"
seems to have included not only extraordinary size and compre-
hensiveness but also serious social commentary. This makes
Chaucer's invocation of metaphoric "Bibles" to measure the number
of heralds in his vision in the *House of Fame* and to number an
alchemist's terms in the *Canon's Yeoman's Tale* seem all the more
purposefully absurd.

A more complex instance of the Bible's being used as one of the
terms in a hyperbolical comparison occurs in the *Wife of Bath's
Prologue.* In this case, however, the size of the Bible as a book is not
at issue. The Wife of Bath is speaking about her fifth husband,
Jankyn, who was wont to search his Bible for antifeminist ammu-
nition. The book in question is Jankin's anthology of secular and
ecclesiastical antifeminist texts, which she refers to—or quotes him
referring to—as a "book of wikked wives":

He hadde a book that gladly, nyght and day,
For his desport he wolde rede alway;   670
He cleped it Valerie and Theofraste,
At which book he lough alwey ful faste.
And eek ther was somtyme a clerk at Rome,
A cardinal, that highte Seint Jerome,
That made a book agayn Jovinian;   675
In which book eek ther was Tertulian,
Crisippus, Trotula, and Helowys,
That was abbesse nat fer fro Parys,
And eek the Parables of Salomon,
Ovides Art, and bookes many on,   680

And alle thise were bounden in o volume.
And every nyght and day was his custume,
Whan he hadde leyser and vacacioun
From other worldly occupacioun,
To reden on this book of wikked wyves.   685
He knew of hem mo legendes and lyves
Than been of goode wyves in the Bible.

(III 669–87)

The irony of the last two lines of the Wife's complaint is especially
sharp. As we shall see in chapter 4, the scarcity of unequivocally
"good" wives in the Bible and the further radical claim of Solomon
(in Ecclesiastes 7:29) that there are no good women at all, biblical
or otherwise, provided Chaucer with a running biblical joke. The
fact that Jankin's manuscript collection of antifeminist texts
appears to have included a copy of the biblical Book of Proverbs—
identified by the Wife of Bath by its standard medieval title, "the
Parables of Salomon" (line 679)—compounds the irony of the
biblical metaphor by clouding the issue of Jankin's biblically based
antifeminism. Proverbs is a biblical book that includes a large
number of antifeminist jibes (e.g., 19:13, 23:27-28, 27:15-16, 31:3,
etc.), but it is also the one book in which a famous ideal wife, the
"Mulier Fortis," is praised at some length (Proverbs 31:10–31).

Indeed, the Wife's charge that there is antifeminist slander in
the "Parables of Salomon" has led critics to two passages in the
Book of Proverbs that seem particularly relevant to her depiction
by Chaucer. The first is the description of a "loose woman" who
threatens the well-being of an unsuspecting young man whom the
speaker in Proverbs is trying to educate:

And behold a woman meeteth him in harlot's attire prepared to
deceive souls; talkative and wandering. / Not bearing to be
quiet, not able to abide still at home, / Now abroad, now in the
streets, now lying in wait near the corners. (7:10–12)

According to G. R. Owst, these biblical verses provided Chaucer
with a model for the talkative, restless, gaudily dressed, and sexually active Wife of Bath.[27] The second passage is the description of
the "Good Wife" or "Woman of Valor" in Proverbs 31:10–31.

According to James Boren, Chaucer fashioned the Wife of Bath as a parodic inversion of the ideal wife depicted in the latter passage.[28]

To begin unpacking the layers of irony in the Wife's complaint about Jankin's reading habits we need only be aware that given how the Wife contends with biblical antifeminism throughout her *Prologue*, and in view of how few "good wives" the Bible actually portrays, it seems more than likely that when she refers to "goode wyves in the Bible" she is not comparing something very great (the number of "wikked wives" in Jankin's book) to something only slightly less great (the number of "goode wyves" in the Bible), as we. might at first be inclined to think. Instead, she is comparing a very great number of antifeminist anecdotes, some scriptural and some not, with a very small number of scriptural stories about "goode wyves." Perhaps echoing Jankin's sarcastic terminology, the Wife refers to the stories and anecdotes about "wikked wyves" that have been read out to her by Jankin as "legendes" and "lyves," terms normally used to describe the lives of saints.[29] But as she goes on to say, all of these stories and anecdotes about women, unless they actually do deal with saints, are fundamentally untrustworthy:

> For trusteth wel, it is an impossible
> That any clerk wol speke good of wyves,
> But if it be of hooly seintes lyves,
> Ne of noon oother womman never the mo.

> (III 688–91)

The Wife's protest in these lines is thus aimed not only at Jankin but at all those "clerkly" authors who are responsible for authoritarian antifeminist texts. This includes, by implication, the divinely inspired authors of Scripture, also conceivably covered by the label "clerkes"—that is, all those male authors who are responsible for the scarcity of praiseworthy female figures in the Bible and in other authoritative texts, with an exception having been made only for those clerks who write the lives of female saints![30]

A final instance of Chaucer's variously original and audaciously literal or metaphorical uses of the Bible as a book occurs in the following passage from the *Parson's Tale*, in which Chaucer's Parson sets up a metaphorical equation that defends the Bible against any possible defilement that might result from its having treated a topic that the Parson finds particularly offensive. The Parson is speaking about "unnatural" forms of sexual intercourse, which constitute "the fifth species of lechery." He points out that even though this form of lechery represents an "abominable" vice about which "no man unnethe [scarcely] oghte speke ne write," it is nevertheless "openly reherced in holy writ" (X 910). How is it, then, that Holy Writ can speak of such unspeakable things? Before he proceeds to answer the question, the Parson himself takes the occasion to speak a bit more openly about the unspeakable sin of unnatural sexual intercourse that he has broached: "This cursednesse doon men and wommen in diverse entente [intention, aim, mind] and in diverse manere" (X 911). Only then does he proceed to explain why the Bible can treat of such things without becoming polluted: "but though that hooly writ speke of horrible synne, certes hooly writ may nat been defouled, namoore than the sonne that shyneth on the mixne [dunghill]" (X 911). As Siegfried Wenzel has shown, the probable source of the Parson's comparison of the Bible and its occasional mention of "horrible sin" to the sun shining on a dunghill is an anonymous Latin treatise on the Seven Deadly Sins that Wenzel refers to by its opening word, _Quoniam_.[31] The relevant line in _Quoniam_ reads: "Ibi dicit expositor Radulphus quod non vituperandus stilus Spiritus sancti etsi sordes scribat, sicut nec radius solis cum immunda illustrat" (In the same place the commentator Radulpdus says that the pen of the Holy Spirit is not befouled even when it writes of loathsome things, just as when the rays of the sun shine on a dunghill).[32] The idea that Scripture may treat of loathsome things without itself being diminished or defiled is a commonplace of medieval exegesis, but the expression of this idea by way of the sun-dunghill simile is not.[33] Though Chaucer may have picked the image up from Radulphus, he has made it his own.

According to the Parson, the Bible is an unequivocally privileged text, immune from pollution. Whether or not a secular text like the _Canterbury Tales_ might enjoy a similar immunity to pollution is not something that the Parson explicitly considers. We would hardly expect him to think so, nor would we even expect him to raise the question. Yet the way in which his claim about the Bible analogically provides justification for his own freedom as a preacher to "speke of horrible synne" is also worth mentioning, especially given the complicating fact that the Parson's prose treatise on sin, penitence, and confession is the thickly biblical final act in a work of fiction made up almost entirely of narratives in verse.[34]

IV

Questioning the status of the *Parson's Tale* within the framework of the *Canterbury Tales* points to a more general and much larger problem. How, if at all, are secular works of fiction and didactic works of religion, including the Bible, related? This question was very much of the moment for Chaucer, a secular poet who drew portraits of contemporary people who use the Bible in ways that the Parson would have considered highly inappropriate, if not "abominable," and who also drew comparisons between the *forma tractandi* (literary "mode of treatment") of the Bible and the *forma tractandi* of his own secular compositions.

In three crucial passages of the *Canterbury Tales*—*General Prologue* I 730–42, *Thopas-Melibee* VII 936–52, and *Retraction* X 1081–92— Chaucer speaks about the "bookness" of the Bible in direct relation to his own compositions. Though each passage treats a different aspect of the relationship between biblical and secular writing, they all advert to that relationship in ways that are particularly searching and provocatively self-reflexive. Among others things that they accomplish, these three passages link Chaucer with the tradition of clerical scriptural authority that the Wife of Bath challenges; they also reveal something quite unexpected and generally unacknowledged about what the Bible and biblical poetics meant to Chaucer in relation to his own literary endeavors. But before turning to the passages, we must first consider some important features of the system of medieval biblical poetics within which Chaucer was writing.

Our point of departure, because of its enormous influence on all medieval biblical poetics, is Augustine's *De doctrina christiana*. Though the following outline of the theory of biblical poetics that Augustine set out in the *De doctrina christiana* touches upon some familiar themes, it also affords an opportunity to consider aspects of Augustine's thinking about biblical and secular letters that are often overlooked.

Augustine's *De doctrina christiana* was begun in 396 and completed, after a long hiatus, in 427.[35] The work blends an impressively lucid and theoretically cogent explication of the allegorical approach to biblical exegesis with an equally lucid, succinct, and elegantly formulated Bible-centered rhetorical theory, a blend of exegetical and expository methodology that Augustine elaborated for the use of Christian teachers.[36] In the unlikely event that Chaucer did not know the *De doctrina christiana* firsthand, his knowledge of ideas derived from it must have been considerable.[37]

Chaucer would surely have known, for example, that at the heart of the *De doctrina christiana* is Augustine's definition of "charity" ("the motion of the soul toward the enjoyment of God for His own sake, and the enjoyment of one's self and of one's neighbor for the sake of God") and of its antithesis, "cupidity" ("a motion of the soul toward the enjoyment of one's self, one's neighbor, or any corporal thing for the sake of something other than God"), which together are said to constitute the Bible's univocal and omnipresent theme.[38] Yet even if everything in the Bible either teaches charity or condemns cupidity, Augustine admits that the means by which various biblical authors do so varies. Sometimes the lesson is taught literally and directly; at other times it is taught figuratively and obliquely. Distinguishing literal from figurative, Augustine had explained, "consists in this: that whatever appears in the divine Word that does not literally pertain to virtuous behavior or to the truth of faith you must take to be figurative."[39] This applies of course to any of the "almost shameful" passages in Scripture:

> Those things which seem almost shameful to the inexperienced, whether simply spoken or actually performed either by the person of God or by men whose sanctity is commended to us, are all figurative, and their secrets are to be removed as kernels from the husk as nourishment for charity.[40]

Furthermore, when we read the Bible we may produce an unlimited number of valid interpretations of its figurative language, as long as each of our interpretations yields a validation of the theme of charity or a condemnation of the theme of cupidity. This thematically univocal multivocity of valid interpretations of figurative or obscure statements in the Bible, says Augustine, was God's original intention when he inspired the Bible's human authors.[41]

Having accounted for the difficulty of figurative language in the Bible and having authorized the search for doctrinal "fruit" in the "chaff" of obscure biblical figures of speech, Augustine next addresses the problem of occasionally obscure literal biblical terms. That figurative happens to precede literal in Augustine's account is an apt reminder that in the Bible, as Augustine understood it, Christian has displaced Jew. Indeed, in both the Old and New Testaments the literal Jew is for Augustine a figure for the Christian to come, and Greek and Latin have priority over Hebrew in authority if not in time. Despite these displacements in his exposition, however, Augustine recommends that the order in which we are to apply our reading strategies to the Bible, after we have become familiar with "those things which are said openly in Scripture," is from literal to figurative:

> having become familiar with the language of the Divine Scriptures, we should turn to those obscure things which must be opened up and explained so that we may take examples from those things that are manifest to illuminate those things which are obscure.[42]

But when Augustine speaks about "things that are manifest," to which "language of the Divine Scriptures" is he referring?

In the answer that Augustine finally offers to this fundamental question we also find an explanation for the intriguing fact that the problem of the relative status of biblical languages has been minimized in the *De doctrina christiana* and its solution postponed until well into book 2, where it is introduced obliquely in the context of a continuing analysis of the problematics of literal and figurative expressions. Working back from figurative to literal, and after listing the forty-four canonical books of the Old Testament and the twenty-seven canonical books of the New Testament, Augustine finally explains how the literal language of the Bible is to be understood:

> Against unknown literal signs the sovereign remedy is a knowledge of languages. And Latin-speaking men, whom we have here undertaken to instruct, need two others for a knowledge of the

> Divine Scriptures, Hebrew and Greek, so that they may turn
> back to earlier exemplars if the infinite variety of Latin trans-
> lations gives rise to any doubts.[43]

When biblical obscurity is the result of a mistranslation from Greek
or Hebrew into Latin, Augustine says, one should consult the
original text and emend the Latin, not interpret it.[44] But in order
to do so, we need to get back behind the Latin. We begin, however,
among "the infinite variety of Latin translations," with the *Itala*,
which Augustine preferred over Jerome's Vulgate because it
followed its source, the Septuagint, "word for word."[45] By referring
to a "word for word" translation of this kind, Augustine argues,
"one may test the truth or falsity of those who have sought to
translate meanings as well as words."[46]

Augustine is unequivocal in affirming the superior status and
independent sufficiency of the Bible in relation to "the books of
the pagans":

> the knowledge collected from the books of the pagans, although
> some of it is useful, is also little as compared with that derived
> from Holy Scriptures. For whatever a man has learned elsewhere
> is censured there if harmful; if it is useful, it is found there. And
> although anyone may find everything which he has usefully
> learned elsewhere there, he will also find very abundantly things
> which are found nowhere else at all except as they are taught
> with the wonderful nobility and remarkable humility of the Holy
> Scriptures.[47]

Yet lest it seem that he meant to do away with all secular knowledge,
Augustine further asserts that even though the message of the Bible
is uniquely divine, its mode of expression is nevertheless identical in
kind to that of pagan literature. In order to extract the uniquely
"useful" biblical meaning that always teaches charity and condemns
cupidity, Augustine explains, the proficient reader of the Bible must
therefore become a competent literary critic, familiar with "all
those modes of expression which the grammarians designate with
the Greek word *tropes*."[48]

When Augustine resumed work on the *De doctrina christiana* at
paragraph 35 of book 3 (in the year 427, after a hiatus of some

thirty years), he proceeded to demonstrate the link that he had posited between the Bible and pagan literature through a series of rhetorical analyses of Old and New Testament passages, thereby proving that "eloquence" as traditionally defined in relation to pagan literature was a self-consciously and amply witnessed feature of biblical literature, too. Because Augustine had initially set the Bible and its plenitude of divine truth apart from and above all other writings, he is somewhat ambivalent about the blend of divine "wisdom" and everyday, pagan-style "eloquence" that his rhetorical analyses of biblical passages uncovered. However, in a concluding observation about the relationship between the two key terms of his rhetorical theory, he settles the matter once and for all by elevating wisdom (which for him of course means Christian "charity") over eloquence:

> What therefore is it to speak not only wisely but also eloquently except to employ sufficient words in the subdued style, splendid words in the moderate style, and vehement words in the grand style while the things spoken about are true and ought to be heard? But he who cannot do both should say wisely what he cannot say eloquently rather than say eloquently what he says foolishly.[49]

Immediately preceding this declaration, Augustine had moved effortlessly from rhetorical analysis of the letters of Saint Paul to an analysis of passages from the letters and treatises of Ambrose and Cyprian in order to demonstrate that the three levels of style (subdued, moderate, and grand) can be correlated to the three goals of the Christian rhetorician: to teach, to delight, and to persuade to righteous action.[50] Now, as the fourth and final book of the *De doctrina christiana* draws to a close, the rhetoric of the divinely inspired human authors of the Bible actually merges with the rhetoric of those ideal Christian rhetoriticians whom Augustine was trying to educate.

Whether or not Augustine succeeded in walking the thin line of finding human eloquence in the Bible without reducing the Bible to mere human eloquence, his approach to biblical poetics in the *De doctrina christiana* was of fundamental importance for later writers trying to understand the literary form and meaning of

Scripture and its relation to religious and secular writing alike. As is generally acknowledged, Augustine's bridging of the stylistic gap between various sacred and secular texts in the *De doctrina christiana* influenced the reception of the Bible in the West in a deep and lasting way, directly through the writings of such theologians as Cassiodorus, Rabanus Maurus, Hugh of Saint Victor, and Peter Lombard, and indirectly through the allegorical interpretation of such pagan authors as Virgil and Ovid, and through the poetry and theoretical writings of such Christian humanist authors as Dante, Petrarch, Boccaccio, and Chaucer.[51] Less often acknowledged, however, is the extent to which Augustine's complex and nuanced position in the *De doctrina christiana* was both preserved and, in different ways, also revised by these authors.

Augustine was once again to take up the question of the relationship between secular and biblical poetics in his *De consensu evangelistarum*, a work that had a similarly strong but much less often considered impact on the thinking of Christian authors throughout the Middle Ages and beyond. But before we consider this other crucial Augustinian text, let us begin to see how Chaucer addressed similar questions about the relationship between secular and biblical modes of storytelling.

V

In the *General Prologue* to the *Canterbury Tales*, Chaucer explicitly links his poetry with the Bible as he answers the anticipated criticism of a reader or listener—a hypothetical "querulous objector"[52]— who might take offense at the bawdiness of some of the stories that follow:

> For this ye knowen al so wel as I,   730
> Whoso shal telle a tale after a man,
> He moot reherce as ny as evere he kan
> Everich a word, if it be in his charge,
> Al speke he never so rudeliche and large, [Although he may
>   speak crudely and freely],
> Or ellis he moot telle his tale untrewe,   735
> Or feyne thyng, or fynde wordes newe.
> He may nat spare, althogh he were his brother;

He moot as wel seye o word as another.
Crist spak hymself ful brode in hooly writ,
And wel ye wot no vileynye is it.   740
Eek Plato seith, whoso kan hym rede,
The wordes moot be cosyn to the dede. [must; cousin]

(I 730–42)

Word-for-word fidelity to one's sources is defended on moral
grounds. To be faithfully literal is to be honest, whereas to change
the words of a story, even slightly, would make it "untrue."
Chaucer's faithful adherence to the possibly "rude" speech of his
characters is further authorized here by appeal to Christ and Plato.
The notion that words and deeds should be "cousins" (i.e., that
they should correspond), though attributed to the heavy artillery
of Plato, was a proverbial saying in Chaucer's day; the remark *whoso
kan hym rede* ("let anyone who can, read him [Plato] for himself")
underlines the jocularity of Chaucer's appeal to a Greek authority
whom neither he nor his audience could read in order to
underwrite the wisdom of a readily available proverb.[53] In
combining Plato and the Bible to authorize his defense of bawdy
language, Chaucer was probably following the lead of Jean de
Meun; but Chaucer omits Jean's philosophical and theological
defense of what is mistakenly called "bawdy" or "improper"
language.[54] Instead, he presses a further extraordinary comparison
between biblical and secular style: because Christ spoke *brode*
(openly, frankly?) in the Bible, Chaucer may do the same in
recounting the *Canterbury Tales.*
　But in what sense is a literary work comparable to Scripture?
　Does Chaucer mean to say—taking "Christ" in line 739 as
synonymous with God the author who "speaks" throughout the
entire Bible—that there are sufficient instances of sexually explicit
action and bawdy speech throughout the Bible to justify his own
use of sexually explicit action and bawdy speech? And is he
implying—as Dante and other medieval authors had not merely
implied about their own fictions but asserted outright—that
beyond the matter of style, the Bible and the *Canterbury Tales* are
congruent at the level of content as well, and that what is frivolous
or bawdy (or, in Augustine's terms, "shameful") in his poetry
should also be understood to contain a salvific core of meaning

below the surface?[55] And if Chaucer meant to imply that the laws of biblical style and hidden meanings apply to his bawdy tales, did he also mean to imply the corollary proposition, namely, that by following the exact words of a source one can recover the original intent of its author, as Augustine had said was the case with those biblical translations that were most likely to convey the original divine intent because they follow the original biblical texts "word for word"?

Or does Chaucer mean to say—taking "Christ" in line 739 as primarily referring to Jesus, the incarnate Son of God, who acts and speaks in the Gospels, rather than to God, who speaks through all the characters in the Bible—that Christ's speeches as reported in the *sermo humilis* style of the New Testament Evangelists are in some sense like the "rustic" or "bourgeois" speeches of the Miller, Reeve, Merchant, or Shipman as reported by Chaucer the Pilgrim-Poet?[56] Did Chaucer really think they were comparable? And was the comparison meant to justify Chaucer's stylistic procedure without reference to the very different contents of the Gospels and his own secular compositions?

Chaucer's ambiguous claim about Jesus's "brode" speech seems all the more radical when placed in juxtaposition with the more traditional view that Jesus's decorous manner of speech even when he was cursed and beaten was meant to teach us a lesson about how to speak, or not to speak. The latter traditional view of Christ's speech is in fact explicitly cited later in the *Canterbury Tales*, in Chaucer the Pilgrim's *Tale of Melibee*, when Prudence tries to convince her husband, Melibee, to moderate his response to the injuries his enemies have inflicted on him:

> ". . . ye owen to enclyne and bowe youre herte to take the pacience of oure Lord Jhesu Crist, as seith Seint Peter in his Epistles. / 'Jhesu Crist,' he seith, 'hath suffred for us and yeven ensample to every man to folwe and sewe hym; / for he dide nevere synne, ne nevere cam ther a vileyns word out of his mouth. / Whan men cursed hym, he cursed hem noght, and whan men betten hym, he manaced hem noght.'" (VII 1501–4)

To be sure, when Prudence loosely paraphrases 1 Peter 2:21–23, in which it is asserted that Christ never spoke "a vileyns word,"

Chaucer is closely following his proximate source, Renaud de Louens's *Le livre de Mellibee et Prudence*.[57] Prudence's biblically authorized assertion about Christ's speech nevertheless serves to highlight the very different and fundamentally opaque claim that Chaucer makes in the *General Prologue* when he describes Christ's speech as "brode" but also unquestionably free from "vileynye."

The indeterminacy of the latter assertion is further underwritten by the fact that in the passage where it occurs Chaucer avoids mentioning Augustine's universally acknowledged claim about the significance of everything in the Bible ("that whatever appears in the divine Word that does not literally pertain to virtuous behavior or to the truth of faith you must take to be figurative"), as well as by the fact that Chaucer has put the two meanings of "Christ" the speaker of "brode" words in play—Christ as author of the Bible and Christ as a character who acts and speaks in the Bible.[58] Though Augustine's analysis of the Bible's style and mode of signification in the *De doctrina christiana* equated biblical and secular poetics in most respects, he held back from endorsing secular poetic practice on this account. Instead, he extrapolated from biblical precedent to Christian rhetorical practice. It remained for later writers to take the next step. As A. J. Minnis points out, the humanist revival of the fourteenth century provided the intellectual climate in which "a writer could justify his own literary procedure or *forma tractandi* by appealing to a Scriptural model, without in any way offending against the great *auctoritas* of the Bible."[59]

Yet the convincingly demonstrated truth of the latter statement does not, of course, prove that a fourteenth-century poet who appeals to the precedent of a scriptural model to justify his or her own literary procedure will necessarily avoid "offending against the great *auctoritas* of the Bible"; nor for that matter does it prove that such a poet would even be concerned, necessarily, about avoiding doing so. For by reaching through the *modus loquendi* of the Evangelists to the *ipsissima verba* of Christ himself, Chaucer took a step beyond merely citing "the precedent of the *modus loquendi* . . . [of] the Four Evangelists who had recorded the life of Christ" to justify "his practice of speaking 'rudeliche and large' after the manner of the Canterbury pilgrims," as Minnis alleges.[60] By using the adverb *brode* in reference both to the diction of "Christ" as a character and to the *modus loquendi* of "Christ" as an author, Chaucer implied a number of things: that the Bible treats a wide range of subjects, some of which (as Augustine puts it) might "seem to be shameful"; that Jesus spoke humbly and "frankly," addressing simple people in a low style, using words suited to their experience of plowing, planting, reaping, and fishing; and that Jesus spoke "clearly," "openly," and "without restraint" when addressing those same simple people in what is at times the vocabulary of violence and venality, of lust, fornication, adultery, fire, sword, and woes everlasting.[61] Within this range of implication, the precise terms of the analogy between the Bible and Chaucer's own sometimes bawdy literary creations remain obscure. Chaucer does not specify which of the implied analogies is to be preferred, nor does he indicate which, if any, is out of bounds. If the magnitude of Chaucer's possible "offense" in drawing any of these analogies is hard to assess, the originality of his gesture of justifying bawdy language in a vernacular poem by invoking the example of Christ is plainly evident.

VI

In the second passage in the *Canterbury Tales* in which Chaucer explicitly invokes the Bible to explain and to justify his secular poetic practice, the analogy that he draws between the style and content of the Bible and the style and content of one of his own literary creations is even more complete. This time, however, the analogy is put forward in the introduction to a prose treatise, *The Tale of Melibee*, and we move from considering questions of diction (bawdy or otherwise) to the larger issues of narrative mode and truth content—to what formalist critics call the relationship of *fabula* (raw story matter) and *syuzhet* (the plot constructed out of the raw story matter).[62]

In the link between the interrupted tale of *Sir Thopas* and the *Tale of Melibee*, which Chaucer offers in its place, Harry Bailey objects to Chaucer's "drasty speche" in *Sir Thopas* and demands something better, either of "mirth" or of "doctrine," in verse or in prose. And Chaucer assents, "Gladly":

... by Goddes sweete pyne!
I wol yow telle a litel thyng in prose

That oghte liken yow, as I suppose,
Or elles, certes, ye been to daungerous [hard to please].
It is a moral tale vertuous,   940
Al be it told somtyme in sondry wyse
Of sondry folk, as I shal yow devyse.
 As thus: ye woot that every Evaungelist,
That telleth us the peyne of Jhesu Crist,
Ne seith nat alle thyng as his felawe dooth;   945
But nathelees hir sentence is al sooth [meaning],
And alle acorden as in hire sentence,
Al be ther in hir tellyng difference.
For somme of hem seyn moore, and somme seyn lesse,
Whan they his pitous passioun expresse—   950
I meene of Mark, Mathew, Luc, and John—
But doutelees hir sentence is al oon.

                                              (VII 936–52)

The *Tale of Melibee*, Chaucer asserts, is a "moral tale vertuous," even though—as with the Gospel narratives vis-à-vis one another—there may be some discrepancies of detail between Chaucer's version of *Melibee* and its source.[63]

This assertion must strike a reader as odd. To begin with, in the defense of a kind of photographic literalism in narrative that he had put forward in the *General Prologue* Chaucer had argued that the "morality" of a story depends upon its perfect fidelity to the words of its source rather than upon its subject and its mode of treatment. There, as we saw, Chaucer asserts that he is obliged to repeat "[e]verich a word" of the tales that were told on the pilgrimage (I 731–33). And Chaucer repeats the same argument, though feigning reluctance and claiming that he is under duress, immediately after recounting the stylistically elevated but severely abbreviated *Knight's Tale* and before beginning (ostensibly) to repeat (rather than actually to invent) the sometimes obscene language used by the Miller in the *Miller's Tale* (see I 3167–75).[64] Furthermore, Chaucer adds, those readers or listeners who object to the *Miller's Tale* and the other "cherles tales" should skip these and choose from among the many other tales that won't offend them. Now that he has warned us, the responsibility for any possible offense is, in any case, our own ("Blameth nat me if that ye chese amys," etc.; I 3176–85). Finally, Chaucer adds with a wink: "And eek men shal nat maken ernest of game" (I 3186).

The latter closing advice to the reader not to take seriously what is meant to be taken only in jest serves as Chaucer's extra insurance, in case we should read and be offended even after we have been warned to choose among the tales carefully. But the advice also undercuts Chaucer's ostensibly "earnest" prior claim that he must tell everything or else falsify his sources, as well as the claim that Plato and Christ had authorized his strict fidelity to the words of his sources—even his "churlish" sources. In the following passage from the introduction to *Melibee*, Chaucer explicitly revokes the call for word-for-word fidelity in narrative that he had issued earlier in relation to his potentially offensive tales:

> Therfore, lordynges alle, I yow biseche,
> If that yow thynke I varie as in my speche,
> As thus, though that I telle somwhat moore
> Of proverbes than ye han herd bifoore
> Comprehended in this litel tretys heere,
> To enforce with th'effect of my mateere [strengthen],
> And though I nat the same wordes seye
> As ye han herd, yet to yow alle I preye
> Blameth me nat; for, as in my sentence,
> Shul ye nowher fynden difference
> Fro the sentence of this tretys lyte [little treatise]
> After the which this murye tale I write.
>
> (VII 953–64)

As Chaucer had tried to deflect criticism in advance of telling potentially offensive tales such as those of the Miller and the Reeve by claiming that he was obliged to report these tales word for word, by declaring, furthermore, that the reader has been forewarned ("arette it nat my vileynye" [I 726]; "I moot reherce / Hir tales alle, be they bettre or werse" [I 3173–74]; 'Blameth nat me. . . . Avyseth yow, and put me out of blame" [I 3181, 3185]), and by asserting, finally, that these "offensive" tales were not meant to be taken seriously in the first place, so he now tries to deflect criticism in advance of telling the *Tale of Melibee* ("Therfore, lordynges alle, I yow biseche"; "blameth me nat") for the opposite reason. This time, Chaucer says, the narrative source has *not* been rendered verbatim (in "the same wordes . . . As ye han herd") but has been "enforced" (i.e., reinforced or strengthened) with "proverbs"; and yet, even so, its *sentence* (meaning) has been faithfully reproduced.

A further connection between these two contradictory defenses of narrative strategy is that even though they both adduce the Bible for support, they do so for opposing purposes. The irony is sharp, not to say daringly intense. Fidelity to different aspects of the literary precedent of the Gospels yields differing results. On the one hand, when the stress is on word-for-word fidelity to a source, the outcome is an impious, entertaining fabliau like the *Miller's Tale*. On the other hand, when the stress is on following the *sentence* or "essential meaning" of a source rather than its exact words, the outcome is a pious, edifying personification allegory like the *Tale of Melibee*.

For Chaucer and his contemporaries, the ultimate authority on the potentially problematic relationship between and among the various gospel narratives would once again have been Augustine, who had addressed the matter around the year 400—in a gap left open, as it were, by the still-to-be completed *De doctrina christiana*—in a work entitled *De consensu evangelistarum* ("On the Harmony of the Gospels").[65] The profound influence of Augustine's *De consensu evangelistarum* throughout the Middle Ages on narrative theory in general and on biblical poetics in particular has been routinely overlooked in favor of that of the *De doctrina christiana*. To see how Chaucer's defense of his handling of the source for the *Tale of Melibee* is related to the Augustinian defense of the sacred gospel narratives, we need to look into the *De consensu evangelistarum*.

There, in a series of remarkable passages, Augustine fully equates sacred and secular narratives as he defends the four often mutually contradictory Gospel accounts of the life of Christ against the charge that they might be "unreliable." Augustine explains that because God chose to reveal "the truth of the Gospel" through "temporal symbols, and by the tongues of men," it stands to reason that the four Gospels will differ in their details; but these differences in no way prove "that any one of the writers is giving an unreliable account":

Neither should we indulge such a supposition, although the order of the words may be varied; or although some words may be substituted in place of others . . . or although something may be left unsaid . . . or although, among other matters which . . . he decides on mentioning rather for the sake of the narrative, and in order to preserve the proper order of time, one of them may introduce something which he does not feel called upon to expound as a whole at length . . . or although, with the view of illustrating his meaning, and making it thoroughly clear, the person to whom authority is given to compose the narrative makes some additions of his own, not indeed in the subject-matter itself, but in the words by which it is expressed; or although, while retaining a perfectly reliable comprehension of the fact itself, he may not be entirely successful, however he may make that his aim, in calling to mind and reciting anew with the most literal accuracy the very words which he heard on the occasion.[66]

Responding to a problem in biblical narrative poetics, Augustine nervously balances divine intention against human execution, the "exalted height of authority" that axiomatically must underlie the Gospels, balanced against the fallible human recorder who "for the sake of the narrative" occasionally "makes some additions of his own" and may even fail to recall "with the most literal accuracy the very words which he heard on the occasion." Augustine then goes on to address a parallel problem in biblical poetics with profound consequences for the literary theory and practice of a Christian author such as Chaucer, and for the development of subsequent Western narrative theory and practice. After confirming (in passing) the central claim of the *De doctrina christiana* regarding literal and figurative meaning in the Bible (i.e., that God speaks in the Bible through "the instrumentality of temporal symbols and by the tongues of men"), Augustine implicitly equates the Bible and secular texts when he asserts that the gospels include material that has been put in "for the sake of the narrative."

One of the more notable instances of Augustine's attempt in the *De consensu evangelistarum* to deal with inconsistencies in the gospel narratives comes in his handling of the conflicting accounts of the Passion—the variously recounted incident in Christ's life which Chaucer specifically alludes to in the passage under discussion.[67] According to the Gospel of Luke (23:32–43), one of the two thieves crucified on either side of Christ "blasphemed him, saying: If thou be Christ, save thyself and us." The other thief asked Jesus, "Lord, remember me when thou shalt come into thy kingdom." Jesus replied: "Amen I say to thee, this day thou shalt be with me in paradise." As Augustine points out, however, there is a "discrepancy" between this account and the accounts of Matthew and Mark, both of whom report (as does Luke) that two thieves were crucified on either side of Jesus; but neither Matthew nor Mark says anything about one of the thieves being saved. They assert instead that the thieves joined "the chief priests, with the scribes and ancients" in mocking Jesus.[68] Yet if Luke's account is the true one, Augustine says, the accounts in Matthew and Mark are nevertheless also true. In fact, they are equally true. Indeed, Augustine asserts, they are all really identical in what they report about the Passion. To prove that this difficult proposition is the case, Augustine uses the following tortured logic: when Matthew and Mark said that "thieves" reproached Christ they were using the plural verb for the singular, "according to a familiar method of speech," thereby linking *one* of the thieves with those others looking on who were mocking Jesus, whereas the second thief, as Luke reports, neither mocked nor reproached Christ but repented and was saved.[69]

Throughout the *De consensu evangelistarum*, Augustine resolves the many similar inconsistencies among the Gospels by similarly distorting an obvious literal sense to suit his apologetic purposes.[70] The example of the conflicting biblical accounts of what happened to the thieves crucified with Christ is especially interesting to consider because the story had a lively afterlife in the apocrypha and later medieval literature and art. By the thirteenth century the names of the two thieves and their respective damnation and salvation were well established as widely held pseudo-biblical facts.[71] Though Chaucer does not mention the thieves in his allusion to the Passion in the *Sir Thopas–Melibee Link* (let alone refer to the apocryphal tradition in which they are named Dismas and Gesmas, the former saved and the latter damned), he does allude to the biblical episode of the crucified thieves in an original and humorous way earlier in the *Canterbury Tales*.

In the *Friar's Tale*, an old widow curses a corrupt summoner along with the "panne" he has been trying to extort from her, sending both the summoner and the pan to hell. The devil, who is about to carry the summoner off to hell in fulfillment of the widow's sincerely meant curse, reassures the corrupt and rapacious summoner that soon all of the questions he had been asking about the nature of fiends and their habitation will be answered:

> "Now, brother," quod the devel, "be nat wrooth;
> Thy body and this panne been myne by right.
> Thou shalt with me to helle yet tonyght.
> Where thou shalt knowen of oure privetee
> Moore than a maister of dyvynetee."
>
> (III 1634–38)

That these lines recall Christ's words to the repentant and believing crucified thief: "Amen I say to thee, this day thou shalt be with me in paradise" (Luke 23:43)—with "this day" changed into "tonyght" and the direction of the repentant thief's impending journey reversed from "in paradise" to "to helle"—renders their use in reference to the unrepentant, thieving summoner especially piquant. The fact that there are discrepant accounts in the Gospels concerning the fate of the thief with whom this summoner is associated adds additional point to the humor. Chaucer may well have believed, with Augustine and with the apocryphal tradition, that one of the two thieves was saved, as Luke says explicitly—even though Matthew and Mark make no mention of this, reporting instead that both thieves crucified alongside of Jesus "reproached him" or "reviled him." In the *Parson's Tale* the fact that one of the two thieves crucified alongside Jesus was saved is adduced by the Parson to encourage the reader not to despair, and Chaucer even makes the Parson quote the very same words from Luke 23:43 that he, Chaucer, had parodied earlier by placing them in the mouth of the fiend in the *Friar's Tale*: "'For sothe,' seyde Crist, 'I seye to thee, to-day shaltow been with me in paradys'" (X 702).

The allusions in the *Friar's Tale* and *Parson's Tale* make it reasonable to infer that Chaucer, like Augustine, had paused to ponder the discrepant gospel accounts of the fates of the two thieves crucified alongside of Jesus. Whether or not a religious and philosophically sophisticated poet like Chaucer was prone to theological speculations of the kind that occupied Augustine, it is clear that as a narrative artist Chaucer perceived the contradictions between the gospel accounts and perhaps even savored them, weighing their implications in aesthetic and strictly technical terms of narrative construction in a manner that Augustine would surely not have been willing to entertain.

VII

Yet drawing too sharp a distinction between Chaucer the narrative artist and Augustine the theologian in their responses to the question of gospel narrative inconsistencies would be a mistake. Augustine's attempt throughout the *De consensu evangelistarum* to explain variations among the Gospels went beyond theological harmonization and apologetics. For Augustine extends and extrapolates from his argument about biblical narrative modes in a most unexpected way. In an extraordinary passage enumerating ways that the Evangelists may "seem to err," Augustine boldly extrapolates from biblical narrative to a theory of narrative in general:

> when several parties happen to narrate the same circumstances, none of them can by any means be rightly charged with untruthfulness if he differs from the other only in such a way as can be defended on the ground of the antecedent example of the evangelists themselves. For as we are not at liberty either to suppose or to say that any one of the evangelists has stated what is false, so it will be apparent that any other writer is as little chargeable with untruth. . . . And just as it belongs to the highest morality to guard against all that is false, so ought we all the more to be ruled by an authority so eminent, to the effect that we should not suppose ourselves to come upon what must be false, when we find narratives of any writers differ from each other in the manner in which the records of the evangelists are proved to contain variations. At the same time, in what most seriously concerns the faithfulness of doctrinal teaching, we should also understand that it is not so much in mere words, as rather truth in the facts themselves, that is to be sought and embraced; for as to writers who do not employ precisely the same modes of statement, if they only do not present discrepancies with respect to the facts and the sentiments themselves, we accept them as holding the same position in veracity.[72]

Starting from the premise that all four Evangelists speak only what is true even when they appear to contradict one another, Augustine moves on to a most unexpected and momentous inference. Though he ends by distinguishing "truth in the facts themselves" from "mere words" in matters "of doctrinal teaching," along the way he has offered nothing less than a theoretical foundation— indeed, a kind of etiological foundation myth—for secular historical writing and secular narrative in general (the "narratives of any writers").

Augustine's preeminent position as a teacher of doctrine in the Catholic Middle Ages would have made his striking claim about the divinely supported position of the secular writer immediately palatable. Yet even if Chaucer was adapting this Augustinian idea, there is still something extraordinary in the way he has applied it.[73] For the self-importance and "seriousness" of the analogy Chaucer draws between the Gospels vis-à-vis one another and his *Tale of Melibee* vis-à-vis its French source is, by virtue of its sheer audacity, provocative of thoughts in precisely the opposite direction. That is, Chaucer's comical inflation of the *Tale of Melibee* by biblical analogy accords with the obvious additional deflationary comic touches in the link prior to the tale itself, as Chaucer returns from the lofty heights of authorial self-importance to his characteristically ironic and self-denigrating posture ("this litel tretys," "this murye tale"[VII 957, 964]), and reassumes his familiar role as the self-effacing and apologetic narrator of the previously interrupted *Tale of Sir Thopas.*

VIII

In the prose *Retraction* at the end of the *Canterbury Tales* (X 1081–92), Chaucer quotes the Bible and links it explicitly with his own compositions one last time:

Now preye I to hem alle that herkne this litel tretys or rede, that if ther be any thyng in it that liketh hem, that therof they thanken oure Lord Jhesu Crist, of whom procedeth al wit and al goodnesse, / And if ther be any thyng that displese hem, I preye hem also that they arette [attribute] it to the defaute of myn unkonnynge and nat to my wyl, that wolde ful fayn have seyd bettre if I hadde had konnynge. / For oure book seith, 'Al that is writen is writen for oure doctrine,' and that is myn entente. (X 1081-83)

In line 1083 Chaucer quotes Romans 15:4: "For what things soever were written, were written for our learning: that through patience and the comfort of the scriptures, we might have hope." Though lines 1081–83 refer to the *Parson's Tale*, they also hark back to previous tales. Earlier, with his tongue planted firmly in his cheek, Chaucer had referred to the lengthy *Tale of Melibee*, too, as a "litel tretys." And earlier still, in the *General Prologue*, he had asked us not to *arette* (attribute) his bawdy tales to his "vileynye" (I 726), and to forgive him for failing to observe decorum in depicting his fellow pilgrims because he has really done the best he could: "My wit is short, ye may wel understonde" (I 746). In addition, at the conclusion of the *Nun's Priest's Tale*, the Nun's Priest had also quoted from Romans 15:4, drawing an analogy between Paul's sacred text and his own secular fable of a cock and fox and encouraging his audience to search out the secular fable's deeper meaning:

"For Seint Paul seith that al that writen is,
To oure doctrine it is ywrite, ywis;
Taketh the fruyt, and lat the chaf be stille."

(VII 3441–43)

In the *Retraction*, where Chaucer makes his second and final reference to Romans 15:4, the referent of the biblical verse remains ultimately ambiguous. Its possible objects include: (1) Chaucer's own edifying *Parson's Tale*; (2) possibly some if not all of the other *Canterbury Tales*, and especially the *Nun's Priest's Tale*, where Paul's global claim regarding the doctrinal pith in all scriptural writings had been adduced explicitly by the Nun's Priest to validate a seemingly trivial piece of secular writing; and (3) as always, the edifying works of Scripture to which all, or some, or at the very least one of Chaucer's *Canterbury Tales* is being compared. Chaucer's second and final quotation from Paul's Epistle to the Romans thus reopens the question of how a privileged biblical text stands in relation to a secular text—a question that Chaucer had explored in the *General Prologue* and the *Sir Thopas–Melibee Link*—

even as the rest of the Retraction is purportedly seeking, once and for all, to close it.[74]

In the three passages from the *Canterbury Tales* that we have considered in this chapter, Chaucer speaks about the Bible in ways that reveal something quite unexpected about what the Bible meant to him in relation to his own literary endeavors. On the one hand, his claims about the relevance of biblical precedents for his poetic practice set him apart from characters like the Wife of Bath, the two summoners (one in the frame of the *Canterbury Tales* and the other in the *Friar's Tale*), the Pardoner, and the two friars (one in the frame of the *Canterbury Tales* and the other in the *Summoner's Tale*) who read and interpret the Bible in bad faith, misappropriating it—sometimes quite brazenly, and at other times quite subtly—as they try to avoid the sanctions that a good-faith reading of it would entail. On the other hand, however, these claims also set him apart from characters like the Prioress, the Second Nun, Prudence in the *Tale of Melibee*, and the Parson, all of whom advert to the Bible in conventionally pious ways that bespeak a conventionally pious view of the Bible's status as a textual nonpareil.

Chaucer's uses of the Bible in these three passages link him instead to a tradition of learned biblical interpretation in the Latin West that reaches as far back as Jerome and Augustine.[75] And beyond this exegetical tradition, the claims that Chaucer advances in these passages also link him to the divinely inspired authors of Scripture themselves—those very scriptural authors whose authority Chaucer's fictional preachers and exegetes frequently challenge. How and why Chaucer portrayed many of his characters as adepts of biblical translation, quotation, and interpretation, and portrayed himself as a writer whose literary practice is authorized by biblical precedent, are questions that I try to answer in the following chapters.

CHAPTER 3

Biblical Translation, Quotation, and Paraphrase

Ryȝtwysly quo con rede,
He loke on bok and be awayed.
(Let whoever can read righteously
Look to the Bible and be informed.)

Pearl 709–10

Scholars and critics routinely overlook the fact that Chaucer translated a large number of biblical verses into English. They therefore also tend to ignore the fact that Chaucer's biblical translations—whether he made them directly from the Vulgate, from a French Bible, or, as was most often the case, from his miscellaneous intermediate sources—are among the finest to appear before the great age of Reformation biblical translation.[1] Indeed, since W. Meredith Thompson's infrequently cited study of "Chaucer's Translation of the Bible" (1962), in which Chaucer's extensive biblical translation was surveyed and his unacknowledged but important place in the history of English biblical translation asserted, hardly anything more has been said on the subject. Though hundreds of notes and essays on the alleged thematic significance of various biblical quotations in Chaucer have since been written, these studies almost never consider Chaucer's technique as a translator.[2] A comprehensive study of Chaucer's methodology in his biblical translations therefore remains a desideratum of Chaucer scholarship; such a study would also fill a gap in the history of English Bible translation.

By analyzing some of Chaucer's biblical translations in relation both to their most likely intermediate sources and to their ultimate sources in the Bible, I hope to elucidate the specific function of these biblical translations in their immediate contexts. More generally, by concentrating on Chaucer's methods of translating the Bible and biblically saturated intermediate sources, I hope to shed further light on his attitude to the poetics of the Bible in relation to his own secular poetic enterprise.

<h2 style="text-align:center">I</h2>

Oaths and asseverations like "God my soule save," "God that made Adam," and so on, spoken by Pandarus, Harry Bailey, and other Chaucerian characters, are obviously mundane colloquialisms. But these seemingly innocuous expressions add vitality to Chaucer's rendering of dialogue and an authenticating tone of informality to his first-person narration. They therefore contribute to the design of his poetry by enhancing "the effect of the real."[3] Yet even if they are not quotations or paraphrases of specific verses in the Bible, these expressions would just as obviously have been recognized by Chaucer's audience as deriving from and echoing the language of that foundational text. When Chaucer places biblically allusive colloquialisms of this kind in contexts that can semantically rejuvenate their biblical origin and activate, or problematize, their religious authority, they may begin to function at another stylistic level—a level at which their otherwise transparent biblical diction and contextual meaning begin to carry weight and significance that their colloquial form and function ordinarily conceal. A few examples will help to clarify this point.

When Chaucer's narrator in the *Nun's Priest's Tale* takes the time to specify that the nearly fatal events in the story he is telling occurred in the month of March, "whan God first maked man" (VII 3188), he is setting the time of his tale and stating a commonplace medieval notion about when the Creation took place; but Chaucer may also be encouraging us to take a second look at the appositionally added biblical detail. This is how some critics respond to the Nun's Priest's allusion to the Creation of Man when they find in it a hint that a deeper meaning of the *Nun's Priest's Tale* lies in an implicit parallelism between Chauntecleer, Pertelote, and Reynard the Fox and Adam, Eve, and the Serpent.[4]

Another example of Chaucer's potentially evocative use of colloquially familiarized biblical diction occurs in the *Pardoner's Tale*. Concluding his sermon against cupidity, the Pardoner rebukes the sinful man who forgets God and Christ, "thy creatour, which that the wroghte / And with his precious herte-blood thee boghte" (VI 901–2). In the context of the Pardoner's biblically thick sermon diction, the colloquially familiar epithets in these lines might also be felt to evoke the authoritative force of their biblical origins, both in the Creation story (Gen. 1:26–27; 2:7, 21–22) and in the repeated explications of the Atonement in the Pauline Epistles (Rom. 5:9, 1 Cor. 6:20, Col. 1:20, etc.).

A related phenomenon is Chaucer's use of less commonly heard phrases or expressions whose ultimate biblical origins also prove to be surprisingly apt in their contexts. A striking example occurs in the pagan world of the *Knight's Tale*, where Palamon and Arcite both vie for the hand of an angelic Emily, Theseus's sister-in-law. After being released from prison and returning to Thebes, Arcite later returns in disguise to Athens and enters his beloved Emily's service as her page. The narrator says of the disguised Arcite: "Wel koude he hewen wode, and water bere" (I 1422). In its context, with the motif of a disguise that will later be exposed, it seems plausible that the expression "hewen wode, and water bere" was meant to recall the biblical story of the Gibeonites, who came in disguise to Joshua's camp and tricked him into signing a treaty but were eventually found out and were sentenced to "hewe trees and to bere watris" (Josh. 9:27).[5]

Similarly, when the nameless Old Man in the Second Nun's Tale orders Valerian, Saint Cecilia's husband, to "Sey ye or nay" (VIII 212), it seems reasonable to suspect that he is paraphrasing Jesus's injunction in Matthew 5:37: "But let your speech be yea, yea: no, no." Considering that this Old Man has miraculously appeared out of nowhere, is "clad in white clothes cleere," and carries "a book with lettre of golde in honde" from which he reads a gilt-lettered paraphrase of Ephesians 4:5–6, the likelihood that what sounds like a biblical expression in his speech was actually intended to be heard as such becomes very strong indeed. In a later scene in the *Second Nun's Tale* there is a similar example of a contextually evoked biblical allusion. When Cecilia, the heroine of the tale and saint-to-be, defiantly answers her interrogator, the Roman prefect Almachius, she tells him that the reason she is answering his questions in what seems to him to be a rude manner is because her answers come "Of conscience and of good feith unfeyned" (VIII

434). Though the words "conscience" and "unfeigned good faith" are both general and appropriate enough in their context to escape special notice, they acquire an additional level of meaning once we recognize that Cecilia is paraphrasing the martyred apostle Saint Paul, who wrote to Timothy about the importance of having "a good conscience, and an unfeigned faith" (1 Tim. 1:5).

II

Chaucer leaves no doubt about his wish to echo biblical language when he introduces quotations from the Bible with "For Seint Paul seith," "and Salomon seith," "as seith Jeremye," "as it is written in the seconde book of kynges," or the like. These and similar identifying tags appear before scores of the most obvious and indisputable instances of quotation or paraphrase of specific biblical passages throughout Chaucer's works, especially in the *Parson's Tale*.[6] The effect that Chaucer usually achieves with these labeled quotations— added to that produced by the hundreds of passages in which his narrators or characters within their narratives quote the Bible to support a claim or to illustrate a point without citing the source of their quotations—is that of a learned author self-consciously heightening the tonality and promoting the thematic seriousness of his own literary creations by adducing the authoritative weight of the *ipsissima verba* of Scripture. But sometimes Chaucer's biblical quotations occur in contexts where they contribute to stylistic and thematic effects that go well beyond (and sometimes even directly in opposition to) elevating the stylistic level of a speaker's discourse or providing a prooftext to support a didactic position.

Chaucer's characters occasionally quote biblical Latin tags that were impressed on their consciousness through repetition in the liturgy, expressions like *benedicite* (Dan. 3:57, etc.), *in principio* (Gen. 1:1; John 1:1), and *placebo* (Ps. 114[116]:19). The biblical context of *benedicite* is the canticle of Daniel 3:52–90, sung by Sidrach, Misach, and Abdenago, the three young men who survive being cast into a fiery furnace by Nabuchodonosor for refusing to bow down to an idol (Daniel 3:1). In this canticle, the word *benedicite* opens verses 57–73, 75–82, 84–88, and 90, and is repeated thirty times. For Chaucer's churchgoing audience, the proximate liturgical source of *benedicite* was the "Canticum iii. puerorum" recited at lauds between Psalms 66(67) and 148; the phrase *in principio*, from Genesis 1:1 and John 1:1, introduced the first lesson at matins for Septuagesima Sunday; and *placebo*, from Psalm 114(116):9, was the first word of the antiphon that began vespers for the Office of the Dead.[7] On the whole, these Latin words and phrases in Chaucer's poetry carry nothing like the pervasive stylistic and thematic weight borne by the more substantial quotations of Latin in the "macaronic sublime" of Langland's *Piers Plowman*.[8] But there are nevertheless a few instances in which even Chaucer's most seemingly trivial biblical Latin expressions can play a more than trivial role.

Take, for example, the case of "*benedicite(e)*." From its use in the liturgy, where it meant "let us bless (the Lord)," by Chaucer's day the Latin expression "benedicite" (also: "bendicite," "benediste," "bendiste," or even "benste") had long since been domesticated into English as a colloquial asseveration, roughly equivalent to "bless my soul!" or "my goodness!" or "by God!"[9] In a soliloquy by the pagan Theseus in the *Knight's Tale*, "benedicite" occurs in the context of mocking praise of Cupid's power to make people miserable by enslaving them to love:

"The god of love, a benedicite!
How myghty and how greet a lord is he!
Ayeyns his myght ther gayneth none obstacles. [avail]
He may be cleped a god for his myracles,
For he kan maken, at his owene gyse,
Of everich herte as that hym list divyse."

(I 1785–90)

Theseus's reason for sarcastically singing the praise of Cupid is that the pagan "god of love" has enslaved Palamon and Arcite and "[b]roght hem hyder [i.e., to exile in Athens] bothe for to dye" (I 1797). It is a small but pointed irony that Theseus should use the expression "benedicite"—originally uttered by the three young men in the Book of Daniel as they praised God for rescuing them from certain death in a fiery furnace—in circumstances where the expected outcome of Cupid's influence over Palamon and Arcite is death rather than deliverance.

There are similarly implicit but no less pointed ironies in at least three of Chaucer's other uses of the same biblically derived and liturgically familiarized oath of deliverance. The first occurs in the *Miller's Tale*, in the following tauntingly jocular speech by Gervays, the village smith:

> "What, Absolon! for Cristes sweete tree, [dear cross]
> Why rise ye so rathe? Ey, benedicitee! [early]
> What eyleth yow? Som gay gerl, God it woot,
> Hath broght yow thus upon the viritoot. [astir?]
> By Seinte Note, ye woot wel what I mene." [Saint Neot]
>
> (I 3767–71)

Gervays is addressing Absolon, the foppish clerk who has come to the village forge with revenge on his mind for having been rebuffed in a humiliating fashion by the carpenter's high-spirited wife, Alisoun. Absolon wants to borrow a hot poker, with which he will soon scald the buttocks of hende Nicholas, the too-clever clerk who will expose his buttocks in order to fart in fastidious Absolon's face.[10] The smith Gervays's "benedicitee," uttered as he stands before his flaming furnace, thus becomes uncannily and inappropriately evocative of the prayer uttered by the young men rescued from a fiery death in the Book of Daniel. Gervays's "benedicitee" may also have had an added pseudo-biblical resonance. Chaucer and many in his audience would have probably been familiar with the Christian legend according to which Noah had uttered an apotropaic "benedicite" in order to expel the Devil from the ark.[11]

The apocryphal tradition of Noah's "benedicite" against the Devil also enhances the slyly covert (in)appropriateness of the ineffective use of the same oath in the *Friar's Tale*, when a rapacious summoner queries the identity of a "feend" whose "dwellyng is in helle" and who will soon carry this summoner off, "body and soule," to eternal damnation:

> "A . . . benedicite! What say ye?
> I wende ye were a yeman trewely."
>
> (III 1456–57)

That a vicious summoner speaking to a devil casually tosses off a colloquial Latinism that means "Let us bless (the Lord)" is funny enough. That *benedicite* was sung in the Bible by pious young men upon their liberation from a furnace, a standard typological icon of Hell, makes the summoner's uttering of the same oath moments before he is about to descend eternally into "the furnace" funnier still—though perhaps with just a shade of the terror that all of this greedy summoner's blasphemous words and actions might have been expected to evoke. Finally, the audience of the *Friar's Tale* might have especially enjoyed the fact that unlike the magically effective *benedicite* that Noah aimed at the Devil, the summoner's utterance of the same charm has no impact at all—on either character.

A final example of a seemingly casual and transparent "benedicite" that is actually resonant with unexpected and this time more grimly topical thematic overtones occurs in the *Nun's Priest's Tale*:

> So hydous was the noyse—a, benedicitee!—
> Certes, he Jakke Straw and his meynee
> Ne made nevere shoutes half so shrille
> Whan that they wolden any Flemyng kille,
> As thilke day was maad upon the fox.
>
> (VII 3393–97)

The Nun's Priest's "a, benedicitee!" is spoken as an asseveration that emphasizes the "hideous shrillness" of the noise made by a mob of peasants and animals as they rush to rescue the rooster Chauntecleer, who, like the pious youths in Daniel, will escape from a seemingly certain death. But the oath also refers to the less impressive loudness of the imagined or remembered "shoutes" (the present commotion is twice as "shrille," the narrator avers) that were uttered by Jack Straw "and his meynee" when, in the course of the Peasants' Revolt, they rushed to kill the hapless Flemings, human victims whose shouts remain unheard. According to the hyperbolic application of the Nun's Priest's simile, the victims' shouts are doubly stifled, for they are implicitly drowned out both by the shouts of their killers as well as by the shouts of the peasants effecting the mock-heroic rescue of a chicken that the Nun's Priest is encouraging us to imagine. That some of this chicken's shouting peasant rescuers may have been among those shouting as killers with "Jakke Straw and his meynee" makes the Nun's Priest's "benedicite" doubly ironic.[12]

Chaucer's most shockingly literal and comically audacious uses of Latin biblical expressions are found in the *Summoner's Tale* and *Pardoner's Tale*, narrated by two of Chaucer's most cynical exploiters of the *verbum Dei* as an instrument of power. In the *Summoner's Tale* a paradigmatically corrupt friar, "frere John," tries to extract money from a bed-ridden peasant named Thomas. Friar John's appeal for a donation from Thomas includes a strategic attack on "possessioners," the property-owning monks who are among Friar John's rivals for Thomas's pecuniary favor:

> "Whan they [i.e., monks] for soules seye the psalm of Davit:
> Lo, 'buf!' they seye, '*cor meum eructavit!*'"
>
> (III 1933–34)

When monks use the biblical expression "Eructavit cor meum" ('My heart hath uttered [a good word, etc.]'; Psalm 44[45]:2[1])— Friar John sarcastically claims—they use the Latin verb *eructo, eructare* with an alternative and prior "literal" sense, meaning "to belch," rather than with the derived sense of the verb, meaning "to utter."[13] With his defamilarizing reading of a belch out of a biblical Latin expression, Friar John also manages to foreshadow the unlucky but poetically just outcome of his own extortionary effort, which ends in his receiving from Thomas the gift of a fart.

The Pardoner, a paradigmatically corrupt seller of indulgences and false relics, proposes a similar defamiliarization of biblical Latin. In deploring the vice of drunkenness, he suggests that a nasalized form of the name "Sampsoun" (first named in Judges 13:24) provides an onomatopoetic equivalent of the snorting sound made by a drunkard:[14]

> O dronke man, disfigured is thy face,
> Sour is thy breeth, foul artow to embrace,
> And thurgh thy dronke nose semeth the soun
> As though thou seydest ay "Sampsoun, Sampsoun!"
>
> (VI 551–54)

That the name of a teetotaling Nazirite biblical hero should convey the aural effects of overindulgence in wine is especially curious: "And yet, God woot, Sampsoun drank nevere no wyn" (VI 555).

Like the scatological humor at the expense of Absolon in the *Miller's Tale*, the crudely comic deformations of biblical Latin in the *Summoner's Tale* and the *Pardoner's Tale* bring the sacred Word of God down into the unloveliest regions of the creatural realm. All three of these comically "low" biblical allusions by Chaucer illustrate what Mikhail Bakhtin observes about parodic uses of the Bible in the Middle Ages in general: "Not a single saying of the Old and New Testaments was left unchallenged as long as it could provide some hint of equivocal suggestion that could be travestied and transposed into the language of the material bodily lower stratum."[15]

III

Chaucer's characters also cite more substantial samples of biblical Latin. In the *Pardoner's Prologue* (VI 334), for example, the Pardoner famously cites as the text for his sermon what appears to be a complete sentence of biblical Latin, *radix malorum est cupiditas* (1 Tim. 6:10). But the Latin version of that portion of the verse which the Pardoner is quoting actually reads: "Radix *enim omnium* malorum est cupiditas" (emphasis added). Though the Pardoner elsewhere proves himself to be especially adept at partial and distorted biblical quotations, in the present instance the disparity has a more innocent explanation. By eliminating the phrase "enim omnium" Chaucer has tapered the Latin saying to fit a decasyllable line. Metrical constraints also appear to have shaped the Pardoner's translation of a substantial passage from Philippians 3:18–19, in which Saint Paul warns members of the Church at Philippi against the fatal vice of gluttony. The biblical passage reads:

> For many walk of whom I have told you often (and now tell you weeping), that they are enemies of the cross of Christ; / Whose end is destruction; whose God is their belly.

The Pardoner's skillful translation reads:

Ther walken manye of whiche yow toold have I—
I seye it now wepyng, *with pitous voys*—
they been enemys of Cristes croys,
Of whiche the ende is deeth; wombe is hir god!

(VI 529–33)

With only minor differences of word order (biblical "I have told you," "cross of Christ," and "God is their belly" becoming the Pardoner's "yow toold have I," "Cristes croys," and "wombe is hir god"), the addition of "with pitous voys" (to make the rhyme with "croys"), omission of the biblical "often," and substitution of "Of whiche" for "whose," Chaucer has done a remarkable job of versifying his biblical source.[16]

Unhampered by the requirements of rhyme, Chaucer's Parson is even more faithful to his biblical model when he cites the same passage:

"Manye," seith Saint Paul, "goon, of whiche I have ofte seyd to yow, and now I seye it wepynge, that been the enemys of the croys of Crist; of whiche the ende is deeth, and of whiche hire wombe is hire god, and hire glorie in confusioun of hem that so savouren erthely thynges." (*Parson's Tale* X 820)

Except for a reversal of the order of the two nouns in the clause "of whiche hire wombe is hire god" (instead of Paul's "whose God is their belly"), the Parson's word order and syntax are closely modeled on the biblical Latin, which Chaucer presumably consulted to complete the abbreviated reference to "Phil. 3[:19] 'Quorum deus venter est,' etc." provided by his proximate source.[17]

In another passage in the *Pardoner's Tale*, the Pardoner makes the mysterious Old Man call explicit attention to the Bible as his source and then skillfully translate a biblical passage into verse:

In Hooly Writ ye may yourself wel rede:
"Agayns an oold man, hoor upon his heed,
Ye sholde arise."

(VI 742–44)

The biblical verse reads:

> Rise up before the hoary head, and honour the person of the
> aged man.(Lev. 19:32) (Vulgate: "Coram cano capite consurge,
> et honora personam senis.")

The Pardoner's principal modification of his biblical source is the
combination of the two parallel hemistichs of Leviticus 19:32 into a
single commandment, eliding the biblical phrase "and honour the
person" and subsuming the biblical commandment to "honour the
person of the aged man" into the parallel commandment to "rise
up before the hoary head"—a change that leaves the sense of the
original sufficiently intact to pass muster as a close biblical paraphrase, if not an exact translation.

A similar instance of close paraphrase within the constraints of
iambic pentameter verse occurs in the *Man of Law's Tale*:

> Ther dronkenesse regneth in any route,
> Ther is no conseil hyd, withouten doute.

> (II 776–77)

In these lines Chaucer translates the latter half of Proverbs 31:4:

> there is no secret where drunkenness reigneth.
> (Vulgate: "nullum secretum est ubi regnat ebrietas.")

Chaucer translates "ubi regnat ebrietas" literally: "Ther dronkenesse
regneth"; he closely paraphrases "nullum secretum" (nothing is
[kept] secret): "Ther is no conseil hyd"; and, in order to fit the
meter, he expands upon the biblical original by adding the
rhyming phrases "any route / . . . withouten doute." In the prose
Tale of Melibee, Chaucer has Dame Prudence translate the same
portion of Proverbs 31:4: "Ther is no privetee ther as regneth
dronkenesse" (VII 1194). In the *Livre de Mellibee et Prudence*,
Chaucer's proximate French source for the *Tale of Melibee*, the
Vulgate's "nullum secretum est ubi regnat ebrietas" is rendered a
bit more scrupulously: "Nul secret n'est la ou regne yvresse."[18]
Prudence's "Ther is no privetee" and the Man of Law's "Ther is no
conseil hyd" are less exact renditions of the Vulgate's "nullum

secretum est," but "privetee" and "conseil" each add a social specificity that was lacking in both the original Latin and the French translation.

IV

On several occasions Chaucer quotes or paraphrases specific passages in the Bible and misattributes them. For example, in a quotation from Matthew 3:8 in the *Parson's Tale*—"Crist seith in his gospel, 'Dooth digne fruyt of Penitence'" (X 115)—the actual speaker of the verse that the Parson closely paraphrases is John the Baptist, not Christ. Kate Petersen suggests that Chaucer's mistake might have resulted from his having confounded what John the Baptist says about penitence in Matthew 3:8—"Bring forth therefore fruit worthy of penance"—with what Jesus says on the same subject in Matthew 4:17: "Do penance, for the kingdom of heaven is at hand"; but as Douglas Wurtele points out, Chaucer may have picked up the misattribution from a later citation in Pennaforte.[19] A similar error occurs in *Parson's Tale* X 142, "as seith Seint Peter, 'whoso that dooth synne is thral of synne," where the verse quoted is not from the Epistles of Saint Peter but from the Gospel of John: "whosoever committeth sin, is the servant of sin" (8:34). Though Chaucer was apparently following Pennaforte in making the erroneous attribution, there is a somewhat similar verse in 2 Peter 2:19, "For by whom a man is overcome, of the same also he is the slave," which may have helped them both to overlook their mistake.[20]

In *Melibee* Dame Prudence misattributes the following saying from Seneca to the Epistle of James:

> For Seint Jame seith in his Episteles that "by concord and pees the smale richesses wexen grete, / and by debaat and discord the grete richesses fallen doun." (VII 1675–76)

Here too Chaucer was no doubt following his proximate source in mistakenly assigning verses from Seneca ("Seneques") to Saint James ("St. Jacques").[21] But as in the previous two examples, the mistake may have slipped past Chaucer more easily because he was recalling a similar biblical saying: "For where envying and contention is, there is inconstancy, and every evil work" (James 3:16–18).

A recurrent error throughout the *Canterbury Tales*, and one that was frequently passed on to Chaucer by his proximate sources, is the misattribution to Solomon of verses from Ecclesiasticus, attributed in the Vulgate to "Iesu filii Sirach," Jesus son of Sirach (see *Melibee* VII 1003, 1159–60, 1161, 1572, 1589, 1671, etc.; and *Parson's Tale* X 854).[22] An epithet that Chaucer sometimes uses when he quotes Solomon is "the wise," "a wise man," or "the wise man" (e.g., in *Man of Law's Prologue* II 117–18; *Parson's Tale* X 539, 569).[23] In *Parson's Tale* 640, however, Chaucer credits "the wise man" with words from a parallel passage in the *Summa vitiorum* that are spoken by Peraldus *in propria persona*. Chaucer's error in this case can be explained by the fact that in the parallel passage Peraldus quotes several thematically related biblical verses from Ecclesiasticus and Proverbs, verses that Chaucer apparently decided to omit.[24]

When there are erroneous biblical quotations in Chaucer's works, trying to split the blame for ignorance or carelessness and the credit for subtly purposeful misprision among Chaucer, his narrators, and his characters is a dubious game with no clearly fixed rules. In the *Wife of Bath's Prologue*, for example, the Wife claims that the Gospel of Mark specifies that Jesus used "barley bread" in the miracle of the loaves and fishes (III 144–46); but the detail is actually found in John 6:9 ("There is a boy here that hath five barley loaves"). Most readers would probably agree that this mistake was simply Chaucer's slip, and not his subtle way of indicating the Wife's unreliability, or her carelessness.

But how to evaluate a similar type of error in the *Legend of Good Women* is more difficult to say. In praising the fidelity of Lucrece and denigrating the tyranny and fickleness of men (*LGW* 1874–85), Chaucer mistakenly refers Jesus's remark about not having found "so great faith in Israel" to the Syro-Phoenician woman of Matthew 15:28, rather than to the Roman centurion of Matthew 8:10. This mistake, like the Wife of Bath's, might also best be written off as the effect of Chaucer's mere carelessness or faulty memory. Yet because the erroneous change of the sex of Christ's exemplary believer from male to female occurs in a work in which Chaucer's single avowed purpose was to praise women, one is

tempted to regard the "error" as a subtle ploy of Chaucer's erst-
while philofeminism.

V

Chaucer's "An ABC," traditionally considered to be his earliest
extant work, is a poem that seems as if it were formed almost
entirely on a biblical template.[25] Though earlier critics tended to
stress the fact that "An ABC" is a fairly close translation by Chaucer
of his proximate source, a prayer to the Virgin in Guillaume
Deguilleville's *La pelerinaige de vie humaine*, some indications of
Chaucer's originality in adapting this source have more recently
come to be appreciated.[26] In addition to its biblical subject matter
and its pervasive biblical language, a further reflex of the biblical
nature of "An ABC" is its abecedarian form. Each stanza of the
poem begins with a different letter of the alphabet, starting with
"Almighty" and ending with "Zacharie," a structural feature that
evokes the form of such well-known and influential biblical alphabetic poems of praise, penance, and prayer as Psalm 118(119),
Proverbs 30:10–31, and Lamentations 1:1–22 and 3:1–66.[27] Though
this basic structural feature of "An ABC" was carried over by
Chaucer from his proximate French source, there are in fact two
variations in Chaucer's handling of Deguilleville's abecedarian
form that suggest a direct link with Psalm 118(119). First, while
Deguilleville's poem is written in twelve-line stanzas, "An ABC" uses
an eight-line stanza, paralleling the units of eight verses for each
letter of the Hebrew alphabet that are indicated in Latin
renderings of Psalm 118(119).[28] Second, while Deguilleville's poem
includes two additional stanzas for the two additional letters that
normally follow *z* in medieval alphabets, *e(t)* and *c(etera)*, Chaucer's
poem, like the psalm, ends with the last letter of the alphabet.
These formal changes make Chaucer's poem seem more
restrained than Deguilleville's. They are in line with Chaucer's
shortening and alteration of Deguilleville's stanzas for "Xristus"
and "Ysaac," modifications of the French source that tone down its
emotionalism.[29]

Besides numerous other changes in form and content, Chaucer
expanded or fleshed out the biblical texture of Deguilleville's
prayer to the Virgin by introducing the following noteworthy

additions and elaborations to the biblical diction, imagery, and narrative references in his French source: a periphrastic allusion to a vivid legal image of the Crucifixion from Colossians 2:14 ("ABC" 59–61); mention of the angel Gabriel, in a scene that "stages an Annunciation" in place of a more "abstract" reference to the Incarnation ("ABC" 113–15); the singular use of the word "ancille," copied from the Latin *ancilla* of Luke 1:38 and 48 ("ABC" 109–10); and a reference to the wounding of Christ on the cross by the apocryphal centurion "Longius" ("ABC" 161–63).[30] Of course, Chaucer could have added these and the other brief biblical phrases and allusions in "An ABC" that are not paralleled in Deguilleville without even opening the Bible. Because Chaucer was adding biblical language and imagery to a liturgical structure of personal devotion and prayerful pleading, his allusive obliquity in "An ABC" was perfectly suited to his artistic goals.

Later in Chaucer's career, in the *Prioress's Prologue* and *Tale* and the *Second Nun's Prologue* and *Tale*, he would represent a similar kind of pious devotion to the Virgin Mary by a similar fluency of biblical diction. In the case of the Prioress, however, Marian piety and fluency of biblical diction are embodied in a story that blends fervid devotion with bloodcurdling violence—a story told by a character whose ruling passions according to her portrait in the *General Prologue* are sentimentality, fastidiousness, and an inappropriate concern with aristocratic bearing.[31] For our present purposes, the noteworthy fact about "An ABC" is that it locates Chaucer's religious sensibility squarely (and without irony) in the popular Marian piety of his age. And if it shows Chaucer wholeheartedly committed to producing a work of sincere religious sensibility, it also testifies to his wide-ranging and easy command of the diction, imagery, and narrative content of the Bible.

Interestingly, "An ABC" is not one of the "translaciouns" by Chaucer named by Queen Alceste in the *Prologue to the Legend of Good Women*. Defending Chaucer against the charge that he has defamed women by translating the *Roman de la rose* and the story of Troilus and Criseyde, Alceste provides the following list of the poet's inoffensive translations:

. . . He hath in prose translated Boece,
And Of the Wreched Engendrynge of Mankynde,

As man may in Pope Innocent yfynde;
And mad the lyf also of Seynt Cecile.
He made also, gon is a gret while,
Orygenes upon the Maudeleyne.

(G 413–18)

In addition to two extant works—that is, *Boece* (a translation in prose and verse of Boethius's *Consolation of Philosophy*) and the *Second Nun's Tale* (a translation in verse of the Life of Saint Cecilia)—Alceste also mentions two works that are no longer extant, "Of the Wreched Engendrynge of Mankynde" (presumably a translation of Innocent III's *De miseria condicionis humane*) and "Orygenes upon the Maudeleyne" (probably a translation of the pseudo-Origen homily *De Maria Magdalena*).[32]

Among the immediately obvious characteristics that Chaucer's translation of the *De Maria Magdalena* homily would have shared with his translation of Innocent III's *De miseria condicionis humane* are a highly artificial rhetorical surface and an abundant supply of biblical allusions and quotations. John McCall, Margaret Jennings, and Rosemary Woolf have given us a plausible and fairly detailed sense of the kind of biblically inspired work that Chaucer's "Orygenes upon the Maudeleyne" must have been.[33] They demonstrate that the pseudonymous homily that Chaucer was presumably following offers its readers a highly emotive dramatization and poetic elaboration of a single passage in the Gospel of John that vividly evokes Mary Magdalene's intense love and pitiful devotion to Christ—a dramatization and poetic elaboration of the biblical scene that interweaves biblical allusions and quotations from Matthew, Luke, John, Lamentations, Song of Songs, Job, and other biblical books. As Jennings writes: "The most apparent stylistic feature of this homily is its widespread use of biblical quotation and allusion; no less than sixty separate citations are easily discernible."[34]

As Robert Lewis points out, Innocent III's *De miseria condicionis humane* is in fact "a kind of commentary on various passages from the Bible," containing some five hundred biblical verses, or parts of verses, drawn from almost every book of the Bible.[35] The biblical quotations gathered by Pope Innocent are grouped around themes like the Seven Deadly Sins, Hell, Judgment Day, and related topics. Chaucer's derivation of biblical materials from the

De miseria is evident in the *Man of Law's Prologue* and *Tale* and the *Pardoner's Tale*, but many of Innocent's biblical quotations also appear in various passages throughout the *Canterbury Tales*.[36] Chaucer's English version of the *De miseria* would in fact have provided him with a veritable collection of *distinctiones* on biblically defined themes—a thematically ordered anthology of biblical verses larger than any other intermediate source of biblical quotations and allusions he is known to have consulted, including even Jerome's biblically enriched *Epistola adversus Jovinianum*.[37]

We obviously do not know how the English versions of biblical passages in Chaucer's lost translations of *De Maria Magdalena* and the *De miseria condicionis humane* would have compared with their proximate and their ultimate sources in the Vulgate. However, having translated so many biblical passages into English, Chaucer would have had a large stock of vernacular biblical materials to compare with the Latin quotations in his other biblically enriched intermediate sources (Jerome's *Epistola adversus Jovinianum*, John of Wales's *Communiloquium*, and the biblically suffused works that lie behind the *Tale of Melibee* and the *Parson's Tale*). We can only speculate that Chaucer would have adapted the biblical passages he had rendered into English in these works for repeated use elsewhere in his poetry. But until Chaucer's "Origenes upon the Maudeleyne" and his "Wretched Engendrynge of Mankynde" come to light, the question of the intertextual relations between their biblical quotations and the corresponding passages in the Bible and in Chaucer's other works will have to remain unanswered.

VI

The most extensive examples of biblical translation and paraphrase in Chaucer's extant works are found in two of the *Canterbury Tales*, the *Tale of Melibee* and the *Parson's Tale*. These two prose tales were written by the learned Chaucer, a scholarly and pious layman who is understandably less familiar to contemporary readers, and also less likely to attract sustained critical attention, than the better-known Chaucer, a brilliant innovator in comic and dramatic verse narrative. An additional barrier that may get in the way of our giving the didactic soundness and devotional piety of *Melibee* and the *Parson's Tale* the serious attention they deserve is their dramatic placement. *Melibee* is narrated by Chaucer's easily bullied pilgrim alter ego in place of an interrupted but brilliant parody of tail-rhyme romance, the *Tale of Sir Thopas*. Similarly, the *Parson's Tale* is offered by its adamant and uncompromising teller as an alternative to, and in explicit repudiation of, the artistry of all the tales in verse that have preceded it.

Yet the fact remains that Chaucer "spak hem so"—and at length, with what was obviously a serious investment of thought and artistic skill and effort. For the purposes of the present study, there are two facts about *Melibee* and the *Parson's Tale* that are especially significant. The first is that Chaucer not only incorporated these biblically rich tales into the framework of the *Canterbury Tales* but drew upon them for some of the biblical verses quoted or alluded to in other tales within that most strikingly original of his works.[38] The second is that although both *Melibee* and the *Parson's Tale* follow their known sources fairly closely, they also contain numerous passages in which Chaucer appears to have omitted, abbreviated, or sometimes even expanded and fleshed out the biblical quotations that he found in his sources, occasionally even introducing his own quotations in addition to, or sometimes even instead of, those that his sources had provided him.[39] The following examples from *Melibee* and the *Parson's Tale* illustrate how Chaucer sometimes pursued each of these options.

In the source of *Melibee*, Renaud de Louens's *Livre de Mellibee et Prudence*, Mellibee blends translation and paraphrase when he quotes from a substantial passage in Ecclesiasticus, misattributed to Solomon, which advises men against giving anyone power over themselves or their property:

> Salemon dit, "A ton fil, a ta femme, a ton frere, a ton amy ne donne puissance sur toy en toute ta vie, car il te vaut mieux que tes enfans te requierent ce que mestier leur sera que toy regarder es mains de tes enfans."[40]

The four verses that Mellibee abbreviates and splices are Ecclesiasticus 33:19–22:

> Hear me, ye great men, and all ye people, and hearken with your ears, ye rulers of the church. / Give not to son or wife, brother or friend, power over thee while thou livest; and give not thy

estate to another, lest thou repent, and thou entreat for the
same. / As long as thou livest, and hast breath in thee, let no
man change thee. / For it is better that thy children should ask
of thee, than that thou look toward the hands of thy children.

Chaucer's rendering of this passage of biblical counsel—counsel
whose neglect would be immortalized two centuries later in
Shakespeare's *King Lear*—is almost identical with Renaud's,
including the misattribution to Solomon:

> And Salomon seith: "Nevere in thy lyf to thy wyf, ne to thy child,
> ne to thy freend ne yeve no power over thyself, for bettre it were
> that thy children aske of thy persone thynges that hem nedeth
> than thou see thyself in the handes of thy children." (VII 1060)

But because Chaucer's translation of Renuad is slavishly, even
awkwardly literal (e.g., "aske of thy persone thynges that hem
nedeth"), his moving of "wyf" to the head of the list of those not to
be given power over oneself and his failure to translate Renaud's "a
ton frere" (the biblical "brother") are minor points that become
worth noting. The wish to read these minor changes as Melibee's
"mistake" rather than Chaucer's eye-skip finds some basis in the
repeated but corrected use of the same passage by Prudence at the
end of the tale. In Renaud's version, Prudence quotes from and
paraphrases a portion of Ecclesiasticus 33:19–22 when she advises
Mellibe's enemies to put themselves at her husband's mercy. She
concedes that in itself this advice might seem unreasonable, and all
the more so because submission to one's enemy goes against the
advice of "Salemon:"

> Car Salemon dit, "'Oyez moy,'" dit il, "tuit pueple et toutes gens et
> gouverneurs d'Eglise: a ton fil, a ta femme, a ton frere, a ton
> cousin, et a ton amy, ne donne puissance sur toy en toute ta vie."[41]

And Chaucer's Prudence makes the same a fortiori argument:

> For Salomon seith, "Leeveth me, and yeveth credence to that I
> shal seyn: I seye," quod he, "ye peple, folk, and governours of
> hooly chirche, / to thy sone, to thy wyf, to thy freend, ne to thy

broother / ne yeve thou nevere myght ne maistrie of thy body whil thou lyvest." (VII 1754–56)

Chaucer follows Renaud even to the point of breaking up the quote from "Solomon" with a "quod he," placed in the same relative position as Renaud's "dit il." But instead of Renaud's succinct "Oyez moy" Chaucer's Prudence says, "Leeveth me, and yeveth credence to that I shal seyn: I seye," which seems to echo the opening of the biblical passage behind Chaucer's proximate source: "Hear me, ye great men, and all ye people, and hearken with your ears."

The five people Renaud's Prudence warns against entrusting with power over oneself are: "ton fil," "ta femme," "ton frere," "ton cousin," and "ton amy." Chaucer's Prudence names four people, "thy sone," "thy wyf," "thy freend," and "thy broother," matching four of the five cited by Renaud's Prudence. Chaucer's Prudence gets the biblical quote right, whereas Renaud's Prudence got it wrong, since the verse in Ecclesiasticus refers to the four people listed in Chaucer's version: "Give not to son or wife, brother or friend, power over thee while thou livest" (v. 20).

Is it far-fetched to insist that in the latter instance Chaucer must have turned from his proximate source and had recourse to the Bible? The evidence may simply indicate his better recall of the exact wording of the passage; it is also possible, though not likely, that Chaucer was working from a manuscript of Renaud's *Livre de Mellibee et Prudence* in which the quotation from Ecclesiasticus was given more accurately. But whether or not Chaucer turned from Renaud to the Bible for Prudence's quotation from Ecclesiasticus, when Melibee's inaccurate foregrounding of "wyf" and omission of "brother" in his earlier quotation of the same passage from Ecclesiasticus are set against Prudence's more accurate biblical recall, the idea that Chaucer intended to invest their differing degrees of translational accuracy with a gendered thematic significance begins to seem more plausible.[42]

Indeed, Prudence's quotations from the Bible in *Melibee* are not only more frequent than her husband's—some ninety-five biblical quotations and allusions against Melibee's ten—they are also, as in the latter example, more accurate. Moreover, as the following examples illustrate, Prudence's biblical translations in *Melibee* are not only more accurate than her husband's but also more accurate, and more extensive, than the corresponding quotations by Prudence in the French source.

For example, in the *Livre de Mellibee et Prudence* there is a brief and somewhat vague allusion by Prudence to a passage in Second Corinthians:

> la gloire que l'on acquiert pour voir pacience est pardurable, selon ce que l'apostre en l'epistre seconde dit a ceulz de Corinte.[43]

The biblical text Renaud apparently has in mind was 2 Corinthians 4:17, which reads: "For that which is at present momentary and light of our tribulation, worketh for us above measure exceedingly an eternal weight of glory." Chaucer's Prudence eliminates the specificity of Renaud's "l'epistre seconde . . . a ceulz de Corinte," but she comes closer to the biblical verse even as she is explicating and expanding upon it:

> and the joy that a man seeketh to have by pacience in tribulaciouns is perdurable, after that the Apostle seith in his epistle. / "the joye of God," he seith, "is perdurable," that is to seyn, everlastynge. (VII 1509–10)

Prudence's use of the word "tribulaciouns," not found in Renaud, echoes Paul's "tribulation." But Prudence's quotation of the sentence "the joye of God is perdurable"—with "perdurable" glossed as "everlastynge"—is actually an extrapolation of the biblical phrase "laetitia sempiterna" (joy everlasting), from Isaiah (35:10, 51:11, 61:7). Like a typical preacher, Chaucer's Prudence takes the occasion of Renaud's Prudence's quote from Corinthians to use a concording biblical quotation in order to explain and elaborate upon Paul's ideas about "the joye of God."

In the climactic scene of *Melibee*, Chaucer introduces a biblically based coda found neither in Renaud nor in Albertanus's original Latin version. In Renaud's version, which follows the Latin, the story ends with Mellibee forgiving his enemies:

> Et pour ce nous vous recevons en nostre amitié et en nostre bonne grace, et vous pardonnons toutes injures et tous voz

meffaiz encontre nous, a celle fin que Dieu, ou point de la mort, nous vueille pardonner les nostres.[44]

This speech, which Chaucer translated fairly closely in *Melibee* VII 1881–84, loosely paraphrases Matthew 6:14–15:

"For if you will forgive men their offences, your heavenly Father will forgive you also your offences. But if you will not forgive men, neither will your Father forgive you your offences."

But Chaucer's version of the story continues with a transformed Melibee addressing his enemies as follows:

"For doutelees, if we be sory and repentant of the synnes and giltes which we han trespassed in the sighte of oure Lord God, / he is so free and so merciable / that he wolde foryeven us oure giltes / and bryngen us to the blisse that nevere hath ende." (VII 1885–88)

With the concluding phrase, "the blisse that nevere hath ende," Melibee repeats the previously introduced idea of "joy everlasting" in slightly different but also liturgically familiarized terms that evoke biblical diction (cp. Ephesians 3:21, Matthew 25:46, etc.). In lines 1885–87, however, the underlying biblical reference is unmistakably more specific:

"If we confess our sins, he is faithful and just, to forgive us our sins, and to cleanse us from all iniquity." (1 John 1:9)

As Melibee paraphrases the verse in the Epistle of John, he also abbreviates, expands, and alters it.

Melibee's use of doublets where the Bible uses a single term—"if we be sory and repentant" for the biblical "if we confess," and "synnes and giltes" for the biblical "sins"—is typical of Chaucer's general translational practice.[45] Like the doublets Chaucer often uses elsewhere, "sory and repentant" and "synnes and giltes" are redundant in a way that leaves the biblical meaning unchanged. However, this is not the case with Melibee's substitution of "so free and so merciable" to characterize God, in place of the biblical "faithful and just" (Vulgate: "fidelis est, et iustus"). In 1 John 1:9 the characterization of God as "just" (Lat. *iustus*) rather than "merciful" (Lat. *misericors*) when he is ready to forgive the person who confesses his or her sins reverses a classic New Testament justice/mercy opposition (see Luke 6:36, etc.); John's rhetorically effective point is that in this case God's "justice" *is* "mercy." As Melibee courteously forgives his enemies for their trespasses against him, his use of "free" and "merciable"—epithets that Chaucer uses elsewhere in reference to the Virgin Mary (e.g., "ABC" 1, 13; *Prioress's Prologue* VII 467)—serves to convey the salubriously feminized courtly ethos that Chaucer apparently wished to promulgate in the *Tale of Melibee*.[46] Melibee's omission in line 1887 of the biblical "cleanse us from all iniquity" would work in the same direction—both God and man can forgive what Melibee calls "giltes," but God alone can "cleanse." Though Chaucer's Melibee may be less adept at quoting the Bible than his wife, Prudence, he proves to be more adept than Renaud's Mellibee—especially after Prudence has won him over to her way of looking at the world.

The suggestion that Chaucer had a specifically didactic purpose for subtly altering and adding to the biblical quotations at the end of Renaud's *Livre de Mellibee et Prudence* is rendered more plausible by other evidence indicating that Chaucer's practice in *Melibee* was not that of an uncritical translator. An example that shows his attention to what might be called practical rather than purely artistic considerations is the dropping of Renaud's quotation of Ecclesiastes 10:16, a biblical quotation potentially offensive to King Richard II.[47] More relevant for our present purpose are Chaucer's departures from Renaud in the double citation of the same biblical passage, Ecclesiasticus 33:19–22. As we have seen, it was Prudence who corrected Melibee's inaccurate quotation from the latter passage, even as she rejected its counsel against submitting to one's enemy (VII 1757–61). In *Melibee*, as in Chaucer's source, it is Prudence who does most of the quoting from the Bible. Furthermore, in both the English and French versions it is Prudence who works hard to set aside her husband's antifeminist biblical canards in order to pursue her larger goal of convincing him to be "free" and "merciable."[48] By introducing a disparity between Melibee's careless but accepting masculine appropriation of the passage in Ecclesiasticus and Prudence's accurate but unaccepting feminine appropriation of the same passage, Chaucer reinforced the gendering of biblical translation and appropriation that was already a feature of Renaud's moral treatise.

VII

Though the exceptions in *Melibee* are important, its relatively few omissions or alterations of the biblical quotations in Renaud's *Livre de Mellibee et Prudence* highlight the fact that Chaucer for the most part translated or paraphrased the verses in his single source almost verbatim. The *Parson's Tale*, however, presents a more complicated case. As K. O. Petersen first pointed out, the framing sections of the Parson's discussion of penitence (*Parson's Tale* X 80–386 and 958–1080) closely resemble the treatment of the same topic in Raymund of Pennaforte's "De poenitentiis et remissionibus," the third book of his *Summa casuum poenitentiae* (c. 1222/29).[49] However, Petersen's further suggestion that William Peraldus's *Summa vitiorum* (1236) was the ultimate source of the Parson's intervening discussion of the sins and their "remedies" (*Parson's Tale* X 390–955) proved to be more problematic.[50]

Siegfried Wenzel has brought to light and analyzed three works, named by him after their first words as *Quoniam*, *Primo*, and *Postquam*, that are closer to Chaucer's treatment of the sins (*Quoniam* and *Primo*) and their remedies (*Postquam*) than any of the other putative sources for these portions of the *Parson's Tale*.[51] Still, we cannot draw hard and fast conclusions about Chaucer's methods of composition on the assumption that we are reading and analyzing the exact same texts that Chaucer read and adapted. As Wenzel reminds us, "perhaps a lucky find will yet reveal a treatise or sermon which actually combines material on the sins from *Quoniam* with material on the virtues from *Postquam*, and perhaps even with material on Penance from Pennaforte or a similarly derived work"; nevertheless, as Wenzel concludes, "the suggestion that Chaucer may have combined these ingredients himself still remains a distinct possibility."[52]

Yet even if a more direct source for the *Parson's Tale* were to turn up, the conclusions that Wenzel has drawn about how Chaucer treated the biblical materials in his sources are unlikely to change: "In comparison with *Quoniam*, *Primo*, or Peraldus, the *Parson's Tale* handles biblical authorities not only with freedom but with knowledge, often quoting a longer text than that furnished by these Latin treatises (e.g., lines 820, 869) or even substituting a different and more fitting quotation (e.g., lines 750–51)."[53] Some consideration of the evidence that Chaucer was more than just a "slavish translator" of the biblical quotations in the proximate sources of the *Parson's Tale* is therefore in order.[54]

In our first example, the Parson is explaining the need for confession, "the seconde partie of penitence," by looking back to the origin of sin in the story of the Fall. His initial approach to this point of origin is by way of a quotation from Paul:

> Of the spryngynge of synnes seith Seint Paul in this wise: that "Right as by a man synne entred first into this world, and thurgh that synne deeth, right so thilke deeth entred into alle men that syneden." (X 322)

Except for the last clause, the Parson is closely translating Romans 5:12:

> Propterea sicut per unum hominem peccatum in hunc mundum intravit, et per peccatum mors, et ita in omnes homines mors pertransiit, in quo omnes peccaverunt. [Wherefore as by one man sin entered into this world, and by sin death; and so death passed upon all men, in whom [i.e., through Adam] all have sinned.]

Chaucer's alteration of the last clause has major theological implications, since it elides Paul's statement of inherited sin and death through Adam and instead implies that "deeth" is an analogous consequence ("right so") suffered by men for their own sins.[55] As Alfred Kellogg points out, a quotation from Romans 5:12 (unattributed to Paul or his Epistle to the Romans) occurs also in a discussion of penitence in Richard de Wetheringsett's *Summa de officio sacerdotis* (c. 1235?); and like Chaucer in *Parson's Tale* X 323–34, de Wetheringsett follows the quotation from Romans 5:12 with additional echoes of Romans 5:12 and 5:14 and with summary mention of Adam ("Homo iste primus parens") and the dire consequences of the Fall.[56] However, the discussion of the Fall in the *Parson's Tale* differs from the analogous one in the *Summa de officio*

sacerdotis in that Chaucer proceeds to translate and closely paraphrase from a block of verses in Genesis 2:24–3:7:

> Looke that in th'estaat of innocence, whan Adam and Eve naked
> weren in Paradys, and nothyng ne hadden shame of hir naked-
> nesse, / how that the serpent, that was moost wily of alle othere
> beestes that God hadde maked, seyde to the womman, "Why
> comaunded God to yow ye sholde nat eten of every tree in
> Paradys?" / The womman answerde: "Of the fruyt," quod she, "of
> the trees in Paradys we feden us, but soothly, of the fruyt of the
> tree that is in the myddel of Paradys, God forbad us for to ete, ne
> nat touchen it, lest per aventure, we sholde dyen." / The serpent
> seyde to the womman, "Nay, nay, ye shul nat dyen of deeth; for
> sothe, God woot that what day that ye eten therof, youre eyen shul
> opene and ye shul been as goddes, knowynge good and harm." /
> The womman thanne saugh that the tree was good to feedyng,
> and fair to the eyen, and delitable to the sighte. She took of the
> fruyt of the tree, and eet it, and yaf to hire housbonde, and he eet,
> and anoon the eyen of hem bothe openeden. / And whan that
> they knewe that they were naked, they sowed of fige leves a maner
> of breches to hiden hire membres. (X 325–30)

As Kellogg observes, treatises like the *Summa de officio sacerdotis* "are
generally tightly constructed, and the commentator will very rarely
indeed give more than a short quotation with reference."[57] This
leads Kellogg to draw the persuasive conclusion that the latter translation and close paraphrase of some eight consecutive biblical verses
is therefore "almost certainly attributable to Chaucer himself."[58]

In a note on the same passage in the *Parson's Tale*, Skeat compares
the Later Wycliffite translation of Genesis 3:1–7; but, as Grace
Landrum correctly points out, the significance of the putative resem-
blance "is lessened by the difference in the *descriptive passages.*"[59]

CHAUCER'S VERSION	THE WYCLIFFITE VERSION
. . . the serpent, that was most wily of alle othere beestes that God hadde maked;	. . . the serpent was feller than alle lyuynge beestis of erthe, which the Lord God hadde maad;

. . . the tree was good to feedyng, and fair to the eyen, and delitable to the sight	. . . the tre was good, and swete to ete, and fair to the iȝen, and delitable in to biholdyng;
. . . they sowed of fige leves a maner of breches to hiden hire membres.	. . . thei sewiden the leeues of a fige tre, and made brechis to hem silf.

As the differences listed above suggest, Chaucer worked independently of the Wycliffite Bible translation, rendering what must have been virtually the same Latin text as was before the Lollard translators with the predictably slight variations that would naturally arise between two independent versions of the same text.

It should also be noted, however, that Chaucer's close and fluent translation includes a few slight but noteworthy departures from the Latin source. In keeping with the Parson's homiletical purposes, Chaucer gives the serpent a colloquially emphatic and contentious "Nay, nay, ye shul nat dyen of deeth," in reply to Eve's demurral regarding the fruit of the tree of knowledge, which also happens to translate quite closely the Vulgate's "Nequaquam morte moriemini," translated in the Douay Bible as "No, you shall not die the death" (3:4), and even more freely in the Wycliffite Bible as "For sothe . . . ȝe schulen not die bi deeth."[60] Chaucer's doubled negation, "Nay, nay," renders the serpent's emphatic Latin adverbial *nequaquam* (in nowise, by no means, not at all); but Chaucer also adds an "anoon"—"and anoon the eyen of hem bothe openeden"—to his translation of the Vulgate's "Et aperti sunt oculi amborum" (3:7), thereby heightening the immediacy of the enlightening effect on Adam and Eve of eating the forbidden fruit.[61] Finally, by adding: "to hiden hire membres," Chaucer makes explicit what the "breeches" sewed by Adam and Eve were for, while the Vulgate and Wycliffite authors are both satisfied to let the covering of Adam and Eve's "members" remain obviously implicit ("cumque cognovissent se esse nudos" [3:7], "and whanne thei knewen that they weren naked").

Like the Pardoner before him (in *Pardoner's Tale* VI 505–11), the Parson adduces the biblical story of Adam and Eve and the loss of Paradise to exemplify the disastrous effects of the sin of Gula (Gluttony):

This synne [gluttony] corrumped al this world, as is wel shewed
in the synne of Adam and of Eve. (X 819).

Having previously explained the origin of sin by translating and
paraphrasing the story of the Temptation and Fall in Genesis
2:24–3:1–7, the Parson can now begin his treatment of the
particular sin of gluttony by merely adverting to the same biblical
point of origin. Thus far Chaucer's summary reference is
extremely close to what he would have found in *Quoniam*, which
reads at a parallel point in its treatment of the same vice: "[Gula]
totum mundum corrumpit, ut patet in primis parentibus."[62] The
minor changes here (which are similar to those one repeatedly
finds when one compares the *Parson's Tale* with its sources) include
Chaucer's explicit and twice-repeated mention of "synne" and his
explicit use of the names of our "primi parentes," Adam and Eve,
instead of the circumlocution "our first parents."[63] *Quoniam* continues with an abbreviated allusion to Paul's condemnation of
gluttony in Philippians: "Phi. 3[:19]: 'Quorum deus venter est,'
etc."; whereas Peraldus's *Summa vitiorum* has virtually the same
brief biblical allusion in roughly parallel position: "juxta illud
apostoli ad. Phil., iii . . . quorum deus venter est."[64] Chaucer's
Parson, however, adds a close translation of a sizable block of the
biblical text in Philippians 3:18–19:

"Manye," seith Saint Paul, "goon, of whiche I have ofte seyd to
yow, and now I seye it wepynge, that been the enemys of the
croys of Crist; of which the ende is deeth, and of whiche hire
wombe is hire god, and hir glorie in confusioun of hem that so
savouren erthely thynges." (X 820)[65]

Like the reference to Adam and Eve's gluttony immediately
preceding it, parts of this same passage from Philippians are also
paraphrased in the section of the Pardoner's sermon on gluttony.[66]
Chaucer's method of composition might have been as follows.
While translating *Quoniam* or a work very much like it for the
Parson's Tale, he found the reference to the lead-in words "Quorum
deus venter est," etc. of Philippians 3[:18–19], went to the Vulgate
and closely translated the two relevant verses, then drew upon his

translation for the animadversions on gluttony in the Pardoner's sermon.

A comparison of the following two passages on the sin of lechery provides a more complicated illustration of how Chaucer treated the biblical prooftexts in his sources. Here we find that the overall similarities between Chaucer and *Quoniam* confirm Chaucer's indebtedness, but at the same time the slight differences show how Chaucer sometimes purposefully adapted the material he found in *Quoniam* by compressing it, introducing anachronistic details, and occasionally even mistakenly altering a biblical injunction as he expanded it:

Parson's Tale:

> God woot, this synne is ful displesaunt thyng to God; for he seyde hymself, "Do no lecherie." And therefore he putte grete peynes agayns this synne in the olde lawe. / If womman thral were taken in this synne, she sholde be beten with staves to the deeth; and if she were a bisshopes doghter, she sholde been brent, by Goddes comandement. / Forther over, by the synne of lecherie God dreynte al the world at the diluge. And after that he brente fyve citees with thonder-leyt, and sank hem into helle. (X 837–39)

Quoniam:

> Valde detestabile est hoc vitium, . . . quia displicet deo, et nocet proprio subiecto, nocet proximo, et multum placet diabolo. Quod multum displiceat deo, per hoc probatur quodprohibet illud. . . . Exo. 20[:14]: "Non mechaberis." . . . Deut. 22[:21], ubi preceptum est nobilem mulierem fornicantem lapidari; si ancilla esset, vapularet. In prophetis vero non solum prohibetur luxuria, sed statuitur pena ei. . . . Item . . . propter luxurie immunditiam diluvium induxit mundo et delevit incendio, igne, et sulphure.[67]

The sequence of biblical references in the *Quoniam* passage— Exodus 20:14, Deuteronomy 22:21, a nonspecific reference to the Prophets, a summary reference to the narrative of the Flood (Genesis 6–7), and a similarly brief reference to the destruction of Sodom and Gomorrah (Genesis 19)—is repeated in the *Parson's*

Tale, but with the following individually slight but cumulatively important modifications. Chaucer renders the seventh commandment, which appears in the Vulgate (Exodus 20:14) and in *Quoniam* as "Non Moechaberis" (Thou shalt not commit adultery), by the more general "Do no lecherie"; he drops the nonspecific reference to the Prophets; he makes the concluding two Genesis references more grimly emphatic. Furthermore, there is no mention in Chaucer's adaptation of *Quoniam* of the saving of humanity from the Flood, and the five cities are not only destroyed "with thonder-leyt"—that is, with a thunderbolt, a simplification of *Quoniam*'s more detailed "incendio, igne, et sulphure"—they are also "sunk into helle."

Chaucer's major departure is his expanded but likewise mistaken handling of the faulty reference in *Quoniam* to Deuteronomy. For Deuteronomy 22[:21] treats neither of the two cases of fornication to which *Quoniam* refers, the first involving a noblewoman who is to be stoned ("nobilem mulierem fornicantem lapidari"), the second a bondwoman who is to be beaten ("si ancilla esset, vapularet"). Instead, Deuteronomy 22:21 has to do with the execution by stoning of *any* wife who turns out not to have been a virgin when she married. Elsewhere, however, the Mosaic law does distinguish between cases of fornication involving a "bondservant" (Lat. *ancilla*) or a "free woman" (Lat. *libera*). The passage in question—and the one actually alluded to both in *Quoniam* (but mistakenly referred to Deuteronomy 22) and in the *Parson's Tale* (without a specific citation of biblical book and chapter)—is found in Leviticus 19:20:

> Homo, si dormierit cum muliere coitu seminis, quae sit ancilla etiam nubilis, et tamen pretio non redempta, nec libertate donata: vapulabunt ambo, et non morientur, quia non fuit libera. [If a man carnally lie with a woman that is a bondservant and marriageable, and yet not redeemed with a price, nor made free: they both shall be scourged, and they shall not be put to death, because she was not a free woman.]

It will be evident that the distinction of punishments based on social status drawn in this verse in Leviticus 19 is the same one drawn in *Quoniam* but mistakenly referred to Deuteronomy 22: the "free woman" is to be stoned to death and the "bondservant" is not put to death but beaten (as is the man she has lain with). Chaucer modifies the cases presented in *Quoniam* in several striking details. Though Chaucer's Parson retains the "bondwoman" found in *Quoniam*, he alters the class (or, more correctly, the "estates") divisions noted in this putative source by substituting a "bisshopes daughter" in place of *Quoniam*'s "nobilem mulierem." The Parson then metes out capital punishment in both cases (in *Quoniam*, however, as in the Bible, the "bondwoman" is sentenced to a nonlethal beating).

These modifications of *Quoniam* are especially interesting to consider in light of evidence regarding the contemporary legal response to sexual misconduct. Richard Helmholz shows that punishments for adultery and fornication imposed by fourteenth-century ecclesiastical courts were far less severe than biblical law demanded.[68] Helmholz's study, which is based on the evidence in the "Act books" and "Cause papers" of church courts in Ely, York, and Canterbury from the thirteenth to fifteenth centuries, deals almost entirely with cases involving lay men and women of the peasant and bourgeois estates, since the offenses of aristocrats and clergy were likely to be handled by the bishop directly.[69] Helmholz's data suggest that in late medieval England adultery was hard to prove, and when proved, the most common court actions were fines and warnings not to repeat the offense.[70] For fornication, the court might impose a fine and it might also require the fornicators to contract a "conditional marriage"—that is, if they were then to repeat the sinful act they would automatically be married.[71]

In bringing in the case of a fornicating "bisshopes doghter" who is to be "brent, by Goddes comandment," Chaucer follows Leviticus 21:9: "Sacerdotis filia si deprehensa fuerit in stupro, et violaverit nomen patris sui, flammis exuretur" (If the daughter of a priest be taken in whoredom and dishonor the name of her father, she shall be burnt with fire)—a biblical passage referred to neither in *Quoniam* nor in Peraldus's *Summa*. The Parson thereby adds a third category to the anatomy of lechery and its punishment that was adduced neither in *Quoniam* nor in Peraldus's *Summa*. The Parson's treatment of the female offender in a crime of fornication thus becomes unfoundedly harsher but at the same time also curiously less comprehensive than in either Peraldus or *Quoniam*.

He deals only with women who are servants or daughters of high church officials, leaving out "free women"—for example, women like Chaucer's sister-in-law, Katherine Swynford, the mistress of John of Gaunt, or other courtly ladies to whom, according to *Quoniam*, the harsh biblical legislation against sexual intercourse outside of marriage might otherwise apply.[72]

A more substantial alteration of the biblical sources of the *Parson's Tale* occurs under the heading of the same sin, "thylke stynkynge synne of Lecherie," where the Parson is discussing adultery as a species of "theft" (X 877–79). Here the Parson partly translates and partly paraphrases closely an exemplary biblical passage that relates the popular story of how Joseph resisted the sexual advances of Potiphar's wife:

In Chaucer's version:

> Soothly, *of this thefte douted gretly Joseph, whan that his lordes wyf preyed hym of vileyne, whan he seyde,* "Lo, *my lady,* how my lord hath take to me under my warde *al that he hath in this world,* ne *no thyng of his thynges* is out of my power, but oonly ye, that ben his wyf. / And how sholde I thanne do this wikkedness, and synne so *horribly agayns God and agayns my Lord? God it forbeede!* . . ." (X 880–81)

The passage in Genesis 39:8–9 (Vulgate) reads:

> *Qui neququam acquiescens operi nefario, dixit ad eam:* Ecce dominus meus, omnibus mihi traditis, *ignorat quid habeat in domo sua:* / nec quidquam est quod non in mea sit potestate, vel non tradiderit mihi, praeter te, quae uxor eius es: quomodo ergo possum hoc malum facere, et peccare *in Deum meum?* [But he, in no wise consenting to that wicked act, said to her: Behold, my master hath delivered all things to me, and knoweth not what he hath in his own house: / Neither is there anything which is not in my power, or that he hath not delivered to me, but thee, who art his wife: how then can I do this wicked thing, and sin against my God?]

As a comparison of the two passages shows—and as Grace Landrum long ago observed[73]—Chaucer appears to have translated directly and closely from the Vulgate, with a few slight modifications (identified by italics and discussed below). At the parallel point in their respective treatments of adultery, neither Peraldus's *Summa vitiorum* nor *Quoniam* quoted from Joseph's words of rebuke and resistance to Potiphar's wife; but under the "remedies" for lechery Peraldus's *Summa vitiorum* did include a bare reference to Joseph and a biblical book and chapter citation, "Gen 39": "Tertium remedium est, ut homo elonget se ab igne luxuriae . . . exemplo Joseph, de quo legitur Gen. 39" (The third remedy [for lechery] is for one to remove oneself from the fire of lechery . . . as Joseph did, of whom we read in Genesis 39).[74] Perhaps this was the hint that Chaucer's manuscript of the *Summa vitiorum* contained; in any case, if there were some mention of the episode of Joseph and Potiphar's wife at the parallel point in Chaucer's source, it would most likely have been in this summary form. The significant difference between this or a similarly bare allusion to "Joseph . . . of whom we read in Genesis 39" and the Parson's detailed quotation of Joseph's actual words lies in the fact that Chaucer's Parson has moved from apodictic moralization about the evils of lechery to a vivid exemplification of the moral principle he is trying to inculcate by way of casuistical rhetorical exemplification, drawn from the authoritative repertoire of biblical narrative.[75]

In addition to his slight but dramatically vivifying expansions of Joseph's righteously modest demurral ("my lady," "al that he hath in this world," "no thyng of his thynges"), the Parson takes another step in the direction of rhetorical amplification by ending not with the one overriding inhibitor to the act of adultery cited by Joseph in Genesis 39:9, namely "my God," but with two inhibitors, divine and human—"God" and "my lord" Potiphar. To keep to his initial point about adultery being a kind of "theft," it makes good sense for the Parson to have Joseph refer to "my lord" Potiphar even when the biblical Joseph—at least according to the Latin text in the Vulgate—does not.[76] The Parson's Joseph also adds, for extra measure, an emphatic "God it forbeede!" These slight amplifications have their formal and dramatically motivated didactic point: as an expositor of ethical teachings, Chaucer's Parson wishes to make the full nature of the crime that Joseph avoids as explicit and as humanly and colloquially vivid—as experientially authentic and as "felt"—as he possibly can.

Yet the Parson stops short of encouraging his readers to join Joseph imaginatively in his struggle against the temptations of Potiphar's Wife—as readers of the contemporary Middle English translation of Aelred of Rievaulx's *De institutione inclusarum* and other contemporary affective works of religious meditation are encouraged to do, when they are imagining themselves present at the scene of Christ's Passion or when they are imaginatively projecting themselves into other biblical stories.[77] Given the power of the techniques of affective meditation and imaginative self-projection that Aelred and his translators were using to arouse strong emotions and individually immediate responses, it is easy to understand why the Parson would *not* employ them in the present erotically charged instance. Indeed, the popularity of the story of Joseph and Potiphar's wife depends on the presumption that unimpeachably chaste and trustworthy men like Joseph are hard to find.[78]

In my analysis of passages from the *Parson's Tale* thus far, I have intentionally been alternating "Chaucer" and "the Parson" when assigning responsibility for the divergences of the *Parson's Tale* from its intermediate biblical sources. The alternation is meant to leave open the fundamentally undecidable question of whether Chaucer introduced these divergences for the purpose of stating his own views on pressing and controversial matters facing the Christian community or views of the fictional Parson—views with which Chaucer either identified fully or from which he wished to distance himself somewhat. For example, in the last of the passages from the *Parson's Tale* which I have so far discussed, the upper-class and anticlerical biases implicit in the mistakes that the Parson makes regarding the biblical punishments meted out for lechery may be interpreted either as purposefully Chaucer's or the Parson's; in the latter case it is difficult if not impossible to say whether or not the Parson's mistakes reveal a bias that was shared by the real Geoffrey Chaucer, Katherine Swynford's brother-in-law.

Would it not be safer, then, and perhaps also more plausible, to regard the Parson's departures from *Quoniam* and Peraldus in the treatment of the sin of lechery simply as Chaucer's mistakes? There is certainly a confusing enough variety of cases of capital punishment for various sexual crimes defined in Leviticus and Deuteronomy to account for Chaucer's blundering over the fate of a fornicating "womman thral" without assuming that the blunders reveal Chaucer's subtle purposiveness—especially if when Chaucer expanded, altered, or added to the biblical texts he found in *Quoniam* he was working from memory.

Yet there is some further justification for regarding the expanded treatment of the topic of lechery in the *Parson's Tale*—the confused synthesis in this section of the tale of several biblical passages, the uniform but biblically unfounded sentence of death meted out both to a "womman thral" and a "bisshopes daughter" guilty of fornication, and the translation and amplification of Genesis 39:8–9—all as the Parson's work, whether or not expressive of the views of Chaucer. Separating the persona of the Parson from that of his creator and discovering significant departures from the sources of the *Parson's Tale* that Chaucer intentionally introduced behind the cover of the character—including blunders in biblical quotations like those in *Parson's Tale* X 837–39—is more plausible in view of other features of Chaucer's invention of the Parson. When the Parson introduces his treatise on penitence by scorning storytelling and poetry and privileging "[m]oralitee and vertuous mateere" in prose (*Parson's Prologue* X 30–60), we obviously are encouraged to segregate his opinions from those of Chaucer the poet. Furthermore, elsewhere in the *Parson's Tale* there are other subtle and purposeful manipulations of biblical authority that imply controversial opinions with which Chaucer, as distinct from his Parson, may or may not have agreed. Though there are many examples, two from the Parson's explication of the sin of Avarice (*Parson's Tale* X 739–803) are especially revealing.

The first, from the Parson's exposition of the idolatry inherent in the sin of avarice, involves several complicated nuances of Chaucer's biblical translation and his apparently purposeful alteration of his proximate source. The Parson says:

> What difference is bitwixe an ydolastre and an avaricious man, but that an ydolastre, per aventure, ne hath but o mawmet or two, and the avaricious man hath manye? For certes, every floryn in his cofre is his mawmet. / And certes, the synne of mawmettrie is *the firste thyng that God deffended in the ten comaundementz,* as bereth witnesse in *Exodi capitulo vicesimo.* / "Thou shalt have no false goddes bifore me, ne thou shalt make to thee no grave

thyng." Thus is an avaricious man, that loveth his tresor biforn
God, an ydolastre. (X 749–51; emphasis added)

In *Quoniam* Chaucer would have found a similar equation of
avarice with idolatry, but the equation there is supported with an
inappropriate quotation from the beginning of Exodus 20:7: "Non
assumes nomen Dei in vanum" (Thou shalt not take the name of
the Lord thy God in vain); and as Wenzel points out, this same
inappropriate quotation occurs also in Peraldus's *Summa.*[79] Chaucer
has apparently gone back to the Bible, to the chapter in Exodus
quoted in his source, and translated those verses from the passage
listing the Ten Commandments that were more suitable to his
theme: "Non habebis deos alienos coram me. / Non facies tibi
sculptile" (Exodus 20:3–4; Thou shalt not have strange gods before
me. / Thou shalt not make to thyself a graven thing).

The Parson's blend of Exodus 20:3–4, introduced as "the firste
thyng that God deffended in the ten comaundementz," follows the
system of numbering the Ten Commandments—the usual orthodox
(i.e., Augustinian) medieval Christian one—according to which
the first commandment, covered in Exodus 20:3–6, forbids "false
worship" and "the worship of false gods" as a "single subject" and
the second commandment, covered in Exodus 20:7, forbids use of
the Lord's name in vain.[80] But by mentioning the prohibition in
Exodus 20:4 against worshiping "a graven thing" the Parson takes a
small step toward entering some very stormy theological waters.
Though Lollard propagandists also followed Augustinian usage in
counting Exodus 20:3–4 as part of the first commandment, they
nevertheless tended to single out and stress the prohibition in
Exodus 20:4 against "graven images," which they accused their
orthodox antagonists of having violated by what they call
"idolatrous" worship of images—gold and jewel-encrusted cruci-
fixes, reliquaries, statues of saints, and the like.[81]

The Parson's assertion that "the synne of mawmettrie is the
firste thyng that God deffended in the ten comaundementz"(X
750) and his brief distributive account of two elements in the first
commandment—translating Exodus 20:3–4: "Thou shalt have no
false goddes bifore me" and "ne thou shalt make to thee no grave
thyng" (X 751)—place him between the heretical and orthodox
positions, but implicitly closer to the Wycliffite one than at least

some of Chaucer's noble friends and patrons would have cared to consider.[82] That Chaucer knew he was touching on fiercely contested matters when he had the Parson discuss the Ten Commandments is confirmed by the fact that some two hundred lines later, when the Parson concludes his account of the "sevene deedly synnes" and their "remedies," he returns to the subject of the Ten Commandments with a revealingly cautious but inaccurate summary, wrapped around an *occupatio*:

> Now after that I have declared yow, as I kan, the sevene deedly synnes, and somme of hire braunches and hire remedies, soothly, if I koude, I wolde telle yow the ten comandementz. / But so heigh a doctrine I lete to divines. Nathelees, I hope to God, they been touched in this tretis, everich of hem alle. (X 956–57)[83]

The Parson's "hope" to have covered all of the Ten Commandments ("everich of hem alle") is frustrated by his never actually saying anything about either the third (Exodus 20:8–11, "Remember that thou keep holy the sabbath day") or the fourth commandments (Exodus 20:12, "Honour thy father and thy mother"). More noteworthy, however, is his deferral of any further commentary or exposition of the Ten Commandments to his intellectual betters ("so heigh a doctrine I lete to divines"). The Parson's explicit disavowal of the role of theologian in this passage is also matched a bit later on by a similar disavowal of his competence to treat the Pater Noster, the prayer that Jesus teaches to his disciples in Matthew 6:9–13 (cp. Luke 11:2–4): "The exposicioun of this hooly preyere, that is so excellent and digne, I bitake to thise maistres of theologie" (X 1043).

Chaucer's avoiding any exposition of the Pater Noster in the *Parson's Tale* contrasts amusingly, and revealingly, with his two other allusions to this Latin prayer, both of which occur in the *Miller's Tale*. There Chaucer depicts an Oxford carpenter and clerk who use the opening words of the prayer in a comically superstitious oath or charm: "the white pater-noster!" (I 3485), and "Now, *Pater-noster, clom!*" (3638). Like the Ten Commandments, the Pater Noster in Chaucer's day was a frequent site of both orthodox and competing Lollard translation, paraphrase, and exegesis.[84] By leaving exposition of these two essential but disputed biblical texts to "divines" and "maistres of theologie" the Parson steers clear of contemporary religious doctrinal controversy and stays focused instead on his priestly goal of leading the individual members of his flock toward penitence.

In the second example, Chaucer is once again not blindly following his source. He is displaying the same tact that he displayed when he dropped the potentially offensive quotation of Ecclesiastes 10:16 in *Melibee*.[85] The specific case of avarice under discussion is tyranny of "lords" over "hooly chirche:"

> What seye we thanne of hem that pilen and doon extorcions to hooly chirche? Certes, the swerd that men yeven first to a knyght, whan he is dubbed, signifieth that he sholde deffenden hooly chirche, and nat robben it ne pilen it; whoso dooth is traitour to Crist. (X 767)

Thus far Chaucer has been following *Quoniam* closely.[86] But he omits the next link in the chain of the argument in *Quoniam*: "Et omnes qui sic gladium acceperunt, gladio peribunt, Matt. 26[:52; for all that take the sword shall perish with the sword]." *Quoniam* mitigates these frightening words a bit by explaining that "hoc est, quod nullo iubente vel concedente in sanguinem innocentium armantur, ut ait Augustinus contra Manicheos" (that is, no one under arms should rejoice in or allow innocent blood to be shed, as Augustine says in *Contra Manicheos*).[87] Chaucer omits this as well. Where he resumes translating, however, the trace of what he has skipped over is visible:

> And as seith Seint Augustyn, "they ben the develes wolves that stranglen the sheep of Jhesu Crist"; and doon worse than wolves. For soothly, whan the wolf hath ful his wombe, he stynteth to strangle sheep. But soothly, the pilours and destroyours of the godes of hooly chirche no [*sic*] do nat so, for they ne stynte nevere to pile. (X 768–69)

This comparison of despoilers of "hooly chirche" to insatiable wolves (based ultimately on John 10:12, Matthew 10:16, Acts 20:29, and similar biblical verses) is also found in *Quoniam*, immediately following the quotation of Matthew 26:52 and the mitigating gloss that Chaucer skipped:

Item, qui subiectos iniuste spoliant, proditores sunt. . . . Ecce quod lupi sunt predones, immo lupis rapaciores, quia lupi aliquando cessant et satiantur, isti vero numquam. [Likewise, those who unjustly despoil their subjects are traitors. . . . Indeed, though wolves are predators, those who despoil their subjects are more rapacious than wolves, for wolves sometimes cease despoiling when they are satiated, but these never cease.][88]

Chaucer has dropped the offensive quotation of Matthew 26:52 along with the mitigating gloss from Augustine's *Contra Manicheos*, while keeping Augustine in the picture by attributing to him a more commonplace saying, one that *Quoniam* leaves unattributed.[89]

Though Chaucer quotes from or alludes to verses from Matthew 26 in some fifteen different passages in the *Canterbury Tales*, he avoids verse 52, "Put up again thy sword into its place: for all that take the sword shall perish with the sword." Why these words might make sword-wielding aristocrats more than a bit uncomfortable is obvious. In the 1380s and 1390s it would have been especially impolitic for Chaucer to cite Matthew 26:52. For Jesus' apparently radical antiwar statement in this verse was frequently cited by Lollard authors in support of their controversial pacifistic arguments against the right of noblemen to participate in the crusades, in the war against the French, or indeed to commit "homicydes" and "manslaughteres" of any kind.[90] Interestingly, the Lollards also invoked the authority of Christ's command in Matthew 26:52 to prove that the Church was forbidden to wield military or, by extrapolation, any sort of temporal power. In a Lollard tract that presents a debate between a Knight and a Clerk over the rights of the Church to secular dominion, the Knight's winning argument includes the following exposition of Matthew 26:52:

"Saynte Mari!" said þe Kniȝt, "it es litel wonder þof ȝe ouerlede þe comone lewde pepil wiþ sich fals exsposiciones of holi writt! [The Clerk has just quoted Luke 22:36–38 to prove that the clergy should wield both temporal and spiritual power.] Parde, þou wost wele þat, when þat Crist schuld be take, Peter drowe his swerde for to fiȝt and smote of Malkus here, and onone Crist repreued him and bad him putt vp his swerd, in token þat þe temperale swerde langid not to him, ne to none oþer prestre for to fiȝt ne smyte wiþ no temperall swerd. But þe swerde þat he schuld smyte wiþ schuld be þe swerde of þe goste, þat es Goddes worde, as saynte Poule saiþ [i.e., in Eph. 6:17].[91]

Whether interpreted in relation to ecclesiastical rights and responsibilities, as in this Lollard tract, or with respect to secular rights and responsibilities, as in *Quoniam*, a quotation of Matthew 26:52 in the court of Richard II would have had a controversial and telltale Wycliffite ring to it. Chaucer would thus have had good reason to make the Parson avoid Matthew 26:52, especially since the point of *Parson's Tale* X 767–69 was neither to condemn all forms of violence nor to second the Wycliffite claim that the Church should not wield temporal power or hold property, but (following *Quoniam*) to condemn only those lords who avariciously "despoil" the Church of its wealth.[92]

In his tale, the Parson quotes from the Bible more than any character in the *Canterbury Tales,* and sometimes, as we have seen, he even expands or embellishes the biblical quotations that were in his sources.[93] Thomas Bestul has explicated two particularly significant additions to the known sources of the *Parson's Tale:* (1) a passage derived from Anselm's *Meditation on the Last Judgment* (X 169–73) describing the terrors of Judgment Day; and (2) a longer passage on the Passion (X 255–82), in which Chaucer draws on a sermon of Saint Bernard and translates and adapts a number of commonplaces from affective literature of meditation on the Passion.[94] Bestul points out that the *Parson's Tale* is twice referred to in its *Prologue* as a "meditacioun," first by the Parson himself (X 55), and then by Harry Bailly (X 69); and he draws attention to Harry Bailly's urging the Parson to be "fructuous" in his tale (X 71). The terms "meditacioun" and "fructuous" are clues, Bestul suggests, that link the *Parson's Tale* to "the late-medieval tradition of *meditatio.*"[95] Like the *Parson's Tale,* late medieval "meditations" were sometimes also compendious compilations from different sources that were increasingly likely to focus on "the virtues and vices and self-examination as part of or prefatory to penitential discipline, even though by the fourteenth century meditations on the humanity of Christ may have been the dominant type."[96]

Affective and religious or politically scrupulous modifications aside, Chaucer seems to have gone out of his way to make the

Parson a translator of the plain text of the Bible into English. D. W. Robertson, Jr., agrees that this is the case, but he tilts the Parson's biblicism back in the direction of allegory: "It is true that most of the [Parson's] authorities are clear on the surface without exposition, and this is as it should be in a manual addressed to laymen; but it is also true that insofar as it is exegetical, it makes no departures from the traditions of Pauline allegory."[97] This passes lightly over a crucial point: the *Parson's Tale* is far more "literal" than "exegetical." The Parson does frequently take for granted the traditional exegetical understanding of the biblical verses he cites.[98] More noteworthy is the fact that Chaucer's ideal churchman renders hundreds of biblical verses, or parts of verses, from Latin into English for a lay audience, concentrating most often on the literal level of interpretation. In doing so, the Parson fulfills the reiterated foreshadowing of his biblically centered speech in the *General Prologue:*

> He was also a lerned man, a clerk,
> That Cristes gospel trewely wolde preche;
> His parisshens devoutly wolde he teche.
> . . . .
> This noble ensample to his sheep he yaf,
> That first he wroghte, and afterward he taughte.
> Out of the gospel he tho wordes caughte . . .
> . . . .
> But Cristes loore and his apostles twelve
> He taughte.
>
> (I 480–82, 496–98, 527–28)

Though the Parson's uses of the Bible are mainly literal, they are nevertheless also faultless in the light of fourteenth-century medieval Christian orthodoxy. Often, however, as we shall see in the following two chapters, when Chaucer's characters use the Bible, they eschew the literal in favor of patently self-interested varieties of glossing and figural interpretations that are frequently unorthodox or contentious.

CHAPTER 4

Partial or Oblique
Quotations and Allusions

Experience proves surely that the Bible does not answer a purpose for which it was never intended. It may be accidentally the means of the conversion of individuals; but a book, after all, cannot make a stand against the wild living intellect of man.

John Henry Newman, *History of My Religious Opinions*

Unlike the substantial and generally self-sufficient biblical quotations discussed in the previous chapter, Chaucer's partial or oblique biblical quotations and allusions seem to call for the completion or clarification provided by their absent scriptural contexts.[1] The frequency with which quotations of this kind appear in Chaucer's works, especially in the *Canterbury Tales*, shows that he was sensitive to the problematic application of institutionally defined and monitored biblical authority. Almost half a millennium later, Cardinal Newman offered both a striking formulation and an implicit solution of the same problem. For when Newman had come to believe that the Bible "cannot make a stand against the wild living intellect of man" he was ready to renounce his Protestantism and accept the Catholic view that biblical interpretation must be strictly controlled by the Church. Whether or not Chaucer accepted this view in his personal life, he was aware that quotations from the Bible, by males and females alike, are always to some extent partial and always to some degree self-interested—at least in fiction.

I

In the *Summoner's Tale*, for example, Friar John quotes only the first clause in Matthew 5:3 to bolster his claims about the validity,

and the virtue, of his obviously corrupt attempts at extorting
money from a sick peasant:

> . . . oure sweete Lord Jhesus
> Spak this by freres, whan he seyde thus:
> "Blessed be they that povere in spirit been."
> And so forth al the gospel may ye seen.
>
> (III 1921–24)[2]

But as the friar's own "[a]nd so forth" invites us to discover, the
omitted second clause of Matthew 5:3, "for theirs is the kingdom of
heaven," reveals that the reward he should be seeking is a heavenly
one rather than a material one. Indeed, the further one reads in
"al the gospel" of the Sermon on the Mount (ending at Matthew
7:28), the more one discovers that Friar John—like other characters in Ricardian poetry—is pointing to an absent biblical
context that exposes his gross neglect of his true Christian duty.[3]

Chaucer uses the device of partial or oblique biblical quotation
to achieve more subtle effects elsewhere in the *Canterbury Tales*.
The Pardoner, for example, differs from the corrupt friar of the
Summoner's Tale in that he brazenly and despairingly cites the Bible
as if he has nothing to hide. Thus when he denounces the various
"tavern vices"—"But, certes, he that haunteth swiche delices / Is
deed, whil that he lyveth in tho vices" (VI 547–48)—the Pardoner
is obliquely echoing the first half of Paul's definition of sin as a
living death: "For the wisdom of the flesh is death" (Romans 8:6);
but he omits Paul's hopeful conclusion in the second half of the
verse, "but the wisdom of the spirit is life and peace," as well as
Paul's further reassurance a few lines later on, in Romans 8:9–13,
that even the worst of sinners can repent and win eternal life.[4]

A less obvious partial biblical allusion in the *Pardoner's Tale*—and
one with a very different tone and thematic resonance—occurs in
the Pardoner's account of an unusual trick for extracting money
from a gullible audience. The trick involves what he alleges to be
the salubrious effects of the shoulder bone from a "holy Jewes
sheep" in his possession. Several possible biblical sources for this
"holy Jewes sheep" have been proposed, but none has been widely
accepted; a vague suggestion of some remote and indefinite but
magical Old Testament event seems to have been precisely the

effect that Chaucer wanted the Pardoner to convey.[5] Leaving its biblical origin unspecified, the Pardoner then claims that when this sheep's bone has been dipped in water, the water will cure sick cattle (VI 353–60). But that is not all. Next he asserts that if the owner of the sick cattle drinks a draught of the same water, every week (he neglects to say for how many weeks!) before cockcrow, while fasting, then his livestock will multiply (he neglects to say how fast!). Then the Pardoner concludes:

> And, sires, also it heeleth jalousie;
> For though a man be falle in jalous rage,
> Lat maken with this water his potage,
> And nevere shal he moore his wyf mystriste,
> Though he the soothe of hir defaute wiste,
> Al had she taken prestes two or thre.
>
> (VI 366–71)

In the "cure" for jealousy that the Pardoner outlines there is an oblique and hitherto unnoticed biblical allusion. The ritual he is describing is in fact a sly inversion of a biblical trial by ordeal initiated by a "husband stirred up by the spirit of jealousy" and imposed on a wife suspected of adultery (Numbers 5:11–31). The passage is unfamiliar enough to quote at length:

> And the Lord spoke to Moses, saying: Speak to the children of Israel, and thou shalt say to them: The man whose wife shall have gone astray, and contemning her husband, Shall have slept with another man, and her husband cannot discover it, but the adultery is secret, and cannot be proved by witnesses. . . . *If the spirit of jealousy stir up the husband against his wife, who either is defiled, or is charged with false suspicion,* He shall bring her to the priest. . . . *And he shall take holy water in an earthen vessel, and he shall cast a little earth of the pavement of the tabernacle into it.* And when the woman shall stand before the Lord, he shall uncover her head, and shall put on her hands the sacrifice of remembrance, and the oblation of jealousy: and he himself shall hold the most bitter waters, whereon he hath heaped curses with execration. And he shall adjure her, and shall say: If another man hath not slept with thee, and if thou be not defiled by

forsaking thy husband's bed, these most bitter waters, on which I have heaped curses, shall not hurt thee. But if thou hast gone aside from thy husband, and art defiled, and hast lain with another man: These curses shall light upon thee: The Lord make thee a curse, and an example for all among his people: may he make thy thigh to rot, and may thy belly swell and burst asunder. Let the cursed waters enter into thy belly, and may thy womb swell and thy thigh rot. . . . And he shall give them to her to drink. . . . And when she hath drunk them, if she be defiled, and having despised her husband be guilty of adultery, the malediction shall go through her, and her belly swelling, her thigh shall rot: and the woman shall be a curse, and an example to all the people. But if she be not defiled, she shall not be hurt, and shall bear children. *This is the law of jealousy. If a woman hath gone aside from her husband, and be defiled, And the husband stirred up by the spirit of jealousy bring her before the Lord, and the priest do to her according to all things that are here written: The husband shall be blameless, and she shall bear her iniquity.*

This trial by a ritual ordeal, the only instance of the practice in the Bible, caused considerable embarrassment to canonists who wished to restrict or eliminate trials by ordeal entirely.[6] Though Chaucer's Pardoner never refers to the biblical ritual explicitly, his cure for jealousy inverts it in a most ingenious way, solving the problem of the woman suspected of adultery by her husband with a minimum of inconvenience to the parties involved. In the Pardoner's inversion of the ritual it is the husband instead of the wife who drinks the potion ("Lat maken with this water his potage"), and there is no waiting to see if his "belly swells" or his "thigh rots." What the Bible prescribes as an adulterous woman's ordeal has become, in the Pardoner's inverted adaptation, a cuckolded husband's surefire cure.

In what seems like a sudden outburst of diabolical honesty, the Pardoner admits that he is the quintessential antibiblical man: "I wol noon of the apostles countrefete; / I wol have moneie, wolle, chese, and whete" (VI 447–48). But then, throughout the *Pardoner's Prologue* and *Tale*, the Bible serves the Pardoner as a disguise behind which he can go about his work as a self-proclaimed apostle of Antichrist. To distract and deceive his victims, he repeatedly flaunts his knowledge of both traditionally cited and out-of-the-way scriptural authority. As the biblical exempla come rolling off his tongue, he encourages his audience—even taunts or dares them— to read the Bible and see for themselves (VI 483, 485–555, 742, etc.). Thus, for example, the Pardoner encourages his imaginary church audience to read "the Olde Testament" to learn about all the "victories" that were achieved, with God's help, "in abstinence and preyere": "Looketh the Bible, and ther ye may it leere" (VI 575–577). But then, without dropping a stitch, he immediately adds:

> Looke, Attilla, the grete conquerour,
> Deyde in his sleep, with shame and dishonour,
> Bledynge ay at his nose in dronkenesse.
>
> (VI 578–81)

This would allow for the Pardoner's presumably illiterate imaginary audience to think that the Bible would fill them in on the death of Attila the Hun (reported in Jordanes's *De getarum gestis* and Paul the Deacon's *De gestis romanorum*).[7] At the same time, however, it might also remind the educated members of Chaucer's audience that in biblically derived works such as Peter Comestor's *Historia scholastica*, the French prose *Bible historiale complétée*, or the versified *Bible* of Jean Malkaraume they would indeed find what was traditionally regarded to be truly historical pagan subject matter correlated with what was considered to be the chronologically related events of canonical biblical history.[8]

Whatever the effect of his allusion to Attila the Hun immediately after his call for "looking to the Bible," the Pardoner immediately proceeds to flaunt the depth and accuracy of his knowledge of the Bible by alluding to "King Lamuel" and the advice he received from his mother on the dangers of drink:

> And over al this, avyseth yow right wel
> What was comaunded unto Lamuel—
> Nat Samuel, but Lamuel, seye I;
> Redeth the Bible, and fynde it expresly
> Of wyn-yevyng to hem that han justise.
>
> (VI 583–87)

Yes, the Pardoner reiterates, he means Lamuel, anticipating his audience's possible perplexity over the name, which they might think he has confused with the more familiar sound-alike Samuel. *You* may only have heard of Samuel, he implicitly chides his listeners, but *I'm* talking about Lamuel. You don't remember him? Look it up![9]

There are numerous other examples of oblique allusion and similar kinds of partial and decontextualized quotation of Scripture by the Summoner, Friar, Pardoner, and other characters in the *Canterbury Tales*, but the locus classicus of Chaucer's use of the device is unquestionably the *Wife of Bath's Prologue*. This text not only includes more partial and decontextualized quotations of Scripture than any of Chaucer's other works but also puts those quotations to use—whether they came by way of Jerome's *Epistola adversus Jovinianum* or other intermediate sources—in a manner that is thematically central but also intriguingly vexed.[10] When the Pardoner, the Friar, or the Summoner and their ilk distort and misappropriate Scripture, there is generally no mistaking it, but how Chaucer expected us to judge the Wife of Bath's uses of biblical allusion is another matter. The Wife's challenging ideas about valid interpretation as opposed to fallacious "glossing" of the Bible is considered in detail in the next chapter. In the present chapter our focus is on her uses of partial and decontextualized quotations, especially in her unorthodox but powerful exploitation of contradiction and inconsistency in the teachings of Saint Paul in 1 Corinthians 7.

Using Jerome's *Epistola adversus Jovinianum* (one of her fifth husband's favorite books) as her unacknowledged guide to most of the relevant biblical texts she cites, the Wife confronts head on the arguments from biblical authority that advocate chastity over marriage.[11] This entails, as the Wife realizes, a confrontation with the teachings of Paul, especially in 1 Corinthians, chapter 7, portions of which she manipulates with a subtlety and dexterity that put the similar attempts at partial quotation of Langland's Lady Meed and Gower's careless nuns to shame:

For sothe, I wol nat kepe me chaast in al.   46
Whan myn housbonde is fro the world ygon,
Som Cristen man shal wedde me anon,

For thanne, th'apostle [i.e., Paul] seith that I am free
To wedde, a Goddes half, where it liketh me. [1 Cor. 7:7–8, 39]
He seith that to be wedded is no synne; [1 Cor. 7:28]
Bet is to be wedded than to brynne. [1 Cor. 7:9]

(III 46–52)

As indicated in brackets, the Wife of Bath partially quotes or echoes five verses in 1 Corinthians 7 in the space of a mere seven lines—affirming what suits her, negating what does not. In their context, however, these verses do not make the straightforward case for sexual indulgence within the marriage bond, or for remarriage in the event of a husband's death, that the Wife claims they do.

In lines 46–50 the Wife summarily rejects what is Paul's repeated recommendation in favor of chastity, for virgins and widows alike, in 1 Corinthians 7:7–8 and 39, to which she partially alludes:

> For I would that all men were even as myself: but everyone hath his proper gift from God; one after this manner, and another after that. *But I say to the unmarried and to the widows: It is good for them if they so continue, even as I.* . . . A woman is bound by the law as long as her husband liveth; but *if her husband die, she is at liberty: let her marry to whom she will;* only in the Lord.

In saying that she will marry the Christian man whom she chooses ("Som Cristen man . . . where it liketh me" (lines 48 and 50), the Wife tacitly accepts the restriction to remarriage "only in the Lord" that Paul sets in 1 Cor. 7:39. But what she ignores is that in 1 Cor. 7:40 Paul qualifies his concession to remarriage even further, elevating widowhood over the married state: "But more blessed shall she be, if she so remain, according to my counsel; and so I think that I also have the spirit of God." The Wife opts instead, in lines 51–52 ("He seith that to be wedded is no synne; / Bet is to be wedded than to brynne"), for Paul's concessive advice favoring marriage in 1 Cor. 7:28 and the second half of 1 Cor. 7:9:

> But if thou take a wife, thou hast not sinned. And if a virgin marry, she hath not sinned: nevertheless such shall have tribulation of the flesh. But I spare you. . . . But if they [the unmarried and the

widows; see v. 8, above] do not contain themselves, let them marry. *For it is better to marry than to be burnt.* (emphasis added)

By dividing up and omitting the minor premise of Paul's recommendation in verse 9, that those who "do not contain themselves" should marry, from its major premise, "it is better to marry than to be burnt," the Wife not only evades the stigmatizing force of Paul's teaching on marriage but also ignores the more immediately relevant advice that Paul addressed to widows like herself in verse 8: "But I say to the unmarried and to the widows: It is good for them if they so continue, even as I." Later on, in lines 83–86 of her *Prologue*, the wife once again refers to 1 Cor. 7:39, and again to only part of the verse:

And for to been a wyf he yaf me leve
Of indulgence; so nys it no repreve
To wedde me, if that my make dye, [mate]
Withouten excepcion of bigamye.

In this case, a paraphrase of a part of verse 39 has been spliced together with a part of 1 Corinthians 7:6: "But I speak this by indulgence." Similarly, in line 51 ("He seith that to be wedded is no synne") the Wife had used only a part of the verse to which she alludes ("But if thou take a wife, thou hast not sinned"), ignoring the intractable portion in which Paul warns those who marry that they will suffer "tribulation of the flesh." Though here the Wife omits Paul's warning, she picks it up later on, in lines 156–57 of her *Prologue*, when she declares that her husband will "have his tribulacion withal / Upon his flessh, whil that I am his wyf"; and she and Paul are echoed by the Pardoner, when he interrupts her, in line 167: "What sholde I bye it [pay for it] on my my flessh so deere?"[12]

The assault on 1 Corinthians 7 in the Wife's *Prologue* continues with more than a dozen mostly partial and misleading quotations or allusions to this same New Testament chapter packed tightly in just over one hundred lines of Chaucer's text (lines 64–167), with several additional allusions to 1 Corinthians 7, alongside numerous other biblical allusions, in the remainder of the *Prologue*. We need to remember that in the Vulgate Bibles of Chaucer's day these verses would have appeared as sentences within a closely written page or column of text, and not numbered and set apart from their context. By darting around, picking, choosing, and splicing her biblical sources, the Wife fashions a mosaic of Paul's teachings that finally resembles her own image of what they ought to mean.

Implicit in the Wife's vetting of verses from 1 Corinthians 7 is her belief that when the Bible records the views of Paul it is merely endorsing what men accept, and not enunciating the commandments of God: "Why sholde *men* elles in *hir* bookes sette / That man shal yelde to his wyf hire dette?" (III 129–30; emphasis added). Her struggle against the authority of Paul and other men reaches a kind of anticlimax in lines 337–47 of her *Prologue*, as she quotes and defiantly dismisses her husband Jankin's unwelcome advice about how she should dress:[13]

> Thou seyst also, that if we make us gay
> With clothyng, and with precious array,
> That it is peril of oure chastitee;
> *And yet—with sorwe!—thou most enforce thee,*   340
> *And seye thise wordes in the Aposteles name.*
> "In habit maad with chastitee and shame
> Ye wommen shul apparaille yow," quod he,
> "And noght in tressed heer and gay perree,
> As perles, ne with gold, ne clothes riche."   345
> *After thy text, ne after thy rubriche,*
> *I wol nat wirche as muchel as a gnat.*
>
> (III 337–47; emphasis added)

In rejecting what she credits as Jankin's "text" and "rubriche" the Wife is of course also quite explicitly rejecting the authoritative teaching of Saint Paul, the man who stands behind Jankin and— most importantly—the man whose voice has sounded throughout the *Prologue* thus far. Indeed, in spurning biblical morality as enunciated by Paul, the Wife sounds much like the Pardoner, who later will proclaim: "I wol noon of the apostles countrefete" (VI 447).

Yet if we pause for a moment at the "gnat" of line 347, we shall find that more is going on here than at first meets the eye. For the "gnat" that makes its appearance here (and in several late Middle

and early Modern English proverbial phrases as well) is surely
derived from the biblical "gnat" of Matthew 23:24, in Jesus's attack
on the Pharisees as "Blind guides who strain out a gnat, and
swallow a camel."[14] And before we swallow Jankin's camel—by
which I mean the Pauline text from 1 Timothy 2:9 that the Wife of
Bath says Jankin quotes to her "in the Aposteles name" and that
she finds so infuriating (lines 340–45, quoted above)—we need to
examine this seemingly antifeminist quotation in its context. For
what we shall find is that Paul's advice in the passage Jankin
partially quotes is actually critical of men and women alike, and
that it relates specifically to the comportment of men and the dress
of women when they pray:

> I will therefore that men pray in every place, lifting up pure
> hands, without anger and contention. / In like manner women
> also in decent apparel: adorning themselves with modesty and
> sobriety, not with plaited hair, or gold, or pearls, or costly attire, /
> But as it becometh women professing godliness, with good
> works. (1 Tim. 2:8–10)

Though the Wife of Bath's partial quotations from 1 Corinthians 7
may be blatantly self-serving, it is also true that the reading strategy
she brings to bear on this chapter is superbly attuned to the
hesitancies, inconsistencies, and spaces for maneuver that Paul
(intentionally and unintentionally) left open in that text.

A similarly revealing recontextualization of biblical material
partially quoted in the *Wife of Bath's Prologue,* but one that works to
the detriment of the Wife's argument, applies to the following lines,
in which she partially quotes and paraphrases her husband's
quoting of unattributed antifeminist lore from the Book of Proverbs:

> Thou seydest eek that ther been thynges thre,
> The whyche thynges troublen al this erthe,
> And that no wight may endure the ferthe.
> O leeve sire shrewe, Jhesu shorte thy lyf!
> Yet prechestow and seyst an hateful wyf
> Yrekened is for oon of thise meschances.

> (III 362–67)

The allusion here, not identified by the Wife as biblical, is to Proverbs 30:21–23:

> By three things the earth is disturbed, and the fourth it cannot bear: / By a slave when he reigneth: by a fool when he is filled with meat: / By an odious woman when she is married: and by a bondwoman when she is heir to her mistress.[15]

As Bernard F. Huppé points out, the immediately preceding passage, Proverbs 30:18–20, uses numerical proverbs that are similar in their form ("three things . . . the fourth") to the passage that the Wife quotes; and more revealingly relevant to Chaucer's portrait of the Wife than Proverbs 30:23 (the climactic verse of the passage quoted above, paraphrased by the Wife in III 366–67) is the climactic antifeminist content of the nearby but absent Proverbs 30:20:[16] "Such is also the way of an adulterous woman, who eateth, and wipeth her mouth, and saith: I have done no evil."

A few lines later, the Wife quotes and distorts part of another of her husband's ostensible uses of proverbial antifeminist wisdom:

> Thou liknest eek wommenes love to helle,
> To bareyne lond, ther water may nat dwelle.
> Thou liknest it also to wilde fyr;
> The moore it brenneth, the moore it hath desir
> To consume every thyng that brent wole be.
>
> (III 371–75)

Though she does not say so explicitly, the passage to which the Wife alludes and from which she loosely paraphrases some expressions in these lines is found in the same biblical book and chapter she has quoted from only a moment earlier, and once again the passage is one that offers a "numerical" proverb:

> There are three things that never are satisfied, and the fourth never saith: It is enough. / Hell, and the mouth of the womb [i.e., a barren womb?], and the earth which is not satisfied with water: and the fire never saith: It is enough. (Proverbs 30:15–16)[17]

In her partial and distorted quotation the Wife replaces four insatiable things that the Bible lists by one, "wommenes love," which becomes the single tenor of three metaphorical vehicles: hell, barren land, and wildfire.[18] The Wife's dropping of the "the mouth of the womb" from among the insatiable things listed in Proverbs 30:16 follows the similar omission in the *Epistola adversus Jovinianum*; but this minor detail is dramatically well motivated. The Wife is embarrassed by the way the unedited text exposes more bluntly what she has in any case been so eager to reveal: her insatiable sexual appetite.[19]

In the immediately following lines of her *Prologue*, the Wife once again cites a distorted and partial quotation from the same biblical book:

Thou seyest, right as wormes shende a tree,
Right so a wyf destroyeth hire housbonde.

(III 376–77)

The passage in Proverbs 25:20 reads: "As a moth doth by a garment, and a worm by the wood: so the sadness of a man consumeth the heart." Ostensibly following her husband's partial quotation and gratuitous extrapolation from the biblical proverb, the Wife changes it from a general observation about the harmful effect of sadness into a specifically antifeminist one about the harmful effect of wives on their husbands.[20]

In the *Tale of Melibee*, however, Chaucer "corrects" for the Wife of Bath's misleadingly self-denouncing quotation of her husband's distorted partial quotation of Proverbs 25:20. Dame Prudence—a wife who systematically quotes the Bible accurately to underwrite the good advice she gives her husband, Melibee—correctly attributes the latter verse to Solomon and accurately quotes more of it than the Wife of Bath had previously quoted, thereby making its compactly expressed and gender-neutral biblical sense even more explicit: "Salomon seith that right as motthes in the shepes flees anoyeth to the clothes, and the smale wormes to the tree, right so anoyeth sorwe to the herte" (VII 997).[21]

A recent trend in criticism of the Wife of Bath (advancing further along a shrewd line of interpretation first put forward by Alfred David), has stressed the "femininity" of the Wife's reading strategy, and the alliance that is thus forged between the Wife as rebellious feminine reader and her creator, Chaucer, who has imagined reading like a rebellious woman.[22] We have come a long way from D. W. Robertson, Jr.'s condemnation of the Wife of Bath as a "carnal exegete" deaf to the true, univocal sense of Scripture. But opinions regarding the extent to which Chaucer meant to validate the Wife's feminine readerly rebelliousness vary widely among recent interpreters. The variety of opinion seems warranted. Any univocal judgment on the Wife's quotation and exegesis of Scripture will fail to do the complexity of her case, and Chaucer's investment in that case, full justice. For when the context in which we evaluate the Wife's partial biblical quotations has been appropriately extended to include the recurrent questioning of biblical quotation and exegesis throughout the *Canterbury Tales*, the partiality of her reading strategy begins to look more and more like the freedom of invention that Chaucer the poet arrogated to himself as a strong reader and interpreter of the Bible and other texts.

Indeed, when the ramifications of all aspects of her reading strategy are considered in relation to Chaucer's approach to biblical texts elsewhere in his works, it becomes apparent that she shares some of Chaucer's most profound concerns about validity in biblical interpretation in general and the problematic appropriation of the enforcing power of biblical authority for institutional purposes in particular. But for now, having recognized that the Wife of Bath is often quoting her husband's (or husbands') self-serving partial quotations of biblical authority, we can begin to appreciate that Chaucer's depiction of her sermonlike protest against the "textual harassment" of women by men—and especially by Saint Paul and her fifth husband, the clerk Jankin—has more to it than might otherwise be accounted for by stereotypical anti-feminist ideas on the irrationality of womanly pique.[23]

II

The use of partial and oblique biblical quotations and allusions in the *Wife of Bath's Prologue* enabled Chaucer to achieve richly ambiguous ironic effects. In the *Miller's Tale* Chaucer's use of the same device may be less ambiguous, but it is equally impressive.

Throughout the *Miller's Tale*, as R. E. Kaske has demonstrated in detail, ironically oblique allusions to Canticles accompany the representation of sexual desire, becoming especially thick in the portrayal of Absolon's wooing of Alisoun.[24] But that is only one of the strands of partially or obliquely adduced biblical authority in the *Miller's Tale*. As its brilliant plot unfolds, the reader's or listener's sense of dramatic irony, heightened by a number of centrally placed partial and oblique allusions to several different decontextualized biblical authorities, rises to an exquisite pitch.[25]

In the main biblically defined plot motif of the *Miller's Tale*, "hende" Nicholas, a clever clerk who is planning to spend a night with Alisoun, the eagerly adulterous wife of John, a foolish old carpenter, terrorizes his gullible victim into literally setting the stage for his own cuckolding by means of a false prophecy of a second Flood. With partial and oblique references to Genesis, chapters 6–9, Nicholas warns John that this second "Noes flood" will be twice as "greet" as the original biblical one (I 3513–21); but Nicholas also reassures John that if he follows instructions, as Noah once did, this time there will be only three survivors, Alisoun, John's adored wife, "and thee and me" (I 3527–32). Taking advantage of John's sad unfamiliarity with the original account of the Flood in Genesis, Nicholas interlards his summary version of the Flood story with an allusion to the apocryphal scene of fighting between Noah and his wife as she resisted his efforts to get her on board the ark (I 3538–43)—an apocryphal and slapstick antifeminist scene no doubt familiar to Chaucer's audience through its frequent portrayal in medieval vernacular drama.[26]

Like the Wife of Bath's return sallies against proponents of chastity by way of her own selected partial quotations from the teachings of Saint Paul, or like Jankin's smugly decontextualized and similarly partial biblical advice about how Alisoun should dress, Nicholas's make-believe reprise of Noah's Flood plays off of an absent biblical context. Though John the "sely carpenter" claims to have heard the story "ful yoore ago" (I 3537), he seems to have forgotten (or never knew in the first place) that the biblical Flood ended with the Lord's promise to "no more curse the earth for the sake of man" and to "no more destroy every living soul" (Genesis 8:21). In the absent biblical source, the Lord's promise, sealed with the "covenant" of the rainbow, was in fact specifically reassuring with respect to floods ("And God said . . . I will remember my covenant with you, and with every living soul that beareth flesh: and there shall no more be waters of a flood to destroy all flesh"; see Genesis 9:11–15). As long as John forgets why the Bible says that there are rainbows in the sky, Nicholas's scheme can proceed according to its renovated pseudo-biblical blueprint. Presumably, we the audience are more up to date. We know the elementary and biblically based fact that there cannot possibly be another world-destroying flood.

This much is fairly obvious. But the comic play that Nicholas makes out of John's ignorance of the absent verses from Genesis is reinforced by a more subtle but similar partial biblical allusion. When Nicholas quotes Solomon to convince John to prepare for the Second Flood—"For thus seith Salomon, that was ful trewe: / 'Werk al by conseil, and thou shalt nat rewe'" (I 3529–30)—he is once again adducing the Bible in a way that becomes superbly telling only when one considers the full biblical context:

> *My son, do thou nothing without counsel, and thou shalt not repent when thou hast done.* Go not in the way of ruin, and thou shalt not stumble against the stones; trust not thyself to a rugged way, lest thou set a stumbling block to thy soul. And beware of thy own children, *and take heed of them of thy household.* (Ecclesiasticus 32:24–26; emphasis added)

Two obvious and relatively minor features of Nicholas's use of partially adduced biblical authority here are, first, that he misattributes a saying by Jesus, son of Sirach, the author of Ecclesiasticus, to Solomon, the author of Ecclesiastes; and second, that he offers "sely" John a positive form of advice that in Ecclesiasticus is phrased in the negative: "Werk al by conseil" as opposed to "do thou nothing without counsel."[27]

In the *Merchant's Tale* it is doubly ironic that the false counselor, Placebo, who urges January to wed a young bride, should also cite "Solomon's" advice to "Wirk alle thyng by conseil" only to dismiss it in favor of January's own "conseil" (IV 1478–90)—doubly ironic because, first, the biblical counsel is dismissed, and second, because the absent biblical context, in which there is a warning to "take heed of them of thy household," foreshadows the threat to the integrity of January's marriage posed by the two most intimate members of January's "household," his trusted squire, Damian, and his young wife, May. In *Melibee* Dame Prudence also mis-attributes to Solomon the same advice of Ecclesiasticus 32:24, but she quotes more of the verse than either Nicholas in the *Miller's Tale* or Placebo in the *Merchant's Tale*, as she not only advises her husband but reassures him as to the effectiveness of her advice: "Werk alle thy thynges by conseil, and thou shalt never repente" (VII 1003). Though Melibee immediately follows his wife's advice and convenes "a greet congregacion of folk" (VII 1004), Chaucer tells us that among those who joined this "congregacion" were various dissemblers and flatterers (VII 1005–7). Because of the conflicting opinions expressed by various speakers, Melibee learns that Prudence's advice to "Wirk alle thyng by conseil" is easier to give than to follow. Though Prudence's use of the biblical verse is obviously not broadly ironical in the same way as Nicholas's and Placebo's uses of it, Chaucer nevertheless is implying in *Melibee* that when one tries to implement even the wisest of biblical counsels, a degree of caution remains in order.

In the *Miller's Tale*, of course, if John the carpenter does not recall (or has never even read or heard about) the end of the Flood narrative in Genesis, there is little chance of his noticing either Nicholas's misattribution of the saying from Ecclesiasticus or his change of its form from negative to positive. Furthermore, though John might be familiar with the proverb derived from the biblical verse, he would certainly not be likely to know its ominously appropriate biblical context ("and take heed of them of thy household"). For if he had, he would have been forewarned against trusting either his tenant, "hende" Nicholas, or his wife, "sweete" Alisoun, the untrustworthy members of his household who (as Damian and May will do to January in the *Merchant's Tale*) are planning to cuckold him even as they speak.

III

In the envoy to the *Clerk's Tale*, the well-instructed wife is urged to take no heed of a husband's objections to his wife's flaunting herself or spending her husband's money, but to "lat hym care and wepe and waille!" (IV 1212). As if ignited by the shock of recognition, the nameless Merchant of the *General Prologue* suddenly begins to confess—"Wepyng and waylyng, care and oother sorwe / I knowe ynogh, on even and a-morwe" (IV 1213–14)—but he then draws back a bit, assimilating his particular plight to the general one of those similarly afflicted ("and so been many mo"), before going on with further details of his personal misfortune, now seen in the light of what he has heard in the *Clerk's Tale* (IV 1218–25). The movement here from the individual plight of one husband to the general condition of all husbands nicely foreshadows and matches the similar movement at the climax of the *Merchant's Tale* from the wiliness of May in answering for her adultery to the wiliness of all wives in similar circumstances. More immediately, the Merchant's generalization signals that he will be responding to the *Clerk's Tale* not as an allegorical theodicy but (following the lead of Chaucer and the Clerk in their ironic *envoi*) as an exemplum on the biblically explored topic of the proper relation between husbands and wives.

The first allusion to the Bible in the *Merchant's Tale*, like most of those that follow it, is a purposefully oblique and fragmentary one. January, who at sixty is well beyond the age when most men are supposed to be pondering such matters, confidently declares his intention to marry:

> to lyve under that hooly boond
> With which that first God man and woman bond [bound]
> "Noon other lyf," seyde he, "is worth a bene; [bean]
> For wedlok is so esy and so clene [pure]
> That in this world it is a paradys."
>
> (IV 1261–65)

In the first couplet, the *rime riche* of "boond-bond" provides an iconic rendering of the idea from Genesis 2:24b that it expresses: God commanded the first man and woman to unite in marriage, to become as one flesh. But in the final three verses, when January speaks of the "esy" and "clene" nature of the "paradys" of wedlock, he reveals his ignorance of, or his self-deluding obliviousness to, key events in the story from Genesis to which he is alluding, namely, Eve's seduction by the serpent, Adam's fall, and the expulsion from Paradise.

These words prove to have been the opening shot in a biblical Battle of the Book over the virtues and vices of women and marriage. January soon follows them by obliquely adducing another scriptural text to buttress his decision to wed, when he proclaims: "A wyf is goddes yifte [gift] verraily" (IV 1311). But here again his memory seems to fail him, since the source of this unacknowledged quotation is almost certainly Proverbs 19:14, the relevant portion of which reads, "a *prudent* wife is from the Lord" (emphasis added). Also relevant, given the circumstances of the story about to unfold, is the clause ending the verse that immediately precedes the one January has misquoted: "the contentions of a wife are a continual dropping" (Proverbs 19:13).

Though it may be difficult if not impossible to prove conclusively that Chaucer had either of the latter two biblical verses in mind when he placed a distorted piece of one of them in January's mouth, the cumulative evidence presented throughout this book of Chaucer's detailed knowledge of the Bible strengthens that possibility. More direct evidence also comes from a marginal Latin gloss in the Ellesmere manuscript that repeats the partial quotation of Proverbs 19:14, compounds the error by misattributing the verse to Jesus son of Sirach, but then provides a corrective quotation from Albertanus of Brescia: "A wife is to be loved because she is a gift of God. Jesus son of Sirach [error for Prov. 19:14]: 'House and riches are given by parents, but a good or prudent wife is properly from the Lord.'"[28] Perhaps only some members of Chaucer's listening audience knew and remembered the Bible well enough to appreciate all the ramifications of this delicate manipulation of a partial and decontextualized scriptural reference, or the similarly subtle effects of the other partial biblical allusions in the *Merchant's Tale* that I shall soon be proposing. At least for readers of a glossed manuscript like Ellesmere, the task was simplified. We can safely assume that most members of Chaucer's reading and listening audience would have accurately recalled the biblical context in a general way—that is, although they might not remember the specific sources and the exact wording of the biblical passages to which January alludes, they would surely have remembered enough to perceive the *tendency* of the Merchant's partial and distorted quotations.

This would certainly have been the case when January (or the Merchant?) praises Eve and all other wives ever after in the course of an extended and more explicit reference to the story of Adam and Eve in Paradise, previously alluded to only in passing:[29]

> And herke why, I sey nat this for noght,
> That womman is for mannes helpe y-wroght. [created]
> The hye God, whan he hadde Adam maked,   1325
> And saugh him al allone, bely-naked,
> God of his grete goodnesse seyde than,
> "Lat us now make an helpe unto this man
> Lyk to hymself"; and thanne he made him Eve.
> Heere may ye see, and heerby may ye preve,   1330
> That wyf is mannes helpe and his confort,
> His paradys terrestre, and his disport.
> So buxom and so vertuous is she, [obedient]
> They moste nedes lyve in unitee.
> O flessh they been, and o flessh, as I gesse   1335
> Hath but oon herte, in wele and in distresse.
>
> (IV 1323–36)

Having once again omitted Eve's treachery and the loss of Paradise, this time the Merchant offers a fuller and hence a more blatantly truncated and distortingly idealized account of what Genesis says about the origin of vexed relations between the sexes.[30]

The Merchant follows this ominously distorted evocation of the first chapters of Genesis with a broad swipe of antimatrimonial verbal irony:

> A wyf! a, seinte Marie, *benedicite*!
> How myghte a man han any adversitee
> That hath a wyf?   1339

There is nothing particularly remarkable about the speaker's posing of a rhetorical question to which the answer on one level (that of the antimatrimonial "joke") is implicitly the opposite of what we are being led to expect on another level (that of the explicitly promatrimonial claim). Though the invocation of the

Virgin Mary might also seem innocent enough, in the present context the Merchant's asseveration by "seinte Marie" constitutes an oblique biblical allusion with a particularly apt ironic resonance. According to medieval traditions amply attested in Middle English lyrics and vernacular drama, the Virgin Mary's husband, Joseph, was not only a gentle and long-suffering man but also a harassed and skeptical one—a saint, to be sure, but not the best advertisement for what the Merchant says is the adversity-free bliss of married life. Swept up in great events in which he played little or no active part and whose significance he did not fully understand, Joseph was traditionally portrayed as a man somewhat embarrassed by the taint of cuckoldry that less trusting souls perceived in his situation.[31]

Now, if Chaucer had made the Merchant swear by "seinte Joseph" rather than by "seinte Marie" there would be less doubt as to his ironic intentions. As it happens, however, Chaucer's likely ironic purpose in having his narrator swear by "Saint Mary" is underscored when January invokes the Virgin (in line 1899), and when May appeals to her (in line 2334), and when, for a third and final time, she is again invoked by the Merchant-Narrator (in line 2418). Of course the irony implicit in Chaucer's oblique evocation of the biblical and apocryphal marital background of "seinte Marie" is a delicate affair; yet it seems highly plausible that members of Chaucer's audience would have found the reiterated allusion risible for the reasons I have suggested.[32]

Not satisfied with the authorities favoring marriage that he has amassed, the Merchant next offers a series of biblical exempla:

> Lo, how that Jacob, as thise clerkes rede, [recount]
> By good conseil of his mooder Rebekke,
> Boond the kydes skyn aboute his nekke,
> For which his fadres benyson he wan.   1365
> Lo Judith, as the storie eek telle kan,
> By wys conseil she Goddes peple kepte,
> And slow hym Olofernus, whil he slepte. [slew]
> Lo Abigayl, by good conseil, how she
> Saved hir housbonde Nabal, whan that he   1370
> Sholde han be slayn; and looke, Ester also
> By good conseil delyvered out of wo

The peple of God, and made hym Mardochee
Of Assuere enhaunced for to be.

On the surface this passage appears to contain an antidote to the
traditional antifeminist list of biblical exempla alluded to in *Sir
Gawain and the Green Knight* and elsewhere in medieval literature.[33]
On closer inspection, however, the antimatrimonial irony of these
biblical exempla—borrowed but modified by Chaucer from the
similarly ordered list of the same virtuous women in *Melibee*[34]—
proves to be sharp. Though each of the biblical heroines mentioned was traditionally regarded favorably for having done
something noteworthy to advance the Divine Plan, the behavior of
each woman toward her husband or lover—that is, the behavior
that ostensibly justifies her inclusion on the Merchant's list—was
uncooperative or worse: Rebecca tricked her blind husband, Isaac,
when she devised the stratagem by which her son Jacob stole the
blessing intended for Esau, Isaac's favorite; Judith was a widow
who wrought vengeance on her would-be lover and foe of the
Israelites, the pagan general Holofernes; Abigail was lavishly
generous with her husband's property to make up for his
discourtesy to King David, and then, when her husband grew
despondent because of her behavior and shortly thereafter died,
she went off to become David's bride; and Esther manipulated
King Ahasuerus in order to save her people and destroy their
bitter foe, Haman.[35]

After brief allusions by the narrator to Ecclesiasticus and
Ephesians on the joys and obligations of marriage (IV 1381–82,
1384) and an echo by January of Psalms 29:4, 10 (IV 1401),
January uses a strikingly gruesome and obliquely biblical image to
express his dismay at the prospect of dying without an heir:

Yet were me levere houndes had me eten, [I would rather]
Than that myn heritage sholde falle
In straunge hand, and this I telle yow alle.   1440

Now, medieval battlefields, like some modern ones, would have
provided a sufficiently vivid and real-life model for the horrifying
picture of a corpse being devoured by "houndes." In the *Knight's
Tale* Chaucer recounts the cruelty of Creon, who leaves corpses

unburied on a battlefield at Thebes and "maketh houndes ete hem in despit" (I 947). Yet the idea of a man who would prefer to be eaten by dogs rather than lose his "heritage" to a stranger echoes motifs of a biblical story, "the crime of Naboth's vineyard," in which the villains are the infamous King Ahab and his even more infamous queen, Jezebel. As Elijah prophesied, because Ahab and Jezebel had instigated the murder of Naboth and then seized his vineyard, Ahab's blood was one day to be licked by dogs and Jezebel, who was the moving force behind the plot, was actually to be eaten by dogs (1 Kings 21:17–24). And so it was (1 Kings 22:37–38, 2 Kings 9:30–37).[36]

In addition to this biblical source, however, January's image of hounds eating a man also evokes the classical story of Acteon, who was transformed into a stag and devoured by his own hounds because of an accidental act of voyeurism committed against Diana (Ovid, *Metamorphoses* 3.138–252).[37] Again in the *Knight's Tale*, in his description of the Temple of Diana, Chaucer sees a painting of this story:

Ther saugh I Attheon an hert ymaked,
For vengeaunce that he saugh Diane al naked;
I saugh how that his houndes have hym caught
And freeten hym, for that they knew hym naught. (I 2065–68)

The doubly ominous allusion in January's grim oath, "Yet were me levere houndes had me eten," evocative of these equally gruesome biblical and classical stories, is uncannily appropriate in view of the syncretism and scopophilia in the scenes that precede it, where the pagan gods Pluto and Proserpina debate the virtue and wisdom of King Solomon and then January, Acteon-like, beholds his wife and Damian copulating in a tree.

More straightforward than this compressed Ahab-Jezebel-Acteon allusion, but equally ominous, is the comparison a few hundred lines later of May to Queen Esther:

Mayus, that sit with so benyngne a chiere [appearance]
Hire to biholde it semed fayerye. [enchantment]
Queene Ester looked nevere with swich an ye [eye]
On Assuer, so meke a look hath she.   1745

Earlier, as we have seen, January had listed Esther along with Rebecca, Judith, and Abigail as biblical proof of woman's helpfulness to man. Esther was specifically praised for having brought about the salvation of the Jews and her uncle Mordechai's advancement. In the present passage, now that January and May are married, Chaucer adverts to the story of Esther in a more pertinent way: we see Esther and her easily manipulated husband, Ahasuerus, close up, so to speak, and the comparison to May and her soon-to-be-cuckolded husband, January, increases our sense of foreboding.

In the blind January's wooing song, addressed to May in his garden on the very day that she and Damian are to enjoy each other's embraces and January is to regain his sight, lost in the course of his marriage, Chaucer introduces a stream of partial biblical allusions that are then brought up shockingly short:

> "Rys up, my wyf, my love, my lady free!
> The turtles voys is herd, my dowve sweete;
> The wynter is goon with alle his reynes weete.   2140
> Com forth now, with thyne eyen columbyn!
> How fairer been thy brestes than is wyn!
> The gardyn is enclosed al aboute;
> Com forth, my white spouse! out of doute
> Thou hast me wounded in myn herte, O wyf!   2145
> No spot of thee ne knew I al my lyf. [blemish]
> Com forth, and lat us taken oure disport;
> I chees thee for my wyf and my confort."
> Swiche olde lewed wordes used he. [rude, wanton]

(IV 2138–49)

As Skeat and many critics since have pointed out, January's speech is rife with ironic reminiscence of verses from the love songs in Canticles.[38] One obvious dramatic irony is that January, who is blind, can no longer see those physical attributes of May that he is praising: her columbine eyes, her whiteness, or her "spotlessness." But the crowning irony, surely, is the Merchant-Narrator's summary judgment that January's paraphrase of Solomon's love song consists of "olde lewed wordes." Even though it is January's use of Canticles that the Merchant calls "lewed," not Canticles itself, his comment challenges the inviolability of the Bible more bluntly than it has already been challenged by the many troublingly partial, inaccurate, and ironically inappropriate biblical references leading up to it.

The challenge of referring to January's biblically inspired love song as "olde lewed wordes" prepares us for a final and even more violent jolt to scriptural authority. Chaucer's structural and thematic master stroke in the *Merchant's Tale* is the biblically permeated and epiclike intervention of Pluto and Proserpina in the affairs of January, Damian, and May. In their one-hundred-line debate, these *deus ex machina* pagan interlopers provide a counterweight to the biblically permeated deliberations on male-female relations that preceded January's decision to wed (IV 1252–1690). Pluto and Proserpina repeat and exemplify the ideas about marriage that were set out on the opposing sides of the deliberations at the beginning of the *Merchant's Tale*. More specifically, Pluto and Proserpina's debate mirrors the formal exchange between January's two counselors, the flatterer Placebo and the wise man Justinus (IV 1469–1690). In that earlier debate, Placebo had perversely cited and then overridden a verse from Ecclesiasticus, misattributed to Solomon, in which people are advised to seek counsel (IV 1478–90)—the same verse from Ecclesiasticus that "hende" Nicholas of the *Miller's Tale* cites, and also misattributes, in a speech to John the carpenter, another jealous old husband and cuckold-to-be; and that Prudence in the *Tale of Melibee* also quotes, and misattributes, in ineffective advice to her husband, Melibee.[39] In the present debate, both Pluto and Proserpina also cite a biblical text by Solomon (IV 2242, 2277), but this time the attribution of the biblical allusion is correct and the outcome of the story is made to hinge upon its proper interpretation.

Pluto and Proserpina's argument retards the forward movement of the tale at its moment of greatest suspense: January is holding on to May, and Damian is in position, ready and waiting in the pear tree. We know that Damian and May will make a cuckold of January—the *mal marié* plot requires that this happen—but how? Meanwhile, by having us eavesdrop on Pluto and Proserpina while we wait, Chaucer coaxes us through a series of *débats d'amour*. What are the merits or demerits of January, the soon-to-be-cuckolded lecher, and of May, his young and beautiful but faithless and conscienceless wife? Who has committed the greater offense, January or May? What outcome would be most just? What are the virtues and vices of men and women, married or otherwise? What are we to make of a generally misanthropic but especially harsh antifeminist verse from Ecclesiastes? And what are the credentials of the biblical figure, Solomon, who authored the controversial verse?

As several critics have noted, the mismatched January and May are perfect human counterparts to the rapist Pluto and his victim/bride Proserpina in medieval tradition.[40] But even more significant is the fact that by introducing these particular supernatural actors Chaucer has managed to highlight archetypal biblical features in the tableau of human actors who are temporarily frozen in their outrageous places. The highlighting is evident when we view this climactic scene against the typical parallel scene in analogues to the *Merchant's Tale*, where, at the equivalent point, it is Saint Peter and God who enter the action, not the pagan gods Pluto and Proserpina.[41] Typically, the brief role played by Saint Peter and God is this: outraged by the scene and by what impends, Saint Peter urges God to restore the old man's sight. God agrees, but warns Peter that the woman will nevertheless manage to explain her way out of being caught in the act. In a rudimentary way, then, Chaucer is following his putative sources. But the changes he makes are telling. First and foremost is the fact that God and Saint Peter have been replaced by imaginary supernatural beings, the pagan king and queen of the underworld, who perform the miracle of restoring the blind husband's sight and then not only countenance the wife's adultery but also allow her to explain it away. In fact, Proserpina bestows upon May a skill that she will be able to pass along to her descendants. In Chaucer's rendering, then, the old fabliau plot suddenly takes on the character of an ancient archetype, a new version of the Eden story. In the old version of Genesis 3, certain conditions in the lives of women were explained as a consequence of the Fall: "To the woman [God] said: I will multiply thy sorrows, and thy conceptions: in sorrow shalt thou bring forth children, and thou shalt be under thy husband's power, and he shall have dominion over thee" (Gen. 3:16). At the climax of the *Merchant's Tale*, Chaucer refashions the fabliau motif of God foreknowing the wily adulterous wife's quick thinking into an etiological countermyth—not the biblical myth of the origin of female suffering in childbirth or of female domination by males, but a countermyth of how May and all women since were endowed by the pagan goddess Proserpina with the necessary cleverness to talk their way out of any situation in which they have been caught red-handed.

In the *Merchant's Tale*, where God and the Bible have all along been so markedly present (at least in name, by way of liturgical ceremony, and by biblical reference), the sudden withdrawal of divine justice at the crucial climactic moment and substitution of a judgment by pagan deities is more worrying by far than the broadly comic role assigned to God and Saint Peter in the analogues. For if God is absent from the denouement of the *Merchant's Tale*, the Bible is nevertheless there in full force. In a marvelous flight of Chaucerian syncretism, Pluto and Proserpina tie together the loose threads of biblical reference that have accumulated in the tale. From the way they cite Scripture we get the impression that they have been listening all along.

Pluto, for example, reaches back through the debate about marriage with which the *Merchant's Tale* opened, past the *Clerk's Tale*, and all the way back to the Wife of Bath's opening move in the "Marriage Group," as he begins his defense of January with an ironically distorted echo of the Wife of Bath's claim to make do with only what "experience" teaches about marriage:[42]

> "My wyf," quod he, "ther may no wight seye nay;
> Th'experience so preveth every day
> The tresons whiche that wommen doon to man.
> Ten hondred thousand [tales] tellen I kan   2240
> Notable of youre untrouthe and brotilnesse.

Pluto then continues with a double-barreled, biblically supported antifeminist blast, invoking Solomon with a quote from Ecclesiastes, then invoking Jesus Ben-Sira with a quote from Ecclesiasticus:

> O Salomon, wys, and richest of richesse,
> Fulfild of sapience and of worldly glorie,
> Ful worthy been thy wordes to memorie
> To every wight that wit and reson kan.   2245

Thus preiseth he yet the bountee of man:
"Amonges a thousand men yet foond I oon,
But of wommen alle foond I noon."
Thus seith the kyng that knoweth youre wikkednesse.
And Jhesus, *filius Syrak,* as I gesse,   2250
Ne speketh of yow but seelde reverence. [seldom]
A wylde fyr and corrupt pestilence
So falle upon youre bodyes yet to-nyght!
Ne se ye nat this honurable knyght,
By cause, allas! that he is blynd and old,   2255
His owene man shal make hym cokewold. [a cuckold]
Lo, where he sit, the lechour, in the tree!
Now wol I graunten, of my magestee,
Unto this olde, blynde, worthy knyght
That he shal have ayen his eyen syght.

                  (IV 2242–60)

To begin with the second and less substantial biblical allusion (in lines 2250–51), Pluto's nonspecific reference to the antifeminism of "Jhesus, *filius Syrak*" could evoke a number of verses in Ecclesiasticus (especially in chapters 25 and 26) describing the disgrace or defeat of husbands by their wives. Ecclesiasticus 25:30, "A woman, if she have superiority, is contrary to her husband," though less virulent than many of the others, is appropriate in a general way to the current situation of January and his wife, May, and will momentarily also suit the case of Pluto and Proserpina.

Before we consider the source and subtle appropriative maneuvers involved in the first of Pluto's biblical allusions, it is worth noting that both of Pluto's appeals to the authority of the Bible in this passage—and the implicit claims of Christian consensus and individual probity that such appeals entail—are undermined immediately after they have been spoken in two ways. The first is the virulence of Pluto's unqualified curses, as he wishes that all women would be stricken with erysipelas and the plague "this very night" (IV 2252–53). The second is the discrediting effect of his closing references to January as *honurable* (IV 2254) and *worthy* (IV 2259)—epithets that no sensible member of Chaucer's audience could possibly let pass as suitable to the soon-to-be cuckolded *senex amans.*

But the undermining of Pluto's two appeals to biblical authority begins earlier. Indeed, a hint at the process of undermining may be seen as early as in the opening four-line puff devoted to the proverbially great wisdom and wealth of Solomon, when we recall that it was Placebo who had last invoked the wisdom of Solomon when misattributing a verse from Ecclesiasticus before ludicrously rejecting its wisdom and then offering January alternative advice that was merely a form of flattery (IV 1478–90). After praising Solomon, Pluto partially paraphrases Ecclesiastes 7:29 and interprets it as offering unequivocal praise of man's "bountee" and condemnation of woman's "wikkednesse" (IV 2242–49).

Pluto's citation of the antifeminist wisdom expressed by Solomon in a portion of Ecclesiastes 7:29 calls for special attention. The verse occurs in the following passage:

> Lo this have I found, said Ecclesiastes [i.e., Solomon], weighing one thing after another, that I might find out the account, / Which yet my soul seeketh, and I have not found it. One man among a thousand I have found, a woman among them all I have not found. / Only this I have found, that God made man right, and he hath entangled himself with an infinity of questions. Who is as the wise man? and who hath known the resolution of the word? (Ecclesiastes 7:28–30)[43]

As the full context reveals, Solomon's primary purpose in verse 29 was not to utter the generally misanthropic and specifically antifeminist grumble that good men are very rare and good women nonexistent, but rather the philosophically more respectable and fundamentally gender-neutral position that sees all human beings as inevitably flawed, and all human wisdom as seriously limited by its very nature.

Proserpina's swift and stunningly decisive reply to Pluto's antifeminist argument—and her rebuttal of his appeal to the authority of Solomon in Ecclesiastes 7:29 in particular—is worth quoting at length:

> What rekketh me of youre auctoritees?
> I woot wel that this Jew, this Salomon,
> Foond of us wommen fooles many oon.

But though that he ne foond no good womman,
Yet hath ther founde many another man   2280
Wommen ful trewe, ful goode, and vertuous.
Witnesse on hem that dwelle in Cristes hous;
With martirdom they preved hir constance.
The Romayn geestes eek make remembrance
Of many a verray, trewe wyf also.   2285
But, sire, ne be nat wrooth, al be it so,
Though that he seyde he foond no good womman,
I prey yow take the sentence of the man; [meaning]
He mente thus, that in sovereyn bontee
Nis noon but God, but neither he ne she.   2290
Ey! for verray God, that nys but oon,
What make ye so muche of Salomon?
What though he made a temple, Goddes hous?
What though he were riche and glorious?
So made he eek a temple of false goddis.   2295
How myghte he do a thyng that moore forbode is?
Pardee, as faire as ye his name emplastre, [plaster over]
He was a lecchour and an ydolastre, [idolater]
And in his elde he verray God forsook; [the true God]
And if that God ne hadde, as seith the book,   2300
Yspared him for his fadres sake, he sholde
Have lost his regne rather than he wolde. [sooner]
I sette right noght, of al the vileynye
That ye of wommen write, a boterflye!
I am a womman, nedes moot I speke,   2305
Or elles swelle, til myn herte breke.
For sithen he seyde that we been jangleresses [since; chatterboxes]
As evere hool I moot brouke my tresses, [enjoy]
I shal nat spare, for no curteisye,   2309
To speke hym harm that wolde us vileynye. [wishes])

The rhetorical shape of this passage is truly brilliant. Starting with an ad hominem attack on Solomon, in which he suddenly ceases to be the quintessential Old Testament teacher of wisdom and ancestor of Christ and becomes instead an infidel ("this Jew, this Salomon"), Proserpina then adduces the female Christian martyrs to rebut Solomon's claim in Ecclesiastes 7:29 that he had been able to find no good women. Next, she proves that she is familiar not only with the text of Ecclesiastes 7:29 but that she knows some crucial exegesis on it as well, disarming its antifeminist jibe with the interpretation in lines 2286–90. Editors and critics of the *Merchant's Tale* have failed to notice that in these lines Proserpina is repeating part of the interpretation of Ecclesiastes 7:29 in the *Glossa ordinaria*, the standard Bible commentary in Chaucer's day. A marginal comment on this verse in the *Glossa* reads:

> Quacunque rem vel discretionem inter homines et eorum mores: quis perfecte bonus nisi solus Christus? . . . Christum qui caput est omnium bonorum; quod figuratur per millenarium qui perfectus numerus. [What thing of real worth or discretion is there among human beings and their ways? Who besides Christ alone is perfectly good? . . . Christ who is the summit of all goods, as is figured by the perfect number one thousand.][44]

Like the author of this gloss, Proserpina takes Solomon's *sentence* (meaning) in the seemingly antifeminist portion of Ecclesiastes 7:29 that Pluto quotes to be that there is no man or woman, but only God—"Nis noon but God, but neither he ne she"—who is perfectly good. And like the glossator, Proserpina is alluding to a concording verse on the incommensurability of human and divine. For in Mark 10:18, in answer to "a certain man" who addressed him as "Good Master," Christ himself was to say explicitly what Solomon had said here obliquely: "Why callest thou me good? None is good but one, that is God."[45]

Having disposed of Ecclesiastes 7:29, Proserpina then resumes her ad hominem assault, turning to the Bible in search of support for her charge that "this Jew, this Salomon" was "a lecchour and an ydolastre" (IV 2277, 2298, and 2291–2302, alluding to 3 Kings 11:1–12). Rising to the peak of her indignation, she seems to forget that she is speaking to Pluto and defiantly addresses Solomon himself (IV 2303–4). Then, finally regaining her composure, Proserpina justifies her attack on Solomon as an act of self-defense, warning all other potential vilifiers of womankind to beware: they too will not be spared merely for the sake of good manners (IV 2309–10).[46]

That the antagonists who adduce biblical authority and debate its correct interpretation in the *Merchant's Tale* happen to be Pluto and Proserpina, two pagan gods, adds a special fillip to a tale that was already an uneasy blend of fabliau, romance, and sermon styles.[47] With Proserpina's powerful attack on biblical and other antifeminists, on antifeminism in general, and on Solomon and his reputed antifeminist teaching in particular, the ironic accumulation of mistaken or inappropriate biblical references in the *Merchant's Tale* reaches its own crazily appropriate climax: a woman—and no less a woman than the Fairy Queen—wins the debate about women and what the Bible says about them by arguing more learnedly and persuasively from the Bible than any character in the story heretofore. The situation is, to say the least, most unusual: not only does the Queen of Hell explicate a biblical verse in an orthodox fashion in order to rebut an antifeminist slur, but she does so in defense of her plan to allow the predictable but biblically unacceptable and very unorthodox outcome of a plot in which a mismatched young bride will commit adultery and get away with it. Pluto's total surrender before this powerful fusillade confirms our own sense of Proserpina's powers of persuasion:

> "Dame . . . be no lenger wrooth;
> I yeve it up!" [I give up!] (IV 2311–12)[48]

All that remains is for Damian and May to have their brief pleasure and for January to see and then to overlook the bitter fruits of his blindness. Proserpina's expertise at orthodox biblical exegesis notwithstanding, she has become the tutelary goddess not only of the adulterous May but of all those women who will succeed in talking their way out of charges of adultery ever after. In all, a superbly and quintessentially Chaucerian climax.

IV

Ecclesiastes 7:29 is partially quoted and its interpretation disputed a second time in the *Canterbury Tales* and once again in a debate between a husband and wife. This time the verse is highlighted in *The Tale of Melibee* when the not-too-wise eponymous hero of that work is listing reasons to reject his wife Prudence's wise counsel in the matter of whether or not he should go to war. The first reason Melibeus offers for rejecting Prudence's advice against acting hastily is that people would think him a fool if he were to change his mind and not follow through on the advice of "so manye wyse" (i.e., a majority of his council) (VII 1055–56). "Secoundely," Melibeus says, "alle wommen been wikke and noon good of hem alle. For 'of a thousand men,' seith Salomon, 'I foond o *good* man, but certes, of alle wommen, *good* womman foond I nevere'" (VII 1057; emphasis added). In adding the word "good" before "man" and "womman" in his translation of Ecclesiastes 7:29, Melibeus was following his proximate source, Renaud de Louens's *Livre de Mellibee et Prudence.*[49] Though the addition of the word "good" leaves the antifeminist sideswiping point of the biblical verse intact, it also implies that Ecclesiastes 7:29 may be understood as an expression of Solomon's generalized misanthropy. Alternatively, according to the "official" understanding of the verse in the *Glossa ordinaria* in relation to Mark 10:18 and the parallel gospel passages, Solomon was referring to the great gap between all forms of human virtue and the virtue of Christ and not referring to the specific lack of virtue among women.

If the "official" interpretation is only implicit in Melibeus's antifeminist reading of Ecclesisates 7:29, it soon becomes fully explicit when Prudence takes her turn at explaining the verse. In *Melibee*, as in Chaucer's proximate source, Prudence waits "ful debonairly and with greet pacience" (VII 1064), until her husband has finished misappropriating Ecclesiastes 7:29 to slander womankind.[50] When her turn comes, however, Prudence explains the "correct" reading of Ecclesiastes 7:29:

> And though that Salomon seith that he ne foond nevere womman good, it folweth nat therfore that alle wommen ben wikke. / For though that he ne foond no good womman, certes, many another man hath founden many a womman ful good and trewe. / Or elles, per aventure, the entente of Salomon was this: that, as in sovereyn bountee, he foond no womman— / this is to seyn, that ther is no wight that hath sovereyn bountee save God allone, as he hymself recordeth in hys Evaungile. / For ther nys no creature so good that hym ne wanteth somwhat of the perfeccioun of God, that is his makere. (VII 1076–80)[51]

Proserpina's disarming of her husband Pluto's antifeminist reading of Ecclesiastes 7:29 in the *Merchant's Tale* parallels Prudence's disarming of her husband Melibeus's partial quotation of the same verse. In both cases, the debate over Ecclesiastes 7:29 comes as the climax to a series of biblical passages that have been adduced by each anatagonist.[52] That in each tale a woman wins a biblically focused dispute with her husband by interpreting the same biblical quotation suggests that Chaucer drew on one of the works for the parallel motif in the other.[53] More significantly, the battle over the correct quotation and interpretation of Ecclesiastes 7:29 that is won by Prudence in *Melibee* and Proserpina in the *Merchant's Tale* recalls the Wife of Bath's more extensive battles with her several husbands over the correct interpretation of other partially quoted and decontextualized biblical verses. Though the Wife of Bath does not debate the interpretive possibilities of Ecclesiastes 7:29, there is additional evidence of Chaucer's lively interest in this verse that remains to be considered. There is also impressive evidence of the widespread popularity of the verse among other medieval authors that deserves notice.

An allusion to the full antifeminist freight of Ecclesiastes 7:29 occurs in Andreas Capellanus's influential *De amore* (c. 1185): "Therefore Solomon, that wisest of men, who knew all the evils and misdeeds of womankind, made a general statement concerning their crimes when he said, 'There is no good woman.' "[54] The antifeminist reading of the verse is also deployed in the following lines from the Latin satiric poem *De coniuge non ducenda* (c. 1222–50): "Of good wives there's a scarcity— / From thousands there's not one to see."[55] Similarly, in a thirteenth-century French paraphrase and adaptation of Ovid's *Ars amatoria*, Ecclesiastes 7:29 is paraphrased with an explicit attribution of its antifeminist sentiment to Solomon, without the "one in a thousand" formula: "And concerning what we have just said, that there are no, or very few, loyal women, Solomon mentions it in Scripture, where he says: 'Who will find a friendly woman?'; as he openly says: 'There is not one.' "[56] And the same combination of elements from Ecclesiastes 7:29 occurs in Jean de Meun's portion of the *Roman de la rose*, where the figure called Ami (Friend) adds the following ironic disclaimer to the lengthy antifeminist diatribe he delivers to the infatuated Dreamer:

> I do not say these things on account of good women, who establish restraints through their virtues; but I have not yet

found any, however many I may have tested. Not even Solomon could find them, no matter how well he knew how to test them, for he himself affirms that he never found a stable woman. And if you take the trouble to seek one and find her, take her; you will have the pick of sweethearts, one who will be wholly yours.[57]

Earlier in the *Roman de la rose*, the same biblical prooftext was implicitly evoked—but without an antifeminist point—when Reason used the "one in a thousand" formula to tell the Lover that true friends are rare. In the Middle English *Romaunt of the Rose*, the lines read: "And certeyn, he is wel bigon, / Among a thousand that fyndith oon."[58] And another oblique Middle English allusion to Ecclesiastes 7:29 occurs in the late thirteenth-century debate poem called "The Thrush and the Nightingale." The Nightingale ironically inverts Solomon's words as he ostensibly defends women against stock antifeminist charges leveled by the Thrush: "'Night bird,' cried the angry Nightingale, / 'To me you seem loathsome in telling these tales. / Take a line of ladies and count them with care: / Not one in a thousand is evil I swear.'"[59] Finally, closer in time to Chaucer, in Richard Rolle's popular *Form of Living* (written in 1349, the year of Rolle's death, for the spiritual guidance of the female recluse Margaret Kirkby) there is an oblique allusion to Ecclesiastes 7:29 as it was interpreted in the *Glossa ordinaria* and by Chaucer's Proserpina and Prudence. Referring to that rare human being, male or female, "one in a thousand," who wishes to avoid evil and fight the devil, Rolle says:

For þe devyll, þat es enmy till all mankynde, when he sees a man or a woman ymang a thousand turne haly to God, and forsake all þe vanytees and ryches þat men þat lufes þis worlde covaytise, and seke þe joy lastand, a thousand wiles he has on what maner he may desayve þam.[60]

In addition to the partial or oblique quotations of Ecclesiastes 7:29 in the *Merchant's Tale* and *Melibee*, Chaucer also alludes to the verse elsewhere in his works. In passages for which there are otherwise no known proximate sources, Chaucer puts Solomon's statement about the rarity or nonexistence of human virtue (rarity among men, nonexistence among women) to various uses. Thus, in the *Prologue* to the *Legend of Good Women*, the verse is playfully and wittily negated when the God of Love berates Chaucer for having told a story of female treachery (in *Troilus and Criseyde*), instead of telling one "of wemen that were goode and trewe:"

> Yis, God wot, sixty bokes olde and newe
> Hast thow thyself, alle ful of storyes grete,
> That bothe Romayns and ek Grekes trete   275
> *Of sundry wemen, which lyf that they ladde,*
> *And evere an hundred goode ageyn oon badde.*
> This knoweth God, and alle clerkes eke
> That usen swiche materes for to seke.
>
> (*Prologue to the Legend of Good Women*
> G, lines 273–79; emphasis added)

The god of Love's claim that "God and clerics who are experts on the subject" all know that good women outnumber bad ones by a hundred to one is a comically absurd and a heavily ironical pointer to the fact that God and Solomon (the ultimate source and proximate "clerkly" or learned author respectively of the biblical statement in Ecclesiastes 7:29, echoed in the italicized couplet) had actually said that there are no good women at all![61] But in fact the couplet points forward and the irony and comic absurdity are more complex than they at first seem. The God of Love, like Proserpina in the *Merchant's Tale* and Prudence in *Melibee*, proceeds to list both pagan and Christian authors—including Saint Jerome, one of the Wife of Bath's main antagonists—who refute Solomon's blanket condemnation of womankind by celebrating chaste and virtuous virgins, wives, and widows (lines 280–310).

A partial and oblique quotation of Ecclesiastes 7:29 also turns up in the *Miller's Prologue* in the *Canterbury Tales*, though here too editors and critics alike seem to have overlooked the allusion. The passage is one in which Robin the Miller "reassures" Osewold the Reeve, who has protested the Miller's declared intention of telling a tale about a carpenter and his (presumably!) unfaithul wife. "Leve brother Osewold," says the Miller,

> Who hath no wyf, he is no cokewold.
> But I sey nat therfore that thou art oon;

Ther been ful goode wyves many oon,
And evere a thousand goode ayeyns oon badde.

(I 3151–55)[62]

In keeping with all the other signs of the Miller's disregard of
institutionally sanctioned behavior, the "reassurance" that he offers
here is a slyly inverted allusion to an unrecuperated version of the
most unreassuring part of Solomon's statement about men and
women in general.[63]

V

References to the Bible, universally regarded as the one
irrefutable source of history, wisdom, and true doctrine, were
commonplace in medieval poetry. Accounting for the abundance
of partial quotation and oblique biblical allusion in Chaucer's
works is therefore not especially problematic. But if we take the
case of the *Merchant's Tale* as typical, the picture of Chaucer's
practice of adverting to the Bible that emerges is more troubling
and intriguingly complex.

There are over sixty places in the *Merchant's Tale* where the Bible
is evoked, most often in faint and passing echoes, but sometimes in
explicit and extended allusions.[64] Some fifteen books of the Old
Testament and five from the New Testament are quoted. The most
elaborate quotations, which bear almost exclusively on the
relations between the sexes, are taken from the Old Testament,
mainly from Genesis, the Song of Songs, and the Wisdom Books.
The eight or nine New Testament allusions, all on this same theme,
are introduced without the explicit biblical markers that
accompany the Old Testament sources. As we have seen, Solomon
gets special attention. He is cited for his wisdom, but this wisdom is
from the outset devalued (IV 1478–90). Words from his Song of
Songs are parodied and then referred to as "lewed" (IV 2138–49).
And finally, Solomon himself is violently attacked for having been a
lecher and an idolater (IV 2277–2310). Of January's two advisors, it
is Placebo who invokes the Bible to tell January only what he wishes
to hear, while it is the honest advisor, Justinus, who gets along
without any biblical references whatsoever. Meanwhile, though
January, Pluto, and Proserpina all look to the Bible for guidance,

when they act on the fragments of biblical wisdom that they extract, the consequences are dire.

For readers who cannot decide if the tone of the *Merchant's Tale* is comic or bitterly ironic, its repeatedly abusive invocations of biblical authority can provide a clue. On the one hand, they are meant to provoke laughter. That is surely the way we react to January's "lewed" use of the Song of Songs, to Pluto's partial quotation from Ecclesiastes, and to Proserpina's "correction" of Pluto's quotation and her climactic tirade against Solomon. Yet, as with the explicit sexual comedy in the tale, there is also something subversive and threatening in our laughter. So with the *Merchant's Tale* as a whole: it is funny and light-hearted, but at the same time it flirts with blasphemy and the subversion of Christian social norms.[65]

The same duality would seem to apply to the application of partial and oblique allusions by the Miller, the Wife of Bath, and other Chaucerian characters. Using the Bible in this way seems to have been one of Chaucer's radical comic devices for exposing human folly in both its benign and more vicious forms. The more primly pious members of his audience may have been put off, but the majority surely were not. Moreover, the strategy for reading the Bible that the Miller, Pluto, Proserpina, the Wife of Bath, and other Chaucerian characters deploy entails more than simply quoting or alluding to a part of a verse out of context. For, as we shall see in the following chapter, the interpretation of biblical verses, whether partially or more fully quoted, and the figural understanding of biblical narratives, whether explicitly alluded to or only implicitly evoked, prove to be subjects of even greater consequence for Chaucer's poetic practice at large.

CHAPTER 5

Biblical "Glossing" and Poetic Meaning

"What are you here for?" asked Paul. "You don't mind my asking, do you?"
"It's all in the Bible," said the big man. "You should read about it there.
Figuratively, you know," he added. "It wouldn't be plain to you, I don't
suppose, not like it is to me."
"It's not an easy book to understand, is it?"
"It's not understanding that's needed. It's vision."

Evelyn Waugh, *Decline and Fall*

Like other Bible-thumping characters in literature, "the big man" who is conversing with Paul Pennyfeather, the protagonist of Waugh's novel, proves to be a far from ideal figure. In fact, the conversation that serves as the epigraph for this chapter takes place in the exercise yard of a prison, where Paul has been incarcerated for (inadvertent!) white-slave trading; and "the big man," as we soon learn, is a homicidal maniac who happens to ply the biblical craft of carpentry, speaks "a curious blend of cockney and Biblical English," and eventually saws off the head of the prison chaplain. Chaucer's Bible-thumping characters may be less extreme in their antisocial actings out, but, as we shall see, they sometimes prove to be equally enthusiastic claimants of the "vision" necessary to explain the difficult passages in a book that is indeed "not an easy book to understand."

In the present chapter I hope to elucidate some of the ways in which narrators and characters in Chaucer's poetry often appropriate the Bible by the use of "glossing" and "figural" reading both for storytelling and other ostensibly more immediate and personal purposes. Investigating what Chaucer's narrators and characters do in this regard inevitably raises a question that is central to the argument of this book: To what degree are Chaucer's own artistic craft and controlling poetic vision informed by the same biblically honed skills of glossing and figural interpretation that he often attributes to his fictional creatures?

I

The earliest interpreters of the Hebrew, Greek, and Latin Bibles tried to make sense of especially difficult biblical passages by "glossing."[1] In its simplest form, the practice consisted of adding an explanation of a verbal difficulty, a "gloss" (Latin *glossa*), either between the lines and directly over the word to be explained or in the margin opposite the line in which the word occurred. This soon led to the appearance of independent lists or "glossaries" of the hard words in the Bible, compiled mainly from the glosses written between the lines and in the margins of biblical manuscripts. A landmark of the increasing sophistication of European biblical glossaries was the encyclopedic *Etymologiae* (sometimes referred to as *Liber glossarum*) by Isidore of Seville. Completed in 632, Isidore's *Etymologiae* brought classical and other extrabiblical learning to bear on the meaning of individual words and phrases in the Vulgate Bible (and a host of other topics besides).[2] Following in the footsteps of Isidore, and sometimes with equal flair for introducing arcane bits of natural and historical lore, later glossators produced line-by-line running commentaries on one or more entire biblical books. Among dozens of scriptural commentaries of this type, it was the *Glossa ordinaria*, compiled in the twelfth century by Anselm of Laon and others, that emerged as the leading exegetical work of its day. The unrivaled influence of the *Glossa ordinaria*, which was often referred to simply as *Glosa* ("the Gloss"), persisted in Chaucer's day and well beyond.[3]

Because the *Glossa ordinaria* was the most widely used aid for interpreting the Bible in the later Middle Ages, it has sometimes been assumed that historically sound criticism of exegesis of the Bible by characters in Chaucer's works must refer to the *Glossa ordinaria* and other standard biblical commentaries of the late fourteenth century as "control" texts. In D. W. Robertson, Jr.'s classic discussion of literal interpretations of the Bible in the *Wife of Bath's Prologue*, for example, repeated citations from the *Glossa ordinaria* reveal how the Wife's understanding of the texts she adduces are mistaken, even perverse.[4] Robertson's reasoning is certainly convincing as far as it goes: the Wife of Bath interprets certain biblical verses literally for her own selfish purposes, and in Chaucer's day all Christian writers (and all true believers) knew that, when reading the Bible, "the letter killeth, but the spirit quickeneth."

However, Chaucer was not a fourteenth-century exegete, and his allegiance to the orthodox view of biblical interpretation (insofar as there was a single view) needs to be proved, not merely assumed. To be sure, as Robertson and like-minded critics assert, a fundamental premise of orthodox exegesis in Chaucer's day was that since "the letter kills and the spirit gives life" (2 Cor. 3:6), one must interpret the Bible not only according to "the letter" but according to its "spiritual" senses.[5] This was, after all, a premise already established in New Testament exegesis of passages from the Old Testament and elaborated by Augustine, Jerome, and other influential theologians and biblical commentators whose views were enshrined in the *Glossa ordinaria.* Thus, even in the General Prologue to the controversial Wycliffite Bible (c. 1395), the well-established notion that the Bible should be read according to its four "senses"—literal, allegorical, moral, and anagogical—is approvingly mentioned and then illustrated by means of a famous example, the four-fold interpretation of "Jerusalem," derived from Nicholas de Lyra's *Postilla litteralis.*[6] Yet, as modern scholarship has convincingly shown, in the thirteenth and fourteenth centuries orthodox scholars such as de Lyra had moved away from the older Augustinian focus on spiritual interpretation, concentrating instead on a philologically and historically more scientific approach to the biblical text and encouraging their readers to derive religious and ethical instruction from a more "literal" understanding of the Bible than an earlier orthodoxy had allowed.[7]

Focusing on late medieval England, we find that the picture is more complicated. For even though the assumption that the Bible has various layers of spiritual meanings may have remained in force among Wycliffite readers of the Bible, Wyclif and his followers were also advancing truly revolutionary new ideas about the nature of the authority of the Bible, proposing innovative theories about the mode of reading and interpretation proper to it, and challenging older claims of its necessary subjection to institutional control. Most significant in the present context was the Wycliffite challenge to the belief that the Bible must be read primarily for its "spiritual" senses. Indeed, according to the Wycliffites, the interpretive premise that "the letter kills and the spirit gives life" could no longer automatically be relied on as a valid principle for true interpretation, because, in practice, it was often used merely as a slogan by parties within the Church whose biblical exegesis the Wycliffites considered to be invalid. As one Wycliffite document puts it: "These be the arms of Antichrist's disciples against true men: *And the letter slayeth.*"[8]

Consequently, according to the Wycliffites, even the older and indisputably orthodox practice of glossing hard words in the biblical text could be regarded with suspicion. Glossed Latin Bibles presented their readers with a blend of first-order sacred text and second-rank commentary in which the distinction between the two was blurred if not altogether eliminated (see figs. 1a and 1b). In these Bibles, commentary impinges on the sacred words of the Holy Spirit, the *ipsissima verba* of God written down by inspired authors, supplementing but also threatening to displace them. Though this did not stop Wyclif and his followers from relying on the interpretations provided in the *Glossa ordinaria*, they nevertheless seem to have been especially sensitive to the danger of glossing.[9]

The sensitivity of the Wycliffites to the dangers of glossing was well motivated, for they themselves were adept at routinely providing partisan glosses in their biblical manuscripts.[10] Indeed, the danger that such glosses might contaminate the sacred text is forthrightly acknowledged by the scribe of at least one Wycliffite biblical text, in a rubric to Isaiah in Lambeth Palace MS 1033 (see fig. 2):

> Here endith the prologe on Isaye, and here bigynneth the text of Isaye. With a short glose on the derke wordis; and loke eche man, that he wryte the text hool bi itself, and the glose in the margyn, ether leve it al out.[11]

As it happens, Lambeth Palace MS 1033 contains no glosses to Isaiah, and the reference to glosses in the rubric was therefore crossed out.[12] But evidence of the cause of this scribe's concern is

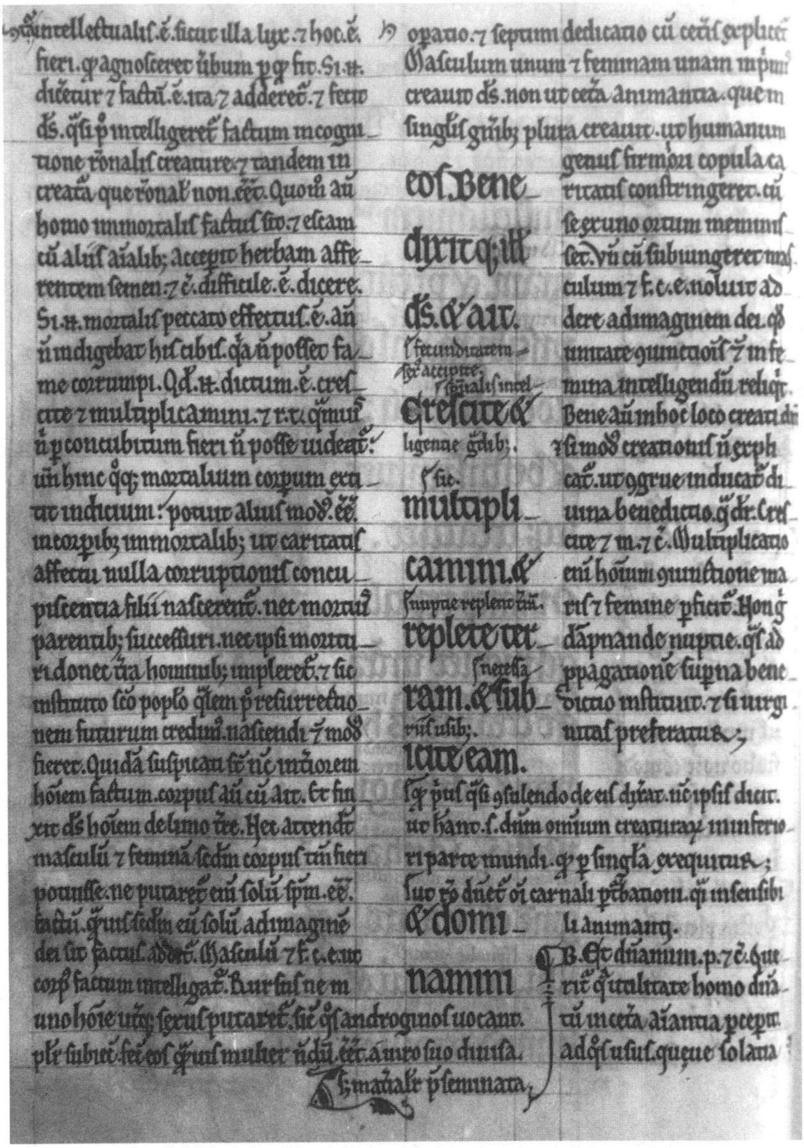

Fig. 1a. Worcester Cathedral Library MS F.76, Bible with *Glossa ordinaria*, fol. 5v, Genesis 1:28 (with abbreviations expanded): ". . . Benedixitque illis Deus, et ait: Crescite et multiplicamini, et replete terram, et subicite eam, et dominamini . . ." Reproduced by permission of the Dean and Chapter of Worcester, Worcester, England.

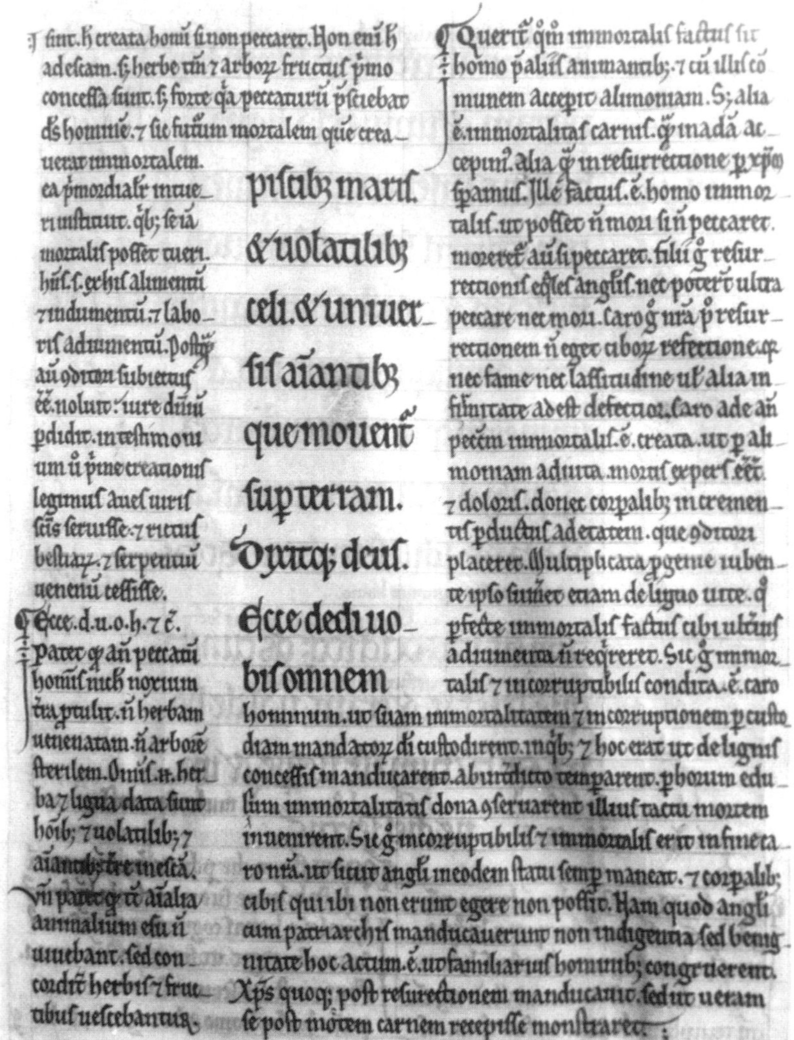
piscibus maris.
& uolatilibus
celi. & uniuer-
sis animantibus
que mouentur
super terram.
Dixitque deus.
Ecce dedi uo-
bis omnem

Fig. 1b. Worcester Cathedral Library MS F.76, Bible with *Glossa ordinaria*, fol. 6r, Genesis 1:28 (continued): ". . . piscibus maris, et volatilibus caeli, et universis animantibus, quae moventur super terram. . . ." Reproduced by permission of the Dean and Chapter of Worcester, Worcester, England.

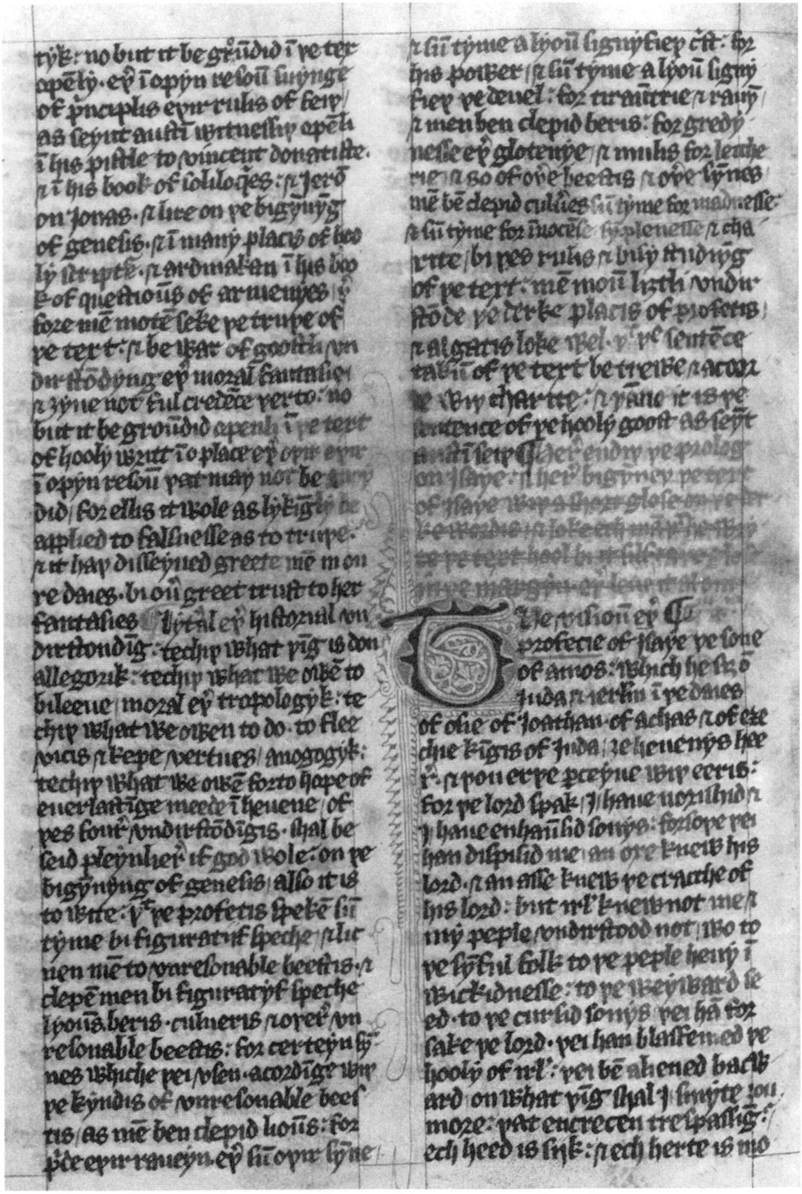

Fig. 2. Lambeth Palace Manuscript 1033, Wycliffite Bible, canceled end of Prologue to Isaiah, fol. 137v. The canceled lines read: "Here endith the prologe on Isaye, and here bigynneth the text of Isaye. With a short glose on the derke wordis; and loke eche man, that he wryte the text hool bi itself, and the glose in the margyn, ether leve it al out" (transcribed by Hargreaves, "The Wycliffite Versions," p. 413). Reproduced by permission of Lambeth Palace Library, London.

not far to seek. In both orthodox and Lollard vernacular biblical translation and paraphrase—as practiced, for example, by Richard Rolle in his translation of Psalms, by Lollard revisers of Rolle's translation, and in the complete Wycliffite Bible translation—the rules regarding the incorporation of occasional bits of exegesis into the biblical text seem to have been relatively relaxed.[13] Though the Lollards' anxiety that glosses might be copied into the texts of biblical manuscripts was no doubt genuine, the inconsistency of their practice suggests that it was really secondary. Their main concern was rather with the way in which friars and other ecclesiastics whom the Lollards regarded as corrupt had taken to substituting what they wanted the Bible to mean for what the Lollards said the Bible was actually saying.[14]

According to the evidence provided in the *Middle English Dictionary*, in the latter half of the fourteenth century it was not only the Lollards who were expressing concern over glossing. The verb *glosen* had come to mean (1) "to gloss, interpret, explain; interpret (a text) falsely; to explain or describe (sth.)"; (2) "to falsify"; (3) "to flatter, deceive." As the illustrative quotations cited for these definitions indicate, the term was most often pejorative. The linguistic evidence therefore suggests that, at the very least, Chaucer and his fellow Englishmen were all aware that there were fraudulent exegetes afoot. When trying to evaluate the interpretation of the Bible in the *Wife of Bath's Prologue* or in any of Chaucer's other works, privileging what were universally conceded to be authoritative interpretations of the Bible in the *Glossa ordinaria* might therefore seem to make good sense. One might even conclude that in view of the widespread fear of controversial glossing, it is the only good sense. But ought one ignore that Chaucer was writing when the very enterprise of "glossing" itself was under attack?

In Chaucer's day, glossing was a practice applicable to the reading of secular texts, too, as witnessed by the survival of some of Chaucer's own works in glossed manuscripts.[15] In the Ellesmere manuscript of the *Canterbury Tales* there are numerous glosses to the *Wife of Bath's Prologue*, "written in as large and as careful a hand as the actual text, which is placed off-centre to make room for the glosses, each of which begins with an illuminated capital in the same colours as those of the text itself."[16] Because Chaucer's profound concern with the issue of biblical glossing is especially evident in the *Wife of Bath's Prologue*, the fact that this work is itself heavily glossed raises intriguing questions. The Ellesmere glosses, which most often identify and fill out partial quotations from the Bible or Saint Jerome's *Epistola adversus Jovinianum*, also appear in other manuscripts of the *Canterbury Tales*, including some that have texts that derive from nonglossed manuscripts.[17] This suggests, as Caie points out, that there was a "gloss tradition" circulating alongside the textual tradition of the *Canterbury Tales*.[18] It has sometimes even been argued that the Ellesmere glosses were Chaucer's "authorial memoranda"; but critics of this view point out that these glosses might very well have emanated from different hands.[19] Furthermore, that many of the glosses express a strongly committed point of view by identifying and sometimes also exposing the abuse of authorities cited, and occasionally by also adding additional prooftexts, suggests that rather than comprising Chaucer's memoranda they record the engaged response of a contemporary reader.[20]

Glossing is a controversial and engaging subject in other Ricardian works of vernacular fiction. In the vision of a "fair feeld ful of folk" at the beginning of *Piers Plowman*, Long Will sees friars of "alle the foure ordres,"

> Prechynge the peple for profit of [the wombe]:
> Glosed the gospel as hem good liked;
> For coveitise of copes construwed it as thei wolde.
> (Prologue 17, 58–61)[21]

Like the friar in Chaucer's *Summoner's Tale*, the friars in this vision preach the Gospel "as they well pleased." As Langland satirically alleges, they construe the Bible "as they wished"—that is, by using "glosing" to support a point of view focused only on their own material profit.[22]

The issue of "glosing" also arises in the works of Chaucer's contemporary and friend, John Gower. In the *Mirour de l'omme*, Gower depicts simoniacs who gloss the Old Testament commandment that "ce q'au dieu fuist commandé, / Ne duist om vendre n'achater" (7478–79; That which has been dedicated to God, / One may neither sell nor buy). This couplet partially translates and interprets Leviticus 27:28: "Whatsoever is once consecrated shall be holy of holies to the Lord." Gower's simoniacs interpret the verse in a way that justifies their thievery:

Le tistre en sciet si bien gloser,
N'est un qui le puet desgloser,
Tanqu'il la lettre ait si glosée.

(7483–85)[23]

[He knows how to gloss the text so well that no one can possibly ungloss it when he has so distorted its literal sense.]

In the *Vox clamantis* Gower once again shows how Bible reading and interpretation can be vexed and spiritually risky pursuits— pursuits for which glossing proves to be of no help, or worse. To illustrate the point, Gower adduces the example of a corrupt rector who takes Genesis 1:28 ("And God blessed them, saying: Be fruitful and multiply") as his license to fornicate:

For God commanded the human race to be fruitful; by His command man is to multiply. Thus, since his seed is copious the rector does multiply, so that he will not be guilty in the light of God's mandate. Through such motives the rector approves the reasons that he may have lady friends, as long as he is in the scholarly profession. First he treats the subject of pregnancy, and in order to bear fruit he is highly repetitious about it. And he reads both the text and the gloss on it, so that the instruction will be clear to his students.[24]

Though the libidinous rector reads "both the text and the gloss" on Genesis 1:28, he clings to the letter of the verse, "Be fruitful and multiply," and apparently ignores its spiritual meaning. In the *Glossa ordinaria*, the marginal comment on Genesis 1:28, "Crescite et multiplicamini et replete terram," reads in part: "In spiritualibus scilicet donis; ut ratio dominetur carni; quasi insensato [*sic*] animanti" (Namely, by means of spiritual gifts; so that the flesh should be ruled by reason; just as living beings rule over lifeless things); and the interlinear gloss reads: "Nuptie replent terram; virginitas celum" (Let them fill the earth by marrying, and fill heaven by virginity). According to its spiritual interpretation, then,

"Be fruitful and multiply" means that Christians should be fruitful and multiply good works and the population of virgins in heaven![25]

Because Gower's glossing rector is a churchman, he should of course be celibate, obeying the spiritual rather than the literal interpretation of the commandment in Genesis 1:28. Gower drives home the irony by telling us that the rector shamelessly makes certain that both the "text" of Genesis 1:28 and its incriminating gloss "will be clear to his students." Like the simoniacs depicted in the *Mirour de l'omme*, who use glossing to justify their thievery, here Gower depicts another ecclesiastical figure who uses glossing to justify sinful behavior rather than to inculcate proper Christian conduct.

Chaucer's uses of *glose* and *glosynge* in the *Canterbury Tales* are for the most part in step with those of Langland and Gower. But the wider range of possibilities in the practice of glossing that Chaucer portrays in the *Canterbury Tales* tells a more complicated story. The clearest instance of Chaucer's pejorative use of *glose* occurs in the *Squire's Tale*, when a "strange knight" ends his listing of the magical properties of a sword he is presenting as a gift to King Cambyuskan by asserting: "This is a verray sooth, withouten glose" (V 166). Here *truth* and *gloss* are antithetical terms. Similarly, in the *Epilogue* to the *Man of Law's Tale*, the Shipman objects to the Host's plan to have the Parson "prechen . . . somwhat."[26] The Shipman is afraid that if the Parson is allowed to "gloss" the Gospel he will spread heresy:

> . . . "Heer schal he nat preche
> He schal no gospel glosen here ne teche.
> We leven alle in the grete God," quod he;
> "He wolde sowen som difficulte,
> Or springen cokkel in our clene corn. . . ." [sprinkle weeds]
> (II 1179–83)

The Shipman's use of *glosen* in reference to what the Parson might preach is unequivocal: it means "to interpret falsely." The Shipman's "springen cokkel in our clene corn" evokes the New Testament parable of the tares among the wheat (Matt. 13:24–30, 36–43); and much later on in the *Canterbury Tales*, when the Parson finally does get a chance to speak, he seems to be refuting the Shipman's earlier impugning of his orthodoxy by rejecting *glosing* ("I wol nat glose") after evoking a related biblical allusion:[27]

Why sholde I sowen draf out of my my fest [chaff; fist]
Whan I may sowen whete, if that me lest?
    (*Parson's Prologue* X 45, 35–36; cp. Matt. 3:12 and Luke 3:17)

Similarly, the Wife of Bath considers "glossing" to be a deplorable reading strategy because it often leads to the evasion of an obviously true literal sense. However, the Wife also shows a subtle awareness of the frequent opacity of so-called literal biblical interpretation. The Wife's opening gambit in her *Prologue* is to privilege personal "experience" over received "authority" as the basis for her remarks on the sad fate of those who marry (III 1–3). After a proleptic glimpse at her five husbands (III 4–8), she postpones her autobiographical reflections on husbands and wives (resumed in III 193–828) and launches instead into a detailed and audaciously critical review of authoritative biblical and exegetical statements on marriage and sexual morality in general (III 9–162). Robertson's summary view of the Wife's exegetical labors in the latter portion of her *Prologue* is that "these lines, taken together, afford a humorous example of carnal understanding and its consequences which is, at the same time, a scathing denunciation of such understanding."[28] But as a close look at some of the Wife's interpretations of Scripture will show, what Robertson calls her "carnal understanding" of the Bible and its exegesis is really the Wife's (and behind her of course Chaucer's) attempt to probe the conflicting appropriations of biblical authority by powerful exegetes whose teachings on marriage and sexual morality were well known to Chaucer and his contemporaries.

The probing begins as early as when the Wife first tells us that she has had five husbands, "[i]f I so ofte myghte have ywedded bee" (III 7). For in addition to clouding the autobiographical question of how many times she has actually been married, the qualifying "if" clause also implicitly raises the vexed matter of biblically derived ecclesiastical attitudes to successive marriages. Patristic writers in the fourth and fifth centuries (including Jerome and Augustine) generally held that second and subsequent marriages in the event of a spouse's death were permissible but should be discouraged.[29] Throughout the Middle Ages this appears to have been the orthodox view regarding widows and widowers, but opinions tended to be sharply divided over the legality of remarriage in cases where the previous marriage had ended in a divorce or annulment rather than with the death of the spouse.[30] Chaucer intentionally leaves the circumstances of the Wife's remarriages ambiguous; and as she proceeds to demonstrate, the biblical basis for the frequently conflicting legal opinions of medieval canonists on the issue of remarriage was also ambiguous.

Loosely following the lead of Jerome's *Epistola adversus Jovinianum*, the Wife opens her *distinctio* on sex and marriage by commenting on two biblical exempla that were sometimes invoked against remarriage: Jesus' attendance at a marriage in Cana of Galilee (John 2:1–11) and Jesus' encounter with the Samaritan woman at the well (John 4:5–19).[31] She cites the first exemplum, together with its exegesis disallowing second and subsequent marriages, without further comment (III 9–13). Perhaps the Wife doesn't bother to attempt a refutation because this interpretation of Jesus' appearance at the wedding in Cana was in fact relatively rare. Indeed, Jesus' presence at the marriage in Cana was more often invoked to explain why marriage is a sacrament. The Parson, for example, observes that "for to halwen [sanctify] mariage he [i.e., Jesus] was at a weddynge, where as he turned water into wyn" (*Parson's Tale* X 919).[32] But the second exemplum, with its truly perplexing dialogue between Jesus and the Samaritan Woman, gets somewhat longer and much rougher treatment:

> Herkne eek, lo, which a sharp word for the nones,
> Biside a welle, Jhesus, God and man,
> Spak in repreeve of the Samaritan:
> "Thou hast yhad fyve housbondes," quod he,
> "And that ilke man that now hath thee
> Is noght thyn housbonde," thus seyde he certeyn.
> What that he mente therby, I kan nat seyn;
> But that I axe, why that fifthe man
> Was noon housbonde to the Samaritan?
> How manye myghte she have in mariage?
> Yet herde I nevere tellen in myn age
> Upon this nombre diffinicioun.

(III 14–25)

Like the powerful Christian exegetes who preceded her, the Wife finds it difficult to determine if John meant to say that Jesus was referring to the Samaritan Woman's currently illegal husband (or lover?) as her fifth or sixth. According to Jerome, Jesus meant to say that the sixth husband of the Samaritan was the man she was currently married to, but Augustine and Gregory concluded that Jesus meant to say that her current husband was her fifth.[33]

Britton Harwood contrasts the Wife's count of the number of husbands in the biblical allusion with Jerome's and concludes that "by reducing the number of the Samaritan's husbands from six to five, the Wife identifies herself with her."[34] Taking a more radical view of the Wife's reading of Jesus' encounter with the Samaritan woman, Priscilla Martin writes: "The Wife of Bath has been criticized for turning Scripture to her own purposes. But in this passage [*Wife's of Bath's Prologue* III 14–23] she senses a gap between the meaning of Christ's words, which she always takes as binding, and the interpretation she has been taught. She has, in fact, put her finger on a very weak link in the chain of clerical exegesis."[35] Though Elaine Hansen also notes the reasonableness of the Wife's confusion over the Samaritan woman passage, Hansen suggests that the Wife is also revealing something about her ambiguous attitude to ecclesiastical authority: "The story of Jesus [the Wife] relates is one that reveals not his loving-kindness, but his apparently gratuitous reproof of the Samaritan woman. The Wife's professed inability to interpret the meaning of his rebuke serves both to challenge its authority and to reveal her own nebulous insecurity."[36] Similarly, Lisa Kiser draws attention to the Wife's repeated use of qualifying "tags"—"I trowe" (III 36), "clepe I" (93), "I seye this" (126), and so on—that show her "hedging" as she reads Scripture; but Kiser highlights an important difference between the Wife's biblical exegesis and the institutionally approved variety: "Never pretending to offer definitive readings of Scripture, the Wife plays the game of 'glosyng up and down' as well as any exegete, but unlike the exegetes, she is willing to expose the fact that her discourse is interested."[37]

After puzzling over the correct interpretation of the strange incident in John 4:5–19, the Wife turns with relief to the injunction of Genesis 1:28 to "increase and multiply, and fill the earth."

Unlike the libidinous rector in Gower's *Vox clamantis*, the Wife has not taken a vow of chastity. She therefore has no reason to hide behind the spiritual gloss on Genesis 1:28. Indeed, *here* is a biblical verse whose interpretation she considers beyond dispute. To gloss it, she says, would be pointless:

> Men may devyne and glosen, up and doun,
> But wel I woot, expres, withoute lye,
> God bad us for to wexe and multiplye;
> That gentil text kan I wel understonde.

> (III 26–29)

There is of course a good prima facie basis for the Wife's bravura claim that Genesis 1:28 is a "gentil text"—what we might nowadays call, following Roland Barthes, a "readerly" as opposed to a "writerly" text—that differs from John 4:5–19 and other similarly obscure biblical texts because it is unshakably univocal and hence naturally resistant to "glossing." In addition, though the matter of when and with whom one should "Increase and multiply" may have been self-evident to Adam and Eve, it was no longer so in the Wife of Bath's day. Yet as the Wife maintains—and as even the most exegetically well-informed and rigorously abstinent members of Chaucer's audience could not deny—"increase and multiply" obviously *does* refer to sexual union for the purpose of procreation.

In fact, despite orthodox spiritual glossing of Genesis 1:28, most canonists, following Augustine and other influential exegetes, held that sex in marriage for the purpose of procreation was not sinful; and more than a few, especially in the later Middle Ages, considered that marital sex in fulfillment of the commandment in Genesis 1:28 might even be a moral good. Commenting on Genesis 1:28 in his popular *Bible historiale* (c. 1291–94/5), Guyart Desmoulins was therefore safely within the bounds of orthodox Christian teaching when he inferred that sexual union between a man and a woman is a good, God-given thing.

> Croissies / et soijes multipliez etc. / Certaine chose est que ilz ne pouoient croistre ne multiplier / sans conIunction dhomme / et de femme / parquoy il appert clerement que dieu ordonna / et estably

le mariage dhomme / et de femme / Et en ce sont confundus aulcuns bougres quy dient que conIunction charnele dhomme / et de femme ne peult estre faite sans pechie [/] Dont vey dieu toutes les choses quil auoit fait / Et chascune estoit bonne a par luy / Et estoient ensamble toutes moult bonnes. [Be fruitful and multiply, etc. Certainly they could not be fruitful and multiply without the sexual union of man and woman, whence it is evident that God ordained and established marriage between man and woman. This confounds any boors who say that carnal union of man and woman cannot take place without sin. For when God saw all that he had created he said that each thing was good by itself (Gen. 1:4, 10, 12, etc.) and that all were "very good" together (Gen. 1:31)].[38]

But then, after affirming the goodness of "conIunction charnele dhomme et de femme," Guyart takes a further step—a step to gladden the heart of the Wife of Bath and those of her "secte"—when he infers that "man" in the Creation story would not have been called "good" were it not for the creation of woman to be his companion:

∫ Et comme Moyse desist que dieu vey que toute choses quil auoit fait estoient bonnes / Il ne le dist pas de lomme [/] Et par aduenture fut ce / pour ce que dieu scauoit bien / que lomme deuoit tost cheir en pechie [/] Ou que lomme nestoit mie ancores du tout parfait / Iusques ad ce que la femme feust faite de luy. / Dequoy Moyse dist cy aprez que dieu dist / Ce nest mie a lomme bon destre seul. [Yet while Moses said that God saw all that He had made as good he did not say this regarding man (see Gen. 1:27). And perhaps this was because God knew well that man would soon fall into sin, or that man was not yet quite perfect, until woman was made from his body—which is why Moses goes on to say after this that God said "It is not at all good for man to be alone" (cp. Gen. 2:18).]

The Wife's second overt rejection of glossing comes in a statement that has no specific biblical source. It is based instead on an argument from the facts of anatomy. "Telle me also," she challenges her audience,

> . . . to what conclusion
> Were membres maad of generacion,
> And of so parfit wys a [wright] ywroght? [maker]
> Trusteth right wel, they were nat maad for noght.
> Glose whoso wole, and seye bothe up and doun.
>
> (III 115–19)[39]

"Gloss as you like and say what you will," she says, you must admit that our "membres of generacion"—a designation that of course already presumes what she is trying to prove—were obviously made for "engendrure" (procreation), and not only for "purgacioun" or to "knowe a femele from a male" (III 120–28). With "[g]lose" parallel to "seye," and hence implicitly emptied of its technical sense (to "gloss," then, is no more than to "say" what one wishes, without any presumption of authority), and with heavy assonance in the clause "[g]lose whoso wole" to underline how fruitless glossing would be against the facts of anatomy, the Wife then turns to the evidence of another "readerly" text, with a partial and defamilarized quotation from 1 Corinthians 7:3:

> Why sholde men elles in hir bookes sette
> That man shal yelde to his wyf hire dette?
>
> (III 129–30)

By attributing Saint Paul's words to "men" in their "books," the Wife naturalizes a biblical precept, or "indulgence" (1 Cor. 7:6), even as she uses it to clinch her case for the use of our "membres" for the purpose of "engendrure."

The Wife's final reference to glossing occurs much later in her *Prologue*, when she describes how her fifth husband, the scholar Jankin, would try to cajole her into making love. Even though he would sometimes beat her, she says, Jankin still had his good points:

> . . . in oure bed he was so fressh and gay,
> And therwithal so wel koude he me glose,
> Whan that he wolde han my *bele chose*,
> That thogh he hadde me bete on every bon,
> He koude wynne agayn my love anon.
>
> (III 508–12)

Rhyming *glose* with *bele chose* (a euphemism for "vulva"), the Wife wins her battle against the coercion of masculine glossing of the biblical text by assimilating it to the "glossing" of her husband's foreplay. Though the masochistic pleasures of a battered wife are ones that Chaucer and his audience were no more likely to regard with equanimity than we are, when the Wife shifts the semantic field of glossing to the realm of sexual play she succeeds in emasculating a fundamentally vexed authoritative form of textual discourse that had seemed to Jankin and other men like him to be invincible.[40] With this step, if we dare to follow where Chaucer has allowed the Wife to lead us, we have transcended the defensive quotation and exegesis of the Bible that the *Wife of Bath's Prologue* so brilliantly exploits and find ourselves instead in a potentially happier world, a world of textual dilatation and generalized sexual play.[41]

In contrast to the Wife's use of "glossing" with reference to a pleasure-giving form of "sexual cajolery," the Summoner's uses of *glose* and *glosynge* imply the pejorative senses of 'to gloss, interpret, explain.' Friar John is trying to swindle money out of a skeptical sick man who bears the biblically resonant name Thomas, and the "glossed" biblical readings that Friar John offers his intended victim are patently self-serving and deceitful.[42] When the Friar alludes to 2 Corinthians 3:6, "For lettre sleeth, so as we clerkes seyn" (IV 1794), one cannot help recalling that the verse had been identified by a Wycliffite reformer as "the arms of Antichrist's disciples against true men." In the *Summoner's Tale* Chaucer has similarly changed the valences of the classic Augustinian dichotomy of biblical "letter and spirit" from the expected minus/ plus to an antifraternal (and coincidentally Wycliffite) plus/minus in order to flesh out his portrait of one particular disciple of Antichrist. Indeed, the sanctimonious and deceitful Friar John proves to be a master of the self-enhancing gloss. "My gloss of the first Beatitude," says Friar John, "is that Jesus meant by it to approve of the friar's vocation; read on in the Sermon on the Mount and see for yourself!" (IV 1918–26)—Chaucer's opinion about this blatantly self-serving and ludicrously "carnal" attempt to interpret the Bible in a way that will justify corrupt clergymen is obvious.[43] Similarly, in the *Monk's Tale* and *Manciple's Prologue* forms of *glosen* are used with the clear and unequivocally pejorative sense of "to flatter, lie, deceive" (VII 2140, IX 34).

In the *Merchant's Tale*, as in the *Wife of Bath's Prologue*, "glossing" is appropriated to the semantic field of sexual behavior, though with a pejorative sense. Before the Merchant provides his listeners with a graphic description of Damian and May's acrobatic act of adultery in a pear tree, he apologizes in advance for any possible offense: "I kan nat glose, I am a rude man" (IV 2351). Here *glose* means something like "to speak euphemistically," rather than "to tell it like it is." It is important to recall, however, that in contrast to this use of *glose* at the climactic moment of the *Merchant's Tale*, the pagan goddess Proserpina has earlier provided us with an exception to the general rule, explicit and implicit elsewhere in the *Canterbury Tales*, that glossing the Bible means interpreting it falsely or deceitfully for some selfish purpose. As we saw in the previous chapter, Proserpina answers her husband Pluto's derogation of women under the sign of Solomon's general biblical antifeminist wisdom by quoting an orthodox gloss to one of Solomon's most notorious antifeminist utterances, Ecclesiastes 7:29. But significantly, while she quotes from the *Glossa ordinaria* to gloss away the literal meaning of Solomon's text, she does so without using the term *glose*. This exceptional case of strong orthodox glossing by a female interpreter who also happens to be the Queen of Hell stands in contrast to all those other instances in the *Canterbury Tales* where Chaucer's male and female characters actually use some form of the word *glose* with pejorative senses. In the context of these cases of false glossing, Proserpina's uncredited quotation from the *Glossa ordinaria* is best viewed as an exception that proves the rule of Chaucer's general distrust of this method of interpretation.

The case Chaucer was building against "glosing" went further (and also in a different direction) than has been suggested by the uses of the term considered thus far. For the last pilgrim to take a stand against *glosynge* is Chaucer's "good man of religioun," the Parson. Not willing to tell a tale in alliterative or rhymed verse, the Parson declares that he will speak in prose:

Thou getest fable noon ytoold for me;
For Paul, that writeth unto Thymothee,
Repreveth hem that weyven soothfastnesse
And tellen fables and swich wrecchednesse.

Why sholde I sowen draf out of my fest, [chaff; fist]
Whan I may sowen whete, if that me lest?
. . . .
I kan nat geeste "rum, ram, ruf," by lettre, [tell a story in alliterative verse]
Ne, God woot, rym holde I but litel bettre;
And therfore, if yow list—*I wol nat glose*—
I wol yow telle a myrie tale in prose
To knytte up al this feeste and make an ende.

(X 31–36, 43–47; emphasis added)

The Parson's reference to Saint Paul's advice to Timothy about avoiding "fables" (1 Tim. 1:4, 4:7 and 2 Tim. 4:4) is straightforward. In context, the Parson's "I wol not glose" means "I won't deceive you with poetic fables," and there is certainly no need for glossing to understand how the quotation from Saint Paul supports his own stand against "fables." Here, in the climactic linking scene of dramatic action that precedes the *Parson's Tale,* Chaucer turns glossing against poetry—that is, against himself—as he prepares for the Parson's hundreds of following quotations from the Bible, free of deceptive glossing and without concern for its potentially dangerous proximity to fabular entertainment.

Chaucer's ideal Parson uses the word *glose* with much the same pejorative force that the term carried when it was used by other characters earlier in the *Canterbury Tales.* It is therefore difficult to accept the unquestioned privileging of the *Glossa ordinaria* and other medieval exegetical sources that many critics assume when they interpret biblical passages in Chaucer's poetry in general, and the Wife of Bath's "carnal" exegesis of the Bible in particular. This is not to say that the Wife of Bath's literal way of reading the Bible was Chaucer's answer to fraudulent *glosynge.* Her way of interpreting the Bible is as selfishly styled to serve her personal ends as the methods of other self-interested interpreters in the *Canterbury Tales.* For example, when she declines the option of perfection through a life of virginity, she does so by alluding to, and then proceeding to reject, Christ's advice to a rich would-be disciple that in order to achieve perfection he should sell all his possessions and give the proceeds to the poor (Matt. 19:21). "Christ was speaking," she says,

. . . to hem that wolde lyve parfitly
And lordynges, by youre leve, that am not I.

(III 107–12)

A similar appeal to the allegedly supporting authority of the same
scriptural text was made by Faux-Semblant in the *Roman de la rose*,
but the chapter in the Gospel of Matthew from which the Wife and
Faux-Semblant both quote ends with Christ reassuring his disciples
that *because* they have abandoned all of their worldly possessions to
follow him they will "receive an hundredfold, and shall possess life
everlasting" (Matt. 19:29).[44] The reading of Matthew 19:21 that the
Wife of Bath and Faux-Semblant propose seems to be a cynical but
logically defensible extension of the traditional exegetical watering
down of Christ's "counsel of perfection." Yet in an interlinear gloss,
the *Glossa ordinaria* all but eliminates the binding force of Jesus'
"give all to the poor" when it generalizes his words as follows: "Non
sufficit relinquere mala nisi sequatur dominum, id est, imitetur" (It
is not sufficient to abandon evil unless you follow God, that is,
imitate Him).[45]

With the exception of the Parson, as we have seen, Chaucer's
characters repeatedly "glose" to argue their self-interested points
of view on controversial questions (virginity or marriage, poverty
or possessions for regular clergy, the relative status of women to
men, etc.). Yet because Chaucer knew just how contentious even
orthodox attempts to validate a claim from a biblical text could
be, and how incorrigibly various the "glossing" of the Bible might
be, he may well have had more respect for the Wife's "carnal"
exegesis than some critics have been willing to allow.[46] It would
therefore be rash to conclude that when Chaucer's characters use
glosynge or *glose* to mean "interpret falsely, lie, deceive (with
'fables'), flatter, cajole sexually, or speak euphemistically" they are
revealing their creator's univocally unsympathetic view of contemporary biblical interpretation. Even if Chaucer's characters
use glossing in ways that repeatedly and disingenuously confirm
that the Bible is "not an easy book to understand" (as Paul
Pennyfeather disingenuously formulates the problem in Waugh's
Decline and Fall), might Chaucer still have meant to condemn only
similarly self-interested and blatantly dishonest uses of glossing
such as these?

Perhaps one final inference is certain. Chaucer's multifaceted poetic explorations of the problem of validity in biblical exegesis exemplify both the demands for and the objections to unmediated access to the Bible over which his Wycliffite contemporaries and their orthodox opponents were struggling. The Wife of Bath's confident way of quoting and commenting on biblical texts gains added relevance in view of the fact that in the 1390s some Lollards were even claiming that women should not only be entitled to read and interpret the Bible but should also be able to serve as priests.[47] Because Chaucer was writing at a time when "glossing" the Bible had become a highly charged social and political undertaking, as the "spiritual" senses of the Bible were being stretched by disputatious male and female interpreters, his literary engagements with conflicted biblical exegesis must have seemed particularly daring. Biblical glossing would continue to occupy English and European intellectuals as a major site of cultural struggle throughout the last quarter of the fourteenth century.[48] For Chaucer, it was a poetic windfall.

CHAPTER 6

"Figura" and the Making of
Vernacular Poetry

Apparently it is impossible for the wit of man to devise a narrative in which the wit of some other man cannot, and with some plausibility, find a hidden sense.

C. S. Lewis, *Reflections on the Psalms*

Throughout the European Middle Ages, a standard exegetical practice involved looking for the Bible's hidden or "figural" senses. As defined in a classic essay by Erich Auerbach, "figural interpretation" of the Bible, the finding of *figurae*, can be taken to include the use of typology, the finding of Old Testament "types" and their New Testament "antitypes" in order "to show that the persons and events of the Old Testament were prefigurations of the new Testament and its history of salvation."[1] Auerbach goes on to explain that figural interpretation "establishes a connection between two events or persons, the first of which signifies not only itself but also the second, while the second encompasses or fulfills the first."[2] He then inserts this definition of figural interpretation within the broader frame of allegory: "Since in figural interpretation one thing stands for another, since one thing represents and signifies the other, figural interpretation is 'allegorical' in the widest sense."[3] Using figural interpretation as a higher-order term that encompasses typology and is roughly synonymous with any kind of allegorical interpretation will prove helpful for our analysis of Chaucer's poetic applications of biblical allegory. Much can be learned about Chaucer's artistry and its relation to medieval biblical poetics by considering his uses of *figura* and figural interpretation *in* his works alongside the frequently contentious application by critics of figural exegesis *to* those works.

I

We can begin by examining Chaucer's own uses of the term *figure* and its derivatives.[4] Limiting ourselves to those passages in which some form of the term *figura* occurs, we find that Chaucer's uses of the interpretive strategies of allegorical interpretation of the Bible include the full range of traditional ecclesiastical approaches to biblical interpretation surveyed by Auerbach. In the following verses from "An ABC," for example, Chaucer uses "figure" to mean an Old Testament "type" or "prefiguration" of a New Testament fulfillment, as he follows his source, Guillaume de Guilleville's *La pelerinaige de la vie humaine*, in linking the burning bush of Exodus 3:2–4 with Mary and the Holy Ghost, and the binding of Isaac in Genesis 22 with the Passion of Christ:[5]

> Thou art the bush on which ther gan descende
> The Holi Gost, the which that Moyses wende
> Had ben a-fyr, and this was in *figure.*
> . . . .
> Ysaac was *figure* of his deth, certeyn,
> That so fer forth his fader wolde obeye
> That him ne roughte nothing to be slayn.
>
> (lines 92–94, 169–71; emphasis added)

In the *General Prologue* to the *Canterbury Tales* we are told that the ideal Parson followed the words of the "gospel" because "first he wroghte, and afterward he taughte" (I 497–98), no doubt an allusion to Matthew 5:19: "He therefore that shall break one of these least commandments, and shall so teach men, shall be called the least in the kingdom of heaven. But he that shall do and teach, he shall be called great in the kingdom of heaven."[6] Chaucer then follows the allusion by quoting the Parson's own words:

> And this *figure* he added eek therto,
> That if gold ruste, what shal iren do?
>
> (I 499–500; emphasis added)

The Parson's "figure," or metaphoric comparison—"If a priest, who is supposed to be like gold, should rust, then what can be expected of his parishioners, who are of baser metal?"—is a "figure" in a more general sense.[7] Rather than referring to an Old Testament type and its New Testament fulfillment, the Parson's "figure" comprises a brief moral allegory that leaves biblical history out of the immediate picture. Yet, as some scholars have maintained, the "figure" may be biblical after all, based ultimately on Lamentations 4:1, "How is the gold become dim, and the finest colour is changed."[8] Perhaps even more to the point, however, are biblical images of the righteous man compared to gold that has been tried and proved true (see Job 23:10, Malachias 3:3, and Wisdom 3:6).

In the *Prologue* to the *Second Nun's Tale*, Chaucer's narrator is following the *Legenda aurea* as she etymologizes the name of the heroine of her tale, Cecile, in various ways.[9] One of the etymologies offered explains the name as a compound,

> . . . by a manere conjoynynge
> Of "hevene" and "Lia"; and heere, in *figurynge*,
> The "hevene" is set for thoght of hoolynesse,
> And "Lia" for hire lastynge bisynesse.
>
> (VIII 95–98; emphasis added)

As the Second Nun uses it here, the phrase "in figurynge" can be translated by our term "symbolically" (as Florence Ridley glosses it), pointing to a blend of figural and typological referents.[10] The "figure" or moral allegory in the Latin form of Saint Cecilia's name is the symbolization of the active and contemplative lifestyles, both embodied, "by a manere conjoynynge," in this saint and martyr. The contemplative lifestyle is "figured" by what is taken (incorrectly) to be the the first element of her name, from Latin *caelum* or "hevene." The active lifestyle is "figured" by what is taken (also incorrectly) to be the second element of her name, from Hebrew *Leah* or "Lia," the Old Testament bride of Jacob who came to be regarded as a paragon of the active life, a "figure" or type of her New Testament antitype, Martha.[11]

For another instance of Chaucerian "figurynge" that blends biblical typology and moral allegory, there is the following passage in the *Parson's Tale*.

it was ordeyned that o man sholde have but o womman, and o womman but o man, as seith Seint Augustyn, by manye resouns. / First, for mariage is *figured* bitwixe Crist and holy chirche. And that oother is for a man is heved of a womman; algate, by ordinaunce it sholde be so. / For if a womman hadde mo men than oon, thanne sholde she have moo hevedes than oon, and that were an horrible thyng biforn God. (X 921–23; emphasis added)

Chaucer's Parson is following his source fairly closely here, but he introduces a small change that is worth noting. For while the Latin source states that matrimony "est figura unionis Christi et Ecclesie," the Parson turns this around and says that "mariage is *figured* bitwixe Crist and holy chirche."[12] Even though the human institution of marriage preceded the coming of Christ and the establishment of the Church, when the Parson speaks he senses no anachronism in taking the relation of Christ and the Church as a "figure" of marriage. This is the case because the institution of marriage was "historically" (i.e., typologically) prefigured by the relationship of Christ to the Church; it was Christ who gave the law of the human institution and not the other way around. Indeed, according to Ephesians 5:22–25, both the form and nature of the institution of marriage were also "prefigured" in Christ's union with the Church:

Let women be subject to their husbands, as to the Lord: Because the husband is the head of the wife, as Christ is the head of the church. He is the saviour of his body. Therefore as the church is subject to Christ, so also let the wives be to their husbands in all things. Husbands, love your wives, as Christ also loved the church, and delivered himself up for it.

If the Latin "[Matrimonium] est figura" in Chaucer's source was meant to imply the inversion, the Parson's "mariage is *figured*" makes it explicit. Chaucer's characters frequently refer to the typological, prefigural meaning of this passage from Ephesians (see *Wife of Bath's Prologue* III 161–62, *Merchant's Tale* IV 1384–88, and *Parson's Tale* X 843 and 929). In the present instance, however, the Parson alludes only to that part of it which leads him to an explanation of the form and nature of matrimony in moral-allegorical, rather than in typological-prefigural terms: man is the head of woman, a woman with more than one man would therefore have more than one head, and a woman with more than one head would be a monstrosity.

A final instance of Chaucer's adaptation of the term *figura*, and one that shows him boldly extrapolating from the semantic field of biblical allegory to secular poetics, occurs in the following passage from *Troilus and Criseyde*:

> This drem, of which I told have ek byforn,
> May nevere outen of his remembraunce.
> He thought ay wel he hadde his lady lorn,
> And that Joves of his purveyaunce
> Hym shewed hadde in slep the signifiaunce
> Of hire untrouthe and his disaventure,
> And that the boor was shewed hym *in figure*.
>
> (5.1443–49; emphasis added)

The "drem" referred to is, of course, Troilus's. It turns out to have been a prophetic dream (first recounted in book 5, lines 1233–41), in which the poem's tragic hero sees a boar with great tusks lying asleep in a forest, embracing and being kissed by his, Troilus's, beloved Criseyde. Like the burning bush and binding of Isaac in "An ABC" 94 and 169, Criseyde's embracing of the boar in Troilus's dream suggests something *in figure*, as a "prefiguration, a foreshadowing or foreboding."[13] And Troilus immediately interprets it as a revelation of Criseyde's unfaithfulness. He thinks that the boar must be a "figure" of something, of another lover to whom Criseyde "hath now here herte apayed" (5.1249). As the reader knows and Troilus does not, it is indeed Diomede who is "figured" by the boar. Moreover, as Cassandra will later explain to Troilus, the boar is a fitting symbol for Diomede because of Diomede's ancestral links to the slaying of the Caledonian boar (5.1513–19).

In all of the occurrences of the term or its variants previously discussed, we have seen how Chaucer used "figure" in a religious, scripturally defined manner. In the example from *Troilus*, the term functions in a secular context but with a blend of its religious senses. On the one hand, "in figure" refers to a kind of typological prefigurement: Diomede is prefigured by the boar because he is, historically, descended from Tydeus and Meleager, the latter of whom killed the Caledonian boar (5.1513–19). On the other hand, "in figure" also implies a kind of moral allegory: the boar is an apt symbol for the inferior Diomede, the uncourtly rival of a true hero like Troilus, who was symbolized earlier in the poem (in Criseyde's dream in 2.925–31) by a noble eagle; Criseyde's being embraced by and kissing the boar, a fierce and ignoble beast, symbolizes her moral failure. Interestingly, though *Troilus* is a secular love story, Chaucer's use of the term "in figure" in a sense that blends prefigurement and moral allegory is analogous to similar uses of that term in the Bible itself (e.g., in 1 Cor. 10:6), in exegetical writings, and in homiletical literature.[14]

This similarity does not by itself prove that *Troilus* is a work with strong affinities to the Bible or to exegetical or homiletical writings. But it does suggest that Chaucer realized that figural composition and reading were adaptable to both secular and religious writing, and that "secular" and "religious" writing were therefore, in this respect at least, not distinctly separate categories.[15] Recent scholarship has made a strong case for the view that Chaucer had thus been taught by his Italian predecessors, Dante, Petrarch, and Boccaccio.[16]

But if a key assumption of Chaucer's biblical poetics was that figural imagery and narrative patterns in sacred and secular writing are to some degree similar, the consequences of that assumption for the critic of Chaucer's poetic practice are vexing. The problem that this assumption poses for Chaucer critics may merely be a special case of the general conundrum of validity in interpretation. When Chaucer seems to one critic or another to be making use of a biblical analogy or a biblical "figure," what are the criteria of corrigibility? How can we decide if and when biblical figural associations are plausible? How do we decide about the intended tonal effects of putative figural associations and their emotive impact?

II

In an early work like the *Book of the Duchess* (c. 1368–72?), as in later works like *Troilus and Criseyde* and the *Knight's Tale*, the death or irrevocable loss of a beloved are tragic facts of life which Chaucer's poetry tries to ameliorate.[17] By the time Chaucer came to write *Troilus* and had revised the early "love of Palomon and of Arcite" for inclusion in the *Canterbury Tales* as the *Knight's Tale*, however, he seems to have adopted a philosophical view of the subject of death that was not evident in the *Book of the Duchess*. This crucial difference between the early poem and the two later ones is explained by the fact that sometime after writing the *Book of the Duchess*, and before he wrote *Troilus* and the *Knight's Tale*, Chaucer had translated the *Consolation of Philosophy* of Boethius and had been won over to a consolatory Boethian view of man's fate—or so the Boethian passages in *Troilus* and the *Knight's Tale* make it reasonable to infer.[18] In the *Book of the Duchess* the consolation for loss that Chaucer offers to the grieving central figure in the poem, and to readers who identify with him, shows no influence of the Boethian perspective.[19] Instead, the poem presents the experience of loss from two alternating and decidedly unphilosophical perspectives: that of an enigmatically uncomprehending narrator, and that of a mysterious Black Knight, who is grieving inconsolably over the loss of his beloved Blanche. In their dream-vision encounter, these two figures act out a prephilosophic and pre-Christian response to death that literally dissolves without any religious or philosophical solution to the problem of premature and undeserved death which the poem confronts. At its conclusion, the only explicit consolation for death that the *Book of the Duchess* has offered the grieving Black Knight and the belatedly empathetic dreamer (and with them, the engaged reader) is the consolation of a courtly love fixed in memory by a rhetorically brilliant gift of poetic art.[20]

Yet from the outset, Chaucer seems in fact to be playing with an opposition between the decorum of inconsolable loss in a pre-Christian, pre-Boethian world and the explicitly withheld consolation for loss that implicit Christian figural patterns afford—that is, the consolation of heavenly reward and resurrection offered to the righteous Christian. For example, in the Ovidian tale of Ceyx and Alcyone that occupies the first third of the poem, there are several mirrorings of pagan and Christian religious practices and beliefs. When Alcyone, whose husband, Ceyx, has drowned, prays for some word of Ceyx's fate to "Juno, hir goddesse" (109), her prayer is answered. Now Chaucer's audience knew, of course, that in fiction, pagan gods can answer prayers, just as the Christian God can do in "real life." But when Ceyx prays to one unnamed God ("I praye God") to soothe his wife's grief and laments the brevity of their worldly joy together (201–11), the overlay of pagan and Christian practices has become, for a moment, explicit. Similarly, the Dreamer's somewhat feeble declaration as a former monotheist, "For I ne knew never god but oon" (237), also brings the world of Christian belief to the surface, but only to obscure it with his immediately following vows to Morpheus, Juno, "or som wight elles" (244). These vows, the Dreamer says in line 238, are uttered in "game" (jest), but by keeping the story on its Ovidian track they effectively block the Christian consolation implicit in the credo of one true God, adverted to in line 237, from being acknowledged or attempted.

The *Book of the Duchess* also includes a significant number of colloquial Christian oaths and asseverations that similarly evoke the world of Christian consolation even as the overtly secular terms of the narrative occlude it. These oaths, expressions such as "By oure Lord" (544, 651), "as wys God helpe me soo" (550), "Before God" (677), "By God," "God Wolde" (665, 814), "By oure lorde" (651), "wys God" (677), "so God me save" (755), "A Goddes half" (758), "by the roode" (924, 992), "a thyng of heven" (308), and others, are uttered mainly by the grieving Black Knight, and a few are spoken by the Dreamer, but they all serve to foreground the fact that an overt Christian consolation for Blanche's death is not being offered.

The seemingly innocuous Christian oaths and asseverations uttered throughout the poem are counterpointed, as James Wimsatt points out, by a series of figural links drawn between the unnamed Blanche and the unnamed but implied Virgin Mary.[21] Chaucer establishes a connection between Blanche and the Virgin Mary through a series of echoes of Canticles, echoes whereby the deceased Blanche is described in terms that evoke the beloved of Solomon, who was traditionally understood to be the typological forerunner of Mary.[22] Other biblical (or putatively biblical) imagery that figurally links Blanche to Mary includes the mention of the biblical heroine Esther (985–88), who, like the bride in Canticles, was also routinely taken to be a type of Mary; the metaphorical identification of Blanche as the "maner principal" and "restyng place" of "Trouthe" (1002–5), perhaps evoking Proverbs 9:1, "Wisdom hath built herself a house," another biblical passage that was taken to prefigure Mary; and the description of Blanche as "lyk to torche bryght / That every man may take of lyght" (963–64), "A chef myrour of al the feste" (974), and a paragon of "godnesse," perhaps evoking Wisdom 7:26, "For she [i.e., Wisdom] is the brightness of eternal light, and the unspotted mirror of God's majesty, and the image of his goodness."[23]

Because the biblical echoes in the *Book of the Duchess* are not found in the sources on which Chaucer drew for other elements of the poem, Wimsatt concludes that "for Chaucer's Duchess, 'immortal light,' 'tower of ivory,' and 'resting-place of Truth' are most appropriate titles, for she *is* Queen of Heaven."[24] Only Chaucer never says this. Instead, he implies it by introducing a largely oblique series of figural texturings that work against the grain of the poem's explicitly secular and Ovidian premises about men and women in love and death and evoke an intentionally occluded Christian worldview. Though A. C. Spearing neglects to mention the biblical basis of figural analogies in the *Book of the Duchess*, his conclusion regarding the way in which Chaucer hinges the poem's central purpose upon the relationship between its figural and literal levels is persuasive: "The possibilities of figuration must be used, and used up, until only the literal is left; and it is, of course, only in the context of the figurative that the literal possesses its full rhetorical power."[25] John of Gaunt's lavish and apparently deeply felt, formal Christian liturgical observances for the prematurely departed Blanche—annual observances in which Blanche was memorialized by the recitation of Vespers of the Dead, Masses, almsgiving, and hospitality—are well attested.[26] What Chaucer was offering his patron John of Gaunt in the *Book of the Duchess* was consolation of another kind.

III

There is a similar but even "thicker" figural texturing in the *House of Fame*, written probably a decade later than the *Book of the Duchess*, perhaps around 1380.[27] As in the *Book of the Duchess*, Chaucer introduces numerous direct and oblique biblical allusions;

but the function of these allusions, which include several especially surprising echoes of prophetic and apocalyptic biblical passages, is as difficult to specify as the thematic center of the *House of Fame* itself. After a playfully comic "Proem" and "Invocation," the "story" of the *House of Fame* begins with a lengthy account of Chaucer's dream one "Decembre the tenthe," a dream in which the poet finds himself in a sumptuous "Temple of Venus." There he sees engraved on the walls and depicted in the statuary a pictorial summary of the *Aeneid* (1.111–475). When he emerges from the Temple of Venus, Chaucer finds himself in a desert, from which he is swept up momentarily by an eagle "with fethres as of gold" (2.530). As Richard Neuse has recently observed, the eagle that seizes Chaucer and takes him on a celestial journey that lands him finally at the House of Fame seems likely to have "flown out of one of Dante's dreams, the one in *Purgatorio* IX, where it carried the pilgrim aloft to the sphere of fire below the moon (IX.30)."[28] And yet, as David Jeffrey's study of the poem has demonstrated, there are also pertinent biblical provenances for the eagle, for the desert landscape from which the eagle rescues (or let us say removes) Chaucer, and for the meaning of Chaucer's visionary experience as a whole.[29]

One New Testament text that seems particularly relevant to the question of whence Chaucer's eagle has flown is Apocalypse 4:7, in which a creature "like an eagle flying" appears as one of four "living creatures" that surround the throne of God. And later on, in the same biblical book, an eagle's wings and a desert both appear in John's vision of the "woman clothed with the sun" (Apoc. 12:1)—only here the direction of flight is *into* rather than *out of* the desert: "And there were given to the woman two wings of a great eagle, that she might fly into the desert unto her place" (12:14). Though the eagle of the Apocalypse might seem to have prior clearance for landing in the *House of Fame,* Jeffrey finds its source in Ezechiel:

> the word of the Lord came to me, saying: Son of man, put forth a riddle, and speak a parable to the house of Israel, And say: Thus saith the Lord God: A large eagle with great wings, long-limbed, full of feathers, and of variety, came to Libanus, and took away the marrow of the cedar. (17:1–3)

In addition to other specific images that seem borrowed from Ezechiel, Jeffrey maintains that the desert, eagle, and Temple of Ezechiel 8, 17, and 37 provided Chaucer with a structural model for the *House of Fame* as a whole. Thus Ezechiel lifted up "between the earth and the heaven" and shown a vision of the corrupted Temple of his day (Ezechiel 8) can be read as a figure for Chaucer, "in a desert, alienated and unsure of his own country."[30] Along these lines, it also becomes noteworthy that Chaucer at the outset refers twice to the date of his dream, "The tenthe day now of Decembre" (63) and "Of Decembre the tenthe day" (111). Counting from March, the month of Creation and the first month of the year according to traditional medieval Christian reckoning, the tenth month of the year is December; and so Chaucer's dream on the tenth day of the tenth month may be read in relation to the biblical dating of the destruction of Jerusalem ("in the tenth month, the tenth day of the month"; 4 Kings 25:1), and therefore in further relation to Ezechiel's vision on the same day of the rebuilding of the Temple to come ("in the beginning of the year, the tenth day of the month"; Ezechiel 40:1). In view of the correspondences, then, Chaucer's vision of the Houses of Rumor and Fame can now also be seen to correspond to Ezechiel's descriptions of the "Outer" and "Inner" courts of the Temple.[31] According to Jeffrey, the biblical paradigms provided by Ezechiel and the Apocalypse do not replace the Virgilian or Dantean design of Chaucer's poem; rather, they provide Chaucer with a "second stage" of reference in light of which he can explore his main subject—the problem of secular and sacred textual traditions and interpretations.[32]

As suggestive as this reading of the *House of Fame* may occasionally seem, it needs to be said that the associations that it proposes between Chaucer's text and its putative biblical subtexts are sometimes unconvincing. Thus Chaucer's December is not the actual month of Ezechiel's vision of the rebuilding of the Temple (which occurs "in the beginning of the year, the tenth day of the month"; Ezech. 40:1), but Jeffrey imports the requisite date from 4 Kings 25:1: "in the tenth month, the tenth day of the month."[33] Nor does a desert figure in the vision of the eagle in Ezechiel 17. There is, instead, a valley of dry bones (but in Ezechiel 37:1–14).[34] Still, Jeffrey's occasionally overzealous reading of the *House of Fame* in the light of its biblical analogies has much to recommend it. Indeed, when Jeffrey suggests that Chaucer's inconclusive ending of the poem institutes "an openness to the final perspective of the full text and Authorial reading"—an "openness" that calls for "silence before the unutterable Word"—his biblically underwritten interpretive grasp of the poem seems especially cogent.[35]

Enhancing the effect of pseudo-biblical elevation, inspiration, and piety in the *House of Fame* is an ironically idolatrous prayer to Venus, "the whiche I preye alwey save us, / And us ay of oure sorwes lyghte!" (466–67). Chaucer utters this prayer in "the temple ymad of glas" in which he dreams that he sees engraved the story of how Venus interceded with Jupiter and thereby helped Aeneas to overcome the malign influence of Juno, defeat Turnus, and win "Lavina to his wif" (458).[36] Chaucer's "idolatry" is further underlined by a shocking asseveration in the name of God the Creator, and by an anachronistic reference to the "temple ymad of glas" as a "chirche:"

> "A Lord," thoughte I, "that madest us
> Yet sawgh I never such noblesse
> Of ymages, ne such richesse,
> As I saugh graven in this chirche. . . ."
>
> (470–73)

Like "chirche" in line 473, many of the religious allusions in the *House of Fame* are commonplace colloquial and anachronistic expressions that serve to evoke the everyday Christian context of Chaucer's audience—e.g., "be Cryste" (271), "Crist . . . that art in blysse" (492), "God . . . that made Adam" (970), "by heven kyng" (1084), and so on. But like the similar Christian oaths and asseverations in the *Book of the Duchess*, those in the *House of Fame* also provide a continuous and implicit counterpoint to the pagan worldview of Virgil's *Aeneid*, Ovid's *Heroides*, and the other secular sources from which Chaucer drew much of the poem's material. Though they were colloquially naturalized, the cumulative weight of these biblically derived expressions also serves to foreground the seriocomic implications of two especially significant biblical allusions.

The first of these is Chaucer's modest disclaimer of a prophetic or otherwise supernatural right to celestial travel—"I neyther am

Enok, ne Elye, / Ne Romulus, ne Ganymede" (588-89)—uttered immediately following Chaucer's characteristically jocular blending of an invocation and querying of the Christian God of creation with an evocation of the pagan Jove, who sometimes "stellifies" people:

> "O God," thoughte I, "that madest kynde,
> Shal I noon other weyes dye?
> Wher Joves wol me stellyfye,
> Or what thing may this sygnifye? . . ." (584–87)

Chaucer's self-promoting and immediately disavowed link to two biblical figures, Enoch, who was taken up to heaven by God (Genesis 5:24; Ecclesiasticus 44:16, 49:16) and Elijah, who ascended to heaven in a flaming chariot (4 Kings 2:11), is balanced by a similarly self-promoting and immediately disavowed link to two pagan ones, Romulus, who was taken up to heaven by Mars (Ovid, *Metamorphoses* 14.816–28) and Ganymede, who was seized by Jove and made into the "botiller" of the gods (Vergil, *Aeneid* 1.28). Well-read members of Chaucer's audience would have recognized that the allusion is a doubled duplication of Dante's similarly half-biblical and half-pagan disclaimer of the right to a supernatural journey: "I am not Aeneas, I am not Paul" (*Inferno* 2.32).[37] In each case, Dante and Chaucer advance a pseudo-biblical claim only to dismiss it. One of the intertextual implications of Chaucer's appropriation and revision of Dante's linking of the *Commedia* with the Bible in the *House of Fame* is the suggestion of an equality of purpose between his humorous English poem and the very serious, much longer Italian one. On the other hand, Chaucer's feigning reluctance to be carried aloft by a fictional eagle and his disclaimer of the biblical stature worthy of such a destiny are in sharp contrast to the sincere posture of humility in Dante's disclaimer of his right to be granted a vision of the fate of souls after death.[38] Dante's disclaimer is serious and helps to establish his credibility as a reporter of the supernatural journey that follows in the *Commedia*; Chaucer's, in turn, is a joke that is tonally suited to the unbelievable but entertaining topsy-turvy vision that follows in the *House of Fame*. Yet because the joke involves the contrastive evocation of Enoch and Elijah, the suggestion of a figural link between the *House of Fame* and the Bible still lingers.

The second biblical allusion has parallel biblical and Dantean intertextual links and a similarly complex function. It occurs while Chaucer is in the grip of the talking eagle who lifts him up in its claws and then flies so high that the world below seems no more "than a prikke" (907). Chaucer begins to grow doubtful. Can this really be happening to him?

> ... "Y wot wel y am here,
> But wher in body or in gost
> I not, ywys, but God, thou wost,
> For more clere entendement [understanding]
> Nas me never yit ysent." (980–84)[39]

As often noted, in these lines Chaucer has made his narrator sound very much like a belated Saint Paul, who also recounted (and, like Chaucer, also somewhat guardedly and ambiguously) a celestial journey in the course of which he heard "secret words" (*verba arcana*):[40]

> I know a man in Christ above fourteen years ago (whether in the body, I know not, or out of the body, I know not; God knoweth), such a one caught up to the third heaven. And I know such a man (whether in the body, or out of the body, I know not; God knoweth): That he was caught up into paradise, and heard secret words, which it is not granted to man to utter. (2 Cor. 12:2–4)

In lines 981–82 Chaucer is quite close to Paul's phraseology, even though his inspiration for the scene was Dante's appropriation of Paul:

> S'i' era sol di me quel che creasti
> novellamente, amor che 'l ciel governi,
> tu 'l sai, che col tuo lume mi levasti.
>
> (*Paradiso* 1.73–75)[41]
> [Whether I was but that part of me which Thou didst create last, O Love that rulest the heavens, Thou knowest who with thy light didst lift me.]

By outdoing Dante, who had repeated Paul's claim in a more oblique and circumlocutory manner, hedged about with pious doxologies, Chaucer almost certainly meant to parody him. But if Chaucer was slyly commenting on Dante's extraordinary claims in the *Commedia*, he was also advancing figurally defined pseudo-biblical claims of his own. Thus Chaucer's formulation—"For more clere entendement / Nas me never yit ysent" (983–84)—replicates Paul's uncertainty as to whether he experienced what he thinks he did "in body or in spirit." At the same time, Chaucer implies that the knowledge he acquired through his supernatural experience is uniquely valuable, like the "secret words" Paul heard and that "it is not granted to man to utter"—all this in the teeth of the eagle's having earlier apprised Chaucer that he is a messenger not of God but of Jove, who has sent him to take Chaucer to the House of Fame, where the poet will hear "wonder thynges" and "of Loves folk moo tydynges" (674–75). Similarly, when Chaucer names the various unsavory biblical figures who are jumbled together with various pagan figures in Fame's court, a purposefully parodic contrast with Dante's vision in *Purgatorio* 29 and elsewhere in the *Commedia* seems paramount. Such is the presumed effect of Chaucer's mention of Joab (1245),[42] the witch of Endor (1261), "Limote" (the magician Elymas of Acts 13:8?) and Simon Magus (Acts 8:9) (named in tandem in line 1274), and, finally, Fame herself, who resembles one of the four beasts around the throne of God described by Saint John in Apocalypse 4:6–8 (echoing the description of the four creatures in Ezechiel 10:4–14).[43] Parodic as it may be, the foregrounded analogy that Chaucer implies between himself and Saint Paul, and between himself and Dante, who made the same analogy, raises serious poetic issues. In both its comic and serious aspects, the analogy reinforces the seriocomic effects of other fantastic events in the *House of Fame*—including the climactically baffled expectation "of love-tydynges" to be told by "[a] man of gret auctorite."[44]

IV

The *Parliament of Fowls* has one-third as many biblical allusions as either the *Book of the Duchess* or the *House of Fame*, and about one-fifth as many biblical allusions as the *Legend of Good Women* (discussed in section V, below).[45] Given the *Parliament*'s relative brevity—699 lines, compared to 1,334 lines in the *Book of the Duchess*, 2,158 in the *House of Fame*, and 2,723 in the *Legend of Good Women*—its inclusion of only a dozen or so either explicit or (mostly) implicit biblical allusions does not preclude its deployment of figural significances similar to those that have been found in the longer dream visions.

The *Parliament* may appear to be a boldly secular poem about nature, Venus, civic virtue, and the natural sexual drives and mating rituals of birds who stand for different classes of human beings—"Chaucer's most philosophical poem," as Peter Dronke calls it, or a poem whose central concern is the "contradictions, ambivalences, and uncertainties of human love," as Larry Benson declares.[46] Yet when Chaucer dates the mating ritual that constitutes the *Parliament*'s central action on "Seynt Valentynes day" (309), he is suggesting that the poem has some religious significance.[47] And religious interpretations of the seemingly secular *Parliament* have not been wanting. Thus, for Huppé and Robertson, the true theme of the *Parliament* is not its concern with the "legitimacy of sexuality" (which is where Derek Pearsall has recently located the poem's thematic center), but its depiction of "the vanity of the world and of the lovers of the world"—human lovers (figured in the poem by different types of birds) who laughably pervert Christian love when they exercise their "natural" will unchecked by reason and revelation.[48] And in another reading that stresses the poem's hidden sense, David Fowler has argued that the *Parliament* must be read in relation to the first chapters of Genesis and the "hexameral" commentary tradition that they inspired.[49]

Huppé and Robertson's understanding of the *Parliament* is disappointingly moralistic and univocal, and Fowler is even more unconvincing when he tries to correlate the exegesis of the six days of Creation in Ambrose's *Hexameron* with corresponding sections of Chaucer's poem. Nevertheless, there is more evidence of biblical diction and imagery in the text of the *Parliament*—and hence more evidence of the poem's specifically Christian thematic concerns— than many recent critics have been willing to admit.[50] Though Chaucer begins by expressing the dizzying perplexity of a personified pagan Love's "wonderful werkynge" (5), he very soon introduces terms that implicitly project that perplexity onto a specifically religious and biblically defined plane of human experience. In the second stanza, Chaucer says that although he is unaware how Love rewards people's efforts ("quiteth folk here hyre"), he does know—because he has read it in books—that Love performs "myrakles," is capable of "crewel yre," and wishes to be the "lord and syre" of his devotees (9, 11, 12).

From their experience of sexual desire and their pursuit of worldly love, Chaucer's audience knew all this as well, though perhaps not quite in these terms, or at least not until they had read the *Book of the Duchess* and similar poems describing how *fin amor* was supposed to be experienced. For Chaucer and his original audience, however, the diction used in the opening two stanzas of the *Parliament* had another bookish source. For example, in line 9, when the narrator claims that the principles according to which the God of Love "quiteth folk here hyre" are inscrutable, his words echo and contrast provocatively with Christ's words to his disciples in Luke 10:7: "for a workman is worthi his hyre." Similarly, the idea of Love as a "lord and syre" recalls and at the same time contrasts provocatively with the biblical conception of Christ the "Lord" and "Sire," as He is addressed by the Samaritan Woman (John 4:11, 15, 19). In the same way, Chaucer's claim that the God of Love is capable of "myrakles" and "crewel yre" evokes the biblical conceptions of God as the "Lord" who performs the "greet myracle" of the Exodus (Exod. 11:7), of God as the frequently "wrooth"-ful and even sometimes seemingly "cruel" Lord about whom Moses repeatedly warns the Israelites (Deut. 1:37, 4:21, 9:8, 9:20), and of God as the "Lord" whose "cruel chastisyng" of the Judeans the prophet Jeremiah justifies (Jer. 30:14).[51]

To bring the two "Lords" in line, Chaucer ends the stanza with a prayer: "God save swich a lord!" (14)—a prayer for the "God of Love" addressed to the "God who is Love" (1 John 4:16). This closing prayer may seem to restore the proper hierarchy that the preceding lines have upset, but the damage has already been done. From here on, Chaucer will in fact repeatedly intertwine partially conflicting and partially complementary poetic conventions and discourses: the fictions of pagan love poetry and courtly love rituals acted out in springtime gardens (derived from such works as Andreas Capellanus's *De amore*, Boccaccio's *Teseida*, and Guillaume de Lorris's portion of the *Roman de la rose*), medieval beast lore (derived from such works as Vincent of Beauvais's *Speculum naturale* and Bartholomew the Englishman's *De proprietatibus rerum*), Neoplatonic philosophical discourses on nature and human destiny (from Macrobius's commentary on Cicero's *Somnium Scipionis*, Alan of Lille's *De planctu naturae*, and Jean de Meun's portion of the *Roman de la rose*), and the discourse of biblically derived Christian diction and imagery.[52] Chaucer intertwines these discourses to render as full and as accurate a poetic correlative of the complex human experience of love as he can possibly achieve.

From the opening lines of the poem, then, with unmistakable evocations of biblical terms and the profoundly central Christian concepts they entail, Chaucer sets in motion a play of pagan fiction and philosophical truth that sometimes coincides with and sometimes conflicts with biblical history and Christian religious truth. The narrator's reported reading of "a bok" (19), the pagan Cicero's "Drem of Scipioun" (31), which immediately follows the opening two stanzas, is given a "Christian coloration" by his claim that the book dealt with "hevene and helle / And erthe, and soules that therinne dwelle" (32–33), by his addition of the phrase "that blysful place" (83) (a reference to Paradise, added by Chaucer to Cicero's uncanny account of a pagan equivalent to Purgatory, paraphrased in lines 78–82), and by his appeal shortly thereafter to God's "grace" (84).[53] Furthermore, because the parliament of birds that Chaucer overhears is set in a walled paradisal garden—a "blysful place / Of hertes hele and dedly woundes cure," leading "unto the welle of grace" (127–29), with "trees clad with leves that ay shal laste, / Ech in his kynde" (173–74), and where "nevere wolde it nyghte, / But ay cler day to any mannes syghte" (209–10)—a number of critics hear Chaucer echoing Genesis (1:11, 2:8–3:24, etc.), Canticles (2:12, 4:12, etc.), and Apocalypse (22:5).[54] The assembly of birds itself— ordered by Dame Nature, who bids "every foul to take his owne place" (316–22)—has been suggestively linked by Huppé and Robertson with the following scene in the Apocalypse of Saint John:

And I saw an angel standing in the sun, and he cried with a loud voice, saying to all the birds that did fly through the midst of heaven: Come, gather yourselves together to the great supper of God. (19:17)[55]

And Bennett hears another possible echo of the Apocalypse in the phrase "by evene noumbres of acord" (381), a phrase that Chaucer uses in reference to nature's proportional distribution of the fundamental qualities of the elements of creation, and that Bennett believes is reminiscent of the repeated symbolic use of the number twelve and its multiples in Apocalypse 7:4–8.[56]

In the last lines of the *Parliament* (693–99) Chaucer awakes to the sound of the birds' shouting as they fly off, and he immediately turns to "othere bokes," in the hope that he may

> ... rede so som day
> That I shal mete som thyng for to fare
> The bet, and thus to rede I nyl nat spare.

As Huppé and Robertson suggest, biblical echoes in the *Parliament* do indeed evoke that higher form of Christian love which problematizes the affirmation of "natural" love. But this "natural" love has been celebrated throughout the poem, and in the scene that brings the visionary portion of the poem to a close (680–92), the celebration of "natural" love is climactically foregrounded in the roundel sung by a select chorus of birds. Like the choice among three noble suitors that the formel eagle will still have to make next year, for Chaucer and the reader the problematic choice among three varieties of love—courtly, natural, and religious, each under the sponsorship of its respective deity, Venus, Nature, and the Christian God—also remains unresolved.[57] Chaucer's deferred effort in the *Parliament* to resolve the conflict among these varieties of love—his effort to choose among them or else somehow to reconcile their perceived disparities—will continue to be a major theme of his later poetry.

V

In the *Legend of Good Women* Chaucer sets out to further the cause of the God of Love by telling stories about women—and they turn out to be all pagan women—each of whom was "trewe in lovyng al hire lyve" (*Prologue* F 437–41; G 427–31). Yet despite this markedly secular purpose, Chaucer deployed more obliquely figural biblical elements in the *Legend of Good Women* than in any of his earlier secular dream visions.[58] Furthermore, if the figural texturing in the *Book of the Duchess* can readily be seen to have served Chaucer's elegiac purpose, the function of the figural texturing in the *Legend of Good Women* is more difficult to explain. For, as in the *House of Fame*, biblical allusions in the *Legend of Good Women* add a figurally constituted level of significance to a work whose meaning is vigorously disputed.[59]

What makes the biblical texture of the *Legend of Good Women* especially puzzling is the way that it operates against the grain of the poem's avowedly antiscriptural program. We can begin to appreciate the importance of figural links between pagan and biblical subjects in the poem by attending to the memorable opening lines of the prologue.[60] Chaucer's narrator's opening move is a colloquially ironic affirmation, "I acorde wel that it ys so," of a fundamental Christian dogma: the belief that "ther ys joy in hevene and peyne in helle" (F-Prologue, lines 1–3). But in lines 4–9 the matter is seen to be less certain. In lines 4–6 Chaucer expresses skepticism about what one is supposed to believe regarding heaven and hell because "no one dwelling in this country" has been there:

> But, natheles, yet wot I wel also
> That ther nis noon dwellyng in this contree,
> That eyther hath in hevene or helle ybe. . . .

Then, in lines 7–9, he constructs a syllogism:

> Ne may of hit noon other weyes witen,
> But as he hath herd seyd or founde it writen;
> For by assay ther may no man it preve.

Since no living person has ever experienced the joy of heaven or the pain of hell, if we continue to believe that there is indeed "joy in hevene and peyne in helle," we must be relying on authority, on what we have "herd seyd or founde it writen," rather than on experience.

For a poem that ostensibly celebrates women who were faithful in worldly love, this sprightly passage of "pop" theology constitutes a surprisingly unexpected introduction. With the seemingly otiose qualifying clause, "dwellyng in this contree," Chaucer amusingly makes allowances for three exceptional and especially pertinent travelers to the otherworld. As we have seen, in the *House of Fame* Chaucer had already placed himself in relation to two of the three: Saint Paul of ancient Palestine and Dante of Italy. The third, who will momentarily enter the poem, is Alceste, the pagan queen who had been to hell and back and who will intercede with the god of Love on Chaucer's behalf and assign him the "penaunce" of composing the stories of "women trewe in lovynge al here lyve" (F 475–91; G 465–81). As V. A. Kolve points out, though Alceste was a pagan queen, she was also considered a type of the Resurrection, and Chaucer's version of her legend therefore shows "a pattern not of courtly loving but of the love that is charity."[61] Furthermore, though Kolve does not discuss the many biblical allusions throughout the *Legend,* their prominence lends support to his suggestion that Chaucer "meant his poem to locate within pagan history certain possibilities of human loving that Christian history would later confirm and redeem."[62]

Having raised the crucial question of whether to believe experience or authority—a question to which Chaucer would return in the *Canterbury Tales,* where it is addressed by the Wife of Bath (III 1–2), by Pluto in the *Merchant's Tale* (IV 2237ff.), and finally by the Parson (X 925–29)—Chaucer answers it with an oblique but unmistakable reference to New Testament doctrine. For as the immediately following asseveration in lines 10 and 11 implies—"But God forbede but men shulde leve [believe] / Wel more thing then men han seen with ye [eye]!"—God does indeed "forbid" that we should believe only what we ourselves have seen or experienced. In the Epistle to the Hebrews, for example, believing the unseen is said to be the essence of "faith":

> the substance of things to be hoped for, the evidence of things that appear not. For by this the ancients obtained a testimony. By faith we understand that the world was framed, by the word of God; that from invisible things visible things might be made. (11:1–3)

And as Peter had formulated the same principle:

you shall greatly rejoice, if now you must be for a little time made
sorrowful in diverse temptations: That the trial of your faith may
be found unto praise and glory and honour at the appearing of
Jesus Christ: Whom having not seen, you love: in whom also now,
though you see him not, you believe: and believing shall rejoice
with joy unspeakable and glorified. (1 Pet. 1:6–8)

Offering the daisy "alle reverence" (F 52), and drawing on the
phraseology of encomia of the Virgin Mary in her praise ("of alle
floures flour," "fulfilled of al vertu and honour" [F 53–54]),
Chaucer continues to imply a parallelism between pagan and Christian values.[63] The parallelism is extended to secular and sacred
forms of writing as Chaucer proceeds to figure himself, in a topos
derived from the Book of Ruth (2:2, etc.), as a belated maker of
love poetry who is like a gleaner come after earlier reapers who
have taken all the "grain" (F 73–77 and G 61–66). As Ellen Martin
has shown, the same image of belated "gleaning," derived from the
Book of Ruth, was a standard figure used to valorize the place of
subsequent biblical commentary and interpretation within a continuous tradition of earlier biblical exegesis.[64] More specifically,
Martin shows how the image of Ruth was used to recuperate the
belatedness and possible exhaustion of the exegetical tradition.
When Chaucer drew on the figure of "gleaning" in Ruth, he was
thus implying that his belatedness in writing vernacular love poetry
had the reassuring precedent of belated but similarly authorized
exegetical compositions.

When Chaucer enthrones the daisy not only as his muse but as a
kind of all-purpose patron goddess, he pushes the parallelism of
pagan and Christian belief to the limit:

> Be ye my gide and lady sovereyne!
> As to myn erthly god to yow I calle,
> Bothe in this werk and in my sorwes alle.
>
> (F 94–96)

From the colloquially discursive theological opening of the
prologue that precedes this passage, as in the biblically suffused
vision of Alceste and her retinue that soon follows (F 213–301, G

142–227), Chaucer repeatedly echoes biblical language and evokes biblical scenes in a way that implies a parallelism between Christian ontological and moral truth and the truth and value of secular love instantiated in pagan literature. Though the parallelism is often noted by critics, what to make of it seems to have become a crux in the criticism of the *Legend of Good Women*. Does the parallelism serve ironically to undermine Chaucer's claim to be praising pagan women who were true in love? Or does it enhance that claim by suggesting that those women true to love who died in the age of natural law were anticipating the values of the age of Christ? A close look at two of the oblique biblical allusions in the poem will suggest that Chaucer wished to do both.

The first occurs in the passage that was Chaucer's major addition to the G-Prologue. In the following words of Cupid, Chaucer introduces a subtle reference to a classic Old Testament antifeminist text:

> But natheles, answere me now to this,
> Why noldest thow as wel han seyd goodnesse
> Of wemen, as thow hast seyd wikednesse?
> Was there no good matere in thy mynde,   270
> Ne in alle thy bokes ne coudest thow nat fynde
> Som story of wemen that were goode and trewe?
> Yis, God wot, sixty bokes olde and newe
> Hast thow thyself, alle ful of storyes grete,
> That bothe Romayns and ek Grekes trete   275
> Of sundry wemen, which lyf that they ladde,
> And evere an hundred goode ageyn oon badde.
> This knoweth God, and alle clerkes eke,
> That usen swiche materes for to seke.
>
> (G 267–79)

Cupid's claim in line 277 that in Chaucer's Greek and Roman sources there are a hundred good women for every bad one plays with the figures and reverses the intention of what we have seen to be Chaucer's favorite Old Testament verse, Ecclesiastes 7:29: "One man among a thousand I have found, a woman among them all I have not found."[65] As if to pinpoint his slyly ironic purpose in evoking Solomon's misogynistic statement, Chaucer puts the name of the Christian God in the mouth of the god of Love on either side of the biblical allusion: "Yis, God wot" (G 273), and "This knoweth God" (G 278). Contrary to what Cupid says, of course, what "God, and alle clerkes eke" know about women is the opposite of what the god of Love claims to be the case. Cupid's inversion of Solomon's teaching on women may thus be seen as the focal point of the many other ironic biblical allusions in the prologue. Indeed, if Chaucer was subtly using Cupid's words to imply his protest against the philofeminist but antibiblical task of praising good women, he may also have expected his readers to recall that the task contrasts amusingly with the antithetical biblical project of Ben Sira: to praise "men of renown" (see Ecclesiasticus 44–50). Though Chaucer never specifically refers to the series of brief narratives in the latter chapters of Ecclesiasticus, there is perhaps an ironic echo of Ben Sira's "Let us now praise men of renown, and our fathers in their generation" (Ecclesiasticus 44:1) in the legend of Lucrece, when Tarquin says: "And let us speke of wyves, that is best; / Preyse every man his owene as hym lest" (1702–3).

The second passage in which Chaucer uses a scriptural analogy to undercut his philofeminist plan comes at the end of the legend of Lucrece. This time the allusion is explicit:

> I telle hyt [Lucrece's story] for she was of love so trewe
> Ne in hir wille she chaunged for no newe;
> And for the stable herte, sadde and kynde,
> That in these wymmen men may alday fynde.
> There as they kaste hir herte, there it dwelleth.
> For wel I wot that Crist himselve telleth
> That in Israel, as wyd as is the lond,
> That so gret feyth in al that he ne fond
> As in a woman; and this is no lye.
>
> (F 1874–82)

Chaucer is here taking leave of Lucrece, who had killed herself because she was raped by Tarquin and feared that she might become a source of ill repute to her husband. According to medieval Christian norms, suicide was the gravest of sins, no matter what the motive. Thus in the *City of God* Augustine points out that even Judas, the paradigmatic sinner, was finally damned for his desperate suicide rather than for his betrayal of Christ; and Augustine then relates specifically to the case of Lucrece, rebutting all the arguments of those who might think that her self-destructive act was virtuous.[66] Still, as Augustine's lengthy debate with the opposing position and the favorable interpretations of Lucrece by other medieval writers demonstrate, if Chaucer expected his audience to view Lucrece's suicide positively, the willing submission to death of the Christian martyrs would have provided a supporting context.[67]

Is Chaucer's Lucrece, then, meant to be viewed as a rash suicide or as a noble pagan who is a prototypical pre-Christian martyr? The answer is that Chaucer allows her to be both, the latter explicitly and the former implicitly, by way of a distortion in the biblical analogy he adduces.[68] For what Chaucer alleges here to be "no lie" regarding Christ's praise of a woman is in fact the language Jesus used to praise a man, the Roman centurion who declared his faith in Jesus' ability to heal the centurion's servant: "And Jesus hearing this, marvelled; and said to them that followed him: Amen I say to you, I have not found so great faith in Israel" (Matt. 8:10; cp. Luke 7:9). The change of genders in Chaucer's allusion is explained by a second biblical passage. When Jesus heals the daughter of the Syro-Phoenician woman, he says: "O woman, great is thy faith: be it done to thee as thou wilt" (Matt. 15:28). But a comparison of the words that Chaucer quotes in Lucrece with both Jesus' words to the Syro-Phoenician woman and with his words to the Roman centurion will show that the words addressed to the centurion are the ones that Chaucer is alluding to.

Misapplying Christ's words to a righteous pagan man to a would-be righteous but finally sinful-because-suicidal pagan woman is Chaucer's way of taking the ground out from under the comic *ad homines* climax of the legend that follows:

And as of men, loke ye which tirannye
They doon alday; assay hem whoso lyste,
The trewest ys ful brotel for to triste. (F 1883–85)

Working against the narrator's explicit claim that women are always faithful and men always tyrannous and untrustworthy, the two verses that Chaucer conflates in his reminiscence of Matthew prove implicitly that men and women are both equally able to show great faith. By obliquely adverting to biblical authority Chaucer subverts the overt ruling premise of the legends: all women are faithful, all men treacherous. This represents a move away from the implications of Chaucer's oblique allusion to Ecclesiastes 7:29 in G 276–77 (what I have called the focal point of biblical references in the work), namely, that there are no good women to be found and only one good man in a thousand. The balanced and conciliatory conclusion thus implied—namely, that both men and women can show great faith—may indicate the direction in which Chaucer would have moved the *Legend of Good Women* had he completed it.

Like Milton proving in his Sixth Prolusion that students should be allowed to mock their philosophical studies, or like Swift recommending cannibalism in his essay on the Irish question, Chaucer in the *Legend of Good Women* sets himself a high literary hurdle. Faced with an unsavory fictional project in terms of traditional Christian ethics and belief, and rather than throw up his hands and plead to Alceste and the god of Love (like Aurelius in the *Franklin's Tale*) "This were an inpossible!," Chaucer agrees to celebrate faithful women; but he does so in a way that evinces his dilemma. Though he proceeds to compose a series of stories that defy biblical teaching on the superior nature of male to female, he nevertheless allusively encodes that biblical teaching even as he explicitly defies it.

VI

The *Nun's Priest's Tale* is the only tale in the entire Canterbury collection that listeners and readers are instructed to interpret figurally. As its learned priestly narrator urges: "Taketh the moralite . . ." and "Taketh the fruyt, and lat the chaf be stille" (VII 3440, 3443). But deciding what the figural message of the tale might be—the "fruyt" hidden within its "chaf"—is another matter. Judson Allen, for example, takes the figural meaning of the fable of Chauntecleer and the fox to be the Nun's Priest's call to repentance; but he regards that call to repentance as a feature of the *Tale*'s generally ironic and entirely humorous effect.[69] On the other hand, there are also critics who tend to play down the comic tone of the *Nun's*

Priest's Tale and take its figural motifs more seriously.[70] For these critics, a series of allusions in the *Tale* to the account of Creation, temptation, and the fall in Genesis 1–3 (VII 3163 and Gen. 1:1?, 3187–88 and Gen. 1, 3257–59 and Gen. 3, 3341 and Gen 1:26–31) justify interpreting the face-off between Chauntecleer and Pertelote, a weak-willed husband and his persuasive wife, as a figural replay of the temptation and fall of Adam and Eve. And in line with this same figural reading, the encounter of Chauntecleer and Reynard the Fox is taken to be an allegorical retelling of the encounter in the Garden of Eden between man and Satan in the form of a serpent—only this time Adam gets away!

Derek Pearsall points out that allegorical readings of the *Nun's Priest's Tale* tend to overlook what was surely Chaucer's main purpose: to give pleasure by provoking laughter, and not to preach a warning against the sins of pride, uxoriousness, concupiscence, and the many other vices that exegesis extracts from the biblical account of the Fall.[71] Pearsall also observes, however, that "exegetical interpretation has also been valuable in alerting us to allusions and levels of meaning which do indeed need recovery."[72] The lesson for readers of this most elusive of Chaucer's tales is clear: without losing sight of Chaucer's comic purpose, strong readings of the *Nun's Priest's Tale* must take account of the allusions and levels of meaning recovered by exegetical interpretation. Furthermore, an added source of comic pleasure in the *Nun's Priest's Tale* is to be found in its dramatic motivation. As Chaucer strongly implies, because the Nun's Priest is subjected to the "petticoat rule" of the Prioress, his motive for telling a figurally encoded antifeminist fable is not far to seek.[73] Like the narrator of the *Legend of Good Women*, who obliquely evokes biblical analogies that work at cross-purposes to his explicit purpose of praising women, the Nun's Priest adduces biblical analogies to prove that "wommanes conseil been ful ofte colde"—and which biblical story could better prove his point than that of Adam, Eve, and the Serpent?

In a concluding address to his audience (VII 3438–46), the Nun's Priest teases them to discover his tale's "moralitee," to get beyond its "chaff" and discover its "fruyt" (VII 3440, 3443). The explicit and implicit "moralitees" of the *Nun's Priest's Tale* are indeed many—too many to yield a single fruit: Don't trust the advice of women, Trust your dreams, Avoid pride, Beware of flatterers, Keep your eyes open and your mouth shut. But twice within the nine lines of the Nun's Priest's concluding challenge to his audience to find his tale's "fruit," he suspiciously limits the challenge to the "goode men" among them (VII 3440, 3445; and cp. the earlier apostrophe to "goode men" in VII 3402). From the surplus of the tale's many possible hidden senses, what finally rises to the surface—underwritten by a quotation from the arch-antifeminist Saint Paul (VII 3441–42)—is its reductive use of "figura" to settle a score. That is how the Nun's Priest implies we are to understand his tale. What Chaucer implies—to our delight—is that a narrator who tries to make *figura* serve patently reductive and univocally petty purposes is bound to fail, because the protean nature of *figura* always enables readings beyond the narrator's grasp.

VII

A more perplexing instance of the figural use of the Bible in the *Canterbury Tales* is found in the extraordinary overlay of biblical archetypes that Chaucer seems to have employed in his depiction of the mysterious Old Man in the *Pardoner's Tale.* Because the fictional speaker of this tale is also a preacher, his use of figural composition is, in principle, no more surprising than the Nun's Priest's. But if most readers find the figural allusions in the *Nun's Priest's Tale* to be relatively transparent and thematically coherent, they also find it much more difficult to decide which explicit or putatively oblique biblical allusions are legitimately implicated in a cogent reading of the *Pardoner's Tale.*

As a preacher whose only desire is to extract money or goods from his audience, the Pardoner says that he uses his tongue as a weapon to attack anyone who would "defame" him or his "bretheren"—"to stynge hym with my tonge smerte [sharply]" (VI 413–16). The image of his tongue as a weapon—this time a serpent's tongue—recurs a few lines later:

Thus spitte I out my venym under hewe
Of hoolynesse, to semen hooly and trewe.

(VI 421–22)

As Skeat and Landrum point out, by using these images of the sharp tongue and poison sting, the Pardoner is implicitly defining himself according to a biblical paradigm of the quintessentially "evil" and "unjust man," a paradigm first set out in the Psalter and cited by Saint Paul:[74]

> Deliver me, O Lord, from the evil man: rescue me from the unjust man. Who have devised iniquities in their hearts: all day long they designed battles. *They have sharpened their tongues like a serpent: the venom of asps is under their lips.* (Ps. 139[140]:4[3]; emphasis added)

> Their throat is an open sepulchre; *with their tongues they have dealt deceitfully. The venom of asps is under their lips.* (Rom. 3:13; emphasis added)

Dolores Noll has noted a further irony working against the Pardoner's posture as a preacher in his use of the images of the sting and the adder, images evocative of another Pauline passage, and one that is central to the theme of a search for Death:[75]

> And when this mortal hath put on immortality, then shall come to pass the saying that is written: *Death is swallowed up in victory. O death, where is thy victory? O death, where is thy sting?* [cp. Osee 13:14; Heb. 2:14] Now the sting of death is sin: and the power of sin is the law. (1 Cor. 15:54–56)

To exemplify his Pauline biblical theme—quoted fairly closely from the Latin of 1 Timothy 6:10: "Radix malorum est cupiditas" (For the desire of money is the root of all evils)—the Pardoner tells the chilling tale of three young "rioters" who become sworn brothers and set out on a journey to find and slay death. Though they have announced and sworn to accomplish their goal of slaying death—"Deeth shal be deed, if that we may hym hente!" (VI 710)—their murderous greed eventuates in their slaying one another. From the outset, their seemingly uncomprehending undertaking of an impossible mission, to slay death, ominously evokes what Paul had prophesied as one of the divine gifts to come at the end of days: "And the enemy death shall be destroyed last"

(1 Cor. 15:26). As several critics have observed, when the three rioters attempt to accomplish a prematurely apocalyptic defeat of Death, they form a kind of unholy Trinity. The figural suggestion of an inverted apocalyptic moment is strongly felt when the two rioters who have murdered the third sit down to eat bread and wine—as if celebrating a Black Mass—over the corpse of their victim, who in turn is about to wreak his revenge through the poisoned wine that he had prepared so he alone would have the gold that the three of them had agreed to share.[76]

These figural associations had been prepared for earlier in the Pardoner's narrative, in a scene whose multilayered potential for figural interpretation has elicited much comment. After the three rioters leave the tavern where the opening and markedly realistic action of the tale is set, the plot shifts to the realm of the supernatural. Of course a shift from realism to allegory may already be observed within the tavern, with the strangely uncomprehending questions that the three rioters and their companions all ask about the identity of the "privee theef men clepeth Deeth" who has been killing their friends, a "thief" whom they swear to seek out and kill (VI 675, 699–701). But the transition from natural to supernatural is more decisively marked shortly after they set out, when the three rioters cross a stile (VI 712) and immediately come upon an "oold man and a povre" (VI 713). This mysterious and ghostlike apparition tells the young men that he has been searching unsuccessfully for a young man who would be willing to exchange his youth for the Old Man's hoary old age (VI 720–26). In addition, the Old Man also reveals to them the shocking fact that he himself has been seeking death, which so far has eluded him (VI 727–38).

Critics agree that the richest vein of figural ore in the encounter between the three rioters and the Old Man lies in the language and imagery that the Pardoner uses to tell the three rioters about the Old Man's dual quest. In a classic article, Robert Miller suggests that the mysterious Old Man is a reflex of the Old Man (the *vetus homo*) of Pauline theology, and thus a figure for the sinful and spiritually dead Pardoner, the narrator of the tale.[77] Though Chaucer does not explicitly quote any of the biblical verses that Miller and other critics adduce, a connection between the Pauline figural metaphorics of "old age/youth" and the Pardoner's imaginative rendering of a confrontation between reckless youth and archetypal, unnatural old age seems plausible enough. But that is not all. It has also been suggested that Chaucer intended the Old Man's account of his failure to find young men willing to trade their youth for his old age to bring to mind Jesus' words to his disciples prior to the Passion: "Greater love than this no man hath, that a man lay down his life for his friends" (John 15:13).[78] And Piero Boitani has recently also suggested that in addition to Leviticus 19:32, which the Old Man actually quotes (VI 742–44), additional biblical verses to which Chaucer alludes in his depiction of the mysterious figure include Matthew 7:12, Job 3:20-22, Romans 7:24, and Apocalypse 9:6.[79]

Some of the ways in which each of these four biblical passages can help to explain facets of the Old Man's complex fashioning are more obvious than others. When the Old Man urges the three rioters not to harm him ("I yeve yow reed, / Ne dooth unto an oold man noon harm now, / Namoore than that ye wolde men did to yow" [744–46]), it seems plausible enough to hear an echo of Matthew 7:12: "All things therefore whatsoever you would that men should do to you, do you also to them, For this is the law and the prophets." Yet the Old Man's words convey a negative form of this "Golden Rule"; and if his words echo any biblical verse, it is perhaps even more likely (as Christine Ryan Hilary suggests) that it is the negative advice offered in Ecclesiasticus 8:7: "Despise not a man in his old age; for we also shall become old."[80] Similarly, the Old Man's lament over his fruitless search for death (VI 721–38), may also seem to resonate with Job's lament in Job 3:20–22:

> Why is light given to him that is in misery, and life to them that are in bitterness of soul? That look for death, and it cometh not, as they that dig for a treasure: And they rejoice exceedingly when they have found the grave. (3:20–22)

Furthermore, Boitani neglects to mention that the linking in these biblical verses of a search for death with digging for treasure and the finding of a grave with rejoicing fortuitously encapsulates the plot of the Pardoner's exemplum. Though the Old Man's lament, "Ne Deeth, allas, ne wol nat han my lyf. / Thus walke I, lyk a resteless kaityf [wretch]" (VI 727–28) may echo Paul's "Unhappy man that I am, who shall deliver me from the body of this death?" (Rom. 7:24)—especially when the contrasting figural senses of "life" and "death" for the *vetus* and *novus homo* are born in mind— the diction and imagery of the passage in which Job questions the justice of God's giving life to those who "look for death" are even closer to Chaucer's text.[81]

As Boitani suggests, another biblical verse that seems relevant to the figural meaning of the Old Man's quest for death is Apocalypse 9:6: "And in those days men shall seek death, and shall not find it: and they shall desire to die, and death shall fly from them."[82] Yet there is certainly nothing explicit in Chaucer's portrayal of the Old Man to establish that he is like the men (and they are not *old* men) who according to this passage will wish to die when the Day of Judgment comes. Similarly, there is nothing about the Old Man that explicitly links him either with Paul praying for deliverance from his sinful flesh or with Job reflecting on how men "in misery" pray for death rather than continued suffering.

The incongruities that vex each of the figural biblical associations of the Old Man discussed thus far leave an opening for yet another attempt to explain his purported biblical origin and figural significance. As Peter Beidler points out, when we identify him with Paul's *vetus homo* or think of him in terms of the other figural interpretations that have been proposed, we overlook three things. First, the Old Man is not immortal (see VI 726); second, he is not evil (in fact, Chaucer emphasizes his "meekness, politeness, patience, and piety"); and third, we are overlooking the significance of his appearance in the plague background in which the Pardoner's exemplum is set.[83] In view of his being presented as an aged survivor of the plague, Beidler argues, Chaucer's audience "may well have been reminded of the biblical Noah," an aged survivor of the Flood—especially as Noah was portrayed in a popular vernacular work like the Wakefield Play of Noah.[84]

VIII

According to John Fleming, Chaucer is hinting at yet another figural layer of meaning in the *Pardoner's Tale* when the Pardoner, after concluding his exemplary tale of the three rioters, urges the members of his pilgrim audience to step right up and buy a pardon:

Myn hooly pardoun may yow alle warice,
So that ye offre nobles or sterlynges,
Or elles silver broches spoones, rynges.
Boweth youre heed under this hooly bulle!
Cometh up, ye wyves, offreth of youre wolle!

(VI 906–10)

In these lines, Fleming claims, the Pardoner has linked himself with the negative side of the biblical figure of Aaron, whose fashioning of the infamous Golden Calf (the Pardoner's "bull"!) is described in the following scene in Exodus:[85]

> And the people seeing that Moses delayed to come down from the mount, gathering together against Aaron, said: Arise, make us gods, that may go before us: for as to this Moses, the man that brought us out of the land of Egypt, we know not what has befallen him. And Aaron said to them: Take the golden earrings from the ears of your wives, and your sons and daughters, and bring them to me. And the people did what he had commanded, bringing the earrings to Aaron. And when he had received them, he fashioned them by founders' work, and made of them a molten calf. (Exod. 32:1–4)

With this "deep" figural reading we have reached a level of biblically inspired interpretation that (as Boitani nervously admits with respect to his own figural readings of the *Pardoner's Tale*) "implies that Chaucer [and, we might add, his imagined 'ideal' reader as well] had the whole Bible at his fingertips and was constantly and deliberately making allusions to it."[86] Nor is Fleming's the last and "deepest" figural association to the Pardoner and his tale, or to other tales, that critics have proposed or are likely to propose in the future.

Indeed, starting with Ralph Baldwin in 1955, a number of scholars have even maintained various different versions of Baldwin's allegorical thesis—namely, that there is a general but nevertheless a crucial structural connection between the Bible and the *Canterbury Tales* as a whole.[87] Like the Bible, which proceeds from Creation in Genesis to the Last Judgment in the Apocalypse, the *Canterbury Tales* also moves, in parallel fashion, from the fructification of spring and the undertaking of a sacred journey in the opening lines of its the *General Prologue* to the homiletical judgment and dismantling of its fictional world in the *Parson's Tale* and *Chaucer's Retraction*.[88] To be sure, a similar movement from creation to judgment and apocalypse can be found in many works of fiction that are not overtly biblical. The Bible in this respect is that "Great Code of all art" which Northrop Frye, following William Blake, takes it to be in his various taxonomical investigations of genres and myths.[89] In a poem such as the *Canterbury Tales*, however, where overt and strongly religious themes are accompanied by an abundance of explicit biblical quotations and allusions, Frye's "Great Code" argument is all the more pertinent. Or, to use historically more relevant terms: because Chaucer himself conceptualized the related tasks of secular literary composition and interpretation in relation to figural biblical exegesis, this mode of medieval biblical reading is a valuable and historically validated tool for the use of critics reading Chaucer today, despite the pitfalls it may present and the blind alleys into which it may sometimes lead.

Conclusion

This is a long lesson . . . and litel am I the wiser
Where Dowel is or Dobet derkiliche ye showen.

Piers Plowman B-Text, 10.369–70

When the dreamer, Long Will, interrupts Scripture's lengthy and difficult lesson on the different requirements for the salvation of Christians and Righteous Heathens with the complaint quoted in the epigraph, his exasperation may be taken to express Langland's readers' similar exasperation at the way in which Scripture's and Will's biblical quotations and counterquotations, both here and throughout Passus 10 and 11 of *Piers Plowman,* have led them into dark alleys of complex and irresolvable scholastic argumentation. Langland's sharply ironic point in creating a personified figure named Scripture who quotes Scripture but fails to resolve the life-and-death issues that are at stake in *Piers Plowman* seems clear enough. Scripture's failure is Langland's way of expressing his own perplexity and frustration in the face of the same variously contentious and conflicting contemporary appeals to biblical authority that Chaucer also responded to with perplexity and frustration.[1]

Yet if the biblical quotations adduced in the poetry of Langland and Chaucer often fail to yield pure and easily accessible doctrine, they nevertheless do frequently serve as vital and dramatically effective narrative ingredients and potent stimuli to religious and philosophical poetic thinking. Indeed, the biblically suffused English poetry that Langland, Chaucer, and other Ricardian poets were writing in the last quarter of the fourteenth century shows some of the innovative and exploratory features that R. W. Southern has taught us to recognize as characteristic of the humanism of the High Middle Ages. Southern's analysis of the rise of what he calls "medieval humanism" includes the following profoundly provocative argument about the central role that the Bible played in the growth and development of the intellectual and social life of the European High Middle Ages. It is an argument that suits the case of late medieval English biblical poetics in every way. "Put in its very simplest terms," Southern says,

> medieval thought became a dialogue between Aristotle and the Bible. Of course it was much more than this, but here lay the main tension which transformed the thought of Europe in the two centuries after 1150. Paradoxical though it may seem, it was the Bible that did most for humanism in its medieval form simply because it provided the most difficult problems. . . . Abraham, Noah, Jacob, David are mystic figures of Christian truth, but scarcely edifying examples of the natural virtues; and a text accepted as the infallible word of God is not a likely vehicle to forward the *studia humanitatis.* But the power of the Bible to provoke thought about human values and human society arose precisely from its lack of interest in these values. The conflict between biblical precepts and the ordinary needs of man in society provided a greater stimulus to independent thought than Aristotle could ever have given: "Take no thought for tomorrow," "Turn the other cheek," "Thou shalt not kill," "Touch not the Lord's anointed," "The powers that be are ordained of God," "Blessed are the poor," "Give all your goods to the poor," "Having food and raiment let us be therewith content"—these and many other precepts forced men to ask the simple question: What in an organized society, and in a rational world, can they mean? These were the precepts and doctrines which first provoked discussion about the ordering of human society and the connection between natural and supernatural virtues. They had the great merit that they presented a challenge. They had to be accepted as inspired words; but they had also somehow to be lived with.[2]

As we have seen, Chaucer knew and worked directly from the Bible with familiarity and great ease, managing to integrate English versions of Latin and French biblically derived devotional and liturgical matter into a wide variety of his works in prose and verse. Yet he also shared—and frequently portrayed in his poetry—the anxiety of his contemporaries as they grappled with what Southern suggests was a central dilemma of their culture: trying to reconcile "the conflict between biblical precepts and the ordinary needs of man in society."

Whether the rise of English vernacular biblical drama and the heavy "biblicism" of other forms of English poetry and prose writings during the reign of Richard II were symptoms, to some degree causes, or mainly the effects of a cultural crisis, it is clear that Chaucer lived through a virtual *Kulturkampf* over the place of the Bible in the lives of his contemporaries. Throughout Europe, this struggle over the role the Bible would play in medieval culture—a struggle that is problematized repeatedly in Chaucer's works and thereby constitutes, as we have seen, a major ingredient of his biblical poetics—was characterized by competing claims about legitimate uses to which the Bible might be put. At all times, believing Christian readers of the Bible have tried to be alert to its most subtle cues, directives from God that were generally assumed to require inspired understanding, to be unlocked by interpretation, lest they be misapplied or even corrupted by heretical interpreters. These dangers had already been anticipated and were warned against in the New Testament itself ("[Jesus] said to them: All men take not this word, but they to whom it is given" [Matt. 19:11]; and "Understanding this first, that no prophecy of Scripture is made by private interpretation" [2 Pet. 1:20]). In Chaucer's lifetime, however, the demands that the Bible makes on the lives of believers were undergoing a particularly vexed and disputed revaluation. In addition to what were perhaps no more than usually disputatious arguments between and among factions about how to interpret the Bible (questions that have arisen throughout the history of its reception), in Chaucer's lifetime there were also heated and acrid arguments focused on the question of whether or not the Bible should be translated into English so as to enable "the people" themselves to settle disputes over problems of its interpretation. Appeals to the Bible are made by Wycliffites and papal apologists, friars and their antagonists, and would-be neutral ecclesiastical authorities alike. In Chaucer's time each of these interpretive subcommunities in conflict pulled at the text in its own different way, each confident that its own reading of a disputed biblical meaning was consistent with the intention of the text's divine author. The Wycliffites held that even if the idea of "inspired" (and hence institutionally monopolized) interpretation was henceforth invalid, there still was no insurmountable difficulty in deciding what the Bible actually meant—as they rather than their opponents knew.

Throughout Chaucer's lifetime, in churches, in parliament, at court, and in the homes of individual men and women, the Bible was still being prayed from, sworn upon, kissed, processed with, and quoted from with full and untroubled devotion. In the same way, the Bible also frequently served Chaucer and other Ricardian poets as a master source of unvexed devotional and didactic materials. But sometimes Chaucer's works, like those of contemporary English authors, reflect a disillusionment with recourse to the Bible that is true to another side of the continuingly complex and vexed role of *sacra scriptura* in late fourteenth-century society. In the second half of the fourteenth century England was beset by repeated visitations of the plague, outbreaks of the war with France, and popular unrest in reaction against repeated demands for higher taxes by an extravagant and ineffective king. Earlier discrepancies between the views on biblical authority of Aristotelian philosophers and more traditional theologians became even sharper. In the last two decades of the century discrepancies between and among the biblically funded and self-justifying but often self-incriminating claims of orthodox priests, friars, Wycliffites, and lay leaders from various factions were also becoming increasingly apparent. Chaucer was thus living in a time of unusually bitter pessimism and widespread weariness—a time in which the safest and surest solutions to be found in biblically inspired writings were those being offered in penitential, devotional, and meditative treatises, works showing the way to individual salvation through penance, prayer, spiritual "exercises," and similar acts of piety.[3]

The perplexities of this situation in the history of biblical interpretation in its fourteenth-century context are parallel in large measure to the debates in our own day over the nature, aims, and politics of literary interpretation. D. W. Robertson, Jr., and most other more recent commentators who take notice of

Chaucer's remarkably heavy use of the Bible—even those whose approaches are not limited by the assumption that Chaucer would share uniformly orthodox views of biblical interpretation—all fail to give sufficient weight to the pervasive effects on Chaucer's poetics of the crisis in biblical authority that accompanied the many other signs of *fin de siècle* strife. That fourteenth-century devotional, mystical, and more obviously "literary" works all shared an approach to the Bible that was informed by extensive knowledge of the biblical text and its traditional interpretation, while at the same time showing daring independence in recasting biblical narratives, is a fact that Chaucer criticism has still not properly appreciated. For when we recognize how vividly and memorably such works as Rolle's *The Form of Living* and *Incendium amoris*, the English version of Aelred's *De institutione inclusarum*, the *Pearl*, and the *Wakefield Noah* involved their readers in the experience of reading imaginatively expanded biblical narratives—narratives in which words, images, and even new scenes were added to the canon of biblical history—we will no longer be likely to overlook or misconstrue Chaucer's similar originality in his adaptations of biblical diction and imagery and his brief but imaginative recreation of selected moments in biblical narrative. We will also cease trying to understand these biblical facets of Chaucer's poetics solely in the light of motifs from medieval biblical exegesis that are all too often either predictably superficial and repetitious or else outlandishly arcane and far-fetched, but in either case irrelevant with respect to the context of the literary work in question.

In the last decade of the twentieth century, now that Chaucer's works are coming to be read in the light of some of our most pressing postmodern cultural and theoretical literary concerns, Chaucer's originality and genius have begun to intrigue us perhaps more than ever before. One result of these latest critical developments is that Chaucer is increasingly viewed in terms of an uncanny or an unconvincingly forced contemporaneity. Neglect of the centrality of the Bible in Chaucer's poetics seems to be endemic, however. For example, in the essays by various scholars in C. David Benson and Elizabeth Robertson's *Chaucer's Religious Tales* (1990), and in John Hill's *Chaucerian Belief: The Poetics of Reverence and Delight* (1991), the place of the Bible is either ignored entirely or it plays a minor and perfunctory role in answering the extraordinarily vexed though seemingly transparent questions of what "Chaucerian belief" or Chaucer's conception (or conceptions) of a "religious tale" might have been.[4] The cognate biblical bases for Chaucer's thinking about literary hermeneutics— repeatedly foregrounded throughout his writings—are also virtually ignored in Judith Ferster's otherwise convincing study of Chaucer's repeated thematization of the problematics of interpretation in its philosophical and theoretical aspects.[5] Similarly, in an otherwise illuminating study of the place of "truth and textuality" in Chaucer's poetry, Lisa Kiser has little to say about questions that for Chaucer and his contemporaries were among the most frequently and widely discussed aspects of her topic— questions such as "What are the institutional and theoretically valid criteria for the 'truth' of translations and interpretations of the Bible?" and "How is the textuality of the Word of God the same or different from that of other textualities?"[6]

Lee Patterson's recent call for the kind of historical criticism that would be adequate for our postmodern age includes these shrewd words on the future of the exegetical approach to Chaucer: "Exegesis . . . is itself one of Chaucer's subjects, and so vulnerable to his characteristic irony; and a fully responsive criticism must accommodate both this interest and the skepticism with which it is regarded."[7] We must now take a further step and acknowledge that not only "exegesis" of the Bible but the Bible itself is "one of Chaucer's subjects" and thus "vulnerable to his characteristic irony."[8] Partly because they were written in reaction against the dead letter of old-style exegetical criticism, otherwise valuable and influential critical studies like Paul Strohm's *Social Chaucer* and Lee Patterson's *Chaucer and the Subject of History* pay little or no attention to Chaucer's biblical "exegesis" or even to the historically central subject of his biblical translation and interpretation.[9]

Similarly, if Jill Mann is right in claiming that Chaucer has bequeathed to modernity "an ideal of feminized masculinity" that can show us "that the reconstruction [of gender relationships] is possible," we need to recognize that the reason Chaucer was able to make this "most valuable contribution" to modernity was because of his engagement with the broader question of how secular and sacred written authorities like Ovid and the Bible, and even his own poetry, are all alike because they are always open to various modes of construction and reconstruction—by men and women alike.[10] Furthermore, critical attention to Chaucer's subtle responses to the Bible will not stand in the way of Professor Mann's recent call for readings of Chaucer that are responsive to contemporary atheistic values and assumptions. On the contrary, such attention might further the project.[11] Writing about the Wife of Bath, Susan Crane asserts that "Chaucer's crossdressing in Alison's feminine rebelliousness is suggestive of the constraints hierarchy imposes on men, but more salient is the ultimate collapse of Alison's specifically feminine effort."[12] But Crane overlooks Chaucer's realignment of the previously restricted claims of women to biblical authority. For Chaucer shows the Wife of Bath, Proserpina, the Prioress, Prudence in the *Tale of Melibee*, and the Second Nun all wielding biblical authority—the primary tool for enforcing male hierarchy—in diverse but equally indefeasible ways.

There is a good deal still to be learned by viewing Chaucer's engagement with controversial questions about gender, social structure, and general hermeneutics through the lens of his biblical poetics. Whether innovatively questioning or piously derivative and affirming, Chaucer's pervasively biblical poetics— understood in relation to the complex mix of old and new ideas about the Bible that were emerging from many different quarters within the larger field of fourteenth-century intellectual life— inscribes themes and motifs on a broad range of complex and controversial religious, political, and social questions, questions that were of the highest moment then, and many of which still remain so now. I do not mean to suggest by this that when Chaucer quotes from or alludes to the Bible directly in his fictions or tells stories that can be read (more or less helpfully and plausibly) in the light of biblical archetypes, he would necessarily have felt that he was flying in the face of received exegetical teachings about the Bible. Nor do I mean to suggest that Chaucer—any more than Aelred of Rievaulx long before him, or Nicholas Love shortly after him—would necessarily have felt that when he adapted biblical sources he was creating those "stories of a new Bible" of which Primo Levi speaks. Yet the freedom and range of approaches to the Bible in late medieval English literature and culture at large, as well as in Chaucer's works, make the latter radical possibilities at least worth considering. Perhaps they are even not so radical after all. To posit a diminution of the Bible's authority once it became available in English has a certain plausibility. This would conform to Ralph Hanna's attractive hypothesis regarding the "cultural pluralism or polyvalence" that developed in the later Middle Ages as a result of the weakening of the authority of other Latin clerical sources when they were translated into the vernacular.[13]

Chaucer has traditionally been implicated in a double paternity suit: he has been named "father of English poetry" and "father of the English language." We now know that English as a language of the court and of its bureaucracy was already alive and well when Chaucer came along and was to develop further under the same official institutional sponsorship under Henry IV and Henry V. To be sure, the medium served Chaucer well; it was supple enough to be shaped and crafted in the most extraordinarily original Chaucerian ways. No doubt, too, his choice of the London variety of the South East Midland dialect gave that dialect a boost in the race for cultural supremacy. But it now seems that burdening Chaucer with the title "Father of the English language" is going too far.[14]

On the other hand, "Father of English poetry" is still appropriate enough as a title for Chaucer if all that we wish to do is reassert that Chaucer stands first in a line of Christian Humanist writers, a line that runs through Spenser, Marlowe, Shakespeare, Milton, and Dryden, and up to Tennyson and Eliot. Today, however, there are fewer interesting observations to be made on this account than there were a generation ago. Seeing Chaucer as the "founder" of this tradition is legitimate even though, of course, English vernacular poetry had been flourishing for centuries before Chaucer. In the *Knight's Tale* Chaucer refers to the difficulty of writing rhyme "in Englyssh proprely" (I 1459–61); and he makes similar remarks about the constraints and hazards of writing poetry in English in *House of Fame* 509–10, *Man of Law's Tale* II 45–50, 778–79; *Squire's Tale* V 37–40; and *Troilus and Criseyde* 5.1793–98. With a highly visible self-awareness, Chaucer played a significant role in promoting and developing English as a newly perceived medium adequate for writing poetry as sophisticated as that which had been written in Latin and had for some time also been written by Chaucer and others in French. Obviously, this paternity is one that Chaucer may be seen to share with Gower.

Anne Hudson has shown how John Wyclif and his followers used the English language to expound sophisticated and complex ideas that had previously been the preserve of Latin authors. As Hudson argues, it was Wyclif who fostered the view that English was not only adequate for the task of biblical translation and exegesis and theological exposition but preferable, because more people could understand it.[15] Chaucer, too, was a pioneer in the use of English prose for expounding philosophical (*Boece*) and scientific subjects (*A Treatise on the Astrolabe*).[16] That Chaucer's two most heavily biblical extant prose works, *Melibee* and the *Parson's Tale*, were written during the years 1386–1400, the same period during which the Wycliffite Bible translations, sermon cycle, and biblically suffused polemical tracts were circulating, is no accident. Chaucer's liminal contributions to the growth of English prose may have been inspired by the Wycliffite example and were surely received by an audience newly schooled through lessons learned from it. The claims of both Wyclif and Chaucer to a share in the title "Father of English Prose" are thus secure.

There is no denying that the title "Father of the English Bible" belongs to Wyclif alone, even though the gestation period was of course quite long, going back to Caedmon and Bede, and even though it was most likely Wyclif's followers who completed the work that Wyclif himself may have only started, or only encouraged others to start.[17] It was, however, Chaucer's translations of hundreds of biblical verses that were read by some of the most influential English noblemen and women and civil servants of the day; it was Chaucer's version of biblical passages, not Wyclif's, that they listened to avidly; and it was Chaucer's English biblical phrases that they heard with pleasure and amusement and remembered with little if any anxiety of the taint of controversy (and possibly even of heresy) that would have accompanied the Wycliffite phrases.

Chaucer thus played a supporting role in the historical process that eventuated in a complete translation of the Bible into English, and the contrast to be drawn between Chaucer's biblically suffused poetry and the Bible-centered Wycliffite program is noteworthy. In Chaucer's plan, the Bible provides a basis for individual reform according to the traditional grid of the seven deadly sins and their remedies, through confession, contrition, and satisfaction within accepted social and religious institutional structures. Chaucer evinces no sense of the need for radical changes on an institutional scale. Still, it is crucial to note just how much of the Bible Chaucer actually translated into English, and the complicity with the Wycliffites that his biblical translations might (incorrectly) be taken to imply.

Chaucer rendered a greater quantity and variety of biblical passages into English prose and verse and achieved a more varied set of tonally diverse literary goals with those translations than had ever been achieved before. While the Wycliffites were translating the Bible to save society, Chaucer and his fellow Ricardian poets were adapting biblical diction, imagery, and story matter to entertain and edify their patrons. The biblically enriched works of these English poets provided their contemporary readers with that ready access to passages of the sacred text in the vernacular which the Wycliffites deemed essential if their broader plan of societal reform was to succeed. Until the sixteenth century the *Canterbury Tales* was most often referred to in manuscripts and early editions as "the boke of the tales of Caunterbury," while the Wycliffite Bible, in at least one Middle English manuscript, is styled in a suggestively similar fashion as "alle the bokes of Goddis storye." In view of the extent to which vernacular biblical materials are to be found throughout the *Canterbury Tales*, the similarity of the titles may look like more than just an uncanny coincidence.[18]

Following the enactment in 1401 of an edict authorizing the death penalty for heresy, and after Archbishop Arundel's *Constitutions* were drafted in 1407 and issued in 1409, the mere possession of unauthorized vernacular biblical translations came to be considered a serious offense.[19] Later in the fifteenth century, as J. A. F. Thomson has shown, "ownership of English books was taken, with some reason, to be evidence of heretical belief and membership in the Lollard sect," and the books confiscated in heresy proceedings were frequently identified only insofar as they were said to be in English and of "reproved reading" (*reprobate leccionis*).[20] Thomson notes that "on one occasion [in 1464] there is evidence that a suspect owned a copy of the *Canterbury Tales* along with two other works which may have been more [!] dubious, and on another a copy of the devotional treatise *The Prick of Conscience* was in Lollard hands."[21]

A linking of the *Canterbury Tales* and *The Prick of Conscience* in this context may at first seem puzzling. The large number of surviving manuscripts suggests that these were two of the most popular vernacular works available in late medieval England.[22] One would therefore expect that the *Canterbury Tales* and *The Prick of Conscience* would both have been considered unexceptionable and irrelevant to the heretical suspicions that the church officials were trying to substantiate. One would further expect that in the eyes of their potential contemporary audiences these two vernacular poetic works would have seemed incommensurable with respect to their literary merits. Furthermore, the differences between the straightforwardly didactic approach of *The Prick of Conscience* and the subtle and frequently blasphemous-seeming artifice of the *Canterbury Tales* would also have been obvious to contemporary readers, even if the religious doctrines stated or implied in both works might, with a little more effort, be seen to be equally orthodox. The juxtaposition of an innovative literary work like the *Canterbury Tales* and an orthodox vernacular penitential treatise like *The Prick of Conscience* makes good cultural-historical as well as bureaucratic-inquisitorial sense. Because *The Prick of Conscience* was sometimes interpolated with Lollard materials, it was in some versions ascribed to Richard Rolle—presumably in order "to cleanse it from heretical taint."[23] Because the *Canterbury Tales* are enriched with hundreds of vernacular biblical passages and because English books in general were cause for suspicion, the bishop's alarmed response to Chaucer's poem and two unnamed vernacular works in John Baron's small library is less anomalous than it might at first appear. As Anne Hudson points out, "if the confiscated copy of *The Canterbury Tales* included, for instance, the Pardoner's Tale or, even more, the Parson's Tale, it could on a rigorous interpretation of [Arundel's Seventh Constitution] rightly have been regarded as indicative of heresy."[24]

This intriguing incident in English social and literary history points ahead to what would soon become the frequent foisting on Chaucer of the paternity of yet another cultural landmark. The Protestant martyrologist John Foxe may have been partially misled by the mistaken attribution to Chaucer of *Jack Upland* and the

Testament of Love when he declared in 1570 that Chaucer was "a right Wicleuian" in his religious opinions. Assertions of Chaucer's premature Protestantism were quite normal among writers in Foxe's day and for a long time thereafter.[25] In a recent essay Linda Georgianna names Thomas Lounsbury as "the key figure" among modern scholarly commentators who have perpetuated the Reformation view of Chaucer as a Protestant poet, and she discusses the century-old mistaken and still-lively scholarly tradition of interpreting Chaucer as "a rational skeptic with no attachment whatsoever to Roman beliefs and devotions."[26] Georgianna also helpfully points out the frequent demonstrations in Chaucer's works of a religious emotionalism and religious "assent" that were typical of the period in which he wrote—demonstrations of what she aptly calls the "immoderate, willed assent of unquestioning love."[27] Nevertheless, she says little about the place of the Bible in Chaucer' religion, and nothing about any of those other facets of Chaucer's biblical poetics, including his occasional problematizing of biblical authority, that we have been exploring.

Around the same time that Foxe and others were proclaiming Chaucer's Protestantism, William Tyndale (d. 1536), the biblical translator and Protestant martyr, was acknowledging that the Bible and Chaucer's poetry were implicated, as it were, by negation. Tyndale attacked the authorities for "forbiddynge the laye people to reade the scripture" while allowing them to read about "troylus with a tousande histories & fables of love & wantones & rybaudry as fylthy as herte can thinke."[28] Similarly, in a prefatory letter to his 1549 reprint of the so-called Matthew Bible of 1537, Edmund Becke contrasts the *Canterbury Tales* with the Bible as he urges his readers to devote "an houre or ii in a day" to Scripture instead of to their presently preferred reading, "Cronicles and Canterbury Tales."[29] As Becke goes on to say, the wished-for result of such a change in reading habits by the "magistrates & the nobilitie," including Edward VI, would be that "then should they also abandone . . . all blasphemyes, swearing, carding, dysing. . . . O what a florishing commune wealth should your grace injoy and have."[30]

In the next century, a court record for the year 1635 pertaining to the alleged atheism of one Brian Walker (who had once supposedly declared, "I doe not beleive there is eyther God or devill, neyhter will I beleive anie thing but what I see") notes that the same Brian Walker spoke "of the booke called Chawcer, which booke he verie much commended, and said he did beleive the same as well as he did the Bible, or wordes to same effect."[31] In this case Chaucer's works and the Bible are once again yoked together but in a very different spirit. The yoking this time seems to have been shared by Walker's accuser, William Hutchinson, "yeoman," and by the High Commission Court before whom he was testifying. For they both appear to have missed what was almost certainly a subtly ironic allusion in Walker's *épatant* declaration. Evidently, Walker was a true Chaucer connoisseur. His allegedly skeptical statement about the truth of the Bible echoes the similarly *épatant* declaration by Chaucer's Nun's Priest, who equates the purported "truth" of his fictional beast fable to that of

> . . . the book of Launcelot de Lake,
> That wommen holde in ful greet reverence.
>
> (VII 3212–13)

Finally, in light of the repeated linking of Chaucer and the Bible throughout the sixteenth and seventeenth centuries, we may need to consider the possibility that Dryden's famous puff of the *Canterbury Tales* in the preface to his *Fables*, "Here we find God's plenty," was intended, and would have been understood by Dryden's original audience, as more than just a rhetorical flourish.[32] Though modern readers may not suspect it, a reference to the *Canterbury Tales* as "God's plenty" for Dryden and his contemporaries would very likely have implied an affinity between Chaucer's poetry and the Bible, an affinity similar to that which was familiar to generations of previous readers. It was an affinity that had been subtly implied by Chaucer himself.

Moving from Tyndale, Becke, Walker, and Dryden to the controversies of Chaucer's twentieth-century critics or to the ongoing debate over the amenability of his texts to biblically derived allegorical approaches is a long leap. Yet, in a way, the older view linking Chaucer's poetry with the Bible has maintained an uncanny hold. Though contemporary acknowledgment of the complex and central role of the Bible and biblical interpretation in Chaucer's poetics may often seem to be lacking, consider a page from the Variorum edition of Chaucer's works currently in progress (see fig. 3). With its gold-edged pages and its Bible-like layout of bits of Chaucer's text overwhelmed by commentary and variants, this edition testifies to a sacralization of Chaucer's poetry (at least among American scholars) that Chaucer himself was sometimes bold enough to hint at. That contemporary scholars still pore over the manuscripts of Chaucer's works, edit and reedit, translate and retranslate them, write books interpreting the *Canterbury Tales* and his other works, develop theories to guide interpreters (theories that sometimes turn into dogmas), divide into schools of competing approaches that then fiercely debate the merits of those approaches, comment on the texts of his works line by line, and even word by word, may not prove that Chaucer himself had similar ideas about the potentially sacral nature of his poetic undertaking. All of these striking examples of the contemporary sacralization of Chaucer's texts are at the very least oblique reflexes of the canonical status his biblically suffused writings have attained. There is indeed a superficial logic to the argument that says it is preposterous to imagine that even a moderately religious medieval Christian author would ever think of his own written words in any sort of relation of propinquity to God's revealed Word or to the diversity of genres of revealed writing represented in the Bible. Yet there is good evidence to suppose that as a Christian author active in England at the end of the fourteenth century Chaucer might well have thought of his works in precisely this audacious way.

In an important study of narrative theory and the rise of early modernism, Allon White makes the compelling Althusserian point that "what seems to be part of the 'code of the real' in a single work may well become a 'symptom' when seen repeated in different works."[33] Chaucer's repeated quests for authority and authoritative interpretation, in the *Book of the Duchess*, the *House of Fame*, the *Legend of Good Women*, throughout the *Canterbury Tales*, and in several of his most profound later lyrics, constitute precisely this: they are symptoms of his desire to find a biblically inspired and biblically modeled vernacular literary solution to the fragmented and fractious flood of biblical translation and interpretation in which his Christian community was adrift. The activities of fourteenth-century philosophers and poets who were

Of thee and of the white lilye flour
Which that the bar, and is a mayde alway,

1651   the] thy Ha[4] He Ne+ CX[1] WR; her that is t. ~ UR   white] *om.*
El+ UR   *Out:* Ad[3] Dd Gg+
1652   the] they ~ TH[3] ST   and] *om.* ~ PN[1]   is] art Pw+   a] *om.* He
Ne+ CX[1,2] WN PN[2]   *Out:* Ad[3] Dd Gg+

---

tions, leading from the humble and temporal to the regal and eternal"; (3) a circular organization beginning at the exact center of the lyric, the descent of the Spirit, in which the end of the *Prologue* is joined to its beginning. In the final stanza, says Burlin, the circular movement draws tight: she speaks as a child, and we are reminded that it was out of the mouth of babes that praise is spoken.

1650–56   Sr. Madeleva (1925:31) suggests that these seven lines utilize an antiphon of matins: "Vouchsafe that I may praise thee, O sacred Virgin; give me strength against my enemies."

1650   laude: As in lines 1645–46 (see note) there is the possibility that *laude* here puns on the office of Lauds.

best kan or may: "Know how to or have the ability to do" (SK).

1651   SK notes that the white lily symbolizes Mary's perpetual virginity, and he refers to Rock's *The Church of Our Fathers* (1849–53:3.245), a rich work on ecclesiology still useful though now superseded by two editions of *The Catholic Encyclopedia* (1910, 1967). Manly observes (1928*a*:625): "The lily as a symbol of the Virgin is common in mediaeval religious verse and prose. According to Alanus de Insulis [*In Cantica Canticorum* (*PL* 210, cols. 64–65)], it was derived from the *Song of Solomon,* ii, 2. For a popular presentation of the influence of the cult of the Virgin upon mediaeval art and life see Henry Adams, *Mont St. Michel and Chartres.*" RB merely quotes Manly on the Song of Solomon. This symbol, common in art and poetry, is related to the symbolism of the unconsumed burning bush in lines 1658–63 (see below). The theology involved in the flower symbolism is discussed by Ferris (1981*b*), who is largely concerned with Mary as *deipara* (mother of God). Although the purity of Mary is widely celebrated in medieval art and literature, the Immaculate Conception—the belief that Mary was conceived without the stain of original sin supposedly the lot of humanity since the Fall—was, as Fisher notes (1977:242), controversial in the fourteenth century. It was not defined as dogma until 1854.

thee: Ferris (1981*b*) points out that here and elsewhere (cf. line 1655) Chaucer is theologically correct in placing the Prioress's praise of Mary second, and secondary, to her praise of God. The antecedent of *thee* is, of course, *Lord,* as addressed in the first line of *PrP* and hence in Ps. 8.

white: Not in El, "obviously by accident," says Manly (1928*a*:625). The same omission occurs in seven other MSS listed in MR, six of these others forming the second of MR's ten lines of textual descent of *PrSeq* (2.354) and hence unrelated to El.   §   Ferris suggests (1981*a*:297) that all of the saints mentioned in *PrT*—Mary, Saint Nicholas (line 1704), Saint John the Evangelist (line 1772), Hugh of Lincoln (line 1874) and Saint John the Baptist (referred to symbolically in the symbol of the Lamb)—were strongly connected to Lincoln.

Fig. 3. Chaucer, *The Prioress's Tale,* ed. Beverly Boyd, in *A Variorum Edition of the Works of Geoffrey Chaucer,* vol. 2, *The Canterbry Tales,* pt. 20, *The Prioress's Tale* (Norman: U of Oklahoma P, 1987), p. 121. Reproduced by permission of the University of Oklahoma Press, Norman.

skeptical about the Bible's unique authority, and the responses of both orthodox and heterodox opponents of these philosophers and poets, were to have consequences, both immediate and far-reaching. On the orthodox side, the efforts of de Lyra, von Oyta, and others (building on the work of Roger Bacon and other thirteenth-century scholars) fed a fourteenth-century revival of Greek and Hebrew biblical studies and a new, more critical attitude to texts in general and to the text of the Bible in particular. This revival helped constitute the cultural shift of the coming European Renaissance and Reformation.[34] On the heterodox side, the activities of Wyclif and his disciples were, as we now realize, fourteenth-century steps leading up to the Reformation side of that cultural shift.[35]

We have long been accustomed to the idea that Chaucer's contribution to progressive pre-Renaissance and pre-Reformation cultural developments in the fourteenth century is evidenced by his openness to a multiplicity of secular humanist poetic influences and by his sharp criticism of various forms of corruption in the Church.[36] More recently, a new generation of scholars sensitive to both literary form and medieval social and economic history have located Chaucer's greatest originality and his major accomplishment as a literary artist in his subtle depiction of the contested social and economic realities of his day.[37] Yet as surely as Chaucer's stylistic innovations and pioneering uses of new literary forms have their social and economic correlatives, they can be fully and properly understood only if they are also seen as evidence of his central concern with, and as facets of his engaged and innovative response to, a problem that had bedeviled Christian culture from the time of Augustine: the problem of the mutual translatability of secular and biblical poetics.

Notes

Unless otherwise indicated, all translations of foreign-language quotations are my own, and all biblical quotations are from the Latin Vulgate or the close English translation of the Vulgate in the Douay-Rheims Bible (with the different numbering of Psalms in the King James version provided in parentheses). The Middle English "Wycliffite Bible" is quoted from the edition of Forshall and Madden, the only complete edition available, and hence indispensable despite its questionable editorial assumptions (see Anne Hudson, *The Premature Reformation* [1988], pp. 231–40). In quoting Middle English I omit diacritic marks of vowel length but follow the conventions of the various editions cited in the use of "thorn" and "yogh" and of *i, y, j, u,* and *v.* Unless otherwise noted, all Chaucer quotations are from *The Riverside Chaucer,* ed. Larry D. Benson (1987).

ABBREVIATIONS

AHDLMA	*Archives d'histoire doctrinale et littéraire du moyen age*
AnM	*Annulae Mediaevale*
BJRL	*Bulletin of the John Rylands Library*
CCSL	Corpus Christianorum, Series Latina
ChauR	*Chaucer Review*
CL	*Comparative Literature*
CSEL	Corpus Scriptorum Ecclesiasticorum Latinorum
EETS	Early English Text Society
ELH	*ELH: A Journal of English Literary History*
ELN	*English Language Notes*
e.s.	extra series
HUSL	*Hebrew University Studies in Literature [and the Arts]*
JEGP	*Journal of English and Germanic Philology*

JMRS	*Journal of Medieval and Renaissance Studies*
JNT	*Journal of Narrative Technique*
MÆ	*Medium Ævum*
MED	*Middle English Dictionary*
M&H	*Medievalia et Humanistica*
MLN	*Modern Language Notes*
MLQ	*Modern Language Quarterly*
MLR	*Modern Language Review*
MP	*Modern Philology*
MS	*Medieval Studies*
NLH	*New Literary History*
NM	*Neuphilologische Mitteilungen*
n.s.	new series
OED	*Oxford English Dictionary*
o.s.	original series
PBA	*Proceedings of the British Academy*
PL	*Patrologia Latina*
PLL	*Papers on Language and Literature*
PMLA	*Publications of the Modern Language Association of America*
PQ	*Philological Quarterly*
RBPH	*Revue belge de philologie et d'histoire*
SAC	*Studies in the Age of Chaucer*
SCH	*Studies in Church History*
SLRev	*Stanford Literature Review*
SP	*Studies in Philology*
StM	*Studia Monastica*
YFS	*Yale French Studies*
ZDP	*Zeitschrift für deutsche Philologie*

INTRODUCTION

1. Quoted in Mary Bosanquet, *The Life and Death of Dietrich Bonhoeffer* (1968), pp. 109–10. References for all further epigraphs are provided in the list of "Works Cited."

2. See Lesley Smith, "The Theology of the Twelfth- and Thirteenth-Century Bible" (1994). The pervasive biblical influence on medieval culture is illustrated and discussed in Hans Rost, *Die Bibel im Mittelalter* (1939), and in the following essay collections: Giovanni Barblan, ed.,

La Bibbia nell'alto medioevo (1962); W. Lourdaux and D. Verhelst, eds., *The Bible and Medieval Culture* (1979); Pierre Riché and Guy Lobrichon, eds., *Le moyen age et la Bible* (1984); Katherine Walsh and Diana Wood, eds., *The Bible in the Medieval World* (1985); André Vernet and Anne-Marie Genevois, eds., *La Bible au moyen age* (1989); and Bernard Levy, ed., *The Bible in the Middle Ages* (1992). On the bibically suffused diction of medieval English vernacular sermons, see G. R. Owst, *Preaching in Medieval England* (1926); id., *Literature and Pulpit in Medieval England*, 2d ed. (1961); and H. Leith Spencer, *English Preaching in the Late Middle Ages* (1993), esp. chapter 4, "Preaching the Gospel," pp. 134–95. Spencer demonstrates that there was a significant late medieval revival of vernacular preaching among the English secular clergy, and her evidence suggests that some of the surviving sermon collections "could have been used as pious lay reading" (pp. 33–49, 259–62; quotation on p. 38). The fundamental influence of the Bible on medieval aesthetics from Boethius to Aquinas is assessed in Edgar de Bruyne, *L'esthétique du moyen age* (1947), pp. 7–12 (with numerous references to the pertinent medieval works discussed more fully in id., *Études d'esthétique médiévale*, 3 vols. [1946]). On the Bible as a primary source of medieval social and political theory, see Walter Ullmann, "The Bible and Principles of Government in the Middle Ages" (1962), and Philippe Buc, *L'ambiguïté du livre: Prince, pouvoir, et peuple dans les commentaires de la Bible au moyen age* (1994).

3. On the scope of Chaucer's biblical allusions, see Grace Landrum's dissertation, "Chaucer's Use of the Vulgate" (1921); Landrum's *PMLA* article of the same title (1924); and Lawrence Besserman, *Chaucer and the Bible* (1988), passim. The independence and high quality of Chaucer's translations of biblical verses is the subject of W. Meredith Thompson's "Chaucer's Translation of the Bible" (1962), and there is a brief assessment of the stylistic and thematic significance of Chaucer's uses of the Vulgate in Derek Brewer, "Chaucer and the Bible" (1988).

4. D. W. Robertson, Jr.'s *A Preface to Chaucer* (1962) is a landmark study of the allegedly biblical-allegorical basis of Chaucer's poetics, but Robertson's methodology is quite different from the one followed in the present book. Though most of the essays by various scholars in David Jeffrey's *Chaucer and Scriptural Tradition* (1984) treat Chaucer's uses of the Bible from a "Robertsonian" perspective, there are several exceptions, including my own contribution to the volume, "*Glosynge Is a Glorious Thyng*: Chaucer's Biblical Exegesis," which offers a brief

critique of the Robertsonian approach. In the same volume, David Jeffrey's introduction and his two essays, "Chaucer and Wyclif: Biblical Hermeneutic and Literary Theory in the XIVth Century" and "Sacred and Secular Scripture: Authority and Interpretation in The House of Fame," raise new and important questions about Chaucer's poetics in relation to late fourteenth-century biblical exegesis, literary theory, theology, and philosophy. (For more on Robertsonian allegorical interpretation, see chapter 4, n. 5.)

5. See Jeffrey, *Chaucer and Scriptural Tradition*, p. 262.

CHAPTER 1. THE BIBLE AND LATE MEDIEVAL LITERARY CULTURE

1. Medieval Latin and Greek manuscripts of the Bible, biblical apocrypha and pseudepigrapha, and biblical commentaries are recorded in Frederick Stegmüller's monumental *Repertorium biblicum medii aevi*, vols. 1–7 (1950–61), and in the *Supplementum*, compiled by Stegmüller with the assistance of N. Reinhardt, vols. 8–11 (1976–80). For a critical survey of manuscripts and textual problems in the history of the Vulgate and other Latin versions, see Bonifatius Fischer's two monographs, *Lateinische Bibelhandschriften im frühen Mittelalter* (1985) and *Beiträge zur Geschichte der lateinischen Bibeltexte* (1986). For more general studies of the Vulgate, see Samuel Berger, *Histoire de la Vulgate* (1893); Raphael Loewe, "The Medieval History of the Latin Vulgate" (1969); and the succinct and up-to-date accounts, with references to more specialized studies, by Margaret Gibson, *The Bible in the Latin West* (1993), pp. 1–2, and Patrick McGurk, "The Oldest Manuscripts of the Latin Bible" (1994). Still valuable, and especially relevant for students of Chaucer's Latin Bible, is Hans Glunz, *History of the Vulgate in England* (1933) (to be used with caution, however, for the reasons explained by Laura Light, "Versions et révisions du texte biblique" [1984], pp. 67–68 et passim).

2. For the view that basic familiarity with the Bible was a feature of lay literacy in the Middle Ages, see Margaret Aston, "Devotional Literacy" (1984), and M. T. Clanchy, *From Memory to Written Record, 1066–1307*, 2d ed. (1993). For the view that literacy (including Bible reading) among medieval women was extremely rare, and limited primarily to "a small fraction at the top of English society," see (with reference mainly to thirteenth-century evidence) Alcuin Blamires,

"The Limits of Bible Study for Medieval Women" (1995), and (with reference mainly to fifteenth-century evidence) Shannon McSheffrey "Literacy and the Gender Gap in the Late Middle Ages: Women and Reading in Lollard Communities" (1995) (quotation on p. 170).

Though private ownership of Bibles in the Middle Ages may have been limited, people seem to have been able to memorize impressively large portions of its sacred words. On the glossed Bible as "a support for the various activities of *memoria,*" see Mary Carruthers, *The Book of Memory* (1990), pp. 80–82 (treating Hugh of St. Victor's instructions on how to memorize the 150 Psalms—a text discussed also by Clanchy, *From Memory,* p. 178), pp. 115–16 (on the mnemonic uses of Jerome's *Index nominorum hebraeorum*—discussed also by Clanchy, along with the similar mnemonic use of the thirteenth-century biblical concordance, ibid., pp. 180–82), and pp. 214–15.

3. On these various biblical works, see discussion and notes, below. On Chaucer's education at court and in baronial households rather than at the universities or Inns of Court, see T. F. Tout, "Learning and Literature in the English Civil Service in the Fourteenth Century" (1929), pp. 381–86, and the summary account of Chaucer's education in Derek Pearsall, *The Life of Geoffrey Chaucer* (1992), pp. 29–34. On the so-called Chaucer circle within the poet's larger audience—a presumed inner circle consisting of highly literate public servants and courtiers such as Bukton, Clifford, Scogan, and Vache and writers such as Gower, Usk, and Clanvowe—see Paul Strohm, *Social Chaucer* (1989), pp. 41–46 et passim; and Pearsall, *Life,* pp. 178–90.

4. See Henderson, *From Durrow to Kells: The Insular Gospel-Books, 650–800* (1987); quotation on p. 198. On one–volume Bibles ("pandects," mainly from the Carolingian period), see Herbert Kessler, *The Illustrated Bibles from Tours* (1977); David Ganz, "Mass Production of Early Medieval Manuscripts: the Carolingian Bibles from Tours" (1994); and Rosamond McKitterick, "Carolingian Bible Production: the Tours Anomaly" (1994). On one-volume Bibles and various other Bible formats in the later Middle Ages, see the discussion and illustrations in Laura Light, *The Bible in the Twelfth Century* (1988), pp. 14–24, 81–101 (glossed Bibles); Barbara Shailor, *The Medieval Book* (1991), pp. 75–80; and Margaret Gibson, *The Bible in the Latin West* (1993), pp. 2–8 et passim.

5. Fourteenth-century illuminated Bibles are illustrated and discussed in Lucy Sandler, *Gothic Manuscripts,* 1285–1385 (1986).

6. Cahn, *Romanesque Bible Illumination* (1982), p. 11.

7. See Samuel Berger, *Histoire de la Vulgate* (1893), p. 3; on summaries, chapter divisions, rubrics, and prefaces typically found in Latin Bibles, see id., *Les préfaces jointes aux livres de la Bible dans les manuscrits de la Vulgate* (1902), and Donatien de Bruyne, *Sommaires, divisions, et rubriques de la Bible latine* (1914). For color illustrations and a detailed description of the Winchester Bible (produced c. 1160–c. 1175 in four "huge" volumes), see Claire Donovan, *The Winchester Bible* (1993). On the origin, format, and contents of the "Paris" Bibles of the early thirteenth–century, see Laura Light, "French Bibles, c. 1200–30: A New Look at the Origin of the Paris Bible" (1994). On the frequently reproduced and adapted "Eusebian Canons," in which Eusebius of Caeserea (d. c. 340) provided ten tables that correlate the corresponding 'sections' of the Gospels, see the brief description and illustration in Gibson, *The Bible in the Latin West*, pp. 30–31, and the definitive study by Carl Nordenfalk, *Die Spätantiken Kanonentafeln*, 2 vols. (1938).

8. On the production of glossed Psalters in the early Middle Ages, see Margaret Gibson, "Carolingian Glossed Psalters" (1994). On the formation of the *Glossa ordinaria*, see Beryl Smalley, "The Bible in the Medieval Schools" (1969), pp. 205–6; and id., *The Study of the Bible in the Middle Ages*, 3d ed. (1983), pp. 46–66 (with new material briefly noted on pp. ix–xi). On the contents and various formats of complete glossed Bibles in the High Middle Ages, see C. F. R. de Hamel, *Glossed Books of the Bible and the Origins of the Paris Booktrade* (1984). New evidence regarding the formation and distribution of the *Glossa ordinaria* is presented by Guy Lobrichon, "Une nouveauté: les gloses de la Bible" (1984); Mary and Richard Rouse, "The Book Trade at the University of Paris, ca. 1250–ca. 1350" (1991), pp. 284–91; and Margaret Gibson, "The Place of the *Glossa ordinaria* in Medieval Exegesis" (1992).

On Nicholas de Lyra's biblical commentaries, see the list of manuscripts in Frederick Stegmüller, *Repertorium biblicum medii aevi*, vol. 4 (1954), nos. 5827–5994, and Edward Gosselin, "A Listing of the Printed Editions of Nicolaus de Lyra" (1970). On de Lyra's career and innovative exegetical methodology, see Herman Hailperin, *Rashi and the Christian Scholars* (1963), pp. 137–246; and for an account that emphasizes the continuities between de Lyra and earlier exegetes, see Henri de Lubac, *Exégèse médiévale*, part 2, vol. 4 (1964), pp. 344–67.

9. Though there were no verse divisions in medieval Bibles, thirteenth-century Paris witnessed the invention of a system for dividing

biblical chapters into proportional segments, each marked by a letter from A to G (or, for shorter chapters, from A to D). The first known use of this system for dividing biblical chapters is in a concordance dated c. 1235, and it is found also in citations of the Bible by exegetes later in the thirteenth century (see Rouse and Rouse, "The Verbal Concordance to the Scriptures" [1974], pp. 10, 17, 22–23). The modern division of the Bible into verses was instituted by the Reformation scholar Robert Estienne, in a Latin octavo Bible printed in 1555 (see M. H. Black, "The Printed Bible" [1963], pp. 442–43). On the inconsistency of the chapter divisions in Bibles produced prior to the middle of the thirteenth century, see Amaury D'Esneval, "La division de la vulgate latine en chapitres dans l'édition parisienne du XIIIe siècle" (1978). (See also n. 19, below.)

10. On the interpolation of glosses into Hebrew, Greek, and Latin Bibles, see Peter Ackroyd, "The Old Testament in the Making" (1970), pp. 76–79; J. N. Birdsall, "The New Testament Text" (1970), pp. 324–25, 344–45; and Raphael Loewe, "The Medieval History of the Latin Vulgate," pp. 122–23. On the frequency with which glosses were incorporated into Middle English (i.e., "Wycliffite") Bibles, see Henry Hargreaves, "The Wycliffite Versions" (1969), pp. 405–6, 412–13. For glosses in Old French biblical translations, see D. A. Trotter, "The Influence of Bible Commentaries on Old French Bible Translations" (1987).

11. On Chaucer's use of the *Glossa ordinaria* in the *Merchant's Tale*, see Lawrence Besserman, "Chaucer and the Bible: The Case of the *Merchant's Tale*" (1978); and for several other suggested instances, see the references in Lynn Morris, *Chaucer Source and Analogue Criticism* (1985), p. 467, s.v. *Glossa ordinaria*. For the suggestion that several biblical passages in Chaucer show the influence of Nicholas de Lyra's *Postilla litteralis*, see Douglas Wurtele, "Chaucer's *Canterbury Tales* and Nicholas of Lyre's *Postillae litteralis*" (1984), and David Hale, "Another Latin Source for the Nun's Priest on Dreams" (1989).

12. Light, "The New Thirteenth–Century Bible," p. 278. On the creation of this "Paris Bible," see Loewe, "The Medieval History of the Latin Vulgate," pp. 145–48; D'Esneval, "La division de la vulgate latine en chapitres dans l'édition parisienne du XIIIe siècle"; and Light, "French Bibles, c. 1200–30: A New Look at the Origin of the Paris Bible."

13. See Light, "The New Thirteenth-Century Bible," pp. 280–88. As de Hamel notes, there are records of one-volume Bibles from the latter

half of the twelfth century (*Glossed Books of the Bible*, p. 37), but as Light points out, the majority of pocket-sized Bibles date from 1230 or later. The size of most of the 250 manuscripts that Light examined for her study of pocket Bibles is "a written space not exceeding 150mm in height," but Light's definition of a "pocket" Bible includes all Bibles with a written space of up to 200mm ("The New Thirteenth-Century Bible," p. 278). On the wide currency in the thirteenth century of slightly larger one-volume Bibles, in addition to the so-called "pocket Bibles," see Light, "Versions et révisions du texte biblique," pp. 79–93.

14. Light, "The New Thirteenth–Century Bible," p. 279, and n. 19.

15. Ibid., p. 286.

16. Ibid., p. 276. In her more recent study, Light shows that thirteenth-century "Paris" Bibles of various sizes were the first to be "arranged in an order that is essentially that of the modern Bible" ("French Bibles, c. 1200–30: A New Look at the Origin of the Paris Bible" [1994], p. 159). In these Bibles, as Light notes (p. 155), the usual order of Old Testament books is Octateuch (Genesis–Ruth), 1–4 Kings, 1–2 Paralipomenon, 1 Esdras, Nehemias (= 2 Esdras), 2 Esdras (= 3 Esdras), Tobit, Judith, Esther, Job, Psalms, Sapiential books (Proverbs, Ecclesiastes, the Song of Songs, Wisdom, and Ecclesiasticus), Prophets (Isaiah, Jeremiah, Lamentations, Baruch, Ezekiel, Daniel, and minor prophets), and 1–2 Maccabees; the usual New Testament order is Gospels, Pauline Epistles, Acts, Catholic Epistles, Apocalypse. (On the origins of this order and various other quite different arrangements that are found in medieval Bibles, see ibid., 159–63, and n. 19, below).

17. Light, "Versions et révisions," pp. 67–68.

18. On private ownership of Bibles in Chaucer's day, see the representative evidence cited from London citizens' wills in D. W. Robertson, Jr., *Chaucer's London* (1968), pp. 201–2, and the extensive survey in Susan Cavanaugh, "A Study of Books Privately Owned in England, 1300–1450" (1980). (For more on the private ownership of Bibles, see nn. 22, 23, and 32, below.)

19. See Light, "Versions et révisions," pp. 92–93 (and id., as in n. 16, above); and especially D'Esneval, "La division de la vulgate en chapitres dans l'édition parisienne du XIIIe siècle." As D'Esneval points out, in Vulgate Bibles from around the year 1150, Genesis is variously divided into 63, 78, 82, 88, or even 156 chapters (instead of the 50 that it would soon come to have in the corrected Vulgate); Exodus has 130 or more

chapters (instead of 40); and the Gospel of Mark has 48 chapters (instead of 16). The corrected system of chapter divisions and the fixed order of biblical books in the Vulgate Bible—which are essentially the same as in modern Catholic Bibles—are attributed to Stephen Langton and his circle (c. 1200). See Smalley, *The Study of the Bible in the Middle Ages*, pp. 222–24, and Loewe, "The Medieval History of the Latin Vulgate," pp. 147–48.

20. See Light, "The New Thirteenth–Century Bible," pp. 285–86.

21. For de Lyra's lament in his *Postilla litteralis* (completed in 1331), see Margaret Deanesly, *The Lollard Bible* (1920), pp. 166–67; and for the Wycliffite claim, see *The Holy Bible*, ed. Forshall and Madden, vol. 1, pp. 57–58. Anne Hudson cites many instances in vernacular Wycliffite sermons where the translation of biblical Latin phrases follows variant Vulgate readings ("Aspects of Biblical Translation in the English [Wycliffite Sermon] Cycle" [1990], pp. lxxii–lxxv).

22. British Library, Harley MS 2807 is a late thirteenth- or early fourteenth-century one–volume octavo Latin Bible, possibly of English provenance. With two oddly colored and stylistically unsophisticated historiated initials, the text of Harley 2807 begins with Jerome's "Frater Ambrosius" prologue and follows the standard order of biblical books from Genesis through 2 Paralipomenon, but it lacks Jeremiah and Psalms, the order of some of the remaining books of the Old Testament is unusual, and the manuscript ends with several blank sheets that were perhaps meant to be used for an *Index nominorum hebraeorum*, a liturgical calendar, canon tables, or some other aid to the Bible reader. Because it lacks the *Glossa ordinaria* and Nicholas de Lyra's commentary—and as its very regular and compact but easily legible script further suggest—Harley 2807 was presumably a Bible that was meant for continuous and uninterrupted private reading, rather than for serious classroom study and discussion. Harley MS 2814 is a similar one-volume octavo English Vulgate that dates from the second half of the thirteenth-century, with blue and red colored initials, beginning with a dominical calendar and Jerome's prologue to "Frater Ambrosius" and ending with an *Index nominorum hebraeorum*. Though it includes all the books of the standard Vulgate in the usual order, it lacks an incipit for Genesis and its text of Psalms is based on the less common "Hebrew Version."

As Lucy Sandler reports (in a letter to Robert Raymo, from which I have kindly been permitted to quote several details about these two manuscripts), Harley 2807 is also unusual in that it places Job, Tobit, Judith, and Esther after Zacharias (on the usual order, see n. 16, above). Sandler further notes that the illustrations on Harley 2807, fol. 3 ("Frater Ambrosius"), which shows Saint Jerome writing, and on fol. 5v (Genesis), which shows the Six Days of Creation, God Enthroned (above), and the Crucifixion (below) are executed in a "reductive, provincial" style and with unusual colors—"strong green, orange, blue, brown, and grey; not English color but not Parisian either." Sandler draws attention to the "lively animated pen work" of Harley 2814's decorated initials and the unusual use of Jerome's "Hebrew" version of Psalms, instead of the more commonly found "Gallican" version.

23. The suggestion that Chaucer owned a Vulgate Bible from which he drew many of his biblical references was first argued in detail by Grace Landrum in her Radcliffe College dissertation, "Chaucer's Use of the Vulgate" (1921); and the case was restated by Landrum with a summary of the evidence in a 1924 *PMLA* article. On the ownership of Bibles (in Latin, English, and French) and biblically suffused devotional works and service books by courtiers and prosperous merchants during Richard II's reign, see Cavanaugh (as in n. 18, above), and V. J. Scattergood, "Literary Culture at the Court of Richard II" (1983), pp. 34–35, 42–43. On the Bibles owned by several of the men condemned by the "Merciless Parliament" in 1388 (including Simon Burley, who was tutor to Richard II, and with whom Chaucer served on a peace commission in 1385), see M. V. Clarke, "Forfeiture and Treason in 1388" (1937), 119–22 et passim.

24. The three gospel harmonies that Chaucer is most likely to have known are Augustine's *De consensu evangelistarum*, the Welshman Clement of Llanthony's *Unum ex quattuor* (composed around the middle of the twelfth century), and the Middle English (Wycliffite?) translation of *Unum ex quattuor* known as *Oon of Foure.* For a survey-account of these and other gospel harmonies, see Elizabeth Salter, *Nicholas Love's "Myrrour of the Blessed Lyf of Jesu Christ"* (1974), pp. 57–71. Augustine's *De consensu evangelistarum* is edited in the Corpus Scriptorum Ecclesiasticorum Latinorum series by F. Weinrich (1904); for a modern English version, see *On the Harmony of the Gospels,* trans. S. D. F. Salmond (1978); and for a critical study, see Heinrich Vogels, *St. Augustinus Schrift De consensu evangelistarum* (1908). Manuscripts of Clement of Llanthony's *Unum ex quattuor* are listed in Stegmüller, *Repertorium,* vol. 2, pp. 249–50, n. 1981 (s.v. *Concordia evangelistarum*);

and for a more detailed account, with a portion of the Latin text reproduced together with its Middle English translation, see P. M. Smith, "An Edition of Parts I–V of the Wycliffite Translation of Clement of Llanthony's Gospel Harmony 'Unum ex Quattuor,' known as *Oon of Foure*" (1984), pp. xv–lxv et passim (Smith treats the indebtedness of Clement's *Unum ex quattuor* to Augustine's *De consensu* on pp. lxxxix–cxxxiii). For the case against assigning *Oon of Foure* to the Lollards, see Anne Hudson, *The Premature Reformation* (1988), pp. 267–68.

25. *Oon of Foure*, the Middle English version of Clement's *Unum ex quattuor*, is sometimes incorporated in the Wycliffite Bible as a Preface to the New Testament (see Smith, as in the previous note, pp. xv–lxv).

26. On the production of *distinctiones*, see L.–J. Battailon, "Intermédiaires entre les traités de morale pratique et les sermons: Les *distinctiones* biblique alphabétiques" (1982); Smalley, *The Study of the Bible in the Middle Ages*, pp. 246–49; and the following studies by Richard and Mary Rouse: "Biblical *distinctiones* in the Thirteenth Century" (1974); "*Statim invenire*: Schools, Preachers, and New Attitudes to the Page" (1991); "The Book Trade at the University of Paris, ca. 1250–ca. 1350" (1991), pp. 284–86; "The Development of Research Tools in the Thirteenth Century" (1991); and *Preachers, Florilegia, and Sermons: Studies on the "Manipulus florum" of Thomas of Ireland* (1979), pp. 3–42.

27. As Robert Pratt demonstrates (in "Chaucer and the Hand That Fed Him" [1966]), Chaucer seems to have drawn biblical references and other authoritative quotations in the *Wife of Bath's Prologue* and *Tale*, *Summoner's Tale*, and *Pardoner's Tale* from the *distinctiones* in the *Communiloquium* of Gerald of Wales.

28. On the earliest Latin concordances, see Rouse and Rouse, "The Verbal Concordance to the Scriptures" (1974); and on the Middle English concordance, produced sometime during the 1390s in conjunction with the Wycliffite Bible translation project, see Hudson, *Premature Reformation*, pp. 234–35.

29. Rouse and Rouse, "The Verbal Concordance to the Scriptures," p. 24.

30. Rouse and Rouse mention an unusually compact mid-thirteenth-century concordance, only four inches by six inches, "truly in the format of the mendicant portable Bibles" (ibid., p. 13).

31. On the origins and distinguishing features of the *Bible moralisée*, *Biblia pauperum*, and *Speculum humanae salvationis*, see the following

editions: *Bible moralisée: Faksimilie im Originalformat des Codex Vindo-bonensis 2554 der Österreichischen Nationalbibliothek,* ed. Reiner Hanssherr, 2 vols. (1973); *Biblia pauperum: A Facsimile and Edition,* ed. Avril Henry (1987); and *A Medieval Mirror: Speculum humanae salvationis, 1324–1500,* ed. Adrian Wilson and Joyce Wilson (1984).

32. Aristocratic ownership of the *Bible moralisée* is documented in Hélène Toubert, "Les bibles moralisées" (1990).

33. On the typological organization of the *Biblia pauperum,* see the essay and informative notes in Avril Henry's edition (as in n. 31, above), pp. 9–17 et passim.

34. On the audience of the *Biblia pauperum* and *Speculum humanae salvationis,* see, resp., *Biblia pauperum,* ed. Henry, p. 3; and *A Medieval Mirror,* ed. Wilson and Wilson, p. 24.

35. On the influence of sermon diction on Chaucer, see Siegfried Wenzel, "Chaucer and the Language of Contemporary Preaching" (1976); and Sabine Volk–Birke, *Chaucer and Medieval Preaching* (1991). For studies that illustrate the bibically suffused diction of medieval English vernacular sermons, see G. R. Owst, *Preaching in Medieval England* (1926); id., *Literature and Pulpit in Medieval England,* 2d ed. (1961); and H. Leith Spencer, *English Preaching in the Late Middle Ages* (1993), esp. chapter 4, "Preaching the Gospel," pp. 134–95. (See also introduction, n. 2, above.)

On the use of the Bible in the liturgy, see Hans Rost, *Die Bibel im Mittelalter* (1939), pp. 79–84; J. A. Lamb, "The Place of the Bible in the Liturgy" (1970), pp. 563–86, 597–98; and David Fowler, *The Bible in Early English Literature* (1976), pp. 11–17; and for an illuminating phenomenological analysis of the effect of recitation of the Gospels in the medieval Latin liturgy, see Daniel Sheerin, "*Sonus* and *Verba*: Varieties of Meaning in the Liturgical Proclamation of the Gospel in the Middle Ages" (1992). On the form and content of various medieval Latin liturgical books (missals, breviaries, lectionaries, hymnaries, *horae,* etc.), see Andrew Hughes, *Medieval Manuscripts for Mass and Office* (1982); and the bibliographic survey in Richard Pfaff, *Medieval Latin Liturgy* (1982). Liturgical books and standard biblical commentaries (from which readings in the liturgy were also sometimes taken) are illustrated and discussed by Light, *The Bible in the Twelfth Century,* pp. 25–78. On Chaucer's use of the liturgy, see Beverly Boyd, *Chaucer and the Liturgy* (1967). For a list of the biblical passages that were quoted in the liturgy of Chaucer's day, see the [Sarum] *Breviarium,* ed. Procter and Wordsworth (1879–86), vol. 3, "Index Biblicus," pp. lii–lxi; and for a list of the biblical characters and Evangelists quoted or referred to in the mass, see *The Sarum Missal*, ed. Legg (1916), "Index II," pp. 557–612; and the Index to *Missale . . . Sarum*, ed. Dickinson (1861–83), pp. 1–11 (unfortunately, neither of the latter two editions of the Sarum missal includes an index of biblical verses, but Dickinson gives copious footnote references to biblical passages throughout). On the origin and content of the English vernacular liturgy, see text and commentary in *The Prymer or Lay Folks' Prayer Book*, parts 1 and 2, ed. Henry Littlehales (1975). The religious and general cultural significance of the laity's use of the Primer has recently been explored by Eamon Duffy, *Stripping of the Altars*, pp. 209–65.

On Chaucer's poetry in relation to the visual arts, and his biblically inspired visual imagination in particular, see V. A. Kolve, *Chaucer and the Imagery of Narrative: The First Five Canterbury Tales* (1984). For an overview of biblically inspired manuscript painting from 600 to 1450, see Francis Wormald, "Bible Illustration in Medieval Manuscripts" (1969). The biblical subjects in cathedral windows that Chaucer must have seen are surveyed in Madeline Caviness, *The Early Stained Glass of Canterbury Cathedral, circa 1175–1220* (1972), especially pp. 101–6 ("The Iconographic Program"), and pp. 107–38 ("Biblical Subjects"); id., *The Windows of Christ Church Canterbury* (1981); and id., "Biblical Stories in Windows: Were They Bibles for the Poor?" (1992). See also Nigel Morgan, "Old Testament Illustration in Thirteenth–Century England" (1992).

36. On the topos of the Book of Nature and the Book of Scripture from the thirteenth through nineteenth centuries, see E. R. Curtius, *European Literature and the Latin Middle Ages* (1953), pp. 319–26. For Saint Bonaventure's especially influential formulation of the topos, see his *Breviloquium* 2.12.1–5, trans. de Vinck, in *Works*, vol. 2 (1963), p. 104; and the discussion in Curtius, *European Literature*, pp. 320–21; and in Kent Emery, Jr., "Reading the World" (1983), pp. 201 et passim.

37. For Chaucer's use of *gospel* in this extended sense (i.e., without restriction to one specific gospel), see *General Prologue* I 481, 498; *Summoner's Tale* IV 1935; *Shipman's Tale* VII 1180; and *Parson's Tale* X 115, 290, 410, etc. For phrases like "the book seith," "as book seith," "oure book seith," etc., see *Melibee* VII 1144–45, 1164, 1177; *Parson's Tale* X 680; *Retraction* X 1083; etc.

38. The word *scripture* meaning "the Bible" occurs in the phrase "holy scripture," in *Romaunt* 6452, within a spurious passage interpolated

within "Fragment C," the non-Chaucerian portion of the Middle English translation of the *Roman de la rose* (see Alred David, in *Riverside Chaucer*, p. 1113, n. 6360–6472).

39. For this reading of "tellen no scripture" in *Troilus* 3.1369, see *The Works of Geoffrey Chaucer*, 2d ed., ed. F. N. Robinson (1957), p. 826, n. 1366–69; and cp. *Boece* 1, pr. 4, 167–68, where Chaucer's "I have put it in scripture and in remembraunce" translates Boethius's "stilo etiam memoriaeque mandaui," which refers to Boethius's answer to the false charges against him (see *Consolation of Philosophy*, trans. H. F. Stewart [1968], book 1, pr. 4.87–88).

40. On relationships between the Bible and secular literature that were coming to be perceived in the literary theory of the later Middle Ages, see Judson Allen, *The Friar as Critic* (1971), pp. 3–28 et passim; A. J. Minnis, *Medieval Theory of Authorship*, 2d ed. (1988); and A. J. Minnis and A. B. Scott, eds., with the assistance of David Wallace, *Medieval Literary Theory and Criticism, c. 1100–c. 1375: The Commentary Tradition*, rev. ed. (1991), pp. 65–112, 197–276, et passim. On the biblical poetics of Jerome and other earlier medieval authors, see E. R. Curtius, *European Literature and the Latin Middle Ages* (1953), pp. 446–58 et passim, and P. B. Salmon, "The Three Voices of Poetry in Mediaeval Literary Theory" (1961).

41. On Giovanni del Virgilio and Albertino Mussato, see Curtius, *European Literature and the Latin Middle Ages*, pp. 214–27; and Minnis and Scott, *Medieval Literary Theory and Criticism*, pp. 316–17, 321–23, 360–66, 390, and 440. On the biblical poetics of Dante, Petrarch, and Boccaccio, see the discussion that follows, and further references in the notes, below.

42. On Chaucer and Dante, see Piero Boitani, "What Dante Meant to Chaucer" (1983); Howard Schless, *Chaucer and Dante* (1984); Karla Taylor, *Chaucer Reads "The Divine Comedy"* (1989); and Richard Neuse, *Chaucer's Dante* (1991). Petrarch's influence on Chaucer has been studied mainly in relation to Chaucer's adaptation of Sonnet 88 as the "*Canticus Troili*" in *Troilus and Criseyde* (1.400–420) and his use of one of Petrarch's Latin letters as a source for the *Clerk's Tale*. See Paul Ruggiers, "The Italian Influence on Chaucer" (1979), pp. 165–66; and David Wallace, " 'Whan She Translated Was': A Chaucerian Critique of the Petrarchan Academy" (1990). On the relationship between Chaucer and Boccaccio, see Hubertis M. Cummings, *The Indebtedness of Chaucer's Works to the Italian Works of Boccaccio* (1965); Piero Boitani,

Chaucer and Boccaccio (1977); and David Wallace, *Chaucer and the Early Writings of Boccaccio* (1985).

43. This is the argument in Barbara Nolan, "The *Vita Nuova*: Dante's Book of Revelation" (1970). See Dante, *Vita nuova*, ed. Michele Barbi (1960), chapters 3, 12, 24, and 42; and *Dante Alighieri: Vita Nuova*, ed. and trans. Mark Musa (1992), pp. 6, 19, 51, and 83.

44. See J. F. Took, *Dante: Lyric Poet and Philosopher* (1990), pp. viii, 43–60 (quotations on pp. 53 and 55). For more on the Bible and the *Vita nuova*, see Jerome Mazzaro, *The Figure of Dante: An Essay on the "Vita Nuova"* (1981).

45. See Dante, *Banquet* (*Convivio*) 2.1.2–15, in *Literary Criticism of Dante Alighieri* (1973), ed. and trans. Haller, pp. 112–14.

46. Dante, *Letter to Can Grande* (*Epistolam X ad Canem Grandem della Scala*) 7–8; in *Literary Criticism of Dante Alighieri*, trans. and ed. Haller, p. 99. For a convincing rebuttal of more recent attempts to question Dante's authorship of the *Epistola a Cangrande*, see Robert Hollander, *Dante's Epistle to Cangrande* (1993). (On Dante and the Bible, see further references in chapter 6, n. 16, below.)

47. *Letter to Can Grande* 10, in *Literary Criticism of Dante Alighieri*, trans. and ed. Haller, pp. 100–101.

48. *Letter to Can Grande* 15, in ibid., pp. 101–2.

49. On the much-discussed topic of Dante's biblically derived allegorical poetics, see the essays by Charles Singleton, "Dante's Allegory" (1950); id., "The Irreducible Dove" (1957); Richard Hamilton Green's attempt to refute Singleton, in "Dante's 'Allegory of the Poets' and the Medieval Theory of Poetic Fiction" (1957); Robert Haller's introduction, in Dante, *Literary Criticism*, trans. and ed. Haller (1977), pp. xxviii–xlv et passim; Robert Hollander, "Dante *Theologus-Poeta*" (1976); Christopher Kleinhenz, "Dante and the Bible: Intertextual Approaches to the *Divine Comedy*" (1986) (with a bibliography of previous work on Dante and the Bible on p. 235, n. 2); Giovanni Barblan, ed., *Dante e la Bibbia* (1986); and two essays by Peter Hawkins: "Scripts for the Pageant: Dante and the Bible" (1988) and "Divide and Conquer: Augustine in the *Divine Comedy*" (1991). Important book-length studies are Alan Charity, *Events and Their Afterlife: The Dialectics of Christian Typology in the Bible and Dante* (1966); Robert Hollander, *Allegory in Dante's "Commedia"* (1969); and John Freccero, *Dante: The Poetics of Conversion* (1986).

50. See Lawrence Besserman, "Biblical Exegesis, Typology, and the Imagination of Chaucer" (1992), pp. 188–99.

51. For Petrarch's views of the Bible in relation to secular authorship, see Hans Baron, *From Petrarch to Leonardo Bruni* (1968), pp. 41–44; Theodor Mommsen, "Petrarch's Conception of the 'Dark Ages'" (1942); and the texts cited and discussed, with additional bibliography, in Minnis and Scott, eds., *Medieval Literary Theory and Criticism*, rev. ed., pp. 413–20 et passim.

52. Baron, *From Petrarch to Leonardo Bruni*, p. 41.

53. Ibid., citing Petrarch, *De otio religioso*, ed. Rotondi (Vatican City, 1958), pp. 103–5.

54. Ibid., pp. 41–42.

55. Ibid.

56. See *Epistolae Familiares* 10.4, in *Petrarch: The First Modern Scholar and Man of Letters*, trans. Robinson and Rolfe (1898), pp. 261–65; quoted and discussed by Minnis, *Medieval Theory of Authorship*, 2d ed., p. 216.

57. When Petrarch points out that biblical authors who call "Christ now a lion, now a lamb, etc." are using metaphor, he is repeating a topos in the exegesis of terms applied to Christ "per similitudinem" (see Curtius, "*Nomina Christi*" [1951]).

58. Translated and discussed by Theodor Mommsen, "Petrarch's Conception of the 'Dark Ages'" (1942), pp. 231–32, with the Latin text at p. 232, n. 1.

59. *Vita di Dante* 21, 12.37–38; translated in Osgood, *Boccaccio on Poetry*, p. xxiii, n. 25. For Boccaccio's linking of secular and biblical poetics in his other writings on Dante, see the extracts from his *Short Treatise in Praise of Dante* and his *Expository Lectures on Dante's Commedia: Prologue*, translated and discussed by David Wallace, in Minnis and Scott, eds., *Medieval Literary Theory and Criticism, c. 1100–c. 1375*, rev. ed., pp. 492–519. On the analogies that Boccaccio draws between his fictions and the Bible in the *Decameron* (discussed below), see Minnis, *Medieval Theory of Authorship*, 2d ed., pp. 203–4, 215–17.

60. Boccaccio, *Decameron*, "The Author's Conclusion," trans. Mark Musa and Peter Bondanella (1982), p. 686.

61. Boccaccio, *Genealogy of the Gods*, trans. in Osgood, preface, in *Boccaccio on Poetry*, p. 11 (and cp. the other analogies that Boccaccio draws between Scripture and secular writing, cited on pp. 49–50).

62. On Middle English summaries, paraphrases, and apocryphal additions to Old and New Testament narratives, see Lawrence Muir, "Translations and Paraphrases of the Bible, and Commentaries" (1970),

pp. 381–403, 535–50. On English "Instructions for Religious" and Saints' Lives, which often include canonical and apocryphal motifs from the lives of biblical figures, see Charlotte D'Evelyn, "[Middle English] Instructions for Religious" (1970); and Charlotte D'Evelyn and Francis Foster, "[Middle English] Saints' Legends" (1970); and on the biblically suffused innovations in liturgical and other forms of late medieval English worship of the saints, see Duffy, *The Stripping of the Altars*, pp. 155–205.

63. For details, and a generous critical appraisal of these two underrated poems, see J. A. W. Bennett, *Middle English Literature*, ed. and completed by Douglas Gray (1986), pp. 30–33 and 35–41, resp.

64. For editions and scholarly commentary on these biblical poems, see Muir, "Translations and Paraphrases of the Bible." On the "principle of disjunction" whereby medieval authors and artists systematically "medievalize" their classical subjects, see Erwin Panofsky, *Renaissance and Renascences in Western Art* (1960), pp. 84–85; and on the same phenomenon and its modifications in the works of Chaucer and his contemporaries, see A. J. Minnis, *Chaucer and Pagan Antiquity*.

65. In defining a "Ricardian" period style, John Burrow identifies a number of stylistic and thematic features that unify the poetry of Chaucer and his great English contemporaries (*Ricardian Poetry: Chaucer, Gower, Langland, and the "Gawain" Poet* [1971]). Yet Burrow says nothing about the uncommonly intense interest in and innovative literary appropriations of the Bible in the works of Chaucer and other Ricardian poets. Though the use of biblical quotation and allusion by these Ricardian poets is often no more extensive than that by many of their lesser-known English predecessors, the approach of the Ricardians to the Bible shows a sufficient number of common features and differs significantly enough from that of their predecessors to warrant further study.

66. For an overview of late medieval English drama in its European context, see William Tydeman, *The Theatre in the Middle Ages* (1988); on biblical drama, see Lynette R. Muir, *The Biblical Drama of Medieval Europe* (1995) ("a detailed survey and analysis of the surviving corpus of biblical drama from all parts of medieval Christian Europe"; p. xiii); and for studies of the theme and structure of the main late medieval English examples of the genre, see V. A. Kolve, *The Play Called Corpus Christi*; Rosemary Woolf, *The English Mystery Plays*; and Martin Stevens, *Four Middle English Mystery Cycles* (1987).

67. See Marianne Briscoe, "Some Clerical Notions of Dramatic Decorum in Late Medieval England" (1991). As Briscoe shows, in contrast to the univocal objections to the drama of Lollard authors, the attitude of orthodox clergy was not entirely hostile. For the Lollard attack on the drama, see selections from *A Tretise of Miraclis Pleyinge*, with excellent notes and references, in *Selections from English Wycliffite Writings*, ed. Anne Hudson, document 19, pp. 97–104; and for the complete text, see *A Tretise of Miraclis Pleyinge*, ed. Clifford Davidson (1993).

68. See Woolf, *English Mystery Plays*, pp. 238–68. For a clear instance of Rolle's influence on Christ's speech in the Towneley play of Thomas, see *Towneley Plays*, ed. George England (1966), pp. 282–83. On the *Meditationes vitae Christi*, the *Vita Jesu Christi*, and the works of Rolle, see discussion and notes, below.

69. See *Towneley Plays*, ed. England, p. 265.

70. Ibid. See Thomas Jambeck, "The Dramatic Implications of Anselmian Affective Piety in the *Towneley Play of the Crucifixion*" (1975).

71. On the Latin and English works of Rolle, see John Alford, "Richard Rolle and Related Works" (1984).

72. See John Alford, "Biblical *Imitatio* in the Writings of Richard Rolle" (1973); and id., "The Biblical Identity of Richard Rolle" (1976).

73. Kieckhefer, *Unquiet Souls* (1984), pp. 99–100. (See also nn. 77 and 82, below.)

74. On English translations and adaptations of the pseudo-Bonaventuran *Speculum meditationes vitae Christi*, Ludolphus of Saxony's *Vita Jesu Christi*, and related works, see Frances Foster, "Legends of Jesus and Mary" (1970); and Robert Frank, "*Meditationes Vitae Christi*: The Logistics of Access to Divinity" (1989).

75. Aelred wrote the *De institutione inclusarum* for his sister, a longtime anchoress who had been elected to supervise a group of anchoresses and had asked her brother to provide her, and them, with practical and spiritual guidance (see Aelred Squire, *Aelred of Rievaulx: A Study* [1981], pp. 118–19). On the *De institutione* and its literary relations, see discussion and references in John Ayto and Alexandra Barratt's introduction to their edition of the Middle English translation, pp. xi–lviii. For the Latin text and a French translation of the *De institutione inclusarum*, see *Aelred de Rievaulx: La vie de recluse, La prière pastorale*, trans. and ed. Charles Dumont (1961).

76. On the essential features of midrash, see James Kugel, *In Potiphar's House* (1990); and on midrash in relation to other forms of

religious and secular writing, see Geoffrey Hartman and Sanford Budick, eds., *Midrash and Literature* (1986).

77. On the rise of meditations on the humanity of Christ "*sicut praesens,*" see Anselme Hoste's introduction to his edition of Aelred's *Quand Jésus eut douze ans* (1958, 1987), pp. 8–10.

78. See Benson, *Riverside Chaucer,* p. xxv; and Aelred, *De institutione,* ed. Ayto and Barratt, p. xvi.

79. See the *Middle English Prose Complaint of Our Lady,* ed. C. W. Marx and Jeanne Drennan (1987), and Nicholas Love, *Mirror of the Blessed Lyf of Jesu Christ,* ed. James Hogg and Lawrence F. Powell (1989).

80. For a study of the *Mirror* in relation to the Gospel Harmony tradition, see Salter, *Nicholas Love's "Myrrour of the Blessed Lyf of Jesu Christ"*; and for a survey of more recent scholarship, see Barbara Nolan, "Nicholas Love" (1984).

81. In his valuable survey of the "ways in which mental images were honored in medieval thought," V. A. Kolve shows how imaginative participation in the life of Christ is not only found in medieval works of private devotion or mystical meditation but is also a prominent feature of Middle English lyric poetry and visual art contemporary with Chaucer. See Kolve, *Chaucer and the Imagery of Narrative,* pp. 24–51 (quotation on p. 31). On the affective strategies of Middle English religious lyrics, see also Rosemary Woolf, *The English Religious Lyric in the Middle Ages* (1969), and Douglas Gray, *Themes and Images in the Medieval English Religious Lyric* (1972).

82. On devotion to "the double passion of Jesus and His Mother" in Franciscan poetry, often based on the Pseudo-Bonaventuran *Meditationes vitae Christi,* see F. J. E. Raby, *A History of Christian-Latin Poetry* (1953), pp. 420–43. On the *Planctus Mariae* form in medieval drama, see Sandro Sticca, *The "Planctus Mariae" in the Dramatic Tradition of the Middle Ages* (1988), and additional sources noted in George Keiser's "The Middle English *Planctus Mariae* and the Rhetoric of Pathos" (1985).

83. On Chaucer's experiments in late medieval, or "gothic," pathos, see Michael Stugrin, "Ricardian Poetics and Late Medieval Cultural Pluriformity: The Significance of Pathos in the *Canterbury Tales*" (1981); Robert Frank, "The *Canterbury Tales* III: Pathos" (1986); and id., "Pathos in Chaucer's Religious Tales" (1990). On the connections between Chaucer's pathetic heroines and Mary in the *Planctus Mariae,*

see Keiser, "The Middle English *Planctus Mariae* and the Rhetoric of Pathos," pp. 184–87.

84. See Bestul, "Chaucer's Parson's Tale and the Late Medieval Tradition of Religious Meditation" (1989), esp. pp. 611–14, where Bestul notes two hitherto unidentified biblical allusions in *Parson's Tale* X 279 (3 Kings 10:24 and 1 Peter 1:12) and discusses some of the possible intermediate sources through which these highly emotive allusions might have reached Chaucer.

CHAPTER 2. THE BIBLE AS BOOK, METAPHOR, AND MODEL FOR POETRY

1. On the Bible and the shaping of the "idea of the book in the Middle Ages," see Jesse Gellrich, *The Idea of the Book in the Middle Ages* (1985), pp. 159–61; and cp. the discussion of Chaucer's consciousness of the "bookness" of the *Canterbury Tales* in Donald Howard, *The Idea of the "Canterbury Tales"* (1976), pp. 63–67.

2. The use of the word *bok* to mean "the Bible" or "any of the individual parts constituting the Bible" is well attested in Middle English. See *MED* s.v. *bok* n. 3a. (a) and 3b. (a); and there are numerous instances of oaths sworn on the Bible in Middle English historical and literary sources; see *MED* s.v. *bok* n. 3a. (d). For oaths on the Gospels (or on missals or other service books) in trials by ordeal, see Robert Bartlett, *Trial by Fire and Water* (1988), pp. 105–6, 121–22, 131, 137–38.

Critical evaluations of the *Man of Law's Tale* are surprisingly diverse. Morton Bloomfield calls it a "typical pathetic tale" and assigns it to the overlapping genres of "Christian comedy" and "tragedy of victimization" ("Man of Law's Tale" [1972], pp. 384–86, 388–89). Similarly, Derek Pearsall takes it to be "an extended *exemplum* of God's grace granted to patience and constant faith" (*Canterbury Tales* [1985], pp. 256–65; quotation on p. 262). Other critics claim that Chaucer's intentions in the *Man of Law's Tale* were satiric, or at least, that he was interested in doing something other than simply exemplifying perfect patience and faith. For variously nuanced satiric readings, see Winthrop Wetherbee, "Constance and the World in Chaucer and Gower" (1989), and Ann Astell, "Apostrophe, Prayer, and the Structure of Satire in *The Man of Law's Tale*" (1991). For a review of earlier scholarship and a discussion of the *Man of Law's Tale* in its contemporary vernacular literary context—a context in which we come to see that "for Chaucer's earliest readers the *Tale* could be either romance or saint's life"—see A. S. G. Edwards, "Critical Approaches to the *Man of Law's Tale*" (1990).

3. For the life of Constance in Trevet's *Chronicle* and a discussion of the relationship between Chaucer's and Trevet's versions of her story, see Margaret Schlauch, "The Man of Law's Tale" (1958), pp. 155–81 (for Trevet's version of the scene of the knight's unmasking, see pp. 171–72); see also Patricia Eberle's explanatory notes to the *Man of Law's Tale*, in *Riverside Chaucer*, p. 857 et passim.

4. For Gower's "Tale of Constance," which was also presumably adapted from Trevet, see *Confessio amantis*, ed. Macaulay, vol. 2, pp. 146–73. On the relationship between Chaucer's and Gower's versions of the Constance legend, see Schlauch, "Man of Law's Tale," pp. 155–56; and Eberle, in *Riverside Chaucer*, esp. notes on pp. 857 and 861–62, n. 834–68 (summarizing more recent scholarship).

5. The fact that Chaucer departed from the versions of Trevet and Gower by making the trial of the false knight a judicial inquest was pointed out by Marie Hamilton, "The Dramatic Suitability of the Man of Law's Tale" (1966), pp. 156–63. Hamilton also notes that Daniel and Susannah (mentioned in *Man of Law's Tale* II 463, 473, and 638–44, respectively) were invoked in prayers by persons about to undergo ordeals of fire or judicial ordeals (pp. 161–63).

6. See *MED* s.v. *Britoun* n. and adj. 2. *Adj.* a) Celtic; b) Breton. On Breton gospel manuscripts, see Jonathan Alexander, "A Note on the Breton Gospel Books," in Francis Wormald, *An Early Breton Gospel Book*, ed. Jonathan Alexander (1977), pp. 13–23.

7. Lines 674 and 676 echo the words of God in Psalm 49, verses 19–22. In verses 19–20 God rebukes the sinner whose "tongue framed deceits" and who spoke "against thy brother, and didst lay a scandal against thy mother's son" (echoed in line 674). In verse 21 God adds: "these things hast thou done, and I was silent" (echoed in line 676). In verse 22 God concludes with the threat: "Understand these things, you that forget God; lest he snatch you away, and there be none to deliver you."

8. Robert Correale's forthcoming edition of Trevet's *Les cronicles* for the Chaucer Library promises to teach us a good deal more about what both Chaucer and Gower took from Trevet in their respective versions of the Constance story. Correale's preliminary report appears

in his essay "Gower's Source Manuscript of Nicholas Trevet's *Les Cronicles*" (1989), pp. 133–57.

9. For a survey of how Wycliffite concerns can be shown to have influenced Chaucer, see Derek Brewer, *Chaucer and His World* (1978), pp. 168–76; id., "The Reconstruction of Chaucer" (1984) (but note Brewer's suggestions regarding Chaucer's "radical literalism" and other ingredients in his poetry that constitute the overlapping intellectual affinities between and among Chaucer, the Lollards, and their Carthusian contemporaries); Anne Hudson, *The Premature Reformation* (1988), pp. 390–94; Alcuin Blamires, "The Wife of Bath and Lollardy" (1989); and Alan J. Fletcher, "The Summoner and the Abominable Anatomy of Antichrist" (1996). And on the links between Wyclif, Chaucer, and other fourteenth-century English writers, see Janet Coleman, *English Literature in History, 1350–1400* (1981), and further in Hudson, *Premature Reformation*, chapter 9, "The Context of Vernacular Wycliffism," pp. 390–445. (See also chapter 5, n. 48, below.)

10. See *MED* s.v. *Ecclesiaste* n. 1. (a) and (b) and 2, with reference to *Wife of Bath's Prologue* III 651, *General Prologue* I 708, *Nun's Priest's Tale* VII 3329, and Gower's *Confessio amantis* 7.4491. The fact that in the Middle Ages Solomon was not only commonly thought to have written Ecclesiastes but was also frequently (if incorrectly) cited as the author of Ecclesiasticus may make the Wife's use of the pronoun "he" in apposition to "Ecclesiaste" seem to point in Solomon's direction.

11. On the medieval mistaking of Solomon as author of Ecclesiasticus and other Wisdom books, see chapter 3, n. 22.

12. The vexed question of the authorship of the Middle English *Romaunt of the Rose* is discussed by Alfred David in *Riverside Chaucer*, pp. 1103–4. Of the three Middle English fragments of the *Romaunt* that survive, fragments "A" and "B" (lines 1–1705 and 1706–5810) correspond to lines 1–5154 of the French, and fragment "C" (lines 5811–7696) corresponds to lines 10679–12360 of the French. Summing up, David writes: "Insofar as one can arrive at any consensus, the evidence argues most strongly that Fragment B cannot be by Chaucer. The evidence is also strong that Fragments B and C are by different authors and fairly strong that C is not by Chaucer. Fragment A is probably by a different author from C, and there is no persuasive evidence that the author of A is *not* Chaucer" (p. 1103). The extensive influence of the *Roman de la rose* on Chaucer is surveyed in D. S. Fansler, *Chaucer and the Roman de la Rose* (1914).

13. See *Riverside Chaucer*, p. 764; and for the French original, see Guillaume de Lorris and Jean de Meun, *Roman de la rose*, ed. Félix Lecoy, vol. 2 (1979), lines 12052–64.

14. On Chaucer's use of other details from Jean de Meun's portrait of Faus Semblant in his portraits of friars and the Pardoner, see Fansler, *Chaucer and the Roman de la Rose*, pp. 162–66. Another character in the *Roman de la rose* who brandishes a book of the Bible is "Poope–Holy" (i.e., Hypocrisy), depicted by Guillaume de Lorris with a "sauter [i.e., Psalter] . . . fast in honde," from which she makes "many a feynt [feigned] praiere / To God and to his seyntis dere" (*Romaunt*, lines 431–34, in *Riverside Chaucer*, p. 691). The latter figure may be compared with the Monk in the *Shipman's Tale* who is carrying his *portehors* (breviary) while he is seducing, and is being seduced by, his best friend's wife (VII 124–33, etc.).

15. The "In principio" of the Friar has been explained as a charm or devotional tag derived from the opening of the Gospel of John (see discussion and references cited by Janette Richardson, *Riverside Chaucer*, p. 808, n. 254).

16. I shall have more to say about Friar John's preference for partial biblical quotation and glossing, and about other instances of partial biblical quotation and glossing, in chapters 4 and 5.

17. In the *Pardoner's Tale* a mysterious Old Man similarly urges his interlocutors to check a biblical quotation for themselves: "In Hooly Writ ye may yourself wel rede: / 'Agayns an oold man, hoor upon his heed, / Ye sholde arise. . .'" (VI 742–44). (For more on the Old Man, see chapter 6, pp. 187–91.)

18. Russell Peck notes an allusion in VI 421 to Romans 3:13–14: "Their throat is an open sepulchre; with their tongues they have dealt deceitfully. The venom of asps is beneath their lips; / Their mouth is full of cursing and bitterness" ("Biblical Interpretation: St. Paul and the *Canterbury Tales*" [1984], pp. 166–67).

19. Friar John's manipulation of the biblical text for his own selfish purposes recalls that of his ancestor Faus Semblant, a fellow friar, who declares: "de religion sanz faille / j'en lés le grain et pregn la paille" (I leave the kernel of religion and take the husk) (*Roman de la rose*, ed. Lecoy, vol. 2, lines 11185–86; and *Romance of the Rose*, trans. Dahlberg [1983], p. 197, line 11216).

20. See *MED* s.v. *scripture* n. 2 (a); on Chaucer's uses of the word, see Norman Davis et al., *A Chaucer Glossary* (1979), s.v. *scripture* n.

21. On the "scriptures" of geomancy, "deplored by churchmen such as Thomas Aquinas and Nicholas Oresme," see Vincent DiMarco, explanatory note to *Knight's Tale* 2045, in *Riverside Chaucer*, p. 836.

22. See Peter of Riga, *Aurora*, ed. Beichner, vol. 2 (1965), p. 39n; for Absalom's description see lines 41–72 of the "Liber secundus regum" (vol. 1, pp. 272–74); Mary's description appears in lines 33–68 of the "Evangelium" (vol. 2, pp. 425–27). On Absalon in the *Miller's Tale* and other medieval allusions to the biblical Absalom, see Beichner, "Absolom's Hair" (1950), pp. 224–27.

23. On Job in the *Clerk's Tale*, see Lawrence Besserman, *The Legend of Job in the Middle Ages* (1979), pp. 111–13.

24. See John Fyler, in *Riverside Chaucer*, pp. 986–87, nn. 1243 and 1246.

25. On the various Bible formats that were available in the later Middle Ages, see chapter 1. Fourteenth-century illuminated Bibles are illustrated and discussed in Lucy Sandler, *Gothic Manuscripts, 1285–1385*, 2 vols. (1986).

26. Medieval French satiric poems with the title "Bible" include Guiot de Provins' *Bible* (c. 1206), which criticizes corrupt secular rulers and (at much greater length) corrupt clergymen, nuns, lawyers, and doctors (see Guiot de Provins, *Oeuvres*, ed. John Orr [1915]). Similarly, in 1210 Hugues de Bérzé wrote a satiric verse "Bible" that treats the biblical stories of Adam and Eve, the life of Christ, and the corruption of the contemporary Christian community (see Amaury Duval, "Hugues de Bersil" [1835]); and around 1243, Geufroi de Paris wrote a seven-book *Bible des sept estats du monde* consisting of summaries of the Old and New Testaments, accounts of Hell, Purgatory, the human condition, Antichrist, and a closing description of the end of the world (Geufroi's *Bible* has been edited by Paul Meyer, in *Notices et extraits des manuscrits de la Bibliothèque Nationale et autres Bibliothèques*, 39, part 1 [1909]). And in the four thousand lines of *Le laie Bible* (c. 1300), an anonymous poet treated the vices and virtues from Adam and Eve to the Last Judgment, with special attention to the sins of his contemporaries (see W. Rothwell, "Notes on the Text of *Le Laie Bible*" [1964]).

27. Owst, *Literature and Pulpit in Medieval England*, 2d ed. (1961), pp. 285–86.

28. Boren, "Alysoun of Bath and the Vulgate 'Perfect Wife'" (1975). More recently, Frances Biscoglio has suggested that Proverbs 31:10–31 is the key to understanding not only the Wife of Bath but Chaucer's

other female heroines (*The Wives of the "Canterbury Tales" and the Tradition of the Valiant Woman of Proverbs 31:10–31* [1993]).

29. See *MED* s.v. *legende* n. 1. (a) "A written account of the life of a saint; (b) a collection of saints' lives"; and *MED* s.v. *lif* n. 5. (d) "A biography, life story, saint's legend." Cp. also the Miller's sarcastic reference to the fabliau he is about to tell as "a legende and a lyf" (*Miller's Prologue* I 3141).

30. The *MED* does not record *clerk* referring to a biblical author, but R. E. Kaske prints and analyzes a medieval Latin poem in which Adam appears both as the man who fell ("primus Adam") and the clerical man who wrote about the Fall ("clericus Adam") (see Kaske, "*Clericus Adam* and Chaucer's *Adam Scriveyn*" [1979]). Though in medieval Latin *clericus* most often seems to have been used to mean "priest, priest in minor orders, monk, or university scholar," it also could refer to a scribe (see *Mittellateinisches Wörterbuch*, vol. 2, fascicule 5 [1973], s.v.) or to any erudite person, whether clerical or secular; see M. T. Clanchy, *From Memory to Written Record, 1066–1307*, 2d ed. (1993), p. 230.

31. See Wenzel, "The Source of Chaucer's Seven Deadly Sins" (1974), p. 376, n. 117.

32. Quoted in Wenzel, ibid.; for Middle English versions of the proverbial notion that "the sun can shine on a dunghill without being defouled," see Whiting, *Proverbs*, S891.

33. In the *De doctrina christiana*, for example, Augustine explained away the apparently "shameful things" mentioned in the Bible by the sanitizing power of allegory (see p. 41, below).

34. One way of solving the "problem" of the *Parson's Tale* has been to posit that whether it was written by Chaucer or by someone else, it was not originally intended for inclusion in the *Canterbury Tales* but was added to the *Tales* by a scribe who felt the need for a conclusion. However, the integral role of the *Parson's Tale* in the literary framework of the *Canterbury Tales* has been ably defended by Lee Patterson, "The *Parson's Tale* and the Quitting of the *Canterbury Tales*" (1978), and Traugott Lawler, *The One and the Many in the Canterbury Tales* (1980), pp. 162–63 et passim. For a summary of the debate, see Traugott Lawler, "Chaucer," (1984), pp. 296–99.

35. Quotations from the *De doctrina christiana* are from Robertson's translation, with references to the Latin text of Martin's CCSL edition also provided.

36. Augustine's ideas on biblical interpretation are analyzed by H.-I. Marrou, *Saint Augustin et la fin de la culture antique* (1938), pp. 469–503; Maurice Pontet, *L'exégèse de S. Augustin prédicateur* (1945), pp. 111–48; and Madeleine Moreau, "Lecture du 'De doctrina christiana'" (1986)—all stressing Augustine's success in harmonizing pagan and Christian cultures. On Augustine's understanding of the "literal" and "figurative" in biblical exegesis, see James Preus, *From Shadow to Promise* (1969), pp. 9–23, and Henri de Lubac, *Exégèse médiévale*, part 1, vol. 1, pp. 177–89. On the place of the *De doctrina christiana* in the development of medieval rhetorical theory, see Harald Hagendahl, *Augustine and the Latin Classics* (1967), pp. 558–68; James Murphy, *Rhetoric in the Middle Ages* (1974), pp. 56–64; and Gerald Press, "The Subject and Structure of Augustine's *De doctrina christiana*" (1980).

37. D. W. Robertson, Jr.'s *Preface to Chaucer* is a classic attempt—now judged by most scholars to be a failed attempt—at understanding Chaucer's poetry in light of the *De doctrina christiana* and other exegetical works. There is little evidence of direct Augustinian or other patristic influence on Chaucer's poetry (*pace* Mary Makarewicz, *The Patristic Influence on Chaucer* [1953]). Still, there is no doubt that as a fourteenth-century intellectual Chaucer would have been familiar with Augustinian ideas. The pervasive influence of *De doctrina christiana* on medieval thought is considered from various perspectives in the recent essays compiled by Edward English, ed., *Reading and Wisdom: The "De doctrina christiana" of Augustine in the Middle Ages* (1995). On the influence of Augustinian ideas in the fourteenth century, and in England in particular, see Christopher Ocker, "Augustinianism in Fourteenth-Century Theology" (1987), and William Courtenay, *Schools and Scholars in Fourteenth-Century England* (1987), pp. 307–24.

38. *On Christian Doctrine*, trans. Robertson, 3.10.15–16, pp. 88–89, and *De doctrina christiana*, ed. Martin, pp. 87–88.

39. Ibid., 3.10.14, pp. 87–88, and Martin, p. 86.

40. Ibid., 3.12.18, p. 90, and Martin, pp. 88–89.

41. Ibid., 3.27.38, p. 102, and Martin, pp. 99–100.

42. Ibid., 2.9.14, p. 42, and Martin, p. 41.

43. Ibid., 2.11.16, p. 43, and Martin, p. 42.

44. Ibid., 2.12.18, p. 45, and Martin, p. 44.

45. Gerald Bonner notes that Augustine's *Itala* seems to have been "a European version of the Old Latin translation used in North Africa

in Augustine's time, but it does not seem possible to be more precise than this" ("Augustine as Biblical Scholar" [1970], p. 545).

46. *On Christian Doctrine,* trans. Robertson, 2.13.19; p. 46; and *De doctrina christiana,* ed. Martin, pp. 44–45. On Augustine's ideas about translation, see Louis Kelly, "Linguistics and Translation in St. Augustine" (1973); and id., *The True Interpreter* (1979), pp. 8–10, 112–14, 205–8, 221–22, et passim. The late antique and medieval distinction between translating "word for word" and translating "meanings" is discussed in W. Schwarz, "The Meaning of *Fidus Interpres* in Medieval Translation" (1944); and Gianfranco Folena, "'Volgarizzare' e 'traddure'" (1973). On Chaucer's work as a translator in relation to the medieval theory and practice of translation, see Rita Copeland, "Rhetoric and Vernacular Translation in the Middle Ages" (1978); id., *Rhetoric, Hermeneutics, and Translation in the Middle Ages* (1991), pp. 142–49, 184–202; R. A. Shoaf, "Notes Towards Chaucer's Poetics of Translation" (1979); and Caroline D. Eckhardt, "The Art of Translation in *The Romaunt of the Rose*" (1984).

47. *On Christian Doctrine,* trans. Robertson, 2.42.63, p. 78, and *De doctrina christiana,* ed. Martin, p. 76.

48. Ibid., 3.29.40, pp. 102–3, and Martin, pp. 100–101.

49. Ibid., 4.28.61, p. 166, and Martin, p. 165.

50. Ibid., 4.18.35–50, pp. 143–58, and Martin, pp. 141–57. On the classical and medieval theories of rhetorical levels, see Murphy, *Rhetoric in the Middle Ages.* The term *sermo humilis,* used to describe the "plain" or "simple" style of the Bible and related to the *submissus* (subdued) style that Augustine is discussing in the present passage, is discussed in a classic essay by Erich Auerbach, "Sermo humilis" (1965) (pp. 33–39 on Augustine's usage in the *De doctrina christiana,* pp. 49–50 on Augustine's "most complete statement" regarding the Bible's use of the *sermo humilis,* in a letter to Volusianus, *Epist.* 137.18).

51. For brief notice of medieval authors from Cassiodorus to Wyclif who were influenced by the *De doctrina christiana,* see Augustine, *On Christian Doctrine,* trans. D. W. Robertson, Jr., p. xii; and Bernard Huppé, *Doctrine and Poetry* (1959), pp. 28–63. On the Christian humanism of "the classicizing friars" in fourteenth-century England, see Beryl Smalley, *English Friars and Antiquity in the Early Fourteenth Century* (1960). The Christian humanist claim that Ovid's *Metamorphoses* contains the same allegorically disguised Christian truths as Scripture

was made in the *Ovide moralisé* (c. 1325) (see Copeland, *Rhetoric, Hermeneutics, and Translation in the Middle Ages*, pp. 107–26). A similar claim was made by Pierre Bersuire, in his influential *Ovidius moralizatus* (c.1350) (see William Reynolds, "Sources, Nature, and Influence of the *Ovidius Moralizatus* of Pierre Bersuire" [1990], pp. 88–90, and for Bersuire's influence on Chaucer, see pp. 94–95).

52. On the "querulous objector" in Chaucer's poetry, see Morton Bloomfield, "The Gloomy Chaucer" (1972). In the *De doctrina christiana* Augustine notes the use of this rhetorical device in Galatians 3:15–22, where Paul anticipates a series of questions and answers them in advance (*On Christian Doctrine*, trans. Robertson, 4.20.39, p. 147, and *De doctrina christiana*, ed. Martin, pp. 144–46).

53. For Middle English proverbial expressions about the need for words and deeds to be "cousins," see Whiting, *Proverbs*, W645; and for the literary and philosophical background of the saying (and a suggested "cousin"-"cozen" pun), see Paul Taylor, "Chaucer's Cosyn to the Dede" (1982). Though Chaucer would not have known Plato's *Timaeus* in Greek, he could have read it in the Latin translation of Chalcidius; but the phraseology of line 742 suggests that in the present instance Chaucer was not drawing on Chalcidius; see further discussion and references in Malcolm Andrew, ed., *The General Prologue* (1993), n. 741–42, pp. 566–67.

54. In Jean de Meun's portion of the *Roman de la rose*, the Bible and Plato are also invoked against a charge of scurrility, when Reason defends her use of words like "testicles" and "penis" with an appeal to Plato's *Timaeus* and an implicit allusion to Genesis 2:19–20 (see Guillaume de Lorris and Jean de Meun, *Le roman de la rose*, ed. Lecoy, lines 7051–88; and *The Romance of the Rose*, trans. Dahlberg, p. 135).

55. On Dante's equation of the *Commedia* and the Bible in the *Epistle to Can Grande*, see chapter 1, n. 46, above.

56. For the use of "Christ" in Middle English referring both to God as author and as protagonist of the Bible, see *MED* s.v. *Crist* n. 1 (a) and 1 (b). On Chaucer's "courtly" and "bourgeois" or, alternatively, "courtly," "civic," and "rustic" styles, see, respectively Charles Muscatine, *Chaucer and the French Tradition* (1957), and John Fisher, "The Three Styles of Fragment I of the *Canterbury Tales*" (1973–74).

57. See J. Burke Severs, "The Tale of Melibeus" (1958), p. 597, lines 760–65.

58. Less evident than the stylistic analogy, but no less plausible, is a further implicit analogy between Christ, who is both author and subject of the Bible, and Chaucer himself, who is both creator and character in the *Canterbury Tales*. As G. K. Chesterton pointedly observes, with the interrupted *Tale of Sir Thopas* Chaucer has introduced into the *Canterbury Tales* a "dark ray of the irony of God" by creating a persona who crosses the boundary between author and character and is mocked—"as He was mocked and killed when He came among his creatures"—when he tries to tell his tale (*Chaucer* [1932], pp. 20–22).

59. Minnis, *Medieval Theory of Authorship*, 2d ed. (1988), p. 167. As Minnis points out (pp. 33–39), affinities between the Bible and secular literature had been discussed by Jerome, Augustine, Gregory the Great, and other early medieval authors, but the late medieval "humanist" approach to the question of how divine and human texts are related was something new. And as Richard McKeon demonstrates in a classic study, throughout the twelfth and thirteenth centuries there was "increasing formalization of the methods of interpreting Scripture and the rules of divine eloquence, and secondarily in the recurrent application of the secular art to Scripture and the recurrent expressions of concern at the excesses of the liberal arts in such application" ("Rhetoric in the Middle Ages" [1942], pp. 19–25 et passim; quotation on p. 20).

On the relationships between biblical and secular literature that were explored in the literary theory of the Middle Ages, see also E. R. Curtius, *European Literature and the Latin Middle Ages* (1953), pp. 446–58 et passim; P. B. Salmon, "The Three Voices of Poetry in Mediaeval Literary Theory" (1961); Judson Allen, *The Friar as Critic* (1971), pp. 3–28 et passim; and A. J. Minnis and A. B. Scott, eds., with the assistance of David Wallace, *Medieval Literary Theory and Criticism, c. 1100–c. 1375: The Commentary Tradition*, rev. ed., pp. 65–112, 197–276, et passim.

60. Minnis, *Medieval Theory of Authorship*, p. 167.

61. For this range of meanings for Christ's "broad" speaking, see the *MED* s.v. *brode* adv. 3 (a), (b), and (c). See also *OED* s.v. *Broad* a. 6. a., b., and esp. c., "Loose, gross, indecent" (however, the earliest citation for the latter entry dates from 1580).

62. On these terms, see Victor Erlich, *Russian Formalism* (1981), pp. 240–42.

63. The text of Chaucer's source for *Melibee,* Renaud de Louens's *Livre de Mellibee et Prudence* (a translation of Albertano of Brescia's *Liber consolationis et consilii*), is edited by Severs, "The Tale of Melibeus." Taking Chaucer's narrator at his word, most scholars have concluded that the minor discrepancies between *Melibee* and its source have no effect on the tale's serious meaning (see Lawler, "Chaucer," pp. 294–96); but a minority of scholars find evidence in *Melibee* of Chaucer's satiric intentions (see chapter 3, n. 42).

64. The *Knight's Tale* actually shows scant regard for "everich a word" of its source, Boccaccio's *Teseida.* As Robert Pratt demonstrates, the *Knight's Tale* is less than one-fourth the length of the *Teseida* ("The Knight's Tale" [1958], pp. 82–105).

65. Chaucer's appeal to the precedent of the Evangelists in the prologue to *Melibee* is discussed in the context of other fourteenth-century references to the Gospel Harmony tradition by Roger Ellis, *Patterns of Religious Narrative in the Canterbury Tales* (1986), pp. 112–13. As A. J. Minnis points out (in *Medieval Theory of Authorship,* pp. 167, 273, nn. 25–26), Chaucer would have found statements about how the four Gospels stand in relation to one another that are similar to those in the *De consensu evangelistarum* in the prologues to commentaries on the Gospels by Hugh of Saint Cher and Nicholas de Lyra. Indeed, as a marginal gloss indicates, the following statement on the harmony of the gospels in the General Prologue to the Wycliffite Bible (c. 1395) derives from de Lyra's prologue to his "literal" commentary on the New Testament:

> hooly scripture tellith ofte the thouȝtis of men, and ofte the wordis and deedis; and whanne the thouȝtis, and wordis, and deedis of men ben contrarie, oo gospeller tellith the thouȝtis, and another tellith the wordis; and bi this equiuocacoun, either diuerse speking, thei ben acordid, ȝhe, whanne thei seemen contrarie in wordis; also ofte in storial mateer scripture rehersith the comune opynyoun of men, and affirmeth not, that it was so in dede. (*Holy Bible,* ed. Forshall and Madden, vol. 1 [1850], p. 56)

66. See *On the Harmony of the Gospels,* trans. Salmond (1888), 2.12.28, p. 118; and *De consensu evangelistarum,* ed. Weihrich (1962), pp. 127–28.

67. Chaucer mentions Christ's "pitous passioun" in VII 950. Moreover, the seemingly innocuous oath "by Goddes sweete pyne!" (VII 936) and the reference to "the peyne of Jhesu Crist" (VII 948) can be read as proleptic signals that of all the incidents in Christ's life treated differently by the various Evangelists, Chaucer's focus will be on the discrepant accounts of the Passion.

68. See Matt. 27:38–44 and Mark 15:27–32. John's Gospel mentions "two others, one on each side" who were crucified with Jesus but does not specify if they were thieves or if they either mocked Jesus or repented (19:18).

69. See *On the Harmony of the Gospels* 3.16.53; pp. 204–5; and *De consensu evangelistarum*, ed. Weihrich, pp. 339–41.

70. Augustine's polemical purpose in his reconciliation of Gospel accounts of the thieves at the crucifixion—as in the *De consensu evangelistarum* in its entirety—was to meet and dismantle explosively radical questions about the truth of Christian history without explicitly raising them. As he says in an earlier chapter:

> we have undertaken in this work to demonstrate the errors or the rashness of those who deem themselves able to prefer charges, the subtlety of which is at least sufficiently observable, against those four different books of the gospel which have been written by these four several evangelists. And in order to carry out this design to a successful conclusion, we must prove that the writers in question do not stand in any antagonism to each other. (1.7.10, p. 81, and *De consensu evangelistarum*, ed. Weihrich, pp. 10–11)

71. In the apocryphal Gospel of Nicodemus, the saved thief crucified alongside Jesus is named Dysmas; the other thief, named Gestas, is not explicitly said to have been damned (see *New Testament Apocrypha*, ed. Hennecke and Schneemelcher [1963], vol. 1, p. 459). By the thirteenth century, the respective salvation and damnation of the two thieves (with a slight change of name for one, from Gestas to Gesmas) had become established facts (see, for a particularly influential example, Jacobus de Voragine, *Legenda aurea*, trans. and adapted by Ryan and Ripperger [1967], p. 208). The tradition is also witnessed by Langland (see *Piers Plowman* C-text, ed. Derek Pearsall [1982], Passus 6.318–25); and the saved and damned thieves are

frequently represented in the visual arts (see Louis Réau, *Iconographie de l'art chrétien*, vol. 2, part 2 [1957], pp. 493–94; and Gertrud Schiller, *Iconography of Christian Art*, trans. Seligman, vol. 2 [1972], s.v. "Dysmas," "Gestas," and "Thieves").

72. *On the Harmony of the Gospels*, trans. Salmond (1888), 2.12.28, p. 119, and *De consensu evangelistarum*, ed. Weihrich (1962), pp. 128–29.

73. Augustine's place in the history of literary theory is still too often defined solely on the basis of a reductive reading of the more widely known ideas about biblical allegory that he formulated in the *De doctrina christiana* (see chapter 6, n. 5, below).

74. On "fruit and chaff" and related terms in medieval literary theory, see D. W. Robertson, Jr., "Historical Criticism" (1980), pp. 8–9; and id., "Some Medieval Literary Terminology" (1980), pp. 58, 72, et passim. A. J. Minnis discusses Chaucer's use of Romans 15:4 in the context of similar appropriations of the verse by de Lyra, Higden, the anonymous author of the *Ovide moralisé*, and Caxton (*Medieval Theory of Authorship*, pp. 205–9). On the allusion to Romans 15:4 in the *Ovide moralisé* in relation to medieval *Heroides* prologues and other related works, see Copeland, *Rhetoric, Hermeneutics, and Translation in the Middle Ages*, pp. 109–10. Marjorie Reeves finds in Chaucer's use of Romans 15:4 an expression of the writer's biblically based "sense of moral purpose," and she suggests that "perhaps there also remained, in the consciousness of an innovative writer who was endowing words with a new human worth, some vestige of the belief that all words take their ultimate value from God's Word" ("The Bible and Literary Authorship in the Middle Ages" [1991], pp. 55–56). Peter Travis is less tentative when he claims that the allusion to Romans 15:4 in the *Retraction* is Chaucer's way of "proffering a defense of the biblically authorized value of all poetry as an apologia pro sua arte. His own scripture is validated by Scripture; his book has been authorized by 'oure book'" ("Deconstructing Chaucer's Retraction" [1991], p. 144).

75. In her essay "Jerome's *Prefatory Epistles* to the Bible and *The Canterbury Tales*" (1993), Brenda Schildgren has suggested that Chaucer's thematization of the problematics of interpretation in the *Canterbury Tales* was influenced by the engagement with interpretive questions in the biblical prefaces of Saint Jerome.

CHAPTER 3. BIBLICAL TRANSLATION, QUOTATION, AND PARAPHRASE

1. On Chaucer's substantial quotations from the Bible by way of Jerome, Innocent III, Renaud de Louens, Raymond of Pennaforte, and William Peraldus, see Besserman, *Chaucer and the Bible.*

2. The neglect of Chaucer's translations from the Bible has yet to be corrected by the recent awakening of critical interest in Chaucer's theory and practice of translation, which has focused on his translations of the *Roman de la rose* and *Consolationis philosophiae.* See Caroline Eckhardt, "The Art of Translation in *The Romaunt of the Rose*"; Tim William Machan, *Techniques of Translation: Chaucer's "Boece"* (1985); Rita Copeland, "Rhetoric and Vernacular Translation in the Middle Ages"; and id., *Rhetoric, Hermeneutics, and Translation in the Middle Ages.*

3. On Chaucer's oaths and asseverations as elements in his native "English" minstrel style, see Derek Brewer, "The Relationship of Chaucer to the English and European Traditions" (1966), pp. 1–38, and Patricia Kean, *Chaucer and the Making of English Poetry* (1972), vol. 1, pp. 1–38. On Chaucer's oaths in relation to their French antecedents, see Larry Benson, "Chaucer's Early Style" (1996).

4. For the overlapping but sometimes conflicting allegorical readings of the *Nun's Priest's Tale* in relation to Genesis 3, see chapter 6, nn. 57 and 58.

5. See *The Holy Bible,* ed. Forshall and Madden, vol. 1, p. 577.

6. For passages in the *Parson's Tale* in which Chaucer quotes biblical Latin tags or identifies his English biblical citations by the Latin name of the biblical book and the Latin form of the chapter number, see X 284, 540, 592, 597, 598, 634, etc. But note Aage Brusendorff's assertion that Latin chapter and verse notations, biblical phrases, and fuller quotations in the *Parson's Tale*—e.g., in X 597, 598, and 639, found in most manuscripts, and in X 588 and 592, found in the Christ Church, Oxford MS—"are certainly not due to Chaucer" (*The Chaucer Tradition* [1925], p. 128, n. 3, with references to the opposing views of Skeat, Pollard, and Koch).

7. See, resp., Sarum Breviary, *Breviarium ad usum Insignis Ecclesiae Sarum,* ed. Procter and Wordsworth, vol. 2, p. 31; vol. 1, col. cccclxxxv; and vol. 1, cols. dxcii–dxciv and vol. 3, col. 271.

8. Langland's artful use of biblical Latin is discussed by A. V. C. Schmidt, in the introduction to his edition of the B-text of *Piers Plowman* (1987), pp. xxx–xxxii (quotation on p. xxxi).

9. See *MED* s.v. *benedicite* interj. Chaucer uses the word some eighteen times (see Besserman, *Chaucer and the Bible*, p. 357, and ibid., pp. 41–42, from which a few sentences in the following discussion have been adapted).

10. On the medieval view of the biblical Absalom, see Paul Beichner, "Absolon's Hair," and Sandra Pierson Prior, "Parodying Typology and the Mystery Plays in the *Miller's Tale*," pp. 61–63. For Middle English and Middle French proverbs on Absalom's beauty, see Whiting, *Proverbs*, A18; and James Woodrow Hassell Jr., *Middle French Proverbs, Sentences, and Proverbial Phrases* (1982), A11.

11. The apocryphal motif of Noah expelling the Devil with a *benedicite* appears in the mid-fourteenth-century *Queen Mary Psalter*, in John Mandeville's *Travels*, and in other works of medieval verbal and visual art. See Anna Mill, "Noah's Wife Again" (1941), pp. 620–21, and Rosemary Woolf, *The English Mystery Plays* (1972), pp. 136–37.

12. On the *Nun's Priest's Tale* as a response to the Peasants' Revolt, see Peter Travis, "Chaucer's Trivial Fox Chase and the Peasants' Revolt of 1381" (1988); and Steven Justice, *Writing and Rebellion: England in 1381* (1994), pp. 207–23.

13. Marie Hamilton observes that Friar John's portrait of gluttonous monks who recite Psalm 44:2 (KJ 45:1) in honor of the dead is funny on two levels: in addition to a punning association of the opening of the Psalm with a belch ("buf"), there is a further joke in the suggestion that monks are reciting a joyous psalm that would be out of place in the Office of the Dead ("The Summoner's 'Psalm of Davit'" [1942]). As Paul Beichner demonstrates, in Peter of Riga's *Aurora* the jocular pun on belching was paired with another biblical instance of the rhetorical figure of *paranomasia*, and from the *Aurora* it seems to have made its way into Matthew of Vendôme's influential *Ars versificatoria*: "Non Alleluia sed allia norunt; / Plus in salmone quam in Salomone legunt." [They (i.e., "monachis sumptuosis") do not know how to utter "Alleluia," but they know how to belch garlic; / they read more in a salmon than in Solomon.] (See Beichner, *"Non Alleluia Ructare"* [1956], and Beichner, ed., *Aurora*, vol. 1, introduction, pp. xxxviii–xxxix, and references.)

14. For the suggestion that Chaucer's Samson came by way of Geoffrey de la Tour Landry's *Enseignements*, see Joseph Grennen, "'Sampsoun' in the *Canterbury Tales*" (1966).

15. See Bakhtin, *Rabelais and His World*, trans. Helen Iswolsky (1968), p. 80. On Chaucer and Bakhtin, see references in Chaucer, *Miller's Tale*, ed. Thomas Ross (1983), p. 12; John Ganim, "Bakhtin, Chaucer, Carnival, Lent" (1986); the articles and response papers by Lars Engle and William McClellan, in *Exemplaria* (1989); Ganim, "Chaucer and the Noise of the People" (1990); and id., *Chaucerian Theatricality* (1990), pp. 17–30.

16. Though many of the Pardoner's biblical quotations are paralleled in Innocent III's *De miseria humane condicionis*, this one is not (see Innocent III, *De miseria humane conditionis*, ed. and trans. Robert Lewis [1978], pp. 8–11).

17. For the parallel passage on gluttony in *Quoniam*, Chaucer's putative source, see Wenzel, "The Source of Chaucer's Seven Deadly Sins," p. 370.

18. See Severs, "The Tale of Melibeus," p. 581, line 373.

19. See Petersen, *The Sources of "The Parson's Tale"* (1901), p. 9, n. 2; and Wurtele, "The Anti–Lollardry of Chaucer's Parson" (1989 [for 1985]), p. 156. For more on Chaucer's errors in the *Parson's Tale*, see Patterson, "The 'Parson's Tale' and the Quitting of the 'Canterbury Tales,'" pp. 351–53.

20. Pennaforte names "Petrus" as the speaker of "Qui facit peccatum, servus est peccati"; but a marginal gloss in Pennaforte reads "*Joan.* 8" (see Petersen, *The Sources of "The Parson's Tale,"* p. 11, n. 1). Patterson notes the error in *Parson's Tale* X 142 and compares Romans 6:16–23, "where Paul contrasts slaves of sin and slaves of righteousness" ("The 'Parson's Tale' and the Quitting of the 'Canterbury Tales,'" p. 362, n. 82).

21. See Severs, "The Tale of Melibeus," p. 606, line 968 and n.

22. For the misattribution of verses from Ecclesiasticus to Solomon in Chaucer's proximate source for the lines of the *Melibee* noted, see Severs, "The Tale of Melibeus," pp. 570, line 64; 579, lines 315–19; 601, lines 850–51; 602, lines 871–72; and 606, lines 961–62. Chaucer's misattribution to Solomon in *Parson's Tale* X 854 of a quote from Ecclesiasticus 26:10, blended with a paraphrase and elaboration of Ecclesiasticus 13:1, is found also in his proximate source (see Wenzel,

"The Source of Chaucer's Seven Deadly Sins," p. 372). The mis-attribution of verses from Job or Ecclesiasticus to Solomon occurs also in Langland's *Piers Plowman* (e.g., B-Text 3.93–96, 9.94a, 10.334a) and Gower's *Confessio amantis* (e.g., 5.2340–44). See also n. 40, below, and chapter 4, n. 27.

23. For the Middle English proverbial expression "As wise as Solomon," see Whiting, *Proverbs*, S460. Chaucer does not use the epithets "wise," "wise man," or "the wise" only with reference to Solomon. He applies them also to Ptolemy (*Wife of Bath's Prologue* III 324), Dante (*Wife of Bath's Tale* III 1125), Seneca (*Monk's Tale* VII 2515), Cato (*Nun's Priest's Tale*, VII 2941), and Plato (*Manciple's Tale* IX 207).

24. In the passage in question, Peraldus quotes from Ecclesiasticus 27:29–30 and Proverbs 26:27 (see Petersen, *The Sources of "The Parson's Tale,"* p. 59). As Dudley Johnson suggests, Chaucer may have considered the entire discussion to be a cento of Solomonic biblical wisdom on the idea that "evil on itself back shall recoil" ("Chaucer and the Bible" [1941], pp. 110–11).

25. "An ABC" echoes some fifty biblical passages (see Besserman, *Chaucer and the Bible*, pp. 284–89). For Skeat's early dating of "An ABC," see his edition of the poem in *Complete Works of Geoffrey Chaucer*, vol. 1, pp. xxx, 58–59. But Alfred David places the poem in the same period as the *Monk's Tale* and *Second Nun's Tale*, when Chaucer was working with Italian sources and experimenting with religious and didactic subjects (i.e., after 1376; see "An ABC to the Style of the Prioress" [1982], pp. 148–49); and Derek Pearsall also rejects an early date: "['An ABC'] was written at a time when Chaucer had begun to experiment with the pentameter, probably in the late 1370s" (*The Life of Geoffrey Chaucer*, p. 83). For more on the dating of "An ABC," see the explanatory headnote by Laila Gross in *Riverside Chaucer*, p. 1076; and Georgia Crampton, "Chaucer's Singular Prayer," pp. 209 and 212, nn. 1 and 38.

26. Deguilleville's prayer to the Virgin is reproduced below the text of "An ABC" in Skeat, ed., *Complete Works of Geoffrey Chaucer*, vol. 1, pp. 261–71. The two poems are also printed in W. E. Rogers's "Geoffrey Chaucer, 'An ABC,' ca. 1369" (1972), pp. 82–94; and Rogers compares them with respect to their unique and shared liturgical elements (pp. 94–106). For an analysis of "An ABC" that also stresses its liturgical affiliations, see Crampton, "Chaucer's Singular Prayer" (1990). In a

recent article ("Chaucer and Deguileville [*sic*]: The *ABC* in Context" [1993]), Helen Phillips has shown that Chaucer might have drawn some of the details in "An ABC" that are not paralleled in Deguilleville's prayer to the Virgin in *La pelerinaige de vie humaine* from another one of Deguilleville's works, the *Pèlerinage de l'ame*. Yet even if Phillips is correct in pointing out that Chaucer's "originality" in "An ABC" is actually less extensive than it was previously thought to be, the evidence for Chaucer's independent addition of biblical allusions to his proximate source—our present concern—seems to remain essentially unchallenged.

27. Biblical and other examples of the abecedarius tradition are discussed in relation to "An ABC" by Crampton, "Chaucer's Singular Prayer," pp. 193–94.

28. In the Canterbury Psalter, for example, Psalm 118(119) has large decorated Latin capitals at the beginning of each eight-verse unit (see George Pace, "The Adorned Initials of Chaucer's *ABC*" [1979], p. 90, n. 5).

29. Ibid., p. 90. Deguilleville and Chaucer lack stanzas for the modern letters *j*, *u*, and *w*. For the "Xristus" and "Ysaac" stanzas, which occupy lines 241–64 in Deguilleville's poem and lines 161–76 in "An ABC," see Skeat, ed., *Complete Works of Geoffrey Chaucer*, vol. 1, p. 270.

30. These and other Chaucerian additions are noted by Gross (as in n. 25, above); Crampton, "Chaucer's Singular Prayer," pp. 203–6; and Rogers, "Geoffrey Chaucer, 'An ABC,' ca. 1369," pp. 97–106. The story of "Longius" or "Longinus" derives from the apocryphal Gospel of Nicodemus, but as Skeat and Gross point out in their notes, it was more readily available to Chaucer in the *Legenda aurea*.

31. The extent of Chaucer's satire on the Prioress is disputed. See Florence Ridley, *The Prioress and the Critics* (1965); and Chaucer, *The Prioress's Tale*, ed. Beverly Boyd (1987), pp. 31–50.

32. "Orygenes upon the Maudeleyne" was probably the earlier of the two works, since it is singled out by Alceste as written "gon is a gret while." John McCall points out that the *De Maria Magdalena* homily and Innocent III's *De miseria condicionis humane* are found together in two "devotional miscellanies," Cambridge MS Peterhouse 219 and Paris MS Lat. 2049 ("Chaucer and the Pseduo Origen *De Maria Magdalena*" [1971], pp. 495, 503, with a list of manuscripts, early editions, and translations of *De Maria Magdalena* on pp. 504–9).

33. See McCall, as in n. 32, above; Jennings, "The Art of the Pseudo-Origen Homily" (1974); and Woolf, "English Imitations of the *Homelia Origenis de Maria Magdalena*" (1974, 1975).

34. Jennings, "The Art of the Pseudo-Origen Homily," p. 140. For analysis of the homily, including its biblical allusions, see also Hans Hansel, "Die Quellen der bayerischen *Magdalenenklage*" (1937); and McCall, "Chaucer and the Pseduo Origen *De Maria Magdalena*," pp. 498–501.

35. See Innocent III, *Lotario dei Segni (Pope Innocent III): De miseria Condicionis Humane*, ed. and trans. Robert Lewis, p. 82, n. 133. Biblical allusions in the *De miseria* are identified in the notes to the latter edition, and in Innocent III, *Lothario Dei Segni (Pope Innocent III): On the Misery of the Human Condition*, ed. Donald Howard, trans. Margaret Dietz (1969).

36. Biblical references in the *De miseria* that Chaucer may have used in the *Man of Law's Prologue* and *Tale*, *Pardoner's Tale*, *Wife of Bath's Prologue*, *Monk's Tale*, and *Parson's Tale* are listed in Emil Köppel, "Chaucer und Innocenz des Dritten Traktat *De Contemptu Mundi sive De miseria Conditionis Humanae*" (1890). On the influence of the *De miseria* on the *Man of Law's Prologue* and *Tale* and on the *Pardoner's Tale*, see also Lewis (as in n. 35, above), pp. 6–8, 8–12. According to Lewis, among the other biblical passages that Chaucer took from Innocent III's treatise are: *House of Fame* 514; *Knight's Tale* I 1303–12; *Man of Law's Tale* II 286 and 488; *Squire's Tale* V 518, *Franklin's Tale* V 880; the stories of Sampson, Nabugodonosor, and Balthasar in the *Monk's Tale*; *Nun's Priest's Tale* B2 4320–25 [VII 3130–35], *Pardoner's Prologue* VI 334, and *Manciple's Tale* IX 344 (ibid., pp. 74–75, n. 71).

37. Referring to the *De miseria* as a *distinctio* may be stretching the term, but as Richard and Mary Rouse have shown (in "Biblical *distinctiones* in the Thirteenth Century"), by the early half of the fourteenth century the term was used to refer to compilations of various kinds of potential sermon material, and not only to the alphabetic finding tools that were earlier described as *distinctiones*.

38. On Chaucer's borrowings from *Melibee* and the *Parson's Tale*, see Emil Köppel, "Chaucer und Albertanus Brixiensis" (1891); and id., "Über das Verhältnis von Chaucers Prosawerken zu seinen dichtungen und die Echtheit der 'Parson's Tale'" (1891). The overlap between biblical quotations in *Melibee* and other tales is noted in the explanatory notes by Sharon DeLong in *Riverside Chaucer*, pp. 924–28; and for

the correspondences between biblical passages in the *Parson's Tale* and Chaucer's other works, see Siegfried Wenzel's explanatory notes to the *Parson's Tale* in *Riverside Chaucer*, pp. 957–65.

39. The history of scholarship on Chaucer's two prose tales and their putative sources is surveyed by Lawler, "Chaucer." On *Melibee*, "a close translation of the *Livre de Melibee et de Dame Prudence*, written by Renaud de Louens sometime after 1336," see DeLong, in *Riverside Chaucer*, pp. 923–28 (quotation on p. 923); and Severs, "The Tale of Melibeus." For a review of the current state of knowledge on the question of the sources of the *Parson's Tale*, see Wenzel, in *Riverside Chaucer*, pp. 956–65. For analogues and possible sources of specific passages in the *Parson's Tale*, see Alfred Kellogg, "St. Augustine and the Parson's Tale" (1952); id., "'Seith Moses by the Devel': A Problem in Chaucer's Parson's Tale" (1953); Germaine Dempster, "The Parson's Tale" (1958); Siegfried Wenzel, "Notes on *The Parson's Tale*" (1981–82); and Thomas Bestul, "Chaucer's Parson's Tale and the Late-Medieval Tradition of Religious Meditation" (1989).

40. Severs, "The Tale of Melibeus," p. 574, lines 164–67. On the frequent misattribution of Ecclesiasticus and Wisdom to Solomon in the Middle Ages, see DeLong, in *Riverside Chaucer*, p. 928, n. 1671, and n. 22, above.

41. Severs, "The Tale of Melibeus," p. 609.

42. The different uses to which Chaucer's Melibee and Prudence put this biblical passage are discussed by Ellis, *Patterns of Religious Narrative in the Canterbury Tales*, pp. 107–8. The style of *Melibee* is compared with that of its French source by Diane Bornstein, "Chaucer's *Tale of Melibee* as an Example of the *Style Clergial*" (1977–78); and Dolores Palomo defends her view of *Melibee* as a satire with a number of convincing stylistic comparisons between Chaucer's tale and its source ("What Chaucer Really Did to *Le livre de Melibee*" [1974]). Similarly, Judson Allen and Teresa Moritz suggest that Chaucer's use of sapiential materials in *Melibee* is not entirely straightforward (*A Distinction of Stories* [1981], p. 216), while Lee Patterson suggests that Chaucer's adaptation of Renaud's *Livre de Mellibee et Prudence* parodies the genre of sapiential children's literature ("What Man Artow?" [1989], pp. 135–60). For differing assessments of the contemporary political message of the *Melibee*, see Gardiner Stillwell, "The Political Meaning of Chaucer's *Tale of Melibee*" (1944); V. J. Scattergood, "Chaucer and the French War: *Sir Thopas* and *Melibee*" (1981); and

Lynn Staley Johnson, "Inverse Counsel: Contexts for the *Melibee*" (1990). See also chapter 2, n. 63.

43. Severs, "The Tale of Melibeus," p. 597, lines 770–72.

44. Ibid., p. 614., lines 1175–79.

45. On doublets in medieval translation, and in Chaucer's translations in particular, see Machan, *Techniques of Translation: Chaucer's "Boece,"* pp. 35–46.

46. Cp. *Troilus and Criseyde*, which ends with a prayer to the Trinity and to Jesus for "love of mayde and moder thyn benigne" (5.1863–69); and the *Prioress's Tale*, which ends with a prayer beseeching "god so merciable" to show mercy on mankind out of "reverence of his mooder Marie" (VII 688–90). For the suggestion that *Melibee* offers Richard II oblique antiwar advice, see Scattergood (as in n. 42, above).

47. For Renaud's quotation of Ecclesiastes 10:16, see Severs, "The Tale of Melibeus," p. 581, lines 381–83.

48. For their extended and biblically suffused debate on women, see *Melibee* VII 1057–1104 (discussed in chapter 4, pp. 131–33).

49. See Petersen, *The Sources of "The Parson's Tale,"* pp. 3–33; and on the structure of the *Parson's Tale*, see Wenzel, in *Riverside Chaucer*, pp. 956–57, nn. 82–83 et passim.

50. See Petersen, *The Sources of "The Parson's Tale,"* pp. 34–81.

51. See Wenzel's "The Source of Chaucer's Seven Deadly Sins," his edition of the *Summa virtutum de remediis anime*, and his notes to the *Parson's Tale* in the *Riverside Chaucer*.

52. Wenzel, "The Source of Chaucer's Seven Deadly Sins," p. 378.

53. Ibid. I shall discuss several examples below.

54. *Summa virtutum*, ed. and trans. Wenzel (1984), p. 30.

55. The difficulties presented by Romans 5:12 are reflected in the more opaque Wycliffite translation: "Therfor as bi o man synne entride in to this world, and bi synne deth, and so deth passide forth in to alle men, in which [man] alle men synneden" (*The Holy Bible*, ed. Forshall and Madden, vol. 4, p. 313).

56. Kellogg, "St. Augustine and the 'Parson's Tale,'" p. 427.

57. Ibid., p. 428, n. 16.

58. Ibid.; and see pp. 428–30 for additional extracts from de Wetheringsett's *Summa* that parallel lines 331–32 and 334–41 of the *Parson's Tale*. Kellogg adduces the *Summa de officio sacerdotis* as an "example" of the kind of work that must have been Chaucer's source

for the commonplace Augustinian ideas on sin that are expounded in lines 322–49 of the *Parson's Tale*, he does not claim that "Chaucer read and followed Richard de Wetheringsett" (p. 427, n. 11).

59. See *Works of Geoffrey Chaucer*, ed. Skeat, vol. 5, p. 453, n. 326–330; and Landrum, "Chaucer's Use of the Vulgate," part 3, pp. 6–7 (quotation on p. 7; her emphasis). For the Wycliffite passage, see *Holy Bible*, ed. Forshall and Madden, vol. 1, p. 83. That Chaucer did not use the Wycliffite Bible for his biblical translations in the *Parson's Tale* is demonstrated convincingly by Wurtele, "The Anti-Lollardry of Chaucer's Parson."

60. See Lewis and Short, *A Latin Dictionary* (1879), s.v. *nequaquam*.

61. In contrast, the Wycliffite rendering is more literal: "And the iȝen of bothe weren openide." Furthermore, Chaucer has run together two clauses: "and he eet, and anoon the eyen of hem bothe opencdcn" (in thc Vulgate: "qui comedit. Et aperti sunt oculi amborum"). Once again, the Wycliffite version follows the Vulgate: "and he eet. And the iȝen of bothe weren openide, etc."

62. Wenzel, "The Source of Chaucer's Seven Deadly Sins," p. 390.

63. Petersen, *Sources of "The Parson's Tale,"* p. 70; Peraldus, however, does mention "Eua" in reference to the first recorded instance of gluttony.

64. Ibid., and Wenzel, "The Source of Chaucer's Seven Deadly Sins," p. 370.

65. Cp. Philippians 3:18–19: "Multi enim ambulant, quos saepe dicebam vobis (nunc autem et flens dico) inimicos crucis Christi: quorum finis interitus: quorum Deus venter est: et gloria in confusione ipsorum, qui terrena sapiunt." [For many walk, of whom I have told you often (and now tell you weeping), that they are enemies of the cross of Christ; Whose end is destruction; whose God is their belly; and whose glory is in their shame; who mind earthly things.]

66. See Besserman, *Chaucer and the Bible*, p. 128; and Patterson, "The 'Parson's Tale' and the Quitting of the 'Canterbury Tales,'" pp. 359–60, n. 75, item 15, noting the correspondence between *Pardoner's Tale* VI 529–33 and *Parson's Tale* X 819–20.

67. Wenzel, "The Source of Chaucer's Seven Deadly Sins," pp. 370–71.

68. See Helmholz, *Marriage Litigation in Medieval England* (1974).

69. Ibid., pp. 6–24.

70. Ibid., pp. 94–98, 185, 208–12.

71. Ibid., pp. 172–81 and 228–29. For a survey of medieval European legislative responses to fornication and adultery among nobles, clergy, and the non–noble laity, see James Brundage, *Law, Sex, and Christian Society in Medieval Europe* (1987).

72. On John of Gaunt's mistress, Katherine (de Roet) Swynford, who was probably the sister of Chaucer's wife, Philippa ("Pan." de Roet?) Chaucer, see Derek Pearsall, *The Life of Geoffrey Chaucer*, pp. 49–51, 90–91, and 141–43. May McKisack, *The Fourteenth Century, 1307–1399*, p. 393, cites among the causes of John of Gaunt's extreme unpopularity in the late 1370s his living "in open sin with his daughters' governess" while still married to his second wife, Constance. Constance died in 1394, and Gaunt married Katherine in 1396.

73. See Landrum, "Chaucer and the Vulgate," part 3.A, p. 14.

74. Quoted by Wenzel, ed., *Summa virtutum*, p. 29, from *Summa vitiorum* 3.4.1–2, Lyons, 1668, p. 34; Petersen, *The Sources of "The Parson's Tale,"* p. 73, lists no parallel passage for X 879–81.

75. Landrum (as in n. 73, above) concludes that Chaucer was translating directly from the Vulgate, but Dudley Johnson points out that in this passage (as in *Parson's Tale* X 155–56, 189, and 680) there are phrases that are closer to the Old Latin Bible; Johnson acknowledges, however, that because Old Latin readings were frequently found in Vulgate Bibles there is no reason to conclude that Chaucer was not using a Vulgate ("Chaucer and the Bible," pp. 121–25).

76. In the Vulgate, the phrase that Chaucer translates "agayns God and my Lord?" is "in Deum meum?," which unambiguously refers to God. In the Old Latin, however, the phrase in the corresponding passage is "coram Domino?," which, as Johnson observes, is ambiguous: "Joseph's concern over sinning both 'agayns God and agayns my Lord' suggests that [Chaucer] had recourse to the Old Latin text, *coram domino*, and, not knowing whether this referred to the temporal or spiritual lord, translated it as both" ("Chaucer and the Bible," p. 123).

77. On Aelred's *De institutione inclusarum* and its literary relations, see discussion and references in John Ayto and Alexandra Barratt's introduction to their edition of the Middle English translation, pp. xi–lviii; and for the Latin text and a modern French translation, see *Aelred de Rievaulx: La vie de recluse, La prière pastorale*, trans. and ed. Charles Dumont (1961). On English translations and adaptations of

the pseudo-Bonaventuran *Speculum meditationes vitae Christi,* Ludolphus of Saxony's *Vita Jesu Christi,* and related works of biblically focused meditative devotion, see Frances Foster, "Legends of Jesus and Mary" (1970), and Robert Frank, "*Meditationes Vitae Christi*: The Logistics of Access to Divinity" (1989). For the late medieval European religious context in which the rise of medieval English meditations on the humanity of Christ "sicut praesens" must be considered, see discussion and references in Anselme Hoste's introduction to his edition of Aelred's *Quand Jésus eut douze ans* (1987), pp. 8–10; and Richard Kieckhefer, *Unquiet Souls: Fourteenth-Century Saints and Their Religious Milieu* (1984), pp. 99–100.

78. On the popularity of the Joseph and Potiphar story in the Middle Ages, see F. E. Faverty, "The Story of Joseph and Potiphar in Medieval Literature" (1931).

79. Wenzel, "The Source of Chaucer's Seven Deadly Sins," p. 367.

80. For Augustine's analysis, see *Quaest. Exodi* 71.1–6; in *Opera,* ed. I. Fraipont (1958), pp. 102–5. The confusing relationship between the differing versions of the Ten Commandments (or "Decalogue") in Exodus and Deuteronomy is clarified in the following note to Exodus 20:1–17, in *The Old Testament of the Jerusalem Bible* (1966), p. 103:

> The Decalogue (or "Ten Words," cf. Ex 34:28; Dt. 4:13; 10:4) has come down to us in two forms: the "Priestly" recension here, and the somewhat different "Deuteronomic" recension in Dt 5:6–21. It is possible that each of the commandments was originally as short as the 5th, 6th, 7th and 8th; the enlargements may be due to editors, whether "Priestly" or "Deuteronomistic." Two systems of division have been proposed: (a) vv. 2–3, 4–6, 7, 8–11, 12, 13, 14, 15, 16, 17, or: (b) vv. 3–6, 7, 8–11, 12, 13, 14, 15, 16, 17a, 17b. The second of these, drawn up by St. Augustine following Deuteronomy, has been adopted by the Church.

Middle English orthodox prose commentaries and metrical translations and paraphrases of the Ten Commandments are surveyed by Robert Raymo, "Ten Commandments" (1986), pp. 2284–90 (texts) and 2512–17 (bibliography).

81. For this Lollard interpretation of the First Commandment, see Margaret Aston, *Lollards and Reformers* (1984), pp. 144–56. Wycliffite commentaries on the Ten Commandments are surveyed by Ernest

Talbert and S. Harrison Thomson, "Ten Commandments" (1970), pp. 362 (texts), 524 (bibliography); and compare the texts cited and briefly discussed by Hudson, *Premature Reformation*, pp. 4–5; 21, n. 75; and 484, n. 226. For a telling contrast, see the pointedly anti-Lollard exposition of the "First Commandement" in Philippe de Mézières's allegorical dream vision, *Le songe du vieil pelerin* (c. 1389; ed. G. W. Coopland, vol. 2, p. 141, where the personified figure of Queen Truth makes no mention of the prohibition in Exodus 20:4 against worship of a "graven thing" and seems to be answering implicitly the heretical separation of the latter verse from its surrounding context and its misapplication to orthodox observances such as worship of religious images and belief in the transubstantiation of bread and wine in the mass.

82. On Wycliffite themes in the *Parson's Tale* and elsewhere in Chaucer, see Wurtele, "The Anti-Lollardry of Chaucer's Parson"; and references in chapter 2, n. 9, above.

83. In his explanatory note, Wenzel points out that "the Parson's discussion of the deadly sins contains clear quotations or allusions to the first (10.750–51), second (588), fifth (887), sixth (837, 867, 887), seventh (795, 798, 887), eighth (795), and ninth (844) commandments" (*Riverside Chaucer*, p. 964). To this list one should add the Parson's further reference to the ninth commandment (the prohibition against coveting one's neighbor's wife) and a reference to the tenth commandment (the prohibition against coveting one's neighbor's material possessions), both of which are compressed in the following line from the Parson's "Remedium contra peccatum Invidie": "Thou shalt not desiren his wyf ne none of his thynges" (X 521). As Wenzel points out, the biblical quotations at a parallel point in *Postquam*, Chaucer's putative source for the *remedia* in the *Parson's Tale*, do not include the ninth and tenth commandments. "It is possible," Wenzel concludes, "that Chaucer found that authority in a copy of *Postquam* which is currently unknown; but it is not unreasonable to think that he might have added the line on his own" (see Wenzel, ed., *Summa virtutum*, p. 27; but with mistaken reference to Exodus 20:17 ["house/ wife etc."] instead of Deut. 5:21 ["wife/house etc."], which provides the Augustinian reading of the ninth and tenth commandments; see n. 80, above). Given the brevity of the line and the fact that the Parson had previously mentioned the ninth commandment, there is not much justification for T. P. Dolan's charge of "special pleading" against

Wenzel's claim that Chaucer went beyond his source for *Parson's Tale* X 521 and added a reference to the ninth and tenth commandments on his own. However, it is important to recall Dolan's warning that because of the distance in time between the *Parson's Tale* and its presently known proximate sources, any claims regarding Chaucer's putative addition or omission of material are subject to doubt (see Dolan's 1986 review of Wenzel's edition of the *Summa virtutum*, pp. 262–63). Indeed, Wenzel makes similar assertions (in "The Source of Chaucer's Seven Deadly Sins," p. 378; and *Riverside Chaucer*, p. 956); as does Judith Shaw, in an important article demonstrating Chaucer's apparent misconstrual of his proximate source ("Corporeal and Spiritual Homicide, the Sin of Wrath, and the Parson's Tale" [1982], p. 300).

84. For orthodox Middle English expositions of the Pater Noster, see Robert Raymo, "Pater Noster," pp. 2279–82 (texts), 2507–9 (bibliography); and for Wycliffite treatments, see Ernest Talbert and S. Harrison Thomson, "Pater Noster," pp. 363 and 371 (texts), and 525 and 529 (bibliography); and Hudson, *Premature Reformation*, pp. 28–29, 310–11, 424–25, et passim (with important bibliographical data on p. 267, n. 198).

85. See *Melibee* VII 1196–1200, and n. 47, above.

86. Wenzel, "The Source of Chaucer's Seven Deadly Sins," p. 368.

87. Ibid.

88. Ibid.

89. Jesus's words in Matthew 26:52, "Put up again thy sword into its place: for all that take the sword shall perish with the sword," are addressed to a nameless disciple who tries to stop the mob that comes to arrest Jesus by drawing his sword and striking off the ear of "the servant of the high priest" (Matt. 26:47–51). In John 18:10 this disciple is identified as Simon Peter and the servant of the high priest who loses an ear is named Malchus.

90. The orthodox understanding of Matthew 26:52, according to which Christ was denouncing tyrannical usurpations of military authority and not outlawing fighting entirely, is represented in the two quotations of the biblical text in John of Salisbury's *Policraticus*, 3.15.18–22 and 6.8.5–15 (ed. Webb, vol. 1, p. 232 and vol. 2, p. 22; ed. and trans. Nederman, pp. 25 and 115–16). For a Wycliffite appeal to the authority of Matthew 26:52 in support of their stand against killing in the crusades or any other kind of warfare, see *Selections from English*

Wycliffite Writings, ed. Anne Hudson (1978), p. 28, lines 135–43. The Lollard position against killing was sometimes even stretched to prohibit capital punishment. For a cautious account of the diversity of Lollard views on war and capital punishment, see Hudson, *Premature Reformation,* pp. 367–70.

91. *Selections from English Wycliffite Writings,* ed. Hudson, p. 134.

92. On the controversy surrounding the Wycliffite claim that the Church should not own property, see Hudson, *Premature Reformation,* pp. 334–46 et passim; and see the Wycliffite text, "The Clergy Should Not Own Property," in *The English Works of Wyclif Hitherto Unprinted,* ed. F. D. Matthew (1902), pp. 359–404.

93. Passages in the *Parson's Tale* where Chaucer seems to delete, fill out, or replace the biblical references that he found in his sources include X 502, 504, 506–7, 631–32, 634, 686, 745–48, and 784.

94. See Bestul, "Chaucer's Parson's Tale and the Late–Medieval Tradition of Religious Meditation."

95. Ibid., p. 600.

96. Ibid., p. 603; contemporary examples that Bestul cites include William Rimington's *Meditationes* or *Stimulus peccatoris* and the Pseudo-Augustinian *Manuale* and *Soliloquia animae ad Deum.*

97. Robertson, *Preface to Chaucer,* p. 336.

98. Robertson, ibid., refers to the tropological interpretation of the narrative of the Fall (X 321ff.) and the spiritual interpretation of the "hundred-fold fruit" of Matt. 13:8 and 23 (X 867ff.) as typical examples of the Parson's use of "Pauline allegory" when citing the Bible. As Wenzel's notes demonstrate (*Riverside Chaucer,* pp. 955–65), when the Parson cites a verse and its exegesis he is usually following Augustine or some other ecclesiastical authority by way of his proximate source.

CHAPTER 4. PARTIAL OR OBLIQUE QUOTATIONS AND ALLUSIONS

1. Because the Bibles available to Chaucer had no verse divisions, the difference between the more complete quotations discussed in the previous chapter and the partial quotations considered in this chapter is a matter of degree. Furthermore, as Judson Allen points out with reference to Chaucer's quotations from other closely written and unindexed authoritative medieval texts, we can safely assume that

Chaucer knows the larger context of his quotations ("Reading and Looking Things Up in Chaucer's England" [1985], p. 2).

2. For a discussion of this passage in relation to Chaucer's dramatization of self-serving biblical glossing, see chapter 5, p. 155.

3. For comparable uses of partial and decontextualized biblical quotations by Chaucer's contemporaries, William Langland and John Gower, see Langland, *Piers Plowman* B-Text, Passus 3.331–53; ed. A. V. C. Schmidt, pp. 34–35 (and cp. the parallel passage, with slight but interesting changes, in the C-Text of *Piers Plowman*, ed. Derek Pearsall, Passus 3.483–97, pp. 86–87); and Gower, *Vox clamantis* 4.567–68, in *Complete Works of John Gower*, ed. Macaulay, vol. 4, *Latin Works*, p. 182; and in *Major Latin Works of John Gower*, ed. and trans. Eric W. Stockton (1962), p. 179.

4. This and other passages in which the Pardoner "breaks off fragments of Paul" are discussed by Russell Peck, "Biblical Interpretation: St. Paul and the *Canterbury Tales*," pp. 166–69. A. J. Minnis considers the Pardoner's self-presentation in the light of thirteenth- and fourteenth-century ideas about the "office of preacher," with notice of key biblical texts that were cited by ecclesiastical writers on the topic ("Chaucer's Pardoner and the 'Office of Preacher'" [1985]).

5. For the suggestion that the "holy Jewes sheep" does not refer to the sheep of some Old Testament personage (as various scholars have held), but is Chaucer's way of implying that the Pardoner is adept at using a pagan divinatory device, see Leo Henkin, "Jacob and the Hooly Jew" (1940).

6. Robert Bartlett explains that medieval canonists favored allegorical interpretations of Numbers 5:11–31, arguing that the ordeal of a woman suspected of adultery outlined in this passage is not a precedent for other judicial ordeals (*Trial by Fire and Water*, pp. 83–85).

7. See Christine Hilary, in *Riverside Chaucer*, p. 908, n. 579.

8. For the biblical molding of early medieval historical consciousness, reflected in the writings of Eusebius, Augustine, Orosius, and others, see Robert Hanning, *The Vision of History in Early Britain* (1966), pp. 1–43. On the biblical influence reflected in medieval and early Renaissance chronicles and other historical writings, see Antonia Gransden, *Historical Writing in England, c. 550 to c. 1307* (1974), Index, s.v. "bible"; and id., *Historical Writing in England II: c. 1307 to the Early Sixteenth Century*, Index, s.v. "bible." On the blending of pagan and biblical authorities in fourteenth-century thought, see Smalley, *English*

Friars and Antiquity in the Early Fourteenth Century, A. J. Minnis, *Chaucer and Pagan Antiquity* (1982); and Patterson, *Chaucer and the Subject of History*, pp. 90–94, 114–26, et passim.

9. As Robert Pratt points out, the Pardoner is not quoting the Bible directly but following Gerald of Wales's *Communiloquium*, despite "his double protestation (lines 578 and 586)" to the contrary ("Chaucer and the Hand that Fed Him," pp. 634–35). On the Pardoner's chiding of his listeners for their presumed confusion between the well-known Samuel and the obscure Lamuel, Pratt writes: "The idea of confusion between the proper names 'Lamuel' and 'Samuel' was not unique with Chaucer, and must have been both aural and ocular; for example, the text of the *Communiloquium* found in Pembroke College, Cambridge, MS 229, fol. 13rb reads 'samuel' with long 's'" (p. 634, n. 42).

10. For intermediate sources of the Wife's biblical quotations, see B. J. Whiting, "The Wife of Bath's Prologue" (1958); Zacharias Thundy, "Matheolus, Chaucer, and the Wife of Bath" (1979); and notes to the *Wife of Bath's Prologue* and *Tale* by Hilary, in *Riverside Chaucer*, pp. 864–74.

11. On the Wife's quarrel with Saint Jerome, see Anne Kernan, "The Archwife and the Eunuch" (1974), and Douglas Wurtele, "The Predicament of Chaucer's Wife of Bath: St. Jerome on Virginity" (1983). See also chapter 5, pp. 149–55.

12. On the Wife's use of 1 Cor. 7:28 and other Pauline statements about marriage and the relationship between the sexes, see James Cotter, "The Wife of Bath and the Conjugal Debt" (1969); Britton Harwood, "The Wife of Bath and the Dream of Innocence" (1972), esp. pp. 248–60 (on the uses of "dette" and "tribulacioun" in the Wife's discourse, deriving from 1 Cor. 7:28); and Priscilla Martin, *Chaucer's Women: Nuns, Wives and Amazons* (1990), pp. 215–17. On the uses of 1 Corinthians 7 here and elsewhere in Chaucer's works, see Besserman, *Chaucer and the Bible*, pp. 82–90, 371–72.

13. Robert Haller observes that the Wife's argument with men covers each of the three estates: her first three (or four?) husbands were presumably commoners (merchants?); Jankin, husband number five, was a member of the clergy, and the protagonist of her tale is a knight ("The Wife of Bath and the Three Estates" [1965]).

14. For Middle English proverbial phrases that include a "gnat," see Whiting, *Proverbs*, G170–78.

15. The quotation of Proverbs 30:21–23 in Jerome's *Epistola adversus Jovinianum* 1.28, adduced by Whiting ("The Wife of Bath's Prologue," p. 210), differs significantly enough from the biblical original to indicate that the Wife is referring to the passage in Proverbs rather than to Jerome's rephrasing of it.

16. Huppé, *A Reading of the Canterbury Tales* (1967), pp. 120–21.

17. On "numerical proverbs" in biblical literature, see *The Old Testament of The Jerusalem Bible*, p. 975, n. "e." For the translation of "*os vulvae*" as "barren womb," see ibid., p. 974. In the Wycliffite Bible, however, as in the later Douay–Rheims version, the phrase is translated as "the mouth of the wombe"; and a marginal gloss explains: "that is, of a leccherouse womman" (*The Holy Bible*, ed. Forshall and Madden, vol. 3, p. 49).

18. A quotation from Proverbs 30:16 also occurs in Jerome's *Epistola adversus Jovinianum* 1.28, preceding a quotation from Proverbs 30:21–23, which the Wife partially quotes in III 362–67. The order in which the Wife adduces the two passages from Proverbs thus reverses their order in the *Epistola adversus Jovinianum.* Jerome, however, substitutes the phrase *amor mulieris* (the love of a woman) for the Vulgate's *os vulvae.* See Whiting, "The Wife of Bath's Prologue," p. 210.

19. In view of the form of Proverbs 30:16 in the Vulgate, in the *Epistola adversus Jovinianum,* in the Wycliffite Bible, and in the Wife's quotation of the verse in III 371–75, there is no merit to Huppé's claim (in *A Reading of the Canterbury Tales,* pp. 120–21) that the Wife has omitted "what comes too close to her . . . a 'barren womb.'"

20. As Skeat points out, the distorted biblical quotation is cited in Jerome's *Epistola adversus Jovinianum:* "Sicut in ligno uermis, ita perdit uirum suum uxor malefica"; and, with *perdet* for *perdit,* it also appears as a gloss in the Ellesmere manuscript (*Complete Works of Geoffrey Chaucer,* vol. 5, p. 301, n. 376).

21. Chaucer is following his source, Renaud's *Livre de Mellibee et Prudence.* See Severs, "The Tale of Melibeus," p. 570, lines 51–53.

22. See Alfred David, *The Strumpet Muse* (1976), pp. 135–58; Charles Owen, *Pilgrimage and Storytelling* (1977), pp. 145–57; Susan Crane, "Alison's Incapacity and Poetic Instability in the Wife of Bath's Tale" (1987); Carolyn Dinshaw, *Chaucer's Sexual Poetics* (1989), pp. 113–31; Jill Mann, *Geoffrey Chaucer (Feminist Readings)* (1991), pp. 70–86; Elaine Hansen, *Chaucer and the Fictions of Gender* (1992), pp. 26–57; and Lynne

Dickson, "Deflection in the Mirror: Feminine Discourse in *The Wife of Bath's Prologue* and *Tale*" (1993).

23. For the phrase "textual harassment," and a thought–provoking analysis of the Wife of Bath's use of the Bible and other authoritative texts, see Robert Hanning, "Roasting a Friar, Mis-taking a Wife, and Other Acts of Textual Harassment in Chaucer's *Canterbury Tales*" (1985). On the *Wife of Bath's Prologue* and medieval sermons, see Lee Patterson, "'For the Wyves love of Bath': Feminine Rhetoric and Poetic Resolution in the *Roman de la Rose* and the *Canterbury Tales*" (1983); and Andrew Galloway, "Marriage Sermons, Polemical Sermons, and *The Wife of Bath's Prologue*: A Generic Excursus" (1992).

24. See Kaske, "The *Canticum Canticorum* in the *Miller's Tale*" (1962); James Wimsatt, "Chaucer and the Canticle of Canticles" (1973), pp. 84–90; Besserman, *Chaucer and the Bible*, pp. 65–71; and Patterson, who points out that Absolon's misappropriation of Canticles is "a characteristically clerical misappropriation: what exegetes typically do *to* the Song of Songs, Absolon here seeks to do to Alisoun *by means of* the Song of Songs" (*Chaucer and the Subject of History*, p. 261). But cp. Pearsall, who maintains that the allusions to Canticles in the *Miller's Tale* are "a gratuitous and very pleasing extra," and *not* (as Kaske had argued) Chaucer's way of adding a "moral edge" to the tale by providing an "implicit orientation toward a controlling set of values" (Pearsall, *The Canterbury Tales*, p. 176, quoting Kaske, "The *Canticum Canticorum* in the *Miller's Tale*," p. 497, for the purpose of refutation).

25. For a classic analysis of the plot of the *Miller's Tale*, see E. M. W. Tillyard, *Poetry Direct and Oblique*, rev. ed. (1977), pp. 85–92.

26. On apocryphal motifs in representations of the Flood narrative in medieval English drama, see Woolf, *The English Mystery Plays*, pp. 132–45. For Chaucer's use of apocryphal biblical motifs in the *Miller's Tale*, see Kelsie Harder, "Chaucer's Use of the Mystery Plays in the *Miller's Tale*" (1956); M. F. Vaughan, "Chaucer's Imaginative One-Day Flood" (1981); and Prior, "Parodying Typology and the Mystery Plays in the *Miller's Tale*."

27. Chaucer misattributes the same positive form of the quotation from Ecclesiasticus to Solomon in *Merchant's Tale* IV 1484–86 and in *Melibee* VII 1003. Indeed, a positive form of the advice in Ecclesiasticus 32:24–26 was proverbial in Chaucer's day. For dozens of instances of the Middle English proverb "Work all things by counsel," see Whiting, *Proverbs*, C 470; and for possible sources and analogues of Chaucer's

various uses of the saying, see Curt Bühler, "Wirk Alle Thyng by Conseil" (1949).

28. Translated by M. Teresa Tavormina, in her note to IV 1311–14, in *Riverside Chaucer*, p. 885. Tavormina points out the misattribution of the first quotation and refers the second to "Albertanus, De amore Dei, fol. 40r."

29. As Tavormina notes (*Riverside Chaucer*, p. 885, n. 1267–1392), the question of whether January or the Merchant is the speaker of these lines (and the "marriage encomium" of which they constitute a part [IV 1267–1392]) is "a major interpretive crux." See Donald Benson, "The Marriage 'Encomium' in the *Merchant's Tale*" (1979). Though the question is not easily decided, I shall follow Pearsall (*The Canterbury Tales*, pp. 195–96) in assuming that the "intrusive voice" heard in these lines is that of the sardonic Merchant.

30. Janette Richardson sums the matter up well when she observes that a laudatory reference to Eve "would immediately connote to a medieval audience an interpretation opposite to that overtly stated, for in conventional antifeminist literature of the age she served as the archtype of womanly frailty, the mother of man's woes, the 'los of al mankynde' as Chaucer himself phrases it in the Wife of Bath's Prologue. The narrator's irony predicts the harsh reality of January's marital paradise, and his allusion to the Garden of Eden foreshadows what is to be the metaphoric conclusion to the tale" (*Blameth Nat Me* [1970], pp. 133–34).

31. See V. A. Kolve, *The Play Called Corpus Christi* (1966), pp. 247–53; Woolf, *English Mystery Plays*, pp. 169–81; and cp. the portrayal of doubting Joseph in "The Cherry-Tree Carol" (*Oxford Book of Ballads*, ed. Arthur Quiller-Couch [1910], no. 101, pp. 431–34).

32. For a different reading of the ironic effect of references to the Virgin in the *Merchant's Tale*, see Emerson Brown, "Biblical Women in the *Merchant's Tale*: Feminism, Antifeminism, and Beyond" (1974).

33. See *Sir Gawain and the Green Knight*, 2d ed., ed. Tolkien and Gordon, revised by Norman Davis (1967), lines 2414–19; Gower, *Confessio amantis* (in *Works of John Gower*, ed. Macaulay, vol. 3, lines 2689–2725; and for other instances of the commonplace, see R. W. King, "A Note on 'Sir Gawayn and the Green Knight,' 2414ff." (1934).

34. See DeLong's explanatory note to *Melibee* VII 1098–1102, in *Riverside Chaucer*, p. 925; and Emerson Brown (as in n. 32, above), pp. 390–91.

35. See Emerson Brown, ibid.

36. The incident was memorable enough to be mentioned in the Latin summary of III Kings LXXXIII in the Vulgate:

> Ubi desecendit helias in samariam domini iussu dicens inproperando regi achab: occidisti insuper et possedisti, et infert: loco quo sanguinem naboth linxerunt canes lingent et tuum; sed et idem de iezabel sueque domus abolitione non tacuit quibus in uerbis humiliatus est achab stans et ambulans demisso capite.

(Donatien de Bruyne, *Sommaires, divisions et rubriques de la Bible latine* [1914], p. 114; and cp. also p. 115, no. 34.)

37. Ovid, *Metamorphoses*, ed. and trans. Frank Justus Miller, vol. 1, pp. 134–43.

38. See *Works of Geoffrey Chaucer*, ed. Skeat, vol. 5, p. 366, n. 2138–2148; and Wimsatt, "Chaucer and the Canticle of Canticles," pp. 84–90. According to Alfred Kellogg, the scene also echoes the attempted rape in a garden in the biblical story of Susannah and the Elders ("Susannah and the 'Merchant's Tale'" [1960]).

39. On the allusion to Ecclesiasticus 32:24–26 in *Miller's Tale* I 3529–30 and Melibee VII 1003, see n. 27, above.

40. On the January/May–Pluto/Proserpina parallelism, see Mortimer Donovan, "The Image of Pluto and Proserpina in the *Merchant's Tale*" (1957); Karl Wentersdorf, "Theme and Structure in the *Merchant's Tale*" (1965); and Marcia Dalbey, "The Devil in the Garden" (1974).

41. See the analogues printed in Germaine Dempster, "The Merchant's Tale" (1958), pp. 341–56; and in *The Literary Context of Chaucer's Fabliaux*, ed. Larry Benson and Theodore Andersson (1971), pp. 203–73.

42. Pluto is echoing lines 1–3 of the *Wife of Bath's Prologue:* "Experience, though noon auctoritee / Were in this world, is right ynogh for me / To speke of wo that is in mariage." As Wenzel demonstrates, the Wife's claim that "experience" confirms what the Bible and other authorities teach by "authority" was a commonplace of sermon rhetoric ("Chaucer and the Language of Contemporary Preaching" [1976], pp. 151–52). On the "Marriage Group" in the *Canterbury Tales*, see George Lyman Kittredge's landmark article, "Chaucer's Discussion of Marriage" (1911–12; rpt. in Schoeck and

Taylor, eds., *Chaucer Criticism*, vol. 1, *The Canterbury Tales* [1960], pp. 130–59, with a brief survey of critical commentary on the idea of the "Marriage Group" through the year 1953, on p. 158, n. 1). Kittredge's suggestion continues to generate discussion. See R. E. Kaske, "Chaucer's Marriage Group" (1973); and the update in Larry Benson's bibliographic note, in *Riverside Chaucer*, pp. 863–64.

43. In the Vulgate, Ecclesiastes 7:29b reads: "Virum de mille unum reperi; mulierem ex omnibus non inveni." Chaucer's iambic pentameter couplet, "Amonges a thousand men yet foond I oon / But of wommen alle foond I noon," renders the Latin more loosely than the Later Wycliffite Bible translator: "I foond o man of a thousynde; y foond not a woman of alle" (*The Holy Bible*, ed. Forshall and Madden, vol. 3, p. 65).

44. *Biblia Latina cum Glossa Ordinaria*, ed. Froehlich and Gibson (1992), vol. 2, p. 703. The marginal and interlinear gloss, however, take the antifeminist tack. On Ecclesiastes 7:28, "Ecce hoc inveni," the marginal gloss comments: "in hac ruina generis humani facilior ad casuum est mulier"; and on "man" and "woman" in 7:29, the interlinear gloss remarks: "Vir a virtute [strength, vigor]. . . . Mulier a mollicie [weakness, wantonness]; molles et inconstantes [(i.e, women are) weak and inconstant]."

45. The reference to Mark 10, absent from the edition of the *Glossa ordinaria* cited in the preceding note, is added in the marginal gloss reproduced in *Glossa ordinaria*, *PL*, vol. 113, col. 1124. The passage in Mark 10:17–18 is paralleled in Matt. 19:16–17 and Luke 18:18–19. Langland quotes the passage, either from Mark or from Luke, as the Latin phrase shows, in *Piers Plowman* B-Text, 10.438 (ed. Schmidt, p. 116): "For sothest word that ever God seide was tho he seide *Nemo bonus. No man is good.*" As we shall see later on, when Prudence in the *Tale of Melibee* quotes Ecclesiastes 7:29, she explains it with explicit reference to Christ's words (though whether she is thinking of Mark 10:18 or the parallel passages in Matthew and Luke is impossible to say); and there are two additional references to the same words of Christ in the *Parson's Tale* (X 301, 1007).

46. Proserpina's attack on Solomon has good medieval precedent. On the mixed reputation and proverbial foolishness of Solomon in his old age, see Robertson, *A Preface to Chaucer*, pp. 323–24 and 324, n. 85 (with references to Jerome, *Adversus jovinianum* 1.30–31; and Augustine, *De doctrina christiana* 3.21.31). On the ambiguities of Solomon's repu-

tation in the Middle Ages, see also Jean Leclercq, *Monks and Love in Twelfth-Century France* (1979), pp. 27–29; and the discussion, with citations from Bonaventure and Boccaccio, in A. J. Minnis and A. B. Scott, eds., *Medieval Literary Theory and Criticism, c. 1100–c. 1375*, rev. ed. (1991), pp. 206–9, 231–33, 503.

47. On the ways in which Chaucer achieved the "amplification, elaboration, and enrichment" of "fabliau-form" in the *Merchant's Tale*, see discussion and references in Pearsall, *The Canterbury Tales*, pp. 193–209.

48. Pluto's surrender recalls Melibee's acknowledged defeat before the superior biblical arguments adduced by his wife Prudence. Melibee says: "Dame . . . dooth youre wil and youre likynge; / for I putte me hoolly in youre disposicioun and ordinaunce" (*Melibee* VII 1725).

49. See Severs, "The Tale of Melibeus," p. 573, lines 158–61: "aprés, car toutes femmes sont mauvaises, et nesune n'est bonne, selon le dit de Salemon: 'De mil hommes,' ce dit il, 'en ay trouvé un preudomme, mais de toutes les femme je n'en ay trouvé une bonne.'" Renaud has added the word "bonne" to the quotation in Albertanus of Brescia, *Liber consolationis et consilii*, ed. Sundby (1873), p. 12, lines 8–11.

50. See Severs, "The Tale of Melibeus," p. 574, lines 174–76.

51. Chaucer was again following Renaud closely (see Severs, "The Tale of Melibeus," p. 575, lines 201–8); and Renaud was following the *Liber consolationis et consilii* (ed. Sundby, pp. 14–15, lines 24–25, 1–6).

52. See *Merchant's Tale* IV 2242–49, 2276–79, and 2287–90; and *Melibee* VII 987–1079 passim.

53. The similar partial quotations and divergent interpretations of Ecclesiastes 7:29 by Pluto and Proserpina in the *Merchant's Tale* come earlier within the framework of the *Canterbury Tales*, at least according to the Ellesmere and Hengwrt manuscripts; but it seems most likely that Chaucer's uses of the verse in the *Merchant's Tale* were "borrowed" from his similarly contrasting and fuller uses of the verse in the husband–wife debate in *Melibee*.

54. See Andreas Capellanus, *The Art of Courtly Love*, trans. John Jay Parry (1941), p. 209; the passage is also quoted in *Andreas Capellanus on Love*, trans. by P. G. Walsh (1982), 3.107; rpt. in Alcuin Blamires et al., eds., *Woman Defamed* (1992), p. 124.

55. See *Gawain on Marriage: The "De Coniuge Non Ducenda"* (1986), p. 89, stanza J7; trans. A. G. Rigg; rpt. in Blamires et al., eds., *Woman Defamed,* p. 127.

56. See *L'art d'amours: Traduction et commentaire de l'Ars amatoria d'Ovide,* p. 145, lines 1890–94; trans. in Leclercq, *Monks and Love,* p. 76.

57. See Guillaume de Lorris and Jean de Meun, *Le roman de la rose,* ed. Lecoy, vol. 2, p. 51, lines 9887–94; and *The Romance of the Rose,* trans. Dahlberg, p. 177.

58. See *Romance of the Rose,* trans. Dahlberg, p. 104, lines 5533–34; and cp. *Roman de la rose,* ed. Lecoy, vol. 1, p. 151, lines 4911–12: "Mes tel ami mout bien se preuvent / s'il entre mil un seul en truevent" (emphasis added). On Chaucer's knowledge of the *Roman de la rose* and the dispute over which part or parts of the Middle English *Romaunt* are his, see chapter 2, n. 12, above.

59. See "The Thrush and the Nightingale," st. 9, lines 49–52; in *Middle English Debate Poetry,* ed. John Conlee (1991), p. 242; rpt. in Blamires et al., eds., *Woman Defamed,* p. 225.

60. See Rolle, *The Form of Living,* in *English Writings of Richard Rolle,* ed. H. E. Allen (1931), p. 85, lines 27–32.

61. For the suggestion that there is a similar allusion to Ecclesiastes 7:29 in F-Prologue 559–61, see A. J. Minnis, "The Legend of Good Women," in Minnis et al., *The Shorter Poems* (1995), p. 323.

62. Cp. the similarly ironic allusion in "The Thrush and the Nightingale" (cited on p. 134, above).

63. "One in a thousand" is not listed in Whiting, *Proverbs*; and I have not found corresponding entries in the collections of medieval French proverbs by Hassell and Morawski, or in the volumes of Latin proverbs compiled by Walther and Schmidt. However, the expression "A man (one) among a thousand" is recorded in Tilley, *A Dictionary of the Proverbs in England in the Sixteenth and Seventeenth Centuries* (1950), M217, with entries dated 1508, 1598, 1616, and 1666. Chaucer's frequent quotations and allusions to Ecclesiastes 7:29 and the similar allusions by other medieval authors suggest that a proverbial saying, something like "One good man among a thousand, (but) no good women," derived from Ecclesiastes 7:29, must also have been current in the High Middle Ages.

Though far removed in time from Chaucer, Anthony Trollope alludes to Ecclesiastes 7:29 in a subtle and very Chaucerian joke when he makes the silly Mr. Gibson say: "your aunt is a woman among a thousand" (*He Knew He Was Right* [1869; Penguin ed., 1993], p. 298). Mr. Gibson is ostensibly praising the rude and unpleasant aunt of the very gentle and pleasant Dorothy Stanbury, the woman to whom Mr. Gibson is proposing marriage, and who will refuse him momentarily.

64. For details, see Besserman, *Chaucer and the Bible*, pp. 111–20.

65. For more on the complex use of authoritative sources in the *Merchant's Tale*, see Robert Edwards, "Narration and Doctrine in the *Merchant's Tale*" (1991).

CHAPTER 5. BIBLICAL "GLOSSING" AND POETIC MEANING

1. See F. G. Vigoroux, s.v. "Glose," in *Dictionnaire de la Bible* (1903), vol. 3, part 1, pp. 252–58.

2. See Isidore of Seville, *Etymologiarum*, ed. W. M. Lindsay (1962). On the text-and-gloss format in Isidore's *Etymologiarum* and other early medieval secular texts, see Martin Irvine, *The Making of Textual Culture* (1994), pp. 209–43, 384–93, et passim. On the blending of Christian (mainly Augustinian) and pagan classical literary theory in Isidore's discussions of biblical poetics, see Jacques Fontaine, *Isidore de Séville* (1983), vol. 1, pp. 157–86.

3. On the formation and influence of the *Glossa ordinaria*, see Beryl Smalley, "The Bible in the Medieval Schools" (1969), pp. 205–6; and id., *The Study of the Bible in the Middle Ages*, 3d ed. (1983), pp. 46–66 (with new material on pp. ix–xi). On the contents and various formats of complete glossed Bibles in the High Middle Ages, see C. F. R. de Hamel, *Glossed Books of the Bible and the Origins of the Paris Booktrade* (1984). New evidence regarding the formation and distribution of the *Glossa ordinaria* is presented by Guy Lobrichon, "Une nouveauté: Les gloses de la Bible" (1984); Mary and Richard Rouse, "The Book Trade at the University of Paris, ca. 1250–ca. 1350" (1991), pp. 284–91; and Margaret Gibson, "The Place of the *Glossa ordinaria* in Medieval Exegesis" (1992).

4. Robertson, *A Preface to Chaucer*, pp. 317–31.

5. See Augustine, *On Christian Doctrine*, trans. and ed. D. W. Robertson, Jr. (1958), 3.9, p. 84. Robertson first enunciated his allegorical approach in a landmark article entitled "Historical Criticism" (1951). Other early influential articles by Robertson are "Some Medieval Literary Terminology, with Special Reference to Chrétien de

Troyes" (1951) and "Chaucerian Tragedy" (1952). In addition to Robertson's classic *A Preface to Chaucer*, see the collaborative study by Bernard Huppé and Robertson, *Fruyt and Chaf: Studies in Chaucer's Allegories* (1963), and Huppé's *A Reading of the Canterbury Tales*. Other scholars of the Robertsonian "school" include Chauncey Wood (*Chaucer and the Country of the Stars* [1970] and *The Elements of Chaucer's "Troilus"* [1984]), Robert Miller ("Allegory in the *Canterbury Tales*" [1979]), and the majority of the authors whose essays appear in David Jeffrey's *Chaucer and Scriptural Tradition*. For a defense of context-sensitive exegetical interpretations of medieval literature in general, and of Chaucer's poetry in particular, see R. E. Kaske, "Patristic Exegesis in the Criticism of Medieval Literature: The Defense" (1960), and id., "Chaucer and Medieval Allegory" (1963). Kaske repeats his call for a context-sensitive approach to medieval biblical and religious imagery in *Medieval Christian Literary Imagery* (1988), pp. xx–xxi. For criticism of the Robertsonian approach, see Morton Bloomfield, "Symbolism in Medieval Literature" (1958); E. T. Donaldson, "Patristic Exegesis in the Criticism of Medieval Literature" (1960); Donald Howard, "Medieval Literature and the History of Ideas," in his *The Three Temptations* (1966), pp. 13–40; and Lee Patterson, "Historical Criticism and the Development of Chaucer Studies," in his *Negotiating the Past* (1987), pp. 3–39.

6. See *The Holy Bible*, ed. Forshall and Madden, vol. 1, pp. 43, 52–53. On the numerous manuscripts of exegetical works by Nicholas de Lyra, see Frederick Stegmüller, *Repertorium biblicum medii aevii*, vol. 4, nos. 5827–5994. For detailed studies of de Lyra's exegesis, see Herman Hailperin, *Rashi and the Christian Scholars* (1963), pp. 137–246; Henri de Lubac, *Exégèse médiévale*, part 2, vol. 4 (1964), pp. 344–67 (emphasizing de Lyra's continuity with orthodox allegorical exegetical tradition); and A. J. Minnis and A. B. Scott, eds., *Medieval Literary Theory and Criticism, c. 1100–c. 1375*, rev. ed. (1991), pp. 66–76 (selections) and pp. 198–99, 203–4 (analysis). On Wycliffite use of de Lyra, see Michael Hurley, "'*Scriptura Sola*': Wyclif and His Critics" (1960); A. J. Minnis, "'Authorial Intention' and 'Literal Sense' in the Exegetical Theories of Richard Fitzralph and John Wyclif" (1975); G. R. Evans, *The Language and Logic of the Bible* (1985), passim; id., "Wyclif on Literal and Metaphorical" (1987); and Hudson, *Premature Reformation*, pp. 271–72.

7. On these developments in late medieval exegesis, see Smalley, *The Study of the Bible in the Middle Ages*, 3d ed., pp. 281–373 (but note

Smalley's qualifying remarks in her preface, pp. xiii–xvii). For an overview of fourteenth–century developments in exegesis, see Frank Rosenthal, "Heinrich von Oyta and Biblical Criticism in the Fourteenth Century" (1950); Beryl Smalley, "Problems of Exegesis in the Fourteenth Century" (1962), and id., "The Bible in the Medieval Schools." Smalley's account is supplemented and in part corrected in William Courtenay, "The Bible in the Fourteenth Century: Some Observations" (1985), and id., *Schools and Scholars in Fourteenth-Century England*, index, s.v. "Bible, study of."

8. Quoted by Margaret Deanesly, *The Lollard Bible* (1920), p. 273.

9. On Wycliffite use of the *Glossa ordinaria*, see Hudson, *Premature Reformation*, pp. 235–37, 243; and for Wycliffite objections to *glosing* by the friars and their other opponents, see ibid., pp. 247–73.

10. On Wycliffite glossing of biblical manuscripts, see Hudson's discussion and references ibid., pp. 247–68.

11. Cited by Henry Hargreaves, "The Wycliffite Versions" (1969), p. 413.

12. Ibid., p. 413, n. 1. Cp. Amaury D'Esneval's suggestion that the omission of standard summaries and rubrics from some thirteenth-century Vulgate Bibles may be the result of a reaction against "glossing" ("La division de la vulgate en chapitres dans l'édition parisienne du XIIIe siècle" [1978], 566, n. 35).

13. For Rolle's version of Psalms, see *The Psalter, or Psalms of David . . . by Richard Rolle of Hampole*, ed. H. R. Bramley (1884). On glosses in Rolle's *Psalter*—glosses that often include controversial Lollard interpretations—see Lawrence Muir, "Translations and Paraphrases of the Bible," pp. 386, 538–39; Hargreaves, "Wycliffite Versions," p. 413; and Michael Kuczynski, *Prophetic Song: The Psalms as Moral Discourse in Late Medieval England* (1995), pp. 165–88. On glosses from Augustine, the *Glossa ordinaria*, and Nicholas de Lyra in the Later Wycliffite Version of Job, Psalms, and Isaiah, see Hargreaves, "Wycliffite Versions," pp. 411–12. On glossing as a source of textual errors and noncanonical narrative materials in Old French biblical translations, see D. A. Trotter, "The Influence of Bible Commentaries on Old French Bible Translations" (1987).

14. For Wycliffite and orthodox criticism of fraternal exegesis, see Penn Szittya, *The Antifraternal Tradition in Medieval Literature* (1986), pp. 176–82, 195–98, et passim. See also n. 9, above.

15. On the glossing of secular texts, see Irvine, *The Making of Textual Culture;* Copeland, *Rhetoric, Hermeneutics, and Translation in the Middle Ages,* pp. 107–26, 189, et passim; and Ruth Morse, *Truth and Convention in the Middle Ages* (1991), pp. 179–230, 277–86. Glosses in manuscripts of the *Canterbury Tales* are surveyed and discussed by Manly and Rickert, eds., *The Text of the Canterbury Tales* (1940), vol. 3, pp. 483–527; Graham Caie, "The Significance of Marginal Glosses in the Earliest Manuscripts of the Canterbury Tales" (1984); and in Stephen Partridge's exhaustive study, "Glosses in the Manuscripts of Chaucer's 'Canterbury Tales'" (1992).

16. Graham Caie, "The Significance of the Early Chaucer Manuscript Glosses" (1975–76), p. 350.

17. Glosses appear not only in Hengwrt 154 (c. 1400–10) and Cambridge Dd.4.24 (c. 1400–20), but were copied throughout the fifteenth century (e.g., in MS Additional 5140, from c. 1470–1500) and were even added to manuscripts such as Cambridge, Trinity College R.3.15, and British Library, Additional 35286, whose texts derive from nonglossed manuscripts (see Caie, ibid., pp. 350–51).

18. For the view that at least some of the glosses in manuscripts of the *Canterbury Tales* are by Chaucer, see Daniel Silvia, "Glosses to the *Canterbury Tales* from St. Jerome's *Epistola adversus Jovinianum*" (1965); Robert Lewis, "Glosses to the *Man of Law's Tale* from Pope Innocent III's *De Misera Humane Conditionis*" (1967), p. 16; and Stephen Partridge, "Glosses in the Manuscripts of Chaucer's 'Canterbury Tales.'"

19. For the phrase "authorial memoranda," see Silvia, "Glosses to the *Canterbury Tales*," p. 37. But cp. Caie's suggestion that glosses in the *Man of Law's Prologue* and *Tale* were meant to expose the Man of Law as a "false exegete," betrayed by his partial biblical quotations and omissions ("The Significance of Marginal Glosses," p. 77). And for a similar interpretation of the glosses in the *Man of Law's Prologue* and *Tale,* see Robert Lewis, "Chaucer's Artistic Use of Pope Innocent III's *De Miseria Humanae Conditionis* in the Man of Law's Prologue and Tale" (1966); and id., "Glosses to the *Man of Law's Tale*" (as in n. 18, above).

20. On the relationship between biblical glossing, glossing of Chaucer's works by characters within the works themselves, and glossing of the manuscripts of the works by early readers, see Susan Schibanoff, "The New Reader and Female Textuality in Two Early Commentaries on Chaucer" (1988).

21. See Langland, *Piers Plowman . . . the B-Text*, ed. A. V. C. Schmidt, p. 3.

22. For evidence that "glosing" was portrayed in a hostile and "anti-clerical" manner by Langland and many other fourteenth-century writers, see Wendy Scase, *Piers Plowman and the New Anticlericalism* (1989), pp. 78–83 and 118–19.

23. See *Works of John Gower*, ed. Macaulay, vol. 1, p. 87.

24. See *The Major Latin Works of John Gower*, trans. Stockton, p. 148. For the Latin text, see *Works of John Gower*, ed. Macaulay, vol. 4, 3.1431–40, p. 145.

25. See *Biblia latina cum Glossa ordinaria*, ed. Froehlich and Gibson, vol. 1, p. 16. For sermons that jokingly refer to lecherous people who cite Genesis 1:28 to justify their desire to fornicate, see Galloway, "Marriage Sermons, Polemical Sermons, and *The Wife of Bath's Prologue*," pp. 21–22. Insofar as Genesis 1:28 relates to laymen, how-ever, Augustine and other Latin exegetes usually interpret it literally, with reference to sexual reproduction. See Jeremy Cohen, *"Be Fertile and Increase, Fill the Earth and Master it": The Ancient and Medieval Career of a Biblical Text* (1989), pp. 243–70. And for a survey of the mainly tolerant views of theologians on the role of sex in marriage for the purpose of procreation, see Brundage, *Law, Sex, and Christian Society in Medieval Europe*, pp. 89, 271–72, 364–65, et passim.

26. On whether or not Chaucer intended this speech for the Shipman, see the explanatory and textual notes by Patricia Eberle and Ralph Hanna, resp., in *Riverside Chaucer*, pp. 862 and 1126.

27. For further discussion of the *Parson's Prologue*, see pp. 156–57, below. For an ingenious but finally unconvincing attempt to show that the *Shipman's Tale* proves that the Shipman himself is extraordinarily adept at perverting biblical counsel, see R. H. Winnick, "Luke 12 and Chaucer's *Shipman's Tale*" (1995).

28. Robertson, *Preface to Chaucer*, p. 330.

29. For the views on remarriage of Augustine, Jerome, and other early medieval authors, see Brundage, *Law, Sex, and Christian Society in Medieval Europe*, pp. 68–69.

30. On the vexed question of second and subsequent marriages according to various medieval authorities, see ibid., General Index, s.v. "Remarriage."

31. The traditional basis for the Wife's reading of John 2:1ff. is evidenced in a Latin gloss in Ellesmere and related manuscripts from

Jerome's *Epistola adversus Jovinianum* 1.40: "For by going once to a marriage he taught that men should marry only once" (quoted by Christine Hilary, in *Riverside Chaucer*, p. 865, n. 13).

32. On the Wife of Bath's performance in relation to medieval sermons on marriage (and on John 2:1 in particular), see Galloway, "Marriage Sermons, Polemical Sermons, and *The Wife of Bath's Prologue.*"

33. As noted by Robertson, who concludes that "Chaucer was following the latter authorities [i.e., Augustine and Gregory] probably through the *Glossa ordinaria*" (*Preface to Chaucer*, p. 324, n. 86; see *Biblia latina cum Glossa ordinaria*, ed. Froehlich and Gibson, vol. 4, p. 233).

34. See Harwood, "The Wife of Bath and the Dream of Innocence," p. 267, n. 29.

35. See Martin, *Chaucer's Women*, pp. 210–15 (quotation on 212).

36. See Hansen, *Chaucer and the Fictions of Gender*, p. 30.

37. See Kiser, *Truth and Textuality in Chaucer's Poetry* (1991), p. 139. For a survey of recent feminist interpretations of the Wife of Bath, see Hansen, *Chaucer and the Fictions of Gender*, pp. 39–52; and further discussion and references in chapter 4, pp. 112–13 and nn. 22 and 23.

38. The quotations in this paragraph are from the transcription of the prologue and opening section of Genesis in Guyart's *Bible historiale*, in Beinecke MS 129, transcribed in Rosemarie McGerr, "Guyart Desmoulins, The Vernacular Master of Histories, and His *Bible Historiale*" (1983), pp. 243–44. As Anne Kernan argues in "The Arch-wife and the Eunuch," the Wife of Bath's literal interpretation of the biblical commandment to "be fruitful and multiply" (Gen. 1:28) is more in line with authoritative orthodox ecclesiastical tradition than Robertson and like–minded interpreters have been willing to allow. See also n. 25, above.

39. The same argument occurs in Jerome's *Epistola adversus Jovinianum* 1.36, and *Roman de la rose* 4401–24 (see Hilary, in *Riverside Chaucer*, p. 866, n. 115–23).

40. On the "suffraunce" and "reverence" due from a husband to his wife, see *Parson's Tale* X 925. Records of medieval English marriage litigation suggest that a husband's violence against his wife, including rape, most often went unpunished; however, there are a few cases on record in which wives were granted divorces on the grounds of repeated physical abuse (see Helmholz, *Marriage Litigation in Medieval England*, pp. 90–94).

41. On the interweaving of sexual and textual themes in the portraits of the Wife of Bath and of La Vieille in the *Roman de la rose* (Chaucer's principal model for the Wife of Bath), see Patterson, " 'For the Wyves Love of Bathe': Feminine Rhetoric and Poetic Resolution in the *Roman de la rose* and the *Canterbury Tales*." For another view of the interplay of sexuality and textuality in the *Wife of Bath's Prologue*, see Carolyn Dinshaw, "*Glose/bele chose*: The Wife of Bath and Her Glossators," in *Chaucer's Sexual Poetics*, pp. 113–31.

42. For passages in the *Summoner's Tale* in which "glossing" occurs (either with or without the words *glose* or *glosing* being used), see III 1789–93, 1794, 1919–24, and 1935–36. On the possible significance of the name of Friar John's victim, see Roy Clark, "Doubting Thomas in Chaucer's *Summoner's Tale*" (1976–77). For a reading of the *Friar's Tale* and *Summoner's Tale* as Chaucer's linked explorations of the question of "lettre" and "entente," see Mary Carruthers, "Letter and Gloss in the Friar's and Summoner's Tales" (1972).

43. A landmark in the critique of fraternal glossing of Scripture is William of Saint Amour's *De periculis* (1256). See Robert Miller, ed., *Chaucer: Sources and Background* (1977), pp. 245–50 (for passages from the *De periculis* in which William of Saint Amour lists "signs" that prove—with the help of many biblical prooftexts—that the friars are "false apostles"); and cp. pp. 259–63 (a selection from Richard de Bury's biblically funded attack on the friars in the *Philobiblon* [1345]). On biblical and exegetical motifs in the satiric depiction of the friar in the *Summoner's Tale*, see further discussion and references in Szittya, *Antifraternal Tradition*, pp. 231–46; and on the similar use of anti-fraternal biblical and exegetical motifs by Jean de Meun in the *Roman de la rose* and by Wyclif and his followers in numerous works, see ibid., pp. 186–90 and 176–82, respectively.

44. See *Roman de la rose*, ed. Lecoy, vol. 2., pp. 95–96, lines 11345–50; and *Romance of the Rose*, trans. Dahlberg, p. 199, lines 11375ff. On Chaucer's use of details from the portrait of Faux-Semblant in his depiction of the Pardoner, the friars in the *General Prologue* and the *Summoner's Tale*, and the Wife of Bath, see Fansler, *Chaucer and the Roman de la Rose*, pp. 162–66.

45. See *Biblia latina cum Glossa ordinaria*, ed. Froehlich and Gibson, vol. 4, p. 62. For other orthodox interpretations of Matthew 19:21 that evade its radical call (e.g., Christ was referring only to people who choose to lead a contemplative rather than an active life, he was

speaking about spiritual rather than temporal matters, etc.), see the patristic and later exegesis cited by Thomas Aquinas, *Catena aurea,* Matthew 19 (Paris, 1537), pp. 86–87.

46. For Jean de Meun's definition of "glossing" as a legitimate mode of interpretation—a definition placed in the mouth of the allegorical figure Reason—see *Roman de la rose,* ed. Lecoy, vol. 1, pp. 218–220, lines 7123–74; and *Romance of the Rose,* trans. Dahlberg, pp. 136–37; and on the tradition of reading for "letter" and "gloss," see Lecoy's and Dahlberg's notes, ibid., pp. 289–90 and 383–84, respectively. As Ellen Martin has recently suggested, openness to invention and multivocity in biblical interpretation were features of orthodox exegetical writings that Chaucer seems to have responded to enthusiastically ("Chaucer's Ruth" [1991]).

47. For a Lollard defense of a woman's right to preach and to consecrate the eucharist, see "The Trial of Walter Brut (1391)," in Blamires et al., eds., *Woman Defamed and Woman Defended,* pp. 250–60. See also Claire Cross, "Great Reasoners in Scripture: The Activities of Women Lollards, 1380–1530" (1978); and Margaret Aston, "Lollard Women Priests?" (1984).

48. For more on Chaucer's thematization of Wycliffite themes, see the introduction and two essays by David Jeffrey, "Chaucer and Wyclif: Biblical Hermeneutic and Literary Theory in the XIVth Century" and "Sacred and Secular Scripture: Authority and Interpretation in *The House of Fame,*" in *Chaucer and Scriptural Tradition,* ed. Jeffrey (1984), and A. J. Minnis, "Chaucer's Pardoner and the 'Office of Preacher,'" pp. 113–18. Anne Hudson's "A Lollard Sect Vocabulary?" (1985) lists Wycliffite terms whose thematically significant uses in Chaucer's poetry have yet to be fully explored. See also chapter 2, n. 9, above.

CHAPTER 6. "FIGURA" AND THE MAKING OF VERNACULAR POETRY

1. Auerbach, "Figura" (1973), p. 30.

2. Ibid., p. 53.

3. Ibid., p. 54. For a critique of Auerbach's definition of *figura,* see Richard Emmerson, "*Figura* and the Medieval Typological Imagination" (1992); and for another attempt to sort out the modalities of typological interpretation, see James Paxson, "A Theory of Biblical Typology" (1991). In an earlier and still valuable essay, Elizabeth Salter

sheds light on some of the ways in which biblical typology and figural thinking are characteristic features of fourteenth-century English poetry ("Medieval Poetry and the Figural View of Reality" [1968]).

4. The *MED* lists twelve distinct senses for *figure* n., including specialized astrological, grammatical, philosophical, musical, legal, and alchemical senses, eight of which are illustrated by citations from Chaucer.

5. See *MED* s.v *figure* n. 3 (b). For a comparison of "An ABC" with its source in Deguilleville, see *Works of Geoffrey Chaucer*, ed. Skeat, vol. 1, pp. 261–71 and 452–57; and Helen Phillips, "Chaucer and Deguileville [*sic*]: The *ABC* in Context" (1993). For another instance of Chaucer's use of the "figure" of the burning bush in relation to Mary, see *Prioress's Prologue* VII 467–68.

6. For Middle English proverbs (no doubt derived from Matt. 5:19) that are even closer to Chaucer's formulation of the principle in *General Prologue* I 497–98, see Whiting, *Proverbs*, L463, L107, etc.

7. See *MED* s.v. *figure* n. 4 (a) "A parable, a comparison or metaphor."

8. See Siegfried Wenzel's note, in *Riverside Chaucer*, p. 819, n. 500, and Edward Bode, "The Source of Chaucer's 'Rusted Gold'" (1962). Whiting identifies "If gold rust, what shall iron do?" as a proverb (*Proverbs*, G304), but cites only the Parson's use of the "figure" in *General Prologue* I 500.

9. See Florence Ridley, in *Riverside Chaucer*, p. 944, n. 85–119. On biblical allusions and figural motifs in the Second Nun's performance, see Paul Clogan, "The Figural Style and Meaning of *The Second Nun's Prologue and Tale*" (1972).

10. See Ridley, ibid., p. 263; and *MED* s.v. *figure* n. 3 (a) and *figuren* v. 3.

11. Among the many allegorical interpretations of Leah and Rachel and Martha and Mary as representatives of the active and contemplative lifestyles, see Gregory the Great, *Moralia in Iob*, 2.6.37, par. 61; in *PL*, vol. 75, col. 764; and Bernard of Clairvaux, *Liber de modo bene vivendi*, chap. 53, par. 126; in *PL*, vol. 184, col. 1277 et passim. For a study of the theme of Mary and Martha, focused on the eleventh and twelfth centuries but spanning the entire Middle Ages, see Giles Constable, *Three Studies in Medieval Religious and Social Thought* (1995), pp. 1–141.

12. For the different order of the "figure" in the source, see Siegfried Wenzel, ed., *Summa virtutum de remediis anime*, p. 23.

13. In its entry s.v. *figure* n. 3 (b), the *MED* cites the phrase "in figure" from both "An ABC" (line 94) and *Troilus* 5.1449. See n. 5, above.

14. On these senses of the term "figure," see Lawrence Besserman, "Chaucer's *Envoy to Bukton* and 'Truth' in Biblical Interpretation" (1991), p. 191.

15. For an interesting attempt to distinguish between allegorical biblical exegesis and medieval literary allegory, see Michael Zink, "The Allegorical Poem as Interior Memoir" (1986), pp. 104–5 et passim. For "figural" readings of Chaucer's dream visions, see (in addition to the works cited below), the totalizing interpretations in Huppé and Robertson, *Fruyt and Chaf: Studies in Chaucer's Allegories* (1963), and F. H. Whitman, "Exegesis and Chaucer's Dream Visions" (1969).

16. For a sampling of the many critical studies on Chaucer's indebtedness to Dante, Petrarch, and Boccacio, see discussion and references in Paul Ruggiers, "The Italian Influence on Chaucer" (1979); Piero Boitani, ed., *Chaucer and the Italian Trecento* (1983); David Wallace, *Chaucer and the Early Writings of Boccaccio* (1985); and id., "'Whan She Translated Was': A Chaucerian Critique of the Petrarchan Academy" (1990).

The bibliography on the views and practices of Dante in relating sacred to secular letters is vast. In addition to the works mentioned in chapter 1, n. 49, see the still-valuable survey and discussion of the range of Dante's biblical allusions in Edward Moore, "Dante and Scripture" (1896); and among more recent studies, see Christopher Kleinhenz, "Dante and the Bible: Intertextual Approaches to the *Divine Comedy*" (1986); Giovanni Barblan, ed., *Dante e la Bibbia* (1988); Peter Hawkins, "Scripts for the Pageant: Dante and the Bible" (1988); and Joan Ferrante, "The Bible as Thesaurus for Secular Literature" (1992), pp. 23–49 (on the significance of Dante's use of Rahab, Solomon, Adam, Peter, and David in the *Commedia*). As Piero Boitani has kindly confirmed in a letter to the author, specific instances of Dante's debt to the liturgy are often noted (especially in relation to *Purgatorio* 29–30), but a detailed study of Dante and the liturgy still remains to be written.

For the "exhaustive testimony [in Petrarch's *De otio religioso* (1347)] . . . about the gradual growth of [Petrarch's] biblical interests," see Hans Baron, *From Petrarch to Leonardo Bruni* (1968), pp. 41–44 (quotation on p. 41). On Petrarch's views and practices in relating sacred to secular letters, see also Theodor Mommsen, "Petrarch's Conception of the 'Dark Ages'" (1942); Ernst Curtius, "*Nomina Christi*" (1951); and Minnis, *Medieval Theory of Authorship*, 2d ed., pp. 211–17 passim. On Boccaccio's similar engagement with ramifications of the relationship between the Bible and secular literature, see his *Vita di Dante* 21, 12.37–38, and the preface to his *Genealogy of the Gods*, trans. in Osgood, *Boccaccio on Poetry*, p. xxiii, n. 25, and p. 11, resp. (and cp. the other analogies that Boccaccio draws between Scripture and secular writing, cited ibid., pp. 49–50); the extracts from his *Short Treatise in Praise of Dante* and his *Expository Lectures on Dante's Commedia: Prologue*, translated and discussed by David Wallace, in Minnis and Scott, eds., *Medieval Literary Theory and Criticism, c. 1100–c. 1375*, rev. ed., pp. 492–519, and Minnis, *Medieval Theory of Authorship*, pp. 203–4 and 215–17 passim.

17. On the date of the *Book of the Duchess*, see Colin Wilcockson's introduction to the poem, in *Riverside Chaucer*, pp. 329–30; and for a critical overview, see Minnis, "The Book of the Duchess," in Minnis et al., *The Shorter Poems*, pp. 73–160.

18. On the Boethian passages in *Troilus* and the *Knight's Tale*, see Bernard Jefferson, *Chaucer and the Consolation of Philosophy of Boethius* (1965), pp. 120–32, 137–40, and 142–43.

19. John Norton-Smith claims that Chaucer's philosophical focus in the *Book of the Duchess* is on the concepts of "Nature" and "moderation" rather than on Boethian or other themes (*Geoffrey Chaucer* [1974], pp. 1–15). Similarly, James Dean argues that Chaucer wrote the *Book of the Duchess* before he knew Boethius well ("Chaucer's *Book of the Duchess*: A Non-Boethian Interpretation" [1985]). For the opposing view, see Frederick Klaeber, "Traces of the *Canticum* and of Boethius' 'De Consolatione Philosophiae' in Chaucer's 'Book of the Duchesse'" (1897), and further references in Wilcockson, *Riverside Chaucer*, p. 971, n. 544. On the indebtedness of the *Book of the Duchess* to French dream visions (primarily the *Roman de la rose* and Guillaume de Machaut's *Jugement dou roy de behaingne, Remede de fortune, Lay de confort*, and *Le dit dou lyon*), see Wilcockson, introduction and explanatory notes to *The Book of the Duchess*, in *Riverside Chaucer*, passim. Wilcockson's notes make use of James Wimsatt's *Chaucer and the French Love Poets* (1968), which lists the many parallels between the *Book of the Duchess* and its French sources and analogues in an appendix, pp. 155–62.

20. John Lawlor finds that the secular consolation offered in the *Book of the Duchess* is based on the ethos of "courtly love" ("The Pattern of Consolation in *The Book of the Duchess*" [1961]). Similarly, Phillip Boardman suggests that "[Chaucer's] refusal to turn to Christianity bespeaks [his] desire to explore for a poetic language which does not call up given philosophical or theological answers" ("Courtly Language and the Strategy of Consolation in the *Book of the Duchess*" [1977], p. 578).

21. See Wimsatt, "The Apotheosis of Blanche in the *Book of the Duchess*" (1967); and id., "*The Book of the Duchess*: Secular Elegy or Religious Vision?" (1981). On Marian and other figurally evocative biblical echoes in the poem, see also Rodney Delasanta, "Christian Affirmation in *The Book of the Duchess*" (1969); and Terence Hoagwood, "Artifice and Redemption: Figuration and Failure of Reference in Chaucer's *The Book of the Duchess*" (1988).

22. See *Book of the Duchess* 904–5 and 971–74 (cp. Cant. 5:10), 945–46 (cp. Cant. 4:4 and 7:4), and 981–84 (cp. Cant. 6:7–8). These correspondences were noted by Wimsatt, "The Apotheosis of Blanche in the *Book of the Duchess*," pp. 35–36; and earlier, in part, by Klaeber (as in n. 19, above).

23. See Wimsatt, "The Apotheosis of Blanche," pp. 37–44. On Esther and Mary as biblical models for real fourteenth-century "queens as intercessors," see Paul Strohm, *Hochon's Arrow* (1992), pp. 96–98.

24. Wimsatt notes that the figurally interpreted imagery of Wisdom 7:26—i.e., images of "light," "mirror," and "goodness"—occurs in the same order in the *Book of the Duchess* ("The Apotheosis of Blanche," pp. 38–40; 44).

25. Spearing, *Readings in Medieval Poetry* (1987), p. 106; and see Spearing's earlier article, "Literal and Figurative in *The Book of the Duchess*" (1984), p. 171.

26. See N. B. Lewis, "The Anniversary Service for Blanche, Duchess of Lancaster, 12th September, 1374" (1937).

27. The slim evidence for dating the *House of Fame* is discussed in John Fyler's introductory headnote to the poem, in *Riverside Chaucer*, p. 978. Biblical allusions in the *House of Fame*, identified by Bennett, Delany, Koonce, Jeffrey, and other scholars cited in the following notes, are listed in Besserman, *Chaucer and the Bible*, pp. 243–47. For a

critical overview of the poem, see Minnis, "The House of Fame," in Minnis et al., *The Shorter Poems*, pp. 161–251.

28. See Neuse, *Chaucer's Dante* (1991), p. 28. The suggestion that the Dantean influence was by way of *Purgatorio* 9.19–21, 28–30, and *Paradiso* 1.61–63 was previously made by J. A. W. Bennett, *Chaucer's Book of Fame* (1968), pp. 50–51; but cp. Howard Schless, *Chaucer and Dante* (1984), pp. 45–50. On the overall influence of Dante on the *House of Fame*, see Piero Boitani, *Chaucer and the Imaginary World of Fame* (1984); Schless, *Chaucer and Dante*, pp. 29–76; and further discussion and references in Fyler's notes, in *Riverside Chaucer*, pp. 977–90.

29. See David Jeffrey, "Sacred and Secular Scripture: Authority and Interpretation in *The House of Fame*." As possible biblical sources for the eagle in the *House of Fame*, Jeffrey (pp. 475–76) suggests Ezechiel 17:3, Apocalypse 4:7 and 12:14, and (perhaps) Isaiah 40:31 (following John Steadman, "Chaucer's Eagle: A Contemplative Symbol" [1960]); and as possible biblical sources for the desert landscape in the poem, Jeffrey suggests Deut. 32:10–12; Jer. 2:6, 17:6–8, 50:12–13; and Ezechiel 37:1–14 (following, in part, Sheila Delany, "Phantom and the House of Fame" [1967]).

30. Jeffrey, "Sacred and Secular Scripture," p. 221. As Jeffrey points out (ibid., n. 26), the word "hous" in Chaucer's title is the Middle English word that renders *Templum* in the Wycliffite Bible translation of Ezechiel 8:10.

31. Ibid., pp. 221–22.

32. Ibid., pp. 223–24.

33. Ibid., p. 220 and n. 22; following Benjamin Koonce, *Chaucer and the Tradition of Fame* (1966), pp. 181–85.

34. This weakens Jeffrey's claim (ibid., p. 211) that Chaucer is depicted "in a desert" like the prophet Ezechiel.

35. Ibid., p. 228. And cp. Martin Irvine's formulation of a similar idea in a different theoretical vocabulary: "Chaucer's critique of literary tradition from within the House of Fame—texts seen *sub specie Famae*—presents an original and important statement about dissemination of authoritative writings viewed on the level of textuality" ("Medieval Grammatical Theory and Chaucer's *House of Fame*," p. 875).

36. James Whitlark suggests that this and other similarly idolatrous prayers in Chaucer's poetry serve to "dramatize the worldliness of Chaucer's characters and to relate it to the condition of pagans and apostates reviled in the Bible and denounced by the early Christians"

("Chaucer and the Pagan Gods" [1977], p. 75). For a more nuanced view of Chaucer's blending of pagan and Christian perspectives, see Minnis, *Chaucer and Pagan Antiquity* (1982).

37. On Chaucer's indebtedness to Dante in this passage, see Fyler, *Riverside Chaucer*, pp. 982–83, n. 588–92.

38. On the Scripture-like status assigned to the *Commedia* by scholars and poets in fourteenth-century Italy, see David Wallace, "Assessing the New Author: Commentary on Dante," in Minnis and Scott, eds., *Medieval Literary Theory*, rev. ed., pp. 439–58. The claim of affinity between the *Commedia* and the Bible might also lead to a parallel claim regarding Dante and divinely inspired biblical authors (see the comments of Guido da Pisa [c. 1340], translated and discussed by Wallace, ibid., pp. 469–76).

39. I have altered the punctuation of the *Riverside Chaucer* text by moving lines 982–83 within the quotation marks.

40. That the "man" obliquely referred to in 2 cor. 12:2–4 was Paul himself is confirmed in vv. 6–7. Piero Boitani refers to 2 Cor. 12:2–4 and observes that the echo of Saint Paul in this passage "shows that Chaucer seems to be thinking of himself as ready for a *raptus* similar to that of the Apostle" ("Introduction: An Idea of Fourteenth–Century Literature" [1983], pp. 18–19).

41. Quotations from Dante's *Commedia* are from the edition and translation by Charles Singleton (1977). In his note to *House of Fame* 981, Fyler refers the reader to 2 Cor. 12:2 and points out that "Paul hears 'secret words (arcana verba) that man may not repeat,' when he is lifted up to the third heaven"; Fyler also cites Dante, *Paradiso* 1.4–9 and 73–75 (*Riverside Chaucer*, p. 985). Similarly, Schless indicates Chaucer's probable reliance on *Paradiso* 1.73–75 for the biblical echo in lines 981–82 and discusses the tone and function of the intertextual echo, with references to additional scholarly commentary (*Chaucer and Dante*, pp. 64–65).

42. Chaucer's view of the Israelite general and trumpeter Joab as an unsavory figure, placed among otherwise more obviously unsavory biblical personages, is confirmed by Joab's appearance as a type of Judas in the *Biblia pauperum* (ed. Avril Henry, p. 90); and by the use of Joab as example of envy and deceit in Gower's *Confessio amantis* 2.3085–88 (ed. Macaulay, vol. 1, p. 21).

43. Though Virgil and Boethius provided most of the details for Chaucer's description of the goddess Fame (see Fyler, in *Riverside*

Chaucer, p. 987, n. 1368–92), Chaucer's allusion to the Apocalypse ("As John writ in th'Apocalips" [line 1385]) suggests that his description of Fame's eyes—as numerous as the feathers on a bird (lines 1380–84)—comes from Apocalypse 4:6, in which "four living creatures, full of eyes before and behind" are seen "round about the throne" of God (see Fyler, ibid., n. 1383–85; and Francis Magoun and Tauno Mustanoja, "Chaucer's Chimera: His Proto-Surrealist Portrait of Fame" [1975]).

44. Various attempts to identify the "man of gret auctorite" are surveyed by Fyler (*Riverside Chaucer,* p. 990, n. 2158). For an earlier attempt to find a "philosophical [Boethian] formula" for the *House of Fame* and the suggestion that the "man of gret auctorite" who is awaited at the end is Boethius, see Paul Ruggiers, "The Unity of Chaucer's *House of Fame*" (1953) (quotation on p. 262). According to Alfred David, Chaucer's self-reflexively literary and playfully inconclusive purpose in the poem is "planned chaos" in the service of a satire of dream vision and courtly love conventions ("Literary Satire in the *House of Fame*" [1960], p. 333). The latter view has gained many adherents (see the review–essay by Laurence Shook, who concludes that "the subject of the *House of Fame* is the art of poetry itself" [*"The House of Fame"* (1979), p. 417]). More recently, this view of the poem has been given a postmodern turn, as "writing" and "the originality of authority itself" are considered to be the *House of Fame*'s principal subjects (Patterson, *Chaucer and the Subject of History,* pp. 19–20, 99–101, and 289–90).

45. On the relative amounts of biblical matter in these poems, see Besserman, *Chaucer and the Bible,* pp. 238–49 and 276–84. The text of the *Parliament* quoted from below is the one edited by Vincent J. DiMarco and Larry D. Benson, *Riverside Chaucer,* pp. 385–94, with explanatory notes by Charles Muscatine, pp. 994–1002. For another excellent edition, with an informative introduction and valuable notes and appendixes, see Chaucer, *The Parlement of Foulys,* ed. D. S. Brewer (1960; rpt. 1972).

46. See Dronke, "Chaucer and the Medieval Latin Poets" (1974/75), p. 164; and Benson, "Introduction to the *Parliament of Fowls,*" in *Riverside Chaucer,* p. 384. Benson has presented new and compelling evidence for the older view that the specific occasion of the *Parliament* was the competition in 1380 among three noble suitors—Richard II, Friedrich of Meissen, and the future Charles VI of France—for the hand of Anne of Bohemia. See Benson, "The Occasion of *The Parlia-*

ment of Fowls" (1982), with supporting astrological evidence in Alan Lazarus, "Venus in the 'North-north-west'? (Chaucer's *Parliament of Fowls*, 117)" (1982). For an exhaustive overview of different critical approaches to the *Parliament*, see Minnis, "The Parliament of Fowls," in Minnis et al., *The Shorter Poems* (1995), pp. 252–321.

47. It has even been suggested that Chaucer invented the tradition of Saint Valentine as the patron saint of birds and humans in the mating season (see Muscatine, *Riverside Chaucer*, p. 999, n. 309, and further discussion and references in Minnis, *The Shorter Poems*, pp. 257–61).

48. See Pearsall, *The Life of Geoffrey Chaucer* (1992), p. 122, and Huppé and Robertson, *Fruyt and Chaf*, pp. 101–48 (quotation on p. 144).

49. See Fowler, "Chaucer's *Parliament of Fowls* and the Hexameral Tradition," in his *The Bible in Middle English Literature* (1984), pp. 128–70.

50. For an interesting explication of the allegorical significance of the *Parliament* (flawed, however, by its neglect of the biblical texture of the poem), see Paul Piehler, "Myth, Allegory, and Vision in the *Parlement of Foules*: A Study in Chaucerian Problem Solving" (1988).

51. Fowler notes that "'miracles' and 'cruel wrath' are strongly reminiscent of the vengeful God of the Old Testament" (ibid., p. 144).

52. On the disparate sources of the *Parliament*, see J. A. W. Bennett, *The "Parliament of Foules": An Interpretation* (1957); and Minnis, *The Shorter Poems*, pp. 265–307. On the key role of Nature, see George Economou, *The Goddess Natura in Medieval Literature* (1972), chapter 5, "Chaucer's *The Parliament of Foules*," pp. 125–50, 200–204.

53. On these lines, see Muscatine, *Riverside Chaucer*, pp. 995–96, nn. 32, 33, and 80–84 (for the phrase "Christian coloration"). As Bennett notes, lines 82–84 were added to Cicero by Chaucer (*The "Parliament of Foules*," pp. 41–42).

54. For these allusions, see Besserman, *Chaucer and the Bible*, pp. 248–49, and Huppé and Robertson, *Fruyt and Chaf*, p. 136.

55. Huppé and Robertson explain the purported allusion as follows: "The assembly [of birds in the *Parliament*] recalls the gathering of birds of all kinds in Apoc. 19.17, where the birds represent the faithful of all classes assembled by the Angel to put down carnal desires so as to be worthy of a place in the feast of the Lamb" (p. 123).

56. Bennett, *The "Parliament of Foules*," p. 133.

57. For the view that a resolution of this conflict is adumbrated in the *Parliament*, see Economou, *The Goddess Natura in Medieval Literature*, pp. 148–50 et passim.

58. See n. 45, above.

59. Interpretation of the *Legend* has concentrated on the question of whether or not Chaucer really meant to praise the pagan women whose stories he tells. For a review of scholarship on this century-old debate, see John Fisher, "The Legend of Good Women" (1979); the headnote to the *Legend of Good Women* by M. C. Shaner and A. S. G. Edwards, in *Riverside Chaucer*, pp. 1059–60; and Donald Rowe, *Through Nature to Eternity: Chaucer's "Legend of Good Women"* (1988), pp. 1–14, 158–65. For a critical overview of the poem, see Minnis, "The Legend of Good Women," in Minnis et al., *The Shorter Poems*, pp. 322–454.

60. On the dating of the "F" and "G" versions of the *Prologue*, see Shaner and Edwards, in *Riverside Chaucer*, p. 1060. In distinguishing between Chaucer and the narrator, I am following Rowe, whose argument for the distinction is central to his cogent interpretation of the poem as a whole (see *Through Nature to Eternity*, chapter 3, "The Narrator as Translator," pp. 47–79).

61. See Kolve, "From Cleopatra to Alceste" (1981), pp. 171–74.

62. Ibid., pp. 177–78.

63. On the Annunciation imagery, see Russell Peck, "Chaucerian Poetics and the Prologue to the *Legend of Good Women*" (1986), pp. 50–51.

64. See Martin, "Chaucer's Ruth."

65. See chapter 4, pp. 126–36, above.

66. See *City of God*, trans. Bettenson, 1.16–23, pp. 26–34.

67. For favorable estimates of Lucrece by Jerome, Jean de Meun, Jacques de Cessoles, the Menagier de Paris, Robert Holcot, Boccaccio, and Gower, see Robert Frank, *Chaucer and "The Legend of Good Women"* (1972), pp. 97–98. Andrew Galloway draws attention to the similarly favorable estimates of Lucrece by Thomas Waleys, John Ridevall, and Ralph Higden, but Galloway argues that for these late medieval authors, as for Chaucer, the story of Lucrece afforded "a social rather than a religious allegory" ("Chaucer's *Legend of Lucrece* and the Critique of Ideology in Fourteenth-Century England" [1993], p. 818).

68. According to Rowe, the legend of Lucrece inscribes the ambiguity of her status by implying conflicting reactions of "pity" ("the narrator's") and "justice" ("Chaucer's") (*Through Nature to Eternity*, p. 67).

69. See Allen, "The Ironic Fruyt: Chauntecleer as Figura" (1969).

70. See Mortimer Donovan, "The Moralite of the Nun's Priest's Sermon" (1953); C. R. Dahlberg, "Chaucer's Cock and Fox" (1954); and Bernard Levy and George Adams, "Chauntecleer's Paradise Lost and Regained" (1967).

71. Pearsall, *The Canterbury Tales*, pp. 235–38. For a classic statement of the now widely held view that "the fruit of the *Nun's Priest's Tale* is its chaff," see E. Talbot Donaldson, "Patristic Exegesis in the Criticism of Medieval Literature: The Opposition" (1960), pp. 16–20 (quotation on p. 20); and Donaldson's expansion of this interpretation of the *Nun's Priest's Tale* in his edition, *Chaucer's Poetry: An Anthology for the Modern Reader*, 2d ed. (1975), pp. 1104–8.

72. Pearsall, *The Canterbury Tales*, p. 237.

73. See Arthur Broes, "Chaucer's Disgruntled Cleric: *The Nun's Priest's Tale*" (1963).

74. See *Works of Geoffrey Chaucer*, ed. Skeat, vol. 5, p. 274, n. 413 (also noting the occurrence of the image of the "adders tongue" in the portrait of Envy in *Piers Plowman* B-text, passus 5.87); and Landrum, "Chaucer's Use of the Vulgate" (1921), p. 165. The quote in Romans is a blend of the verse from Psalms 139[140]:4[3] and Psalm 5:11, "Their throat is an open sepulchre: they dealt deceitfully with their tongues: judge them, O God."

75. See Noll, "The Serpent and the Sting in the *Pardoner's Prologue* and *Tale*" (1982–83).

76. Critics have suggested that Chaucer hints at travesties of the mass not only in the actions of the three rioters in the *Pardoner's Tale* but also in the introduction to the *Tale*, when he shows the Pardoner drinking at an "alestake" and eating from a "cake" (VI 321–22). See Robert Nichols, "The Pardoner's Ale and Cake" (1967); Clarence Miller and Roberta Bux Bosse, "Chaucer's Pardoner and the Mass" (1971–72); Rodney Delasanta, "Sacrament and Sacrifice in the *Pardoner's Tale*" (1973); and, more recently, George Brown, "*Scriptura Rescripta*: The (Ab)use of the Bible by Medieval Writers" (1992), who refers to "the sordid *agape* of bread and poisoned wine consumed by two members of the unholy Trinity after the sacrificial death of the third" (p. 287).

Though he makes no mention of the *Pardoner's Tale*, Emmanuel Le Roy Ladurie recounts an early fourteenth-century murder plot that provides an uncannily realistic analogue to the one carried out by Chaucer's three rioters. In records of the Inquisition in the southern

French village of Montaillou, two shepherds and "another man" were accused of having sworn "an oath of brotherhood" on bread and wine to kill a hostile priest. They even went so far as to hire two Catalan assassins, but the plan went awry (see *Montaillou* [1979], p. 51).

77. See Miller, "Chaucer's Pardoner" (1960), pp. 224–27. The relevant biblical verses that Miller cites are Romans 6:1–11, Colossians 3:1–10, Ephesians 4:17–24, and Apocalypse 9:6 ("Chaucer's Pardoner," pp. 230, 240, 242, and 244 nn. 13 and 31). He is followed by Derek Pearsall, who cites Romans 6:6, Colossians 3:9, and Ephesians 4:22 to explain the Old Man's "unappeased yearning after life, or maybe after spiritual life" ("Chaucer's Pardoner: The Death of a Salesman" [1982–83], p. 363). Pearsall also hears an echo in *Pardoner's Tale* VI 727–28 of Apocalypse 9:6 (*The Canterbury Tales*, pp. 102–3). For other provocative accounts of the function of these and other biblical allusions that Chaucer uses in his description of the Old Man, see Dinshaw, *Chaucer's Sexual Poetics*, pp. 156–84; Piero Boitani, *The Tragic and the Sublime in Medieval Literature* (1989), pp. 4–19; H. M. Leicester, Jr., *The Disenchanted Self* (1990), pp. 48–51; and Patterson, *Chaucer and the Subject of History*, pp. 402–6 (and for more on the Pardoner's allusion to Apocalypse 9:6, see n. 82, below.)

78. See Robert Black, "Sacral and Biblical Parody in Chaucer's Canterbury Tales" (1974), p. 136.

79. Boitani, *Tragic and the Sublime*, pp. 9–11.

80. See Hilary, *Riverside Chaucer*, p. 909, n. 745. On the "Golden Rule" in its positive (New Testament) and negative (rabbinic) formulations, see David Jeffrey, gen. ed., *Dictionary of Biblical Tradition in English Literature* (1992), pp. 313–14.

81. The likelihood of an allusion in *Pardoner's Tale* VI 727–28 to Romans 7:24 is enhanced by Chaucer's translation of this verse in the *Parson's Tale*: "yet seyde [seint Paul], 'Allas, I caytyf man! Who shal delivere me fro the prisoun of my caytyf body?'" (X 344).

82. See Boitani, as in n. 77, above. Apocalypse 9:6 is translated by the Parson and attributed to its putative biblical author: "And therfore seith Seint John the Evaungelist, 'They shullen folwe deeth, and they shul nat fynde hym; and they shul desiren to dye, and deeth shal flee fro hem'" (X 216).

83. Beidler, "Noah and the Old Man in the Pardoner's Tale" (1980–81), p. 250.

84. Ibid., pp. 252–53, with relevant passages from the Noah play cited from *The Wakefield Pagaents in the Towneley Cycle*, ed. A. C. Cawley (1958), p. 15, lines 48–54, 57–64, and 264–76. (On Noah in vernacular drama, see chapter 4, n. 26.)

85. Fleming, "Chaucer and Erasmus" (1985), pp. 161–63.

86. Boitani, *Tragic and the Sublime*, pp. 11–12.

87. On the purported "Genesis-Apocalypse" structure of the *Canterbury Tales*, see Baldwin, *The Unity of "The Canterbury Tales"* (1955), pp. 15–21, 28–37; J. C. Nitzsche, "Creation in Genesis and Nature in Chaucer's *General Prologue* 1–18" (1978); Lawler, *The One and the Many in the Canterbury Tales*, pp. 162–63; Paul Taylor, "The Alchemy of Spring in Chaucer's *General Prologue*" (1982–83); and Morton Bloomfield, "The Canterbury Tales as Framed Narratives" (1983). Donald Howard has also suggested that "the binary or 'diptych' structure" of the *Canterbury Tales* is a feature of the work that recalls the Old Testament/New Testament division of the Bible (*The Idea of the Canterbury Tales*, p. 320).

88. See James Dean, "Dismantling the Canterbury Book" (1985).

89. See Frye, *The Great Code: The Bible and Literature* (1982). On biblical typology as a model for the drawing of character in medieval secular literature, see Warren Ginsberg, *The Cast of Character* (1983), pp. 71–97 and 177–83.

CONCLUSION

1. A more immediate cause of the Dreamer's exasperation may be Scripture's mistranslation of "Non mecaberis" (Thou shalt not commit adultery) as "Thou shalt not kill" (Luke 18:20)—"perhaps," as Schmidt suggests, "through unconscious confusion with *necare* 'kill'" (see Schmidt, ed., *Piers Plowman*, p. 333, n. 364).

2. Southern, "Medieval Humanism" (1970), p. 47. For more on the role of the Bible in defining social issues in the Middle Ages, see Alexander Murray, *Reason and Society in the Middle Ages*, rev. ed. (1985), pp. 328–30, 386–93, 403.

3. Southern: "Curiously enough, therefore, the paradoxes of the Bible did more for rational argument by stimulating discussion than all the reasons of Aristotle which were swallowed whole" ("Medieval

Humanism," p. 48). Though Southern may be correct in claiming that "the paradoxes of the Bible" stimulated "rational argument"—and one might include under this heading the biblically suffused "poetic argument" frequently found in Chaucer, Langland, and other Ricardian poets—he neglects to mention that the Bible was also at the center of a turn away from rational argument, in later medieval Latin and vernacular poetry and prose that uses the diction and imagery of Scripture for mystical and devotional purposes.

4. Though they say little or nothing about Chaucer and the Bible, three essays in the Benson and Robertson volume that define important facets of Chaucer's "religious" sensibility are Linda Georgianna, "The Protestant Chaucer"; Barbara Nolan, "Chaucer's Tales of Transcendence"; and Derek Pearsall, "Chaucer's Religious Tales." For a strong critique of the attempt in the Benson and Robertson volume to define what is "religious" in the *Canterbury Tales*, see H. Marshall Leicester, Jr., "Piety and Resistance: A Note on the Representation of Religious Feeling in the *Canterbury Tales*" (1995).

5. See Ferster, *Chaucer on Interpretation* (1985).

6. See Kiser, *Truth and Textuality in Chaucer's Poetry*, pp. 1, 2.

7. Patterson, *Negotiating the Past*, pp. 6–7.

8. Ibid., p. 6.

9. The late medieval English debate about biblical translation and interpretation gets more attention in the socially focused studies by Coleman, *English Literature in History: 1350–1400, Medieval Readers and Writers*; Olson, *The "Canterbury Tales" and the Good Society*; and Peggy Knapp, *Chaucer and the Social Contest* (1990). For a sharp critique of the neglect of religious concerns in recent "new historicist" and "cultural materialist" studies of early modern literature, see David Aers, "A Whisper in the Ear of Early Modernists, or Reflections on Literary Critics Writing the 'History of the Subject'" (1992), p. 182 et passim.

10. Mann, *Geoffrey Chaucer*, quotations from pp. 171 and 194, resp.

11. See Jill Mann, "Chaucer and Atheism" (1995).

12. Crane, *Gender and Romance in Chaucer's "Canterbury Tales"* (1994), p. 130.

13. Hanna, "*Compilatio* and the Wife of Bath" (1989), pp. 5–7 et passim.

14. See John Fisher, "Chaucer and the Written Language," and id., "A Language Policy for Lancastrian England" (1992).

15. Hudson, "Wyclif and the English Language" (1986), pp. 102–3. The point still holds of course, as Hudson asserts, whether or not any of Wyclif's own English writings survive. For evidence suggesting that some of Wyclif's English writings do in fact survive, see Margaret Aston, "Wyclif and the Vernacular" (1987).

16. See Margaret Schlauch, "Chaucer's Prose Rhythms" (1950); id., "The Art of Chaucer's Prose" (1966); and David Burnley, *The Language of Chaucer* (1989).

17. On Wyclif's role as (at most) the instigator of the Wycliffite Bible, rather than as one of the translators, see Hudson, *Premature Reformation*, pp. 240–41.

18. On the manuscript titles of the *Canterbury Tales*, see Pratt, "Chaucer's Title." For the Middle English biblical manuscript referred to, see *The Middle English Bible*, ed. Lindberg (1978), p. 60.

19. The text of Arundel's *Constitutions* is analyzed in detail in Anne Hudson, "Lollardy: The English Heresy?" (1985), pp. 146–49. The effects on Lollard translation activities of *De heretico comburendo* in 1401 and the drafting and formal issuing of Arundel's *Constitutions* in 1407 and 1409 are discussed by Hudson, *Premature Reformation*, pp. 14–15.

20. See Thomson, *The Later Lollards, 1414–1520* (1967), pp. 241–42.

21. Ibid., p. 243. The case involving John Baron of Amersham, owner of the *Canterbury Tales*, is recorded in Bishop Chedworth of Lincoln's register (f. 62v); it is cited and discussed by Hudson, "Lollardy: The English Heresy?" p. 142.

22. On the uncertain authorship of the *Prick of Conscience*, its contents, and its 133 manuscripts, see discussion and bibliography in Raymo, "Works of Religious and Philosophical Instruction," pp. 2268–70 and 2486–92. On the 82 manuscripts of the *Canterbury Tales*, see Pearsall, *The Canterbury Tales*, pp. 8–23 and Appendix A, pp. 321–25.

23. See Derek Pearsall, *Old English and Middle English Poetry* (1977), p. 139. On Lollard interpolations in other originally orthodox English works of the fourteenth century, see Talbert and Thomson, "Wyclyf and His Followers," pp. 357–59.

24. See Hudson, "Lollardy: The English Heresy?" p. 149.

25. *Jack Upland* is printed alongside other Chaucerian "apocrypha" in *Works of Geoffrey Chaucer*, ed. Skeat, vol. 7, pp. 191–203, 492–96. Foxe's discussion of Chaucer's Protestantism in his *Actes and Monumentes* is reprinted in Brewer, *Chaucer: The Critical Heritage*, vol. 1, pp. 107–9 (quotation on p. 108).

26. See Georgianna, "The Protestant Chaucer," pp. 58–60.

27. Ibid., p. 68.

28. See Brewer, *Chaucer: The Critical Heritage*, vol. 1, p. 87.

29. Ibid., p. 102. Brewer remarks in the headnote to this selection that "the contrast between the Bible and Chaucer is a commonplace of the first half of the sixteenth century."

30. Ibid.

31. Ibid., pp. 151–52.

32. Ibid., p. 167.

33. See White, *The Uses of Obscurity* (1981), p. 4.

34. Aspects of the fourteenth-century English contribution to the rise of humanism are considered in Smalley's *English Friars* and in Courtenay's *Schools and Scholars*, pp. 161–67 et passim. On the role that nominalism and other fourteenth-century philosophical and religious currents played in the birth of the Renaissance and Reformation, see Courtenay, "Nominalism and Late Medieval Religion"; Heiko Ober-man, "Some Notes on the Theology of Nominalism with Attention to its Relation to the Renaissance"; id., "Fourteenth-Century Religious Thought"; and other essays by Oberman in his two collections *Fore-runners of the Reformation: The Shape of Late Medieval Thought* (1966) and *The Dawn of the Reformation: Essays in Late Medieval and Early Reformation Thought* (1986). See also the volume of essays edited by Charles Trinkaus and Heiko Oberman, *The Pursuit of Holiness in Late Medieval and Renaissance Religion* (1974).

35. The Wycliffite legacy of the sixteenth-century Reformation was first demonstrated by A. G. Dickens, *The English Reformation* (1964), pp. 22–37; it has been considered more recently, but with qualifications, by Margaret Aston, "Lollardy and the Reformation: Survival or Revival?" (1964, 1984); and by Hudson, *Premature Reformation*, pp. 60–63, 494–507, et passim.

36. On "Renaissance" features in Chaucer's poetry, see A. C. Spearing, *Medieval to Renaissance in English Poetry* (1985), pp. 1–58.

37. For recent work that relates Chaucer's literary innovations to his social reality, see (in addition to works cited in n. 9, above): Paul Strohm, "The Social and Literary Scene in England" (1986); id., *Social Chaucer* (1989); Lee Patterson, *Chaucer and the Subject of History* (1991); the essays by Patterson and Strohm in Patterson's 1990 collection of essays by various scholars, *Literary Practice and Social Change in Britain, 1380–1530*; Patterson's "Court Politics and the Invention of Literature:

The Case of Sir John Clanvowe" (1992) (which, despite its title, has a good deal to say about Chaucer's role in the late fourteenth-century redefinition of "courtliness" as "literariness"); and the essays in Barbara Hanawalt's *Chaucer's England: Literature in Historical Context* (1992) (reviewed by Steven Justice [1994]).

Works Cited

PRIMARY SOURCES

Aelred of Rievaulx. *Aelred de Rievaulx: La vie de recluse, La prière pastorale. Texte latin, introduction, traduction et Notes.* Trans. and ed. Charles Dumont. Sources Chrétiennes 76, Série des Textes Monastiques d'Occident, 6. Paris: du Cerf, 1961.

———. *Aelred of Rievaulx's De institutione inclusarum: Two English Versions.* Ed. John Ayto and Alexandra Barratt. EETS o.s. 287. London: Oxford UP, 1984.

———. *Quand Jésus eut douze ans.* Ed. Anselme Hoste. Trans. Joseph Dubois. 1958. 2d ed. Sources Chrétiennes 60. Paris: du Cerf, 1987.

Albertanus of Brescia. *Albertani Brixiensis: Liber consolationis et consilii ex quo hausta est fabula gallica de Melibeo et Prudentia quam anglice redditamet "The Tale of Melibee" inscriptum, Gulfridus Chaucer inter "Canterbury Tales" recepit.* Ed. Thor Sundby. Chaucer Society Publications, 2d ser., 2/8. London: Trübner, 1873.

Andreas Capellanus. *The Art of Courtly Love.* Trans. John Jay Parry. 1941. New York: Ungar, 1959.

Aquinas, Thomas. [*Catena aurea.*] *Enarrationes, quas catenam vere auream dicunt in quattuor evangelia.* Paris, 1537.

Augustine. *On the Harmony of the Gospels.* Trans. S. D. F. Salmond. Ed. M. B. Riddle. In *The Works of St. Augustine,* vol. 6. In *A Select Library of the Nicene and Post-Nicene Fathers of the Christian Church, First Series,* ed. Philip Schaff, pp. 65–236. Grand Rapids, Mich.: Eerdmans, 1888; rpt. 1978.

———. *De consensu evangelistarum.* Ed. F. Weihrich. CSEL 43. Vienna: Tempsky, 1904.

———. *Sancti Aurelii Augustini. Quaestionum in heptateuchum libri VII, Locutionum in heptateuchum libri VII, De octo quaestionibus ex veteri testamento.* Ed. I. Fraipont. CCSL 33, Aurelii Augustini Opera, pars 5. Turnholt: Brepols, 1958.

―――. *On Christian Doctrine.* Trans. D. W. Robertson Jr. Indianapolis: Bobbs-Merrill, 1958.

―――. *Sancti Aurelii Augustini. De doctrina christiana, De vera religione.* Ed. Joseph Martin. Corpus Christianorum, Series Latina 32, Aurelii Augustini Opera, pars 4, 1. Turnholt: Brepols, 1962.

―――. *The City of God.* Trans. Henry Bettenson. With an introduction by John O'Meara. 1972. Harmondsworth, Middlesex, Eng.: Penguin Books, 1984.

Bible. Vulgate. *Biblia Sacra iuxta vulgatam Clementinam.* 4th ed. A. Colunga and L. Turrado, eds. Madrid: Biblioteca de Autores Cristianos, 1965.

―――. *The Holy Bible, Containing the Old and New Testaments, with the Apocryphal Books in the Earliest English Versions made from the Latin Vulgate by John Wycliffe and his Followers.* Ed. Josiah Forshall and Sir Frederic Madden. 4 vols. Oxford: Oxford UP, 1850.

―――. *The Middle English Bible: Prefatory Epistles of Jerome.* Ed. Conrad Lindberg. Oslo: Universitetsforlaget, 1978.

―――. *Douay-Rheims version. Old Testament first published at Douay, 1609; New Testament first published at Rheims, 1582.* Baltimore: John Murphy, 1899. Rpt. Rockford, Ill.: Tan Books, 1971.

―――. *The Old Testament of the Jerusalem Bible* [vol. 1]; *The New Testament of the Jerusalem Bible* [vol. 2]. Garden City, N.Y.: Doubleday, 1966. (Translated from *La Bible de Jerusalem.* Paris: du Cerf, 1961.)

―――. *Biblia latina cum Glossa ordinaria: Facsimile Reprint of the Editio Princeps Adolph Rusch of Strassburg 1480/81.* Introduction by Karlfried Froehlich and Margaret T. Gibson. Turnholt: Brepols, 1992.

Bible moralisée. Bible moralisée: Faksimilie im Originalformat des Codex Vindobonensis 2554 der Österreichischen Nationalbibliothek. Commentarium by Reiner Hanssherr. 2 vols. Graz: Akademische Druck; Paris: Club du Livre, 1973.

Biblia pauperum: A Facsimile and Edition. Ed. Avril Henry. London: Scolar; Ithaca, N. Y.: Cornell UP, 1987.

Boccaccio, Giovanni. *Boccaccio on Poetry: Being the Preface and the Fourteenth and Fifteenth Book's of Boccaccio's Genealogia deorum gentilium.* Trans. and ed. Charles G. Osgood. Indianapolis: Bobbs-Merrill, 1956.

————. *The Decameron.* Trans. Mark Musa and Peter Bondanella. With an Introduction by Thomas G. Bergin. New York: New American Library, 1982.

Boethius. *The Theological Tractates. The Consolation of Philosophy.* Trans. H. F. Stewart and E. K. Rand [*Theological Tractates*], with the English translation of "I.T." (1609), revised by H. F. Stewart [*Consolation of Philosophy*]. Loeb Classical Library. 1918. London: Heinemann; Cambridge, Mass.: Harvard UP, 1968.

Bonaventure. *Breviloquium.* In *The Works of Bonaventure: Cardinal, Seraphic Doctor and Saint.* Trans. José de Vinck. 5 vols. Paterson, N.J.: St. Anthony Guild, 1960–70. Vol. 2, 1963.

Bury, Richard de. *The Philobiblon of Richard de Bury.* Ed. and trans. Ernest C. Thomas. London: Kegan Paul, Trench, 1888. Foreword by Michael Maclagan. Oxford: Blackwell (for the Shakespeare Head Press), 1959. Rpt. New York: Barnes and Noble, 1970.

Chaucer. *The Complete Works of Geoffrey Chaucer.* Ed. Walter W. Skeat. 2d ed. 7 vols. 1894, 1897. Oxford: Oxford UP, 1899–1900.

————. *The Text of the Canterbury Tales: Studied on the Basis of All Known Manuscripts.* Ed. John M. Manly and Edith Rickert. Vol. 3. Text and Critical Notes. Part 1. Chicago: U of Chicago P, 1940.

————. *The Works of Geoffrey Chaucer.* Ed. F. N. Robinson. 2d ed. Boston: Houghton Mifflin, 1957.

————. *The Parlement of Foulys.* Ed. D. S. Brewer. 1960. Manchester: Manchester UP, 1972.

————. *Chaucer's Poetry: An Anthology for the Modern Reader.* Ed. E. T. Donaldson. 2d ed. 1958. Glenn View, Ill.: Scott, Foresman, 1975.

————. *The Miller's Tale.* Ed. Thomas W. Ross. In *A Variorum Edition of the Works of Geoffrey Chaucer,* vol. 2, *The Canterbury Tales,* part 3, *The Miller's Tale.* Norman: U of Oklahoma P, 1983.

————. *The Prioress's Tale.* Ed. Beverly Boyd. In *A Variorum Edition of the Works of Geoffrey Chaucer,* vol. 2, *The Canterbury Tales,* part 20, *The Prioress's Tale.* Norman: U of Oklahoma P, 1987.

————. *The Riverside Chaucer.* 3d ed. General editor, Larry D. Benson. Boston: Houghton Mifflin, 1987.

————. *The General Prologue.* Ed. Malcolm Andrew. In *A Variorum Edition of the Works of Geoffrey Chaucer,* vol. 2, *The Canterbury Tales,* part 1 B, *The General Prologue: Explanatory Notes.* Norman: U of Oklahoma P, 1993.

Dante Alighieri. *La vita nuova di Dante Alighieri.* Ed. Michele Barbi. In *Le opere di Dante: Testo critico della Società Dantesca Italiana.* 2d ed. Florence: Società Dantesca Italiana, 1960.

————. *The Divine Comedy.* Trans. Charles S. Singleton. 2d ed. 3 vols. in 6 parts. 1970–75. Bollingen Series 80. Princeton, N.J.: Princeton UP, 1977.

————. *Literary Criticism of Dante Alighieri.* Trans. and ed. Robert S. Haller. 1973. Lincoln: U of Nebraska P, 1977.

————. *Dante Alighieri: Vita nuova.* Trans. Mark Musa. The World's Classics. Oxford: Oxford UP, 1992.

Gawain on Marriage: The "De coniuge non ducenda." Trans. A. G. Rigg. Toronto: Pontifical Institute of Mediaeval Studies, 1986.

Geufroi de Paris. *Bible des sept etats du monde.* Ed. Paul Meyer. In *Notices et extraits des manuscrits de la Bibliothèque Nationale et autres Bibliothèques,* 39, part 1, pp. 255–322. Paris: Klincksieck, 1909.

Gower, John. *The Complete Works of John Gower.* 4 vols. Ed. G. C. Macaulay. Oxford: Clarendon, 1899–1902. (Vol. 1, *The French Works;* vols. 2–3, *English Works* (*Confessio Amantis* and *In Praise of Peace,* issued as EETS, e.s., 81, 82, in 1900 and 1901); vol. 4: *Latin Works,* rpt. London: Oxford UP, 1957.)

————. *The Major Latin Works of John Gower: The Voice of One Crying, and the Tripartite Chronicle.* Ed. and trans. Eric W. Stockton. Seattle: U of Washington P, 1962.

Guillaume de Lorris and Jean de Meun. *Le roman de la rose.* Ed. Félix Lecoy. 3 vols. Les Classiques Français du Moyen Age, 92, 95, 98. Paris: Champion, 1965, 1979, 1982.

————. *The Romance of the Rose.* Trans. Charles Dahlberg. Princeton, N.J.: Princeton UP, 1971. Rpt. Hanover, N.H.: UP of New England, 1983.

Guiot de Provins. *Les oeuvres de Guiot de Provins: Poète lyrique et satirique.* Ed. John Orr. Publications de l'Université de Manchester, 104; Série Française 1. Manchester: Manchester UP, 1915.

Innocent III. *Lothario Dei Segni (Pope Innocent III). On the Misery of the Human Condition.* Ed. Donald R. Howard. Trans. Margaret Mary Dietz. Indianapolis: Bobbs-Merrill, The Library of Liberal Arts, 1969.

————. *Lotario dei Segni (Pope Innocent III). De miseria condicionis humane.* Ed. and trans. Robert E. Lewis. The Chaucer Library. Athens: U of Georgia P, 1978.

Isidore of Seville. *Etymologiarum sive originum libri xx.* Ed. W. M. Lindsay. 2 vols. 1911. London: Oxford UP, 1962.

Jacobus de Voragine. *The Golden Legend* [*Legenda aurea*]. Trans. and adapted by Granger Ryan and Helmut Ripperger. New York: Longmans, Green, 1941. Rpt. Salem, N.H.: Ayer, 1967.

John of Salisbury. *Ioannis Saresberiensis: Episcopi carnotensis policratici, sive De Nugis curialium et vestigiis philosophorum, libri VIII.* Ed. Clemens C. I. Webb. 2 vols. Oxford: Clarendon, 1909.

————. *Policraticus: Of the Frivolities of Courtiers and the Footprints of Philosophers.* Ed. and trans. Cary J. Nederman. Cambridge Texts in the History of Political Thought. Cambridge: Cambridge UP, 1990.

Langland, William. *Piers Plowman by William Langland: An Edition of the C-Text.* Ed. Derek Pearsall. Berkeley: U of California P, 1978, 1982.

————. *The Vision of Piers Plowman: A Complete Edition of the B-Text.* Rev. ed. Ed. A. V. C. Schmidt. London: Dent, Everyman's Library, 1987.

L'art d'amours: Traduction et commentaire de l'Ars amatoria d'Ovide. Ed. Bruno Roy. Leiden: E. J. Brill, 1974.

Lewis, C. S. *Reflections on the Psalms.* 1958. London: Collins-Fontana, 1961.

Literary Context of Chaucer's Fabliaux: Texts and Translations, The. Ed. Larry D. Benson and Theodore M. Andersson. Indianapolis: Bobbs-Merrill, 1971.

Love, Nicholas. *The Mirror of the Blessed Lyf of Jesu Christ.* Ed. James Hogg and Lawrence F. Powell. 2 vols. Analecta Cartusiana 91. Salzburg: Institut für Anglistik und Amerikanistik, Universität Salzburg, 1989.

Mézières, Philippe de. *Philippe de Mézières, Chancellor of Cyprus: Le songe du vieil Pelerin.* Ed. G. W. Coopland. 2 vols. Cambridge: Cambridge UP, 1969.

Middle English Debate Poetry. Ed. John Conlee. East Lansing, Mich.: Colleagues, 1991.

Middle English Prose Complaint of Our Lady and Gospel of Nicodemus, Ed[ited] from Cambridge Magdalene College MS Pepys 2498, The. C. William Marx and Jeanne F. Drennan, eds. Middle English Texts 19. Heidelberg: Carl Winter, 1987.

Newman, John Henry. *History of My Religious Opinions* (1865 ed.). In *Newman: Prose and Poetry,* ed. Geoffrey Tillotson. Cambridge, Mass.: Harvard UP, 1970.

New Testament Apocrypha. Ed. Edgar Hennecke and Wilhelm Schneemelcher. 2 vols. 1959, 1964. English trans. ed. by R. Mcl. Wilson. Philadelphia: Westminster P, 1963, 1965.

Ovid. *Metamorphoses.* Trans. Frank Justus Miller. 2 vols. Loeb Classical Library. London: Heinemann; Cambridge, Mass.: Harvard UP, 1944, 1946.

Oxford Book of Ballads, The. Ed. Arthur Quiller-Couch. Oxford: Clarendon, 1910; rpt., 1951.

Patrologiae cursus completus . . . Series Latina. Ed. J.-P. Migne (and successors). 221 vols. Paris, 1844–64.

Pearl. Ed. E. V. Gordon. Oxford: Clarendon, 1953.

Peter of Riga. *Aurora: Petri Rigae Biblia versificata. A Verse Commentary on the Bible.* 2 vols. Ed. Paul E. Beichner, C. S. C. Publications in Mediaeval Studies 19. Notre Dame, Ind.: U of Notre Dame P, 1965.

Prymer, or Lay Folks' Prayer Book, The. Parts 1 and 2. Ed. Henry Littlehales. Early English Text Society o.s. 105, 109. 1895, 1897. Millwood, N.Y.: Kraus, 1975.

Rolle, Richard. *The Psalter, or Psalms of David and Certain Canticles, with a Translation and Exposition in English by Richard Rolle of Hampole.* Ed. H. R. Bramley. Oxford: Clarendon, 1884.

————. *English Writings of Richard Rolle, Hermit of Hampole.* Ed. Hope Emily Allen. Oxford: Clarendon, 1931; rpt., 1963.

Sarum Breviary, The. *Breviarium ad usum Insignis Ecclesiae Sarum.* Ed. Francis Procter and Christopher Wordsworth. 3 vols. Cambridge: Cambridge UP, 1879 (vol. 2), 1882 (vol. 1), 1886 (vol. 3).

Sarum Missal, The. *Missale ad usum Insignis et Praeclarae Ecclesiae Sarum.* Ed. Francis Henry Dickinson. 1861–63. Farnborough, Hants., Eng.: Gregg International, 1969.

The Sarum Missal, Edited from the Early Manuscripts. Ed. J. Wickham Legg. Oxford: Clarendon, 1916.

Sir Gawain and the Green Knight. Ed. J. R. R. Tolkien and E. V. Gordon. 2d ed. revised by Norman Davis. Oxford: Clarendon, 1967.

Sources and Analogues of Chaucer's Canterbury Tales. Ed. W. F. Bryan and Germaine Dempster. 1941. New York: Humanities P, 1958.

[Speculum humanae salvationis.] A Medieval Mirror: Speculum humanae salvationis, 1324–1500. Ed Adrian Wilson and Joyce Lancaster Wilson. Berkeley and Los Angeles: U of California P, 1984.

Spenser, Edmund. *The Faerie Queene*. In *The Poetical Works of Edmund Spenser*, ed. J. C. Smith and E. De Selincourt. London: Oxford UP, 1912; rpt., 1963.

Summa virtutum de remediis anime. Ed. and trans. Siegfried Wenzel. The Chaucer Library. Athens: U of Georgia P, 1984.

Towneley Plays, The. Ed. George England. EETS e.s. 71. London: Oxford UP, 1966.

Tretise of Miraclis Pleyinge, A. Ed. Clifford Davidson. With commentary on the dialect by Paul A. Johnston Jr. Early Drama, Art, and Music Monograph Series 19. Kalamazoo: Western Michigan U, Medieval Institute, 1993.

Trollope, Anthony. *He Knew He Was Right*. 1869. Harmondsworth, Middlesex, Eng.: Penguin Books, 1993.

Wakefield Pageants in the Towneley Cycle, The. Ed. A. C. Cawley. Manchester: Manchester UP, 1958.

Waugh, Evelyn. *Decline and Fall*. 1928. Harmondsworth, Middlesex, Eng.: Penguin Books, 1970.

Woman Defamed and Woman Defended: An Anthology of Medieval Texts. Ed. Alcuin Blamires, with Karen Pratt and C. W. Marx. Oxford: Clarendon, 1992.

Wyclif, John. *The English Works of Wyclif Hitherto Unprinted*. Ed. F. D. Matthew. 2d ed. EETS o.s. 74. London: Kegan Paul, 1902. Rpt. Millwood, N.Y.: Kraus, 1978.

————. *Selections from English Wycliffite Writings*. Ed. Anne Hudson. Cambridge: Cambridge UP, 1978.

————. *English Wycliffite Sermons*. 3 vols. Ed. Anne Hudson (vols. 1 and 3) and Pamela Gradon (vol. 2). Oxford: Clarendon, 1983 (rpt., 1990), 1988, 1990.

SECONDARY SOURCES

Ackroyd, Peter R. "The Old Testament in the Making." In *Cambridge History of the Bible*, vol. 1 (1970), pp. 67–113.

Aers, David. "A Whisper in the Ear of Early Modernists, or Reflections on Literary Critics Writing the 'History of the Subject.'" In *Culture and History: 1350–1600: Essays on English Communities, Identities and Writing*, ed. David Aers, pp. 177–202. London: Harvester Wheatsheaf, 1992.

Alford, John A[lexander]. "Biblical *Imitatio* in the Writings of Richard Rolle." *ELH* 40 (1973): 1–23.

———. "The Biblical Identity of Richard Rolle." *Fourteenth Century English Mystics Newsletter* 2.4 (1976): 21–25.

———. "Richard Rolle and Related Works." In A. S. G. Edwards, ed., 1984, pp. 35–60.

Allen, Judson Boyce. "The Ironic Fruyt: Chauntecleer as Figura." *SP* 66 (1969): 25–35.

———. *The Friar as Critic: Literary Attitudes in the Later Middle Ages.* Nashville, Tenn.: Vanderbilt UP, 1971.

———. "Reading and Looking Things Up in Chaucer's England." *The Chaucer Newsletter* 7 (1985): 1–2.

Allen, Judson Boyce, and Theresa Anne Moritz. *A Distinction of Stories: The Medieval Unity of Chaucer's Fair Chain of Narratives for Canterbury.* Columbus: Ohio State UP, 1981.

Astell, Ann W. "Apostrophe, Prayer, and the Structure of Satire in *The Man of Law's Tale.*" *SAC* 13 (1991): 81–97.

Aston, Margaret. "Lollardy and the Reformation: Survival or Revival?" *History* 49 (1964): 149–70. Rpt. in Aston, *Lollards and Reformers* (1984), pp. 219–42.

———. "Lollard Women Priests?" *Journal of Ecclesiastical History* 31 (1980): 441–61. Rpt. in Aston, *Lollards and Reformers* (1984), pp. 49–70.

———. "Devotional Literacy." Chapter 4 in Aston, *Lollards and Reformers*, pp. 101–33.

———. *Lollards and Reformers: Images and Literacy in Late Medieval Religion.* History Series 22. London: Hambledon, 1984.

———. "Wyclif and the Vernacular." In Hudson and Wilks, eds., 1987, pp. 281–330.

Auerbach, Erich. "Sermo humilis." In *Literary Language and Its Public in Late Latin Antiquity and in the Middle Ages* (1958), trans. Ralph Manheim, pp. 27–66. New York: Pantheon, 1965.

———. "Figura." 1944. In *Scenes from the Drama of European Literature*, trans. Ralph Manheim (1959), pp. 11–76. Gloucester, Mass.: Peter Smith, 1973.

Bakhtin, Mikhail. *Rabelais and His World.* Trans. Helen Iswolsky. Cambridge, Mass.: MIT P, 1968.

Baldwin, Ralph. *The Unity of "The Canterbury Tales."* Anglistica 5. Copenhagen: Rosenkilde and Bagger, 1955. Rpt. in Schoeck and Taylor, eds., 1960, pp. 14–51.

Barblan, Giovanni, ed. *La Bibbia nell'alto medioevo.* Settimane di Studio del Centro Italiano di Studi sull'Alto Medioevo 10. Spoleto: La Sede del Centro, 1962.

———. *Dante e la Bibbia.* Atti del Convegno Internazionale promosso da "Biblia." Firenze, 26–28 settembre 1986. Biblioteca dell' "Archivum Romanicum." Serie 1: Storia-Letterature-Paleografia 210. Florence: Olschki, 1988.

Baron, Hans. *From Petrarch to Leonardo Bruni: Studies in Humanistic and Political Literature.* Chicago: U of Chicago P (for the Newberry Library), 1968.

Bartlett, Robert. *Trial by Fire and Water: The Medieval Judicial Ordeal.* Oxford: Clarendon, 1988.

Battailon, L[ouis]-J[acques]. "Intermédiaires entre les traités de morale pratique et les sermons: Les *distinctiones* biblique alphabétiques." In *Genres littéraires* (1982), pp. 213–26.

Beichner, Paul E., C. S. C. "Absolon's Hair." *MS* 12 (1950): 222–33.

———. "Non Alleluia Ructare." *MS* 18 (1956): 135–44.

Beidler, Peter G. "Noah and the Old Man in the Pardoner's Tale." *ChauR* 15 (1980–81): 250–54.

Bennett, J. A. W. *The "Parliament of Foules": An Interpretation.* Oxford: Clarendon, 1957.

———. *Chaucer's Book of Fame: An Exposition of "The House of Fame."* Oxford: Clarendon, 1968.

———. *Middle English Literature.* Ed. Douglas Gray. Oxford History of English Literature, vol. 1, part 2. Oxford: Clarendon, 1986.

Benson, C. David, and Elizabeth Robertson, eds. *Chaucer's Religious Tales.* Chaucer Studies 15. Cambridge: Brewer, 1990.

Benson, Donald R. "The Marriage 'Encomium' in the *Merchant's Tale*: A Chaucerian Crux." *ChauR* 14 (1979): 48–60.

Benson, L[arry] D. "The Occasion of *The Parliament of Fowls.*" In Benson and Wenzel, eds., 1982, pp. 123–44, 283–88.

———. "The Beginnings of Chaucer's English Style." In Besserman, ed., 1996, pp. 29–49.

Benson, L[arry] D., and Siegfried Wenzel, eds. *The Wisdom of Poetry: Essays in Early English Literature in Honor of Morton W. Bloomfield.* Kalamazoo: Western Michigan U, Medieval Institute, 1982.

Berger, Samuel. *Histoire de la Vulgate pendant les premiers siècles du moyen âge.* Paris: Hachette, 1893.

————. *Les préfaces jointes aux livres de la Bible dans les manuscrits de la Vulgate.* Paris: Imprimerie Nationale, 1902.

Besserman, Lawrence. "Chaucer and the Bible: The Case of the *Merchant's Tale.*" *HUSL* 6 (1978): 10–31.

————. *The Legend of Job in the Middle Ages.* Cambridge, Mass.: Harvard UP, 1979.

————. "*Glosynge Is a Glorious Thyng*: Chaucer's Biblical Exegesis." In Jeffrey, ed., 1984, pp. 65–73.

————. "Chaucer and the Bible: Parody and Authority in the *Pardoner's Tale.*" In *Biblical Patterns in Modern Literature*, ed. David Hirsch and Nehama Aschkenasy, pp. 43–50. Brown Judaic Studies 77. Chico, Calif.: Scholar's P, 1984.

————. *Chaucer and the Bible: A Critical Review of Research, Indexes, and Bibliography.* Garland Reference Library of the Humanities 839. New York: Garland, 1988.

————. "Chaucer's *Envoy to Bukton* and 'Truth' in Biblical Interpretation: Some Medieval and Modern Contexts." *NLH* 22 (1991): 177–97.

————. "Biblical Exegesis, Typology, and the Imagination of Chaucer." In Keenan, ed., 1992, pp. 183–205.

————. "Augustine, Chaucer, and the Translation of Biblical Poetics." In *The Translatability of Cultures: Figurations of the Space Between*, ed. Sanford Budick and Wolfgang Iser. Irvine Studies in the Humanities. Stanford, Calif.: Stanford UP, 1996.

————, ed. *The Challenge of Periodization: Old Paradigms and New Perspectives.* New York: Garland, 1996.

Bestul, Thomas A. "Chaucer's Parson's Tale and the Late-Medieval Tradition of Religious Meditation." *Speculum* 64 (1989): 600–619.

Bethurum, Dorothy, ed. *Critical Approaches to Medieval Literature: Selected Papers from the English Institute, 1958–59.* New York: Columbia UP, 1960; rpt., 1967.

Birdsall, J. N. "The New Testament Text." In *Cambridge History of the Bible* 1: 366–80.

Biscoglio, Frances Minetti. *The Wives of the "Canterbury Tales" and the Tradition of the Valiant Woman of Proverbs 31:10–31.* San Francisco: Mellen Research UP, 1993.

Black, M. H. "The Printed Bible." In *Cambridge History of the Bible* 3: 408–75.

Black, Robert R. "Sacral and Biblical Parody in Chaucer's Canterbury Tales." Ph.D. diss. Princeton U, 1974.

Blamires, Alcuin. "The Wife of Bath and Lollardy." *MÆ* 58 (1989): 222–42.

———. "The Limits of Bible Study for Medieval Women." In Smith and Taylor, eds., 1995, pp. 1–12.

Bloomfield, Morton W. "Symbolism in Medieval Literature." *MP* 61 (1958): 73–81.

———. "The *Man of Law's Tale*: A Tragedy of Victimization and a Christian Comedy." *PMLA* 87 (1972): 384–90.

———. "The Gloomy Chaucer." In *Veins of Humor*, ed. Harry Levin, pp. 57–68. Harvard English Studies 3. Cambridge, Mass.: Harvard UP, 1972.

———. "The Canterbury Tales as Framed Narratives." In Pearsall, ed., 1983, pp. 44–56.

Boardman, Phillip C. "Courtly Language and the Strategy of Consolation in the *Book of the Duchess*." *ELH* 44 (1977): 567–79.

Bode, Edward L. "The Source of Chaucer's 'Rusted Gold.'" *MS* 24 (1962): 369–70.

Boitani, Piero. *Chaucer and Boccaccio*. Medium Ævum Monographs, n.s., 8. Oxford: Oxford UP, 1977.

———. "Introduction: An Idea of Fourteenth-Century Literature." In Boitani and Torti, eds., 1983, pp. 11–31.

———. "What Dante Meant to Chaucer." In Boitani, ed., 1983, pp. 115–39.

———. *Chaucer and the Imaginary World of Fame*. Chaucer Studies 10. Woodbridge, Suffolk, Eng.: Boydell and Brewer, D. S. Brewer; Totowa, N. J.: Barnes and Noble, 1984.

———. *The Tragic and the Sublime in Medieval Literature*. Cambridge: Cambridge UP, 1989.

———, ed. *Chaucer and the Italian Trecento*. Cambridge: Cambridge UP, 1983.

Boitani, Piero, and Anna Torti, eds. *Literature in Fourteenth-Century England: The J. A. W. Bennett Memorial Lectures*. Tübingen Beiträge zur Anglistik 5. Tübingen: Gunter Narr; Cambridge: Brewer, 1983.

Boitani, Piero, and Jill Mann, eds. *The Cambridge Chaucer Companion*. Cambridge: Cambridge UP, 1986.

Bonner, Gerald. "Augustine as Biblical Scholar." In *Cambridge History of the Bible* 1: 541–63.

Boren, James L. "Alysoun of Bath and the Vulgate 'Perfect Wife.'" *NM* 76 (1975): 247–56.

Bornstein, Diane. "Chaucer's *Tale of Melibee* as an Example of the Style Clergial." *ChauR* 12 (1977–78): 236–54.

Bosanquet, Mary. *The Life and Death of Dietrich Bonhoeffer.* 1968. New York: Harper and Row, Colophon Books, 1973.

Boyd, Beverly. *Chaucer and the Liturgy.* Philadelphia: Dorrance, 1967.

Brewer, Derek. *Chaucer and Chaucerians: Critical Studies in Middle English Literature.* London: Thomas Nelson, 1966, 1970.

———. "The Relationship of Chaucer to the English and European Traditions." In Brewer, ed., 1966, pp. 1–38.

———. *Chaucer and His World.* London: Eyre Methuen, 1978.

———. "The Reconstruction of Chaucer." *SAC, Proceedings* 1 (1984): pp. 3–19.

———. "Chaucer and the Bible." In *Philologica Anglica (Festschrift for Prof. Y. Terasawa),* pp. 270–84. Tokyo: Kenkyusha, 1988.

———, ed. *Writers and their Background: Geoffrey Chaucer.* London: Bell, 1974; Athens: Ohio UP, 1975.

———, ed. *Chaucer: The Critical Heritage.* 2 vols. London: Routledge and Kegan Paul, 1978.

Briscoe, Marianne. "Some Clerical Notions of Dramatic Decorum in Late Medieval England." In *Drama in the Middle Ages: Comparative and Critical Essays,* ed. Clifford Davidson and John H. Stroupe, pp. 210–22. AMS Studies in the Middle Ages 18. New York: AMS, 1991.

Broes, Arthur T. "Chaucer's Disgruntled Cleric: *The Nun's Priest's Tale.*" *PMLA* 78 (1963): 156–62.

Brown, Emerson, Jr. "Biblical Women in the *Merchant's Tale:* Feminism, Antifeminism, and Beyond." *Viator* 5 (1974): 387–412.

Brown, George H. "*Scriptura Rescripta:* The (Ab)use of the Bible by Medieval Writers." In Dean and Zacher, eds., 1992, pp. 285–300.

Brundage, James A. *Law, Sex, and Christian Society in Medieval Europe.* Chicago: U of Chicago P, 1987.

Brusendorff, Aage. *The Chaucer Tradition.* Oxford: Clarendon, 1925.

Bruyne, Donatien de. *Sommaires, divisions et rubriques de la Bible latine.* Namur, Belgium: Auguste Godenne, 1914.

Bruyne, Edgar de. *Études d'esthétique médiévale.* 3 vols. Bruges: Editions "De Tempel," 1946.

———. *L'Esthétique du Moyen Age.* Louvain: l'Institut Supérieur de Philosophie, 1947.

Buc, Philippe. *L'ambiguïté du livre: Prince, pouvoir, et peuple dans les commentaires de la Bible au moyen age.* Preface by Jacques Le Goff. Théologie Historique 95. Paris: Beauchesne, 1994.

Bühler, Curt F. "Wirk Alle Thyng by Conseil." *Speculum* 24 (1949): 410–12.

Burnley, David. *The Language of Chaucer.* The Language of Literature. London: Macmillan, 1989.

Burrow, J[ohn]. A. *Ricardian Poetry: Chaucer, Gower, Langland, and the "Gawain" Poet.* New Haven, Conn.: Yale UP, 1971.

Cahn, Walter. *Romanesque Bible Illumination.* Ithaca, N.Y.: Cornell UP, 1982.

Caie, Graham D. "The Significance of the Early Chaucer Manuscript Glosses (with Special Reference to the *Wife of Bath's Prologue*)." *ChauR* 10 (1975–76): 350–60.

———. "The Significance of Marginal Glosses in the Earliest Manuscripts of *The Canterbury Tales.*" In Jeffrey, ed., 1984, pp. 75–88.

Cambridge History of the Bible, The. Vol. 1. *From the Beginnings to Jerome.* Ed. P. R. Ackroyd and C. F. Evans. Cambridge: Cambridge UP, 1970. Vol. 2. *The West from the Fathers to the Reformation.* Ed. G. W. H. Lampe. Cambridge: Cambridge UP, 1969. Vol. 3. *The West from the Reformation to the Present Day.* Ed. S. L. Greenslade. Cambridge: Cambridge UP, 1963.

Carruthers, Mary J. "Letter and Gloss in the *Friar's* and *Summoner's Tales.*" *JNT* 2 (1972): 208–14.

———. *The Book of Memory: A Study of Memory in Medieval Culture.* Cambridge Studies in Medieval Literature 10. Cambridge: Cambridge UP, 1990.

Carruthers, Mary J., and Elizabeth D. Kirk, eds. *Acts of Interpretation: The Text in Its Contexts, 700–1600: Essays on Medieval and Renaissance Literature in Honor of E. Talbot Donaldson.* Norman, Okla.: Pilgrim Books, 1982.

Cavanaugh, Susan. "A Study of Books Privately Owned in England, 1300–1450." 2 vols. Ph.D. diss. U of Pennsylvania, 1980.

Caviness, Madeline H. *The Early Stained Glass of Canterbury Cathedral, circa 1175–1220.* Princeton, N.J.: Princeton UP, 1972.

———. *The Windows of Christ Church Cathedral Canterbury.* Corpus Vitrearum Medii Ævi, Great Britain, 2. London: Oxford UP (for the British Academy), 1981.

———. "Biblical Stories in Windows: Were They Bibles for the Poor?" In Levy, ed., 1992, pp. 103–47.

Charity, Alan Clifford. *Events and Their Afterlife: The Dialectics of Christian Typology in the Bible and Dante.* Cambridge: Cambridge UP, 1966.

Chesterton, G. K. *Chaucer.* London: Faber and Faber, 1932.

Clanchy, M. T. *From Memory to Written Record, 1066–1307.* 1979. 2d ed. Oxford: Blackwell, 1993.

Clark, Roy Peter. "Doubting Thomas in Chaucer's *Summoner's Tale.*" *ChauR* 11 (1976–77): 164–78.

Clarke, M[aude]. V[iolet]. "Forfeitures and Treason in 1388." In Sutherland and McKisack, eds., 1937, pp. 115–45.

Clogan, Paul M. "The Figural Style and Meaning of *The Second Nun's Prologue and Tale.*" *M&H* 3 (1972): 213–40.

Cohen, Jeremy. *"Be Fertile and Increase, Fill the Earth and Master it": The Ancient and Medieval Career of a Biblical Text.* Ithaca, N.Y.: Cornell UP, 1989.

Coleman, Janet. *English Literature in History: 1350–1400, Medieval Readers and Writers.* London: Hutchinson, 1981.

Constable, Giles. *Three Studies in Medieval Religious and Social Thought: The Interpretation of Mary and Martha, The Ideal of the Imitation of Christ, The Orders of Society.* Cambridge: Cambridge UP, 1995.

Copeland, Rita. "Rhetoric and Vernacular Translation in the Middle Ages." *SAC* 9 (1987): 41–75.

———. *Rhetoric, Hermeneutics, and Translation in the Middle Ages: Academic Traditions and Vernacular Texts.* Cambridge Studies in Medieval Literature 11. Cambridge: Cambridge UP, 1991.

Correale, Robert M. "Gower's Source Manuscript of Nicholas Trevet's *Les Cronicles.*" In Yeager, ed., 1989, pp. 133–57.

Cotter, James Finn. "The Wife of Bath and the Conjugal Debt." *ELN* 6 (1969): 169–72.

Courtenay, William J. "Nominalism and Late Medieval Religion." In Trinkaus and Oberman, eds., 1974, pp. 26–59.

———. "The Bible in the Fourteenth Century: Some Observations." *Church History* 54 (1985): 176–87.

———. *Schools and Scholars in Fourteenth-Century England.* Princeton, N.J.: Princeton UP, 1987.

Crampton, Georgia R. "Chaucer's Singular Prayer." *MÆ* 59 (1990): 191–213.

Crane, Susan. "Alison's Incapacity and Poetic Instability in the Wife of Bath's Tale." *PMLA* 102 (1987): 20–28.

———. *Gender and Romance in Chaucer's "Canterbury Tales."* Princeton, N.J.: Princeton UP, 1994.

Cross, Claire. "Great Reasoners in Scripture: The Activities of Women Lollards, 1380–1530." In *Medieval Women*, ed. Derek Baker, pp. 359–80. SCH, Subsidia 1. Oxford: Blackwell (for the Ecclesiastical History Society), 1978.

Cummings, Hubertis M. *The Indebtedness of Chaucer's Works to the Italian Works of Boccaccio: A Review and Summary.* 1916. New York: Haskell House, 1965.

Curtius, Ernst Robert. *European Literature and the Latin Middle Ages.* 1948. Trans. Willard R. Trask. Bollingen Series 36. Princeton, N.J.: Princeton UP, 1953; New York: Pantheon, 1953. Rpt. New York: Harper and Row, Harper Torchbooks, 1963.

———. "*Nomina Christi.*" In *Mélanges Joseph de Ghellinck, S.J.* 2:1029–32. Museum Lessianum, Section Historique, nos. 13, 14. Gembloux: J. Duculot, 1951.

Dahlberg, C. R. "Chaucer's Cock and Fox." *JEGP* 53 (1954): 277–90.

Dalbey, Marcia A. "The Devil in the Garden: Pluto and Proserpine in Chaucer's *Merchant's Tale.*" *NM* 75 (1974): 408–15.

David, Alfred. "Literary Satire in the House of Fame." *PMLA* 75 (1960): 333–39.

———. *The Strumpet Muse: Art and Morals in Chaucer's Poetry.* Bloomington: Indiana UP, 1976.

———. "An ABC to the Style of the Prioress." In Carruthers and Kirk, eds., 1982, pp. 147–57.

———. "Chaucer's Edwardian Poetry." In Dean and Zacher, eds., 1992, pp. 35–54.

———. Explanatory and Textual Notes to *The Romaunt of the Rose.* In *Riverside Chaucer* (1987), pp. 1103–16, 1198–1210.

Davis, Norman, and C. L. Wrenn, eds. *English and Medieval Studies Presented to J. R. R. Tolkien on the Occasion of His Seventieth Birthday.* London: Allen and Unwin, 1962.

Davis, Norman, Douglas Gray, Patricia Ingham, and Anne Wallace-Hadrill. *A Chaucer Glossary.* Oxford: Clarendon, 1979.

Dean, James [M.] "Dismantling the Canterbury Book." *PMLA* 100 (1985): 746–62.

————. "Chaucer's *Book of the Duchess*: A Non-Boethian Interpretation." *MLQ* 46 (1985): 235–49.

Dean, James, and Christian K. Zacher, eds. *The Idea of Medieval Literature: New Essays on Chaucer and Medieval Culture in Honor of Donald R. Howard.* Newark: U of Delaware P; London: Associated UP, 1992.

Deanesly, Margaret. *The Lollard Bible and Other Medieval Biblical Versions.* Cambridge: Cambridge UP, 1920.

Delany, Sheila. "Phantom and the House of Fame." *ChauR* 2 (1967): 67–74.

————. *Chaucer's House of Fame: The Poetics of Skeptical Fideism.* Chicago: U of Chicago P, 1972. Rpt. with a foreword by Michael Near. Gainesville: UP of Florida, 1994.

Delasanta, Rodney. "Christian Affirmation in *The Book of the Duchess*." *PMLA* 84 (1969): 245–51.

————. "Sacrament and Sacrifice in the *Pardoner's Tale*." *AnM* 14 (1973): 43–52.

DeLong, Sharon Hiltz. Explanatory Notes to the *Tale of Melibee*. In *Riverside Chaucer* (1987), pp. 923–28.

Dempster, Germaine. "The Merchant's Tale." In Bryan and Dempster, eds., 1941, 1958, pp. 333–56.

————. "The Parson's Tale." In Bryan and Dempster, eds., 1941, 1958, pp. 723–60.

D'Esneval, Amaury. "La division de la vulgate en chapitres dans l'édition parisienne du XIIIe siècle." *Revue des sciences philosophiques et théologiques* 62 (1978): 559–68.

D'Evelyn, Charlotte. "[Middle English] Instructions for Religious." In Severs, ed., 1970, pp. 458–81 (texts), 650–59 (bibliography).

D'Evelyn, Charlotte, and Francis A. Foster. "[Middle English] Saints' Legends." In Severs, ed., 1970, pp. 410–29 (texts), 553–649 (bibliography).

Dickens, A. G. *The English Reformation.* New York: Schocken, 1964.

Dickson, Lynne. "Deflection in the Mirror: Feminine Discourse in *The Wife of Bath's Prologue* and *Tale*." *SAC* 15 (1993): 61–90.

DiMarco, Vincent J. Explanatory Notes to *The Knight's Tale*. In *Riverside Chaucer* (1987), pp. 826–41.

DiMarco, Vincent J., and Larry D. Benson, eds. *The Parliament of Fowls*. In *Riverside Chaucer* (1987), pp. 385–94.

Dinshaw, Carolyn. *Chaucer's Sexual Poetics.* Madison: U of Wisconsin P, 1989.

Dolan, T. P. Review of Siegfried Wenzel, ed., *Summa virtutum de remediis anime. SAC* 8 (1986): 260–63.

Donaldson, E. Talbot. "Patristic Exegesis in the Criticism of Medieval Literature: The Opposition." In Bethurum, ed., 1960, pp. 1–26.

Donovan, Claire. *The Winchester Bible.* Toronto: U of Toronto P, 1993.

Donovan, Mortimer J. "The Moralite of the Nun's Priest's Sermon." *JEGP* 52 (1953): 498–508.

————. "The Image of Pluto and Proserpine in the *Merchant's Tale.*" *PQ* 36 (1957): 49–60.

Dronke, Peter. "Chaucer and the Medieval Latin Poets, Part A." In Brewer, ed., 1974/1975, pp. 154–72.

Duffy, Eamon. *The Stripping of the Altars: Traditional Religion in England, c.1400– c.1580.* New Haven, Conn.: Yale UP, 1992.

Duval, Amaury. "Hugues de Bersil." *Histoire littéraire de la France* 18:816–21. Paris: Firmin Didot, 1835.

Eberle, Patricia J. Explanatory Notes to *The Man of Law's Tale.* In *Riverside Chaucer* (1987), pp. 854–63.

Eckhardt, Caroline D. "The Art of Translation in *The Romaunt of the Rose.*" *SAC* 6 (1984): 41–63.

Economou, George D. *The Goddess Natura in Medieval Literature.* Cambridge, Mass.: Harvard UP, 1972.

Edwards, A. S. G., ed. *Middle English Prose: A Critical Guide to Major Authors and Genres.* New Brunswick, N.J.: Rutgers UP, 1984.

————. "Critical Approaches to the *Man of Law's Tale.*" In Benson and Robertson, eds., 1990, pp. 85–94.

Edwards, Robert R. "Narration and Doctrine in the *Merchant's Tale.*" *Speculum* 66 (1991): 342–67.

Ellis, Roger. *Patterns of Religious Narrative in the Canterbury Tales.* Totowa, N.J.: Barnes and Noble, 1986.

Emery, Kent, Jr. "Reading the World Rightly and Squarely: Bonaventure's Doctrine of the Cardinal Virtues." *Traditio* 39 (1983): 183–218.

Emmerson, Richard K. "*Figura* and the Medieval Typological Imagination." In Keenan, ed., 1992, pp. 7–42.

Engle, Lars. "Chaucer, Bakhtin, and Griselda." *Exemplaria* 1 (1989): 429–59.

————. "Bakhtin, Chaucer, and Anti-Essentialist Humanism." *Exemplaria* 1 (1989): 489–97.

English, Edward D., ed. *Reading and Wisdom: The "De doctrina christiana" of Augustine in the Middle Ages.* Notre Dame Conferences in Medieval Studies 6. Notre Dame, Ind.: U of Notre Dame P, 1995.

Erlich, Victor. *Russian Formalism: History-Doctrine.* 1955. New Haven, Conn.: Yale UP, 1981.

Evans, G. R. *The Language and Logic of the Bible.* Vol. 1. *The Earlier Middle Ages.* Vol. 2. *The Road to Reformation.* Cambridge: Cambridge UP, 1984, 1985.

————. "Wyclif on Literal and Metaphorical." In Hudson and Wilks, eds., 1987, pp. 259–66.

Fansler, Dean Spruill. *Chaucer and the Roman de la Rose.* Columbia University Studies in English and Comparative Literature 7. New York: Columbia UP, 1914.

Faverty, F. E. "The Story of Joseph and Potiphar's Wife in Medieval Literature." *Harvard Studies and Notes in Philology and Literature* 13 (1931): 81–127.

Ferrante, Joan M. "The Bible as Thesaurus for Secular Literature." In Bernard S. Levy, ed., 1992, pp. 23–49.

Ferster, Judith. *Chaucer on Interpretation.* Cambridge: Cambridge UP, 1985.

Fischer, Bonifatius. *Lateinische Bibelhandschriften im frühen Mittelalter.* Vetus Latina 11. Freiburg: Herder, 1985.

————. *Beiträge zur Geschichte der lateinischen Bibeltexte.* Vetus Latina 12. Freiburg: Herder, 1986.

Fisher, John H. *John Gower, Moral Philosopher and Friend of Chaucer.* New York: New York UP, 1964.

————. "The Three Styles of Fragment I of the *Canterbury Tales.*" *ChauR* 8 (1973–74): 119–27.

————. "The Legend of Good Women." In Rowland, ed., 1979, pp. 464–76.

————. "Chaucer and the Written Language." In Heffernan, ed., 1985, pp. 237–51.

————. "A Language Policy for Lancastrian England." *PMLA* 107 (1992): 1168–80.

Fleming, John. "Chaucer and Erasmus on the Pilgrimage to Canterbury: An Iconographical Speculation" In Heffernan, ed., 1985, pp. 148–66.

Fletcher, Alan J. "The Summoner and the Abominable Anatomy of Antichrist." *SAC* 18 (1996): 91–117.

Folena, Gianfranco. "'Volgarizzare' e 'tradurre': Idea e terminologia della traduzione dal medio evo italiano e romanzo all'umanesimo europeo." In *La traduzione: saggi e studi*, pp. 57–120. Centro per lo studio dell'insegnamento all'estero dell'italiano, Università degli studi di Trieste. Trieste: Lint, 1973.

Fontaine, Jacques. *Isidore de Seville et la culture classique dans l'espagne wisigothique*. 2d ed. 3 vols. Paris: Études Augustiniennes, 1983.

Foster, Francis A. "Legends of Jesus and Mary." In Severs, ed., 1970, pp. 447–57 (texts), 639–44 (bibliography).

Fowler, David C. *The Bible in Early English Literature*. Seattle: U of Washington P, 1976.

———. *The Bible in Middle English Literature*. Seattle: U of Washington P, 1984.

Frank, Robert Worth, Jr. *Chaucer and "The Legend of Good Women."* Cambridge, Mass.: Harvard UP, 1972.

———. *"The Canterbury Tales* III: Pathos." In Boitani and Mann, eds., 1986, pp. 143–58.

———. *"Meditationes Vitae Christi*: The Logistics of Access to Divinity." In *Hermeneutics and Medieval Culture*, ed. Patrick J. Gallacher and Helen Damico, pp. 39–50. Albany: State U of New York P, 1989.

———. "Pathos in Chaucer's Religious Tales." In Benson and Robertson, eds., 1990, pp. 39–52.

Freccero, John. *Dante: The Poetics of Conversion*. Ed. Rachel Jacoff. Cambridge, Mass.: Harvard UP, 1986.

Frye, Northrop. *The Great Code: The Bible and Literature*. New York: Harcourt Brace Jovanovich, 1982.

Fyler, John M. Explanatory Notes to the *House of Fame*. In *Riverside Chaucer* (1987), pp. 977–90.

Galloway, Andrew. "Marriage Sermons, Polemical Sermons, and *The Wife of Bath's Prologue*: A Generic Excursus." *SAC* 14 (1992): 3–30.

———. "Chaucer's *Legend of Lucrece* and the Critique of Ideology in Fourteenth-Century England." *ELH* 60 (1993): 813–32.

Gameson, Richard, ed. *The Early Medieval Bible: Its Production, Decoration, and Use*. Cambridge Studies in Palaeography and Codicology. Cambridge: Cambridge UP, 1994.

Ganim, John M. "Bakhtin, Chaucer, Carnival, Lent." *SAC, Proceedings* 2 (1986): 59–71.

——. *Chaucerian Theatricality.* Princeton, N.J.: Princeton UP, 1990.

——. "Chaucer and the Noise of the People." *Exemplaria* 2 (1990): 71–88.

Ganz, David. "Mass Production of Early Medieval Manuscripts: The Carolingian Bibles from Tours." In Gameson, ed., 1994, pp. 53–62.

Gellrich, Jesse M. *The Idea of the Book in the Middle Ages: Language, Theory, Mythology, and Fiction.* Ithaca, N.Y.: Cornell UP, 1985.

Genres littéraires dans les sources théologiques et philosophiques médiévales: Définition, critique et exploitation, Les. Actes du Colloque International de Louvain-la-Neuve, 25–27 mai 1981. Publications de l'Institut d'Études Médiévales, 2e serie: Textes, Études, Congrès 5. Louvain-La-Neuve: Université Catholique de Louvain, 1982.

Georgianna, Linda. "The Protestant Chaucer." In Benson and Robertson, eds., 1990, pp. 55–69.

Gibson, Margaret T. "The Place of the *Glossa ordinaria* in Medieval Exegesis." In Jordan and Emery, eds., 1992, pp. 5–27.

——. *The Bible in the Latin West.* The Medieval Book 1. Notre Dame, Ind.: U of Notre Dame P, 1993.

——. "Carolingian Glossed Psalters." In Gameson, ed., 1994, pp. 78–100.

Ginsberg, Warren [S.] *The Cast of Character: The Representation of Personality in Ancient and Medieval Literature.* Toronto: U of Toronto P, 1983.

Glunz, Hans H. *History of the Vulgate in England from Alcuin to Roger Bacon.* Cambridge: Cambridge UP, 1933.

Gosselin, Edward A. "A Listing of the Printed Editions of Nicolaus de Lyra." *Traditio* 26 (1970): 399–426.

Gransden, Antonia. *Historical Writing in England, c. 550 to c. 1307.* London: Routledge and Kegan Paul, 1974.

——. *Historical Writing in England II: c. 1307 to the Early Sixteenth Century.* London: Routledge and Kegan Paul, 1982.

Gray, Douglas. *Themes and Images in the Medieval English Religious Lyric.* London: Routledge and Kegan Paul, 1972.

Green, Richard Hamilton. "Dante's 'Allegory of the Poets' and the Medieval Theory of Poetic Fiction." *CL* 9 (1957): 118–28.

Grennen, Joseph E. "'Sampsoun' in the *Canterbury Tales*: Chaucer Adapting a Source." *NM* 67 (1966): 117–22.

Gross, Laila Z. Explanatory Notes to the Short Poems. In *Riverside Chaucer* (1987), pp. 1076–91.

Hagendahl, Harald. *Augustine and the Latin Classics.* Studia Graeca et Latina Gothoburgensia, XX:I, II. 2 vols. in one. Göteborg: Acta Universitatis Gothoburgensis, 1967.

Hailperin, Herman. *Rashi and the Christian Scholars.* Pittsburgh: U of Pittsburgh P, 1963.

Hale, David G. "Another Latin Source for the Nun's Priest on Dreams." *N&Q* 234 [n.s. 36] (1989): 10–11.

Haller, Robert S. "The Wife of Bath and the Three Estates." *AnM* 6 (1965): 47–64.

Hamel, C. F. R. de. *Glossed Books of the Bible and the Origins of the Paris Booktrade.* Woodbridge, Suffolk, Eng.: Boydell and Brewer, D. S. Brewer, 1984.

Hamilton, Marie P. "The Summoner's 'Psalm of Davit.'" *MLN* 57 (1942): 655–57.

———. "The Dramatic Suitability of the *Man of Law's Tale.*" In *Studies in Language and Literature in Honour of Margaret Schlauch,* ed. M. Brahmer et al., pp. 153–63. Warsaw: PWN, Polish Scientific Publishers, 1966.

Hanawalt, Barbara, ed. *Chaucer's England: Literature in Historical Context.* Medieval Studies at Minnesota 4. Minneapolis: U of Minnesota P, 1992.

Hanna, Ralph III. "*Compilatio* and the Wife of Bath: Latin Backgrounds, Ricardian Texts." In Minnis, ed., 1989, pp. 1–11.

———. Textual Notes to *The Canterbury Tales.* In *Riverside Chaucer* (1987), pp. 1117–35.

Hanning, Robert W. *The Vision of History in Early Britain: From Gildas to Geoffrey of Monmouth.* New York: Columbia UP, 1966.

———. "Roasting a Friar, Mis-taking a Wife, and Other Acts of Textual Harassment in Chaucer's *Canterbury Tales.*" *SAC* 7 (1985): 3–21.

Hansel, Hans. "Die Quellen der bayerischen *Magdalenklage.*" *ZDP* 62 (1937): 363–88.

Hansen, Elaine Tuttle. *Chaucer and the Fictions of Gender.* Berkeley and Los Angeles: U of California P, 1992.

Harder, Kelsie B. "Chaucer's Use of the Mystery Plays in the *Miller's Tale.*" *MLQ* 17 (1956): 193–98.

Hargreaves, Henry. "The Wycliffite Versions." In *Cambridge History of the Bible* 2:387–415.

Hartman, Geoffrey H., and Sanford Budick, eds. *Midrash and Literature.* New Haven, Conn.: Yale UP, 1986.

Hartung, Albert E., gen. ed. *A Manual of the Writings in Middle English, 1050–1500.* Vol. 7. Hamden, Conn.: Archon Books, Shoe String P (for the Connecticut Academy of Arts and Sciences), 1986. Vol. 9. New Haven, Conn.: The Connecticut Academy of Arts and Science, 1993.

Harwood, Britton J. "The Wife of Bath and the Dream of Innocence." *MLQ* 33 (1972): 257–73.

Hassell, James Woodrow, Jr. *Middle French Proverbs, Sentences, and Proverbial Phrases.* Subsidia Mediaevalia 12. Toronto: Pontifical Institute of Mediaeval Studies, 1982.

Hawkins, Peter S. "Scripts for the Pageant: Dante and the Bible." *SLRev* 5 (1988): 75–92.

———. "Divide and Conquer: Augustine in the *Divine Comedy*." *PMLA* 106 (1991): 471–82.

Heffernan, Thomas J., ed. *The Popular Literature of Medieval England.* Tennessee Studies in Literature 28. Knoxville: U of Tennessee P, 1985.

Helmholz, R[ichard]. H. *Marriage Litigation in Medieval England.* Cambridge Studies in English Legal History. Cambridge: Cambridge UP, 1974. Rpt. Holmes Beach, Fla.: Gaunt, 1986.

Henderson, George. *From Durrow to Kells: The Insular Gospel Books, 650–800.* London: Thames and Hudson, 1987.

Henkin, Leo J. "Jacob and the Hooly Jew." *MLN* 55 (1940): 254–59.

Hermann, John P., and John J. Burke, eds. *Signs and Symbols in Chaucer's Poetry.* Tuscaloosa: U of Alabama P, 1981.

Hilary, Christine Ryan. Explanatory Notes to the *Wife of Bath's Prologue and Tale.* In *Riverside Chaucer* (1987), pp. 864–74.

———. Explanatory Notes to the *Pardoner's Introduction, Prologue, and Tale.* In *Riverside Chaucer* (1987), pp. 904–10.

Hill, John M. *Chaucerian Belief: The Poetics of Reverence and Delight.* New Haven, Conn.: Yale UP, 1991.

Hoagwood, Terence Allan. "Artifice and Redemption: Figuration and Failure of Reference in Chaucer's *The Book of the Duchess*." *StM* 11 (1988): 57–68.

Hollander, Robert. *Allegory in Dante's "Commedia."* Princeton, N.J.: Princeton UP, 1969.

———. "Dante *Theologus-Poeta*." *Dante Studies* 94 (1976): 91–136.

———. *Dante's Epistle to Cangrande.* Recentiores: Later Latin Texts and Contexts. Ann Arbor: U of Michigan P, 1993.

Howard, Donald R. *The Three Temptations: Medieval Man in Search of the World.* Princeton, N.J.: Princeton UP, 1966.

———. *The Idea of the "Canterbury Tales."* Berkeley and Los Angeles: U of California P, 1976.

Hudson, Anne. "A Lollard Sect Vocabulary?" In *So Meny People, Langages, and Tonges: Philological Essays in Scots and Mediaeval English Presented to Angus McIntosh,* ed. M. L. Samuels and Michael Benskin, pp. 15–30. Edinburgh, 1981. Rpt. in Hudson, *Lollards and Their Books* , pp. 165–80.

———. "Lollardy: The English Heresy?" *SCH* 18 (1982): 261–83. Rpt. in Hudson, *Lollards and Their Books,* pp. 141–63.

———. *Lollards and their Books.* London: Hambledon P, 1985.

———. "Wyclif and the English Language." In Kenny, ed., 1986, pp. 85–103.

———. *The Premature Reformation: Wycliffite Texts and Lollard History.* Oxford: Clarendon, 1988.

———. "Aspects of Biblical Translation in the English [Wycliffite Sermon] Cycle." In Hudson, ed. *English Wycliffite Sermons* 3:lxix–xcviii.

Hudson, Anne, and Michael Wilks, eds. *From Ockham to Wyclif. SCH, Subsidia* 5. Oxford: Blackwell (for the Ecclesiastical History Society), 1987.

Hughes, Andrew. *Medieval Manuscripts for Mass and Office: A Guide to Their Organization and Terminology.* Toronto: U of Toronto P, 1982.

Huppé, Bernard F. *Doctrine and Poetry: Augustine's Influence on Old English Poetry.* Albany: State U of New York P, 1959.

———. *A Reading of the "Canterbury Tales."* 1964. Rev. ed. Albany: State U of New York P, 1967.

Huppé, Bernard F., and D. W. Robertson, Jr. *Fruyt and Chaf: Studies in Chaucer's Allegories.* Princeton, N.J.: Princeton UP, 1963.

Hurley, Michael. "'*Scriptura Sola*': Wyclif and His Critics." *Traditio* 16 (1960): 275–352.

Irvine, Martin. "Medieval Grammatical Theory and Chaucer's *House of Fame.*" *Speculum* 60 (1985): 850–76.

———. *The Making of Textual Culture: "Grammatica" and Literary Theory, 350–1100.* Cambridge Studies in Medieval Literature 19. Cambridge: Cambridge UP, 1994.

Jambeck, Thomas J. "The Dramatic Implications of Anselmian Affective Piety in the *Towneley Play of the Crucifixion.*" *AnM* 16 (1975): 110–27.

Jefferson, Bernard L. *Chaucer and the Consolation of Philosophy of Boethius.* Princeton, N.J.: Princeton UP, 1917. Rpt. New York: Haskell House, 1965.

Jeffrey, David Lyle. "Introduction." In Jeffrey, ed., 1984, pp. xiii–xvi.

———. "Chaucer and Wyclif: Biblical Hermeneutic and Literary Theory in the XIVth Century." In Jeffrey, ed., 1984, pp. 109–40.

———. "Sacred and Secular Scripture: Authority and Interpretation in *The House of Fame.*" In Jeffrey, ed., 1984, pp. 207–28.

———, ed. *Chaucer and Scriptural Tradition.* Special issue of *Revue de l'Université d'Ottawa* 54 (1983). Rev. ed. Ottawa: U of Ottawa P, 1984.

———, gen. ed. *A Dictionary of Biblical Tradition in English Literature.* Grand Rapids, Mich.: Eerdmans, 1992.

Jennings, Margaret. "The Art of the Pseudo-Origin Homily: *De Maria Magdalena.*" *M&H*, n.s., 5 (1974): 139–52.

Johnson, Dudley R. "Chaucer and the Bible." Ph.D. diss. Yale U, 1941.

———. "The Biblical Characters of Chaucer's Monk." *PMLA* 66 (1951): 827–43.

Johnson, Lynn Staley. "Inverse Counsel: Contexts for the *Melibee.*" *SP* 87 (1990): 137–55.

Jordan, Mark D., and Kent Emery, Jr., eds. *Ad Litteram: Authoritative Texts and Their Medieval Readers.* Notre Dame Conferences in Medieval Studies 3. Notre Dame, Ind.: U of Notre Dame P, 1992.

Justice, Steven. *Writing and Rebellion: England in 1381.* Berkeley and Los Angeles: U of California P, 1994.

———. Review of Barbara Hanawalt, ed., *Chaucer's England: Literature in Historical Context. Speculum* 69 (1994): 790–92.

Kaske, R[obert]. E. "Patristic Exegesis in the Criticism of Medieval Literature: The Defense." In Bethurum, ed., 1960, pp. 27–60.

———. "The *Canticum Canticorum* in the *Miller's Tale.*" *SP* 59 (1962): 479–500.

———. "Chaucer and Medieval Allegory." *ELH* 30 (1963): 175–92.

———. "Chaucer's Marriage Group." In Mitchell and Provost, eds., 1973, pp. 45–65.

———. "*Clericus Adam* and Chaucer's *Adam Scriveyn.* " In Vasta and Thundy, eds., 1979, pp. 114–18.

———, in collaboration with Arthur Groos and Michael W. Twomey. *Medieval Christian Literary Imagery: A Guide to Interpretation.* Toronto Medieval Bibliographies 11. Toronto: U of Toronto P, Centre for Medieval Studies, 1988.

Kean, P[atricia]. M. *Chaucer and the Making of English Poetry*. 2 vols. London: RKP, 1972.

Keenan, Hugh T., ed. *Typology and English Medieval Literature*. Georgia State Literary Studies 7. New York: AMS, 1992.

Keiser, George R. "The Middle English *Planctus Mariae* and the Rhetoric of Pathos." In Heffernan, ed., 1985, pp. 167–93.

Kellogg, Alfred L. "St. Augustine and the 'Parson's Tale.'" *Traditio* 8 (1952): 424–30. Rpt. in Kellogg, 1972, pp. 343–52.

————, "'Seith Moses by the Devel': A Problem in Chaucer's *Parson's Tale*." *RBPH* 31 (1953): 61–64. Rpt. in Kellogg, 1972, pp. 339–42.

————. "Susannah and the 'Merchant's Tale.'" *Speculum* 35 (1960): 275–79. Rpt. in Kellogg, 1972, pp. 330–38.

————. *Chaucer, Langland, Arthur: Essays in Middle English Literature*. New Brunswick, N.J.: Rutgers UP, 1972.

Kelly, L[ouis]. G. "Linguistics and Translation in Saint Augustine." *Bible Translator* 24 (1973): 134–39.

————. *The True Interpreter: A History of Translation Theory and Practice in the West*. Oxford: Blackwell, 1979.

Kenny, Anthony, ed. *Wyclif in His Times*. Oxford: Oxford UP, 1986.

Kernan, Anne. "The Archwife and the Eunuch." *ELH* 41 (1974): 1–25.

Kessler, Herbert L. *The Illustrated Bibles from Tours*. Studies in Manuscript Illumination 7. Princeton, N.J.: Princeton UP, 1977.

Kieckhefer, Richard. *Unquiet Souls: Fourteenth-Century Saints and Their Religious Milieu*. Chicago: U of Chicago P, 1984.

King, R. W. "A Note on 'Sir Gawayn and the Green Knight,' 2414ff." *MLR* 29 (1934): 435–36.

Kiser, Lisa J. *Truth and Textuality in Chaucer's Poetry*. Hanover, N.H.: UP of New England, 1991.

Kittredge, G[eorge]. L[yman]. "Chaucer's Discussion of Marriage." *MP* 9 (1911–12): 435–67. Rpt. in Schoeck and Taylor, eds., 1960, pp. 130–59.

Klaeber, Frederick. "Traces of the *Canticum* and of Boethius' 'De Consolatione Philosophiae' in Chaucer's 'Book of the Duchesse.'" *MLN* 12 (1897): 189–90.

Kleinhenz, Christopher. "Dante and the Bible: Intertextual Approaches to the *Divine Comedy*." *Italica* 63 (1986): 225–36.

Knapp, Peggy. *Chaucer and the Social Contest*. London: Routledge, 1990.

Kolve, V. A. *The Play Called Corpus Christi*. Stanford, Calif.: Stanford UP, 1966.

———. "From Cleopatra to Alceste: An Iconographic Study of the *Legend of Good Women.*" In Hermann and Burke, eds., 1981, pp. 130–78.

———. *Chaucer and the Imagery of Narrative: The First Five Canterbury Tales.* Berkeley and Los Angeles: U of California P, 1984.

Koonce, Benjamin G. *Chaucer and the Tradition of Fame: Symbolism in the House of Fame.* Princeton, N.J.: Princeton UP, 1966.

Köppel, Emil. "Chaucer und Innocenz des Dritten Traktat *De Contemptu Mundi sive De Miseria Conditionis Humanae.*" *Archiv* 84 (1890): 405–18.

———. "Chaucer und Albertanus Brixiensis." *Archiv* 86 (1891): 29–46.

———. "Über das Verhältnis von Chaucers Prosawerken zu seinen dichtungen und die Echtheit der 'Parson's Tale.'" *Archiv* 87 (1891): 33–54.

Kuczynski, Michael P. *Prophetic Song: The Psalms as Moral Discourse in Late Medieval England.* Middle Ages Series. Philadelphia: U of Pennsylvania P, 1995.

Kugel, James. *In Potiphar's House: The Interpretive Life of Biblical Texts.* New York: Harper Collins, 1990.

Lamb, J. A. "The Place of the Bible in the Liturgy." In *Cambridge History of the Bible* 1:563–86.

Landrum, Grace. "Chaucer's Use of the Vulgate." Ph.D. diss. Radcliffe College, 1921.

———. "Chaucer's Use of the Vulgate." *PMLA* 39 (1924): 75–100.

Lawler, Traugott. *The One and the Many in the Canterbury Tales.* Hamden, Conn.: Shoe String P, Archon, 1980.

———. "Chaucer." In A. S. G. Edwards, ed., 1984, pp. 291–313.

Lawlor, John. "The Pattern of Consolation in *The Book of the Duchess.*" *Speculum* 31 (1956): 626–48. Rpt. in Schoeck and Taylor, eds., 1961, pp. 232–60.

Lazarus, Alan J. "Venus in the 'north-north-west'? (Chaucer's *Parliament of Fowls,* 117)." In Benson and Wenzel, eds., 1982, pp. 145–49.

Leclercq, Jean. *Monks and Love in Twelfth-Century France: Psycho-Historical Essays.* Oxford: Oxford UP, 1979.

Leicester, H. Marshall, Jr. *The Disenchanted Self: Representing the Subject in the "Canterbury Tales."* Berkeley and Los Angeles: U of California P, 1990.

———. "Piety and Resistance: A Note on the Representation of Religious Feeling in the *Canterbury Tales.*" In *The Endless Knot: Essays* on *Old and Middle English in Honor of Marie Boroff*, ed. M. Teresa Tavormina and R. F. Yeager. Cambridge, Eng.: D. S. Brewer, 1995, pp. 151–60.

Le Roy Ladurie, Emmanuel. *Montaillou: The Promised Land of Error.* 1975. Trans. Barbara Bray. 1978. New York: Random House, Vintage Books, 1979.

Levi, Primo. *Survival in Auschwitz: The Nazi Assault on Humanity* [*Se questo è un uomo*]. 1958. Trans. Stuart Woolf. New York: Macmillan, Collier Books, 1961.

Levy, Bernard S., ed. *The Bible in the Middle Ages: Its Influence on Literature and Art.* Medieval and Renaissance Texts and Studies 89. Binghamton: State U of New York P, 1992.

Levy, Bernard S., and George R. Adams. "Chauntecleer's Paradise Lost and Regained." *MS* 29 (1967): 178–92.

Lewis, Charlton T., and Charles Short. *A Latin Dictionary, Founded on Andrews' Edition of Freund's Latin Dictionary, Revised, Enlarged, and in Great Part Rewritten.* Oxford: Clarendon, 1879, 1962.

Lewis, C. S. *Reflections on the Psalms.* London: Collins-Fontana, 1958, 1969.

Lewis, N. B. "The Anniversary Service for Blanche, Duchess of Lancaster, 12th September, 1374." *BJRL* 21 (1937): 176–94.

Lewis, Robert E. "Chaucer's Artistic Use of Pope Innocent III's *De Miseria Humanae Conditionis* in the *Man of Law's Prologue* and *Tale.*" *PMLA* 81 (1966): 485–92.

———. "Glosses to the *Man of Law's Tale* from Pope Innocent III's *De Miseria Humane Conditionis.*" *SP* 64 (1976): 1–16.

Light, Laura. "Versions et révisions du texte biblique." In Riché and Lobrichon, eds., 1984, pp. 55–93.

———. "The New Thirteenth-Century Bible and the Challenge of Heresy." *Viator* 18 (1987): 275–88.

———. *The Bible in the Twelfth Century: An Exhibition of Manuscripts at the Houghton Library.* Cambridge, Mass.: Harvard College Library, 1988.

———. "French Bibles, c. 1200–30: A New Look at the Origin of the Paris Bible." In Gameson, ed., 1994, pp. 155–76.

Lobrichon, Guy. "Une nouveauté: les gloses de la Bible." In Riché and Lobrichon, eds., 1984, pp. 95–114.

Loewe, Raphael. "The Medieval History of the Latin Vulgate." In *The Cambridge History of the Bible* 2:102–54.

Lourdaux, W., and D. Verhelst, eds. *The Bible and Medieval Culture.* Mediaevalia Lovaniensia, series I, studia VII. Louvain: Louvain UP, 1979.

Lubac, Henri de. *Exégèse médiévale: Les quatre sens de l'écriture.* 2 parts in 4 vols. Études Publiées sous la Direction de la Faculté de Théologie S. J. de Lyon-Fourvière, vols. 41 (première partie, vols. 1 and 2), 42 (seconde partie, vol. 3), 59 (seconde partie, vol. 4). Paris: Aubier, 1959, 1959, 1961, 1964.

McCall, John P. "Chaucer and the Pseudo Origen *De Maria Magdalena:* A Preliminary Study." *Speculum* 46 (1971): 491–509.

Machan, Tim William. *Techniques of Translation: Chaucer's "Boece."* Norman, Okla.: Pilgrim Books, 1985.

McClellan, William. "Bakhtin's Theory of Dialogic Discourse, Medieval Rhetorical Theory, and the Multi-Voiced Structure of the *Clerk's Tale*." *Exemplaria* 1 (1989): 462–88.

———. "Lars Engle, 'Chaucer, Bakhtin, and Griselda': A Response." *Exemplaria* 1 (1989): 499–506.

McGerr, Rosemarie Potz. "Guyart Desmoulins, the Vernacular Master of Histories, and His *Bible Historiale*." *Viator* 14 (1983): 211–44.

McGurk, Patrick. "The Oldest Manuscripts of the Latin Bible." In Gameson, ed., 1994, pp. 1–23.

McKeon, Richard. "Rhetoric in the Middle Ages." *Speculum* 17 (1942): 1–32.

McKisack, May. *The Fourteenth Century, 1307–1399.* Vol. 5 of *The Oxford History of England.* Oxford: Clarendon, 1959.

McKitterick, Rosamond. "Carolingian Bible Production: The Tours Anomaly." In Gameson, ed., 1994, pp. 63–77.

McSheffrey, Shannon. "Literacy and the Gender Gap in the Late Middle Ages: Women and Reading in Lollard Communities." In Smith and Taylor, eds., 1995, pp. 157–70.

Magoun, Francis P., Jr. and Tauno F. Mustanoja. "Chaucer's Chimera: His Proto-Surrealist Portrait of Fame." *Speculum* 50 (1975): 48–54.

Makarewicz, Mary R. *The Patristic Influence on Chaucer.* Washington, D.C.: Catholic U of America P, 1953.

Mann, Jill. *Geoffrey Chaucer.* Feminist Readings. Hertfordshire, Eng.: Wheatsheaf, 1991.

———. "Chaucer and Atheism." *SAC* 17 (1995): 5–19.

Marrou, Henri-Irénée. *Saint Augustin et la fin de la culture antique.* Bibliothèque des Écoles Françaises d'Athènes et de Rome 145. Paris: E. De Boccard, 1938.

Martin, Ellen E. "Chaucer's Ruth: An Exegetical Poetic in the Prologue to the *Legend of Good Women.*" *Exemplaria* 3 (1991): 467–90.

Martin, Henri-Jean, and Jean Vezin, eds. *Mise en page et mise en texte du livre manuscrit.* [Paris]: Éditions du Cercle de la Librairie-Promodis, Centre National des Lettres, 1990.

Martin, Priscilla. *Chaucer's Women: Nuns, Wives and Amazons.* London: Macmillan, 1990.

Mazzaro, Jerome. *The Figure of Dante: An Essay on the "Vita Nuova."* Princeton Essays in Literature. Princeton, N.J.: Princeton UP, 1981.

Middle English Dictionary. Ed. Hans Kurath, Sherman M. Kuhn, John Reidy, and Robert E. Lewis. Ann Arbor: U of Michigan P, 1954–.

Mill, Anna Jean. "Noah's Wife Again." *PMLA* 56 (1941): 613–26.

Miller, Clarence H., and Roberta Bux Bosse. "Chaucer's Pardoner and the Mass." *ChauR* 6 (1971–72): 171–84.

Miller, Robert P. "Chaucer's Pardoner, the Scriptural Eunuch, and the Pardoner's Tale." *Speculum* 30 (1955): 180–99. Rpt. in Schoeck and Taylor, eds., 1960, 1:221–44.

———. "Allegory in the *Canterbury Tales.*" In Rowland, ed., 1979, pp. 326–51.

———, ed. *Chaucer: Sources and Backgrounds.* Oxford: Oxford UP, 1977.

Minnis, A[lastair]. J. "'Authorial Intention' and 'Literal Sense' in the Exegetical Theories of Richard Fitzralph and John Wyclif: An Essay in the Medieval History of Biblical Hermeneutics." *Proceedings of the Royal Irish Academy* 75, section C, i (Dublin, 1975): 1–31.

———. *Chaucer and Pagan Antiquity.* Chaucer Studies 8. Woodbridge, Suffolk, Eng.: Boydell and Brewer, D. S. Brewer, 1982.

———. "Chaucer's Pardoner and the 'Office of Preacher.'" In Boitani and Torti, eds., 1985, pp. 88–119.

———. *Medieval Theory of Authorship: Scholastic Literary Attitudes in the Later Middle Ages.* 1984. 2d ed. Philadelphia: U of Pennsylvania P, 1988.

———, ed. *Latin and Vernacular: Studies in Late-Medieval Texts and Manuscripts.* Cambridge: Brewer, 1989.

Minnis, A. J., with V. J. Scattergood and J. J. Smith. *The Shorter Poems.* Oxford Guides to Chaucer. Oxford: Clarendon, 1995.

Minnis, A. J., and A. B. Scott, eds., with the assistance of David Wallace. *Medieval Literary Theory and Criticism, c. 1100–c. 1375: The Commentary Tradition.* 1988. Rev. ed. Oxford: Clarendon, 1991.

Mittellateinisches Wörterbuch bis zum Ausgehenden 13. Jahrhundert. Munich: C. H. Beck'sche Verlags Buchhandlung, 1973. Vol. 2, fascicule 5, "cirrus-cognoscibilitas."

Mommsen, Theodor E. "Petrarch's Conception of the 'Dark Ages.'" *Speculum* 17 (1942): 226–42.

Moore, Edward. "Dante and Scripture." In *Studies in Dante, First Series: Scripture and Classical Authors in Dante,* pp. 47–91. Oxford: Clarendon, 1896. Rpt. New York: Greenwood, 1968.

Morawski, Józef. *Proverbes français antérieurs au xve siècle.* Les Classiques Français du Moyen Age 47. Paris: Champion, 1925.

Moreau, Madeleine. "Lecture du 'De Doctrina Christiana.'" In *Saint Augustin et la Bible,* ed. Anne-Marie la Bonnardière, pp. 253–85. Bible de Tous les Temps 3. Paris: Beauchesne, 1986.

Morgan, Nigel. "Old Testament Illustration in Thirteenth-Century England." In Bernard S. Levy, ed., 1992, pp. 149–98.

Morris, Lynn King. *Chaucer Source and Analogue Criticism: A Cross-Referenced Guide.* Garland Reference Library of the Humanities 454. New York: Garland, 1985.

Morse, Ruth. *Truth and Convention in the Middle Ages: Rhetoric, Representation, and Reality.* Cambridge: Cambridge UP, 1991.

Muir, Lawrence. "Translations and Paraphrases of the Bible, and Commentaries." In Severs, ed., 1970, pp. 381–409 (texts), 534–52 (bibliography).

Muir, Lynette R. *The Biblical Drama of Medieval Europe.* Cambridge: Cambridge UP, 1995.

Murphy, James J. *Rhetoric in the Middle Ages: A History of Rhetorical Theory from Saint Augustine to the Renaissance.* Berkeley and Los Angeles: U of California P, 1974.

Murray, Alexander. *Reason and Society in the Middle Ages.* 1978. Rev. ed. Oxford: Clarendon, 1985.

Muscatine, Charles. *Chaucer and the French Tradition: A Study in Style and Meaning.* Berkeley and Los Angeles: U of California P, 1957, 1969.

———. Explanatory Notes to *The Parliament of Fowls.* In *Riverside Chaucer* (1987), pp. 994–1002.

Neuse, Richard. *Chaucer's Dante: Allegory and Epic Theater in "The Canterbury Tales."* Berkeley and Los Angeles: U of California P, 1991.

Nichols, Robert E., Jr. "The Pardoner's Ale and Cake." *PMLA* 82 (1967): 498–504.

Nitzsche, J. C. "Creation in Genesis and Nature in Chaucer's *General Prologue* 1–18." *PLL* 14 (1978): 459–64.

Nolan, Barbara. "The *Vita Nuova*: Dante's Book of Revelation." *Dante Studies* 88. Albany, N.Y.: Dante Society of America, 1970.

———. "Nicholas Love." In A. S. G. Edwards, ed., 1984, pp. 83–95.

———. "Chaucer's Tales of Transcendence: Rhyme Royal and Christian Prayer in the *Canterbury Tales*." In Benson and Robertson, eds., 1990, pp. 21–38.

Noll, Dolores L. "The Serpent and the Sting in the *Pardoner's Prologue* and *Tale*." *ChauR* 17 (1982–83): 159–62.

Nordenfalk, Carl. *Die Spätantiken Kanonentafeln: Kunstgeschichtliche Studien über die Eusebianische Evangelien-Konkordanz in den Vier Erstedn Jahrhunderten ihrer Geschichte.* 2 vols. Die Buchornamentik der Spätantike 1. Gothenburg: O. Isaacsons Boktryckeri, 1938.

Norton–Smith, John. *Geoffrey Chaucer.* London: Routledge and Kegan Paul, 1974.

Oberman, Heiko A. "Some Notes on the Theology of Nominalism with Attention to its Relation to the Renaissance." *Harvard Theological Review* 53 (1960): 47–76.

———. *Forerunners of the Reformation: The Shape of Late Medieval Thought.* New York: Holt, Rinehart and Winston, 1966.

———. "Fourteenth-Century Religious Thought: A Premature Profile." *Speculum* 53 (1978): 80–93.

———. *The Dawn of the Reformation: Essays in Late Medieval and Early Reformation Thought.* Edinburgh: Clark, 1986.

Ocker, Christopher. "Augustinianism in Fourteenth-Century Theology." *Augustinian Studies* 18 (1987): 81–106.

Olson, Paul A. *The "Canterbury Tales" and the Good Society.* Princeton, N.J.: Princeton UP, 1986.

Owen, Charles A., Jr. *Pilgrimage and Story-Telling in the Canterbury Tales: The Dialectic of "Ernest" and "Game."* Norman, Okla.: Pilgrim Books, 1977.

Owst, G[erald]. R[obert]. *Preaching in Medieval England: An Introduction to Sermon Manuscripts of the Period, c.1350–1450.* Cambridge

Studies in Medieval Life and Thought. Cambridge: Cambridge UP, 1926.

——. *Literature and Pulpit in Medieval England: A Neglected Chapter in the History of English Letters and of the English People.* 2d ed. Oxford: Blackweil, 1961.

Oxford English Dictionary, The. Ed. R. W. Burchfield et al. 20 vols. Oxford: Clarendon, 1986.

Pace, George B. "The Adorned Initials of Chaucer's *ABC.*" *Manuscripta* 23 (1979): 88–98.

Palomo, Dolores. "What Chaucer Really Did to *Le livre de Melibee.*" *PQ* 53 (1974): 304–20.

Panofsky, Erwin. *Renaissance and Renascences in Western Art.* Uppsala University, Gottesman Lectures 7. Stockholm: Almqvist and Wiksell, 1960.

Partridge, Stephen Bradford. "Glosses in the Manuscripts of Chaucer's 'Canterbury Tales': An Edition and Commentary." Ph.D. diss. Harvard U, 1992.

Patterson, Lee W. "The 'Parson's Tale' and the Quitting of the 'Canterbury Tales.'" *Traditio* 34 (1978): 331–80.

——. "'For the Wyves Love of Bathe': Feminine Rhetoric and Poetic Resolution in the *Roman de la Rose* and the *Canterbury Tales.*" *Speculum* 58 (1983): 656–95.

——. *Negotiating the Past: The Historical Understanding of Medieval Literature.* Madison: U of Wisconsin P, 1987.

——. "'What Man Artow?': Authorial Self–Definition in *The Tale of Sir Thopas* and *The Tale of Melibee.*" *SAC* 11 (1989): 117–75.

——. *Chaucer and the Subject of History.* Madison: U of Wisconsin P, 1991.

——. "Court Politics and the Invention of Literature: The Case of Sir John Clanvowe." In *Culture and History 1350–1600: Essays on English Communities, Identities and Writing,* ed. David Aers, pp. 7–41. New York: Harvester Wheatsheaf, 1992.

——, ed. *Literary Practice and Social Change in Britain, 1380–1530.* The New Historicism: Studies in Cultural Poetics 8. Berkeley and Los Angeles: U of California P, 1990.

Paxson, James J. "A Theory of Biblical Typology." *Exemplaria* 3 (1991): 359–83.

Pearsall, Derek. *Old English and Middle English Poetry.* Vol. 1 of *The Routledge History of English Poetry.* London: Routledge and Kegan Paul, 1977.

———. "Chaucer's Pardoner: The Death of a Salesman." *ChauR* 17 (1982–83): 358–65.

———. *The Canterbury Tales.* Unwin Critical Library. London: Allen and Unwin, 1985. Rpt. London: Routledge, 1993.

———. "Chaucer's Religious Tales: A Question of Genre." In Benson and Robertson, eds., 1990, pp. 11–19.

———. *The Life of Geoffrey Chaucer: A Critical Biography.* Oxford: Blackwell, 1992.

———, ed. *Essays in Memory of Elizabeth Salter.* Special issue of *Leeds Studies in English,* n.s. 14 (1983).

Peck, Russell A. "Biblical Interpretation: St. Paul and the *Canterbury Tales.*" In Jeffrey, ed., 1984, pp. 143–70.

———. "Chaucerian Poetics and the Prologue to the *Legend of Good Women.*" In Wasserman and Blanch, eds., 1986, pp. 39–55.

Petersen, Kate Oelzner. *The Sources of "The Parson's Tale."* Radcliffe College Monographs 12. Boston: Ginn, Atheneum P, 1901. Rpt. New York: AMS, 1973.

Petrarch. *Petrarch: The First Modern Scholar and Man of Letters.* Ed. and trans. James Harvey Robinson and Henry Winchester Rolfe. 1898. New York: Haskell House, 1968.

Pfaff, Richard W. *Medieval Latin Liturgy: A Select Bibliography.* Toronto Medieval Bibliographies 9. Toronto: U of Toronto P, 1982.

Phillips, Helen. "Chaucer and Deguileville [*sic*]: The ABC in Context." *MÆ* 62 (1993): 1–19.

Piehler, Paul. "Myth, Allegory, and Vision in the *Parlement of Foules:* A Study in Chaucerian Problem Solving." In *Allegoresis: The Craft of Allegory in Medieval Literature,* ed. J. S. Russell, pp. 187–214. New York: Garland, 1988.

Pontet, Maurice. *L'exégèse de S. Augustin prédicateur.* Études Publiées sous la Direction de la Faculté de Théologie S. J. de Lyon-Fourvière 7. Paris: Aubier, 1945.

Pratt, Robert A. "The Knight's Tale." In Bryan and Dempster, eds, 1941, 1958, pp. 82–105.

———. "Chaucer and the Hand That Fed Him." *Speculum* 41 (1966): 619–42.

————. "Chaucer's Title: 'The boke of the tales of Caunterbury.'" *PQ* 54 (1975): 19–25.

Press, Gerald A. "The Subject and Structure of Augustine's *De Doctrina Christiana.*" *Augustinian Studies* 11 (1980): 99–124.

Preus, James Samuel. *From Shadow to Promise: Old Testament Interpretation from Augustine to the Young Luther.* Cambridge, Mass: Harvard UP, 1969.

Prior, Sandra Pierson. "Parodying Typology and the Mystery Plays in the *Miller's Tale.*" *JMRS* 16 (1986): 57–73.

Raby, F. J. E. *A History of Christian-Latin Poetry from the Beginning to the Close of the Middle Ages.* 2d ed. Oxford: Clarendon, 1953.

Raymo, Robert R. "Works of Religious and Philosophical Instruction." In Hartung, ed., 1986, pp. 2255–2378 (texts), 2467–2582 (bibliography).

Réau, Louis. *Iconographie de l'art chrétien.* 6 parts in 3 vols. Paris: Presses Universitaires de France, 1955–59.

Reeves, Marjorie. "The Bible and Literary Authorship in the Middle Ages." In *Reading the Text: Biblical Criticism and Literary Theory,* ed. Stephen Prickett, pp. 12–63. Oxford: Blackwell, 1991.

Reynolds, William D. "Sources, Nature, and Influence of the *Ovidius Moralizatus* of Pierre Bersuire." In Chance, ed., 1990, pp. 83–99.

Richardson, Janette. *Blameth Nat Me: A Study of Imagery in Chaucer's Fabliaux.* The Hague: Mouton, 1970.

————. Explanatory Notes to the Friar's Portrait in the *General Prologue.* In *Riverside Chaucer* (1987), pp. 807–9.

Riché, Pierre, and Guy Lobrichon, eds. *Le moyen age et la Bible.* Bible de Tous les Temps 4. Paris: Beauchesne, 1984.

Ridley, Florence H. *The Prioress and the Critics.* University of California Publications, English Studies 30. Berkeley and Los Angeles: U of California P, 1965.

————. Explanatory Notes to the *Second Nun's Prologue* and *Tale.* In *Riverside Chaucer* (1987), pp. 942–46.

Robertson, D. W., Jr. "Historical Criticism." In *English Institute Essays, 1950,* pp. 3–31. New York: Columbia UP, 1951. Rpt. in Robertson, 1980, pp. 3–20.

————. "Some Medieval Literary Terminology, with Special Reference to Chrétien de Troyes." *SP* 48 (1951): 669–92. Rpt. in Robertson, 1980, pp. 51–72.

————. "Chaucerian Tragedy." *ELH* 19 (1952): 1–37. Rpt. in Schoeck and Taylor, eds., 1961, pp. 86–121.

————. *A Preface to Chaucer: Studies in Medieval Perspectives.* Princeton, N.J.: Princeton UP, 1962.

————. *Chaucer's London.* New York: Wiley, 1968.

————. *Essays in Medieval Culture.* Princeton, N.J.: Princeton UP, 1980.

Rogers, W. E. "Geoffrey Chaucer, 'An ABC,' ca. 1369." *Anglistica* 18 (1972): 82–106.

Rosenthal, Frank. "Heinrich von Oyta and Biblical Criticism in the Fourteenth Century." *Speculum* 25 (1950): 178–83.

Rost, Hans. *Die Bibel im Mittelalter: Beiträge zur Geschichte und Bibliographie der Bibel.* Augsburg: M. Seitz, 1939.

Rothwell, W. "Notes on the Text of *Le Laie Bible.*" *MÆ* 33 (1964): 1–20.

Rouse, Richard H., and Mary A. Rouse. "Biblical *distinctiones* in the Thirteenth Century." *AHDLMA* 41 (1974): 27–37.

————. "The Verbal Concordance to the Scriptures." *Archivum Fratrum Praedicatorum* 44 (1974): 5–30.

————. "The Development of Research Tools in the Thirteenth Century." 1976 (in French). In Rouse and Rouse, 1991, pp. 221–55.

————. *Preachers, Florilegia, and Sermons: Studies on the Manipulus Florum of Thomas of Ireland.* Studies and Texts 47. Toronto: Pontifical Institute of Mediaeval Studies, 1979.

————. "*Statim invenire:* Schools, Preachers, and New Attitudes to the Page." In *Renaissance and Renewal in the Twelfth Century,* ed. Robert L. Benson and Giles Constable, with Carol D. Lanham, pp. 201–25. Cambridge, Mass.: Harvard UP, 1982. Rpt. in Rouse and Rouse, 1991, pp. 191–219.

————. "The Book Trade at the University of Paris, ca. 1250–ca. 1350." 1988. In Rouse and Rouse, 1991, pp. 259–338.

————. *Authentic Witnesses: Approaches to Medieval Texts and Manuscripts.* Publications in Medieval Studies 17. Notre Dame, Ind.: U of Notre Dame P, 1991.

Rowe, Donald W. *Through Nature to Eternity: Chaucer's "Legend of Good Women."* Lincoln: U of Nebraska P, 1988.

Rowland, Beryl, ed. *Chaucer and Middle English Studies in Honour of Rossell Hope Robbins.* London: Allen and Unwin, 1974; Kent, Ohio: Kent State UP, 1975.

————. *Companion to Chaucer Studies.* Rev. ed. New York: Oxford UP, 1979.

Ruggiers, Paul G. "The Unity of Chaucer's *House of Fame.*" *SP* 50 (1953): 16–29. Rpt. in Schoeck and Taylor, eds., 1961, pp. 261–74.

————. "The Italian Influence on Chaucer." In Rowland, ed., 1979, pp. 160–84.

Salmon, P. B. "The Three Voices of Poetry in Mediaeval Literary Theory." *MÆ* 30 (1961): 1–18.

Salter, Elizabeth. "Medieval Poetry and the Figural View of Reality." *PBA* 54 (1968): 73–92.

————. *Nicholas Love's "Myrrour of the Blessed Lyf of Jesu Christ."* Analecta Cartusiana 10. Salzburg: Institut für Anglistik und Amerikanistik, Universität Salzburg, 1974.

Sandler, Lucy Freeman. *Gothic Manuscripts, 1285–1385.* Vol. 1. *Text and Illustration.* Vol. 2. *Catalogue.* A Survey of Manuscripts Illuminated in the British Isles 5, gen. ed. J. J. G. Alexander. London: Harvey Miller; Oxford: Oxford UP, 1986.

Scase, Wendy. *Piers Plowman and the New Anticlericalism.* Cambridge Studies in Medieval Literature 4. Cambridge: Cambridge UP, 1989.

Scattergood, V. J. "Chaucer and the French War: *Sir Thopas* and *Melibee.*" In Glyn S. Burgess, A. D. Deyermon, W. H. Jackson, A. D. Mills, and R. T. Ricketts, eds. *Court and Poet: Selected Proceedings of the Third Congress of the International Courtly Literature Society, Liverpool, 1980,* pp. 287–96. Liverpool: Cairns, 1981.

————. "Literary Culture at the Court of Richard II." In *English Court Culture in the Later Middle Ages,* ed. V. J. Scattergood and J. W. Sherborne, pp. 29–43. London: Duckworth, 1983.

Schibanoff, Susan. "The New Reader and Female Textuality in Two Early Commentaries on Chaucer." *SAC* 10 (1988): 71–108.

Schildgren, Brenda Deen. "Jerome's *Prefatory Epistles* to the Bible and *The Canterbury Tales.*" *SAC* 15 (1993): 111–30.

Schiller, Gertrud. *Iconography of Christian Art.* 2d ed. Trans. Janet Seligman. 2 vols. London: Lund Humphries, 1971–72.

Schlauch, Margaret. "The Man of Law's Tale." In Bryan and Dempster, eds., 1941, 1958, pp. 155–206.

————. "Chaucer's Prose Rhythms." *PMLA* 65 (1950): 568–89.

————. "The Art of Chaucer's Prose." In Brewer, ed., 1966, pp. 140–63.

Schless, Howard. *Chaucer and Dante: A Revaluation.* Norman, Okla.: Pilgrim Books, 1984.

Schoeck, Richard J., and Jerome Taylor, eds. *Chaucer Criticism.* Vol. 1. *The Canterbury Tales.* Vol. 2. *Troilus and Criseyde and the Minor Poems.* Notre Dame, Ind.: U of Notre Dame P, 1960, 1961.

Schwarz, W. "The Meaning of *Fidus Interpres* in Medieval Translation." *Journal of Theological Studies* 45 (1944): 73–78.

Severs, J. Burke. "The Tale of Melibeus." In Bryan and Dempster, eds., 1941, 1958, pp. 560–614.

————, ed. *A Manual of the Writings in Middle English, 1050–1500.* Vol. II. Hamden, Conn.: Shoe String P, Archon (for the Connecticut Academy of Arts and Sciences), 1970.

Shailor, Barbara A. *The Medieval Book: Illustrated from the Beinecke Rare Book and Manuscript Library.* 1988. Medieval Academy Reprints for Teaching 28. Toronto: U of Toronto P, Medieval Academy of America, 1991.

Shaner, M. C. E., and A. S. G. Edwards. Explanatory Notes to *The Legend of Good Women.* In *Riverside Chaucer* (1987), pp. 1059–75.

Shaw, Judith. "Corporeal and Spiritual Homicide, the Sin of Wrath, and the Parson's Tale." *Traditio* 38 (1982): 281–300.

Sheerin, Daniel J. "*Sonus* and *Verba*: Varieties of Meaning in the Liturgical Proclamation of the Gospel in the Middle Ages." In Jordan and Emery, eds., 1992, pp. 29–69.

Shoaf, R. A. "Notes towards Chaucer's Poetics of Translation." *SAC* 1 (1979): 55–66.

Shook, Laurence K. "The House of Fame." In Rowland, ed., 1979, pp. 414–27.

Silvia, Daniel S., Jr. "Glosses to the *Canterbury Tales* from St. Jerome's *Epistola adversus Jovinianum.*" *SP* 62 (1965): 28–39.

Singleton, Charles S. "Dante's Allegory." *Speculum* 25 (1950): 78–83.

————. "The Irreducible Dove." *CL* 9 (1957): 129–35.

Smalley, Beryl. *English Friars and Antiquity in the Early Fourteenth Century.* Oxford: Blackwell, 1960.

————. "Problems of Exegesis in the Fourteenth Century." In *Antike und Orient im Mittelalter,* ed. Paul Wilpert. pp. 266–77. Kölner Mediaevistentagung, Miscellanea Mediaevalia 1. Berlin: de Gruyter, 1962.

————. "The Bible in the Medieval Schools." In *Cambridge History of the Bible* 2:197–220.

———. *The Study of the Bible in the Middle Ages.* 3d ed. Oxford: Blackwell, 1983.

Smith, Lesley. "The Theology of the Twelfth- and Thirteenth-Century Bible." In Gameson, ed., 1994, pp. 223–32.

Smith, Lesley, and Jane H. M. Taylor, eds. *Women, the Book and the Godly: Selected Proceedings of the St. Hilda's Conference, 1993.* Vol. 1. Woodbridge, Suffolk, Eng., and Rochester, N. Y.: Boydell and Brewer, D. S. Brewer, 1995.

Smith, Paul Martin. "An Edition of Parts I–V of the Wycliffite Translation of Clement of Llanthony's Latin Gospel Harmony *Unum ex Quattuor,* known as Oon of Foure." Ph.D. diss. U of Southampton, 1984.

Southern, R. W. "Medieval Humanism." In *Medieval Humanism,* pp. 29–60. New York: Harper and Row, Harper Torchbook, 1970.

Spearing, A. C. "Literal and Figurative in *The Book of the Duchess.*" *SAC Proceedings* 1 (1984): 165–71. Rev. ed. in Spearing, 1987, pp. 94–106.

———. *Medieval to Renaissance in English Poetry.* Cambridge: Cambridge UP, 1985.

———. *Readings in Medieval Poetry.* Cambridge: Cambridge UP, 1987.

Spencer, H. Leith. *English Preaching in the Late Middle Ages.* Oxford: Clarendon, 1993.

Steadman, John M. "Chaucer's Eagle: A Contemplative Symbol." *PMLA* 75 (1960): 153–59.

Stegmüller, Frederick. *Repertorium biblicum medii aevii.* 11 vols. *Supplementum,* vols. 8–11, compiled with the assistance of N. Reinhardt. Madrid: Instituto Francisco Suárez, 1950–80.

Stevens, Martin. *Four Middle English Mystery Cycles: Textual, Contextual, and Critical Interpretations.* Princeton, N.J.: Princeton UP, 1987.

Sticca, Sandro. *The "Planctus Mariae" in the Dramatic Tradition of the Middle Ages.* Trans. Joseph R. Berrigan. Athens: U of Georgia P, 1988.

Stillwell, Gardiner. "The Political Meaning of Chaucer's *Tale of Melibee.*" *Speculum* 19 (1944): 433–44.

Strohm, Paul. "The Social and Literary Scene in England." In Boitani and Mann, eds., 1986, pp. 1–18.

———. *Social Chaucer.* Cambridge, Mass.: Harvard UP, 1989.

———. *Hochon's Arrow: The Social Imagination of Fourteenth-Century Texts.* Princeton, N.J.: Princeton UP, 1992.

Stugrin, Michael. "Ricardian Poetics and Late Medieval Cultural Pluriformity: The Significance of Pathos in the *Canterbury Tales*." *ChauR* 15 (1980–81): 155–67.

Sutherland, L. S., and M. McKisack, eds. *Fourteenth Century Studies by M. V. Clarke*. Oxford: Clarendon, 1937, 1968.

Szittya, Penn R. *The Antifraternal Tradition in Medieval Literature*. Princeton, N.J.: Princeton UP, 1986.

Talbert, Ernest W., and S. Harrison Thomson. "Wyclyf and His Followers." In Severs, ed., 1970, pp. 354–80 (texts), 517–33 (bibliography).

Tatlock, John S. P., and Arthur G. Kennedy. *A Concordance to the Complete Works of Geoffrey Chaucer and to the Romaunt of the Rose*. 1927. Gloucester, Mass.: Peter Smith, 1963.

Tavormina, M. Teresa. Explanatory Notes to the *Merchant's Prologue* and *Tale*. In *Riverside Chaucer* (1987), pp. 884–890.

Taylor, Paul Beekman. "Chaucer's *Cosyn to the Dede*." *Speculum* 57 (1982): 315–27.

———. "The Alchemy of Spring in Chaucer's *General Prologue*." *ChauR* 17 (1982–83): 1–4.

Taylor, Karla. *Chaucer Reads "The Divine Comedy."* Stanford, Calif.: Stanford UP, 1989.

Thompson W. Meredith. "Chaucer's Translation of the Bible." In Davis and Wrenn, eds., 1962, pp. 183–99.

Thomson, J. A. F. *The Later Lollards, 1414–1520*. 1965. London: Oxford UP, 1967.

Thundy, Zacharias P. "Matheolus, Chaucer, and the Wife of Bath." In Vasta and Thundy, eds., 1979, pp. 24–58.

Tilley, Morris Palmer. *A Dictionary of the Proverbs in England in the Sixteenth and Seventeenth Centuries: A Collection of the Proverbs Found in English Literature and Dictionaries of the Period*. Ann Arbor: U of Michigan P, 1950.

Tillyard, E. M. W. *Poetry Direct and Oblique*. 1934. Rev. ed. 1945. Westport, Conn.: Greenwood, 1977.

Took, J. F. *Dante: Lyric Poet and Philosopher: An Introduction to the Minor Works*. Oxford: Clarendon, 1990.

Toubert, Hélène. "Les bibles moralisées." In Martin and Vezin, eds., 1990, pp. 408–11.

Tout, T. F. "Learning and Literature in the English Civil Service in the Fourteenth Century." *Speculum* 4 (1929): 365–89.

Travis, Peter W. "Chaucer's Trivial Fox Chase and the Peasants' Revolt of 1381." *JMRS* 18 (1988): 195–220.

––––––. "Deconstructing Chaucer's Retraction." *Exemplaria* 3 (1991): 135–58.

Trinkaus, Charles and Heiko Oberman, eds. *The Pursuit of Holiness in Late Medieval and Renaissance Religion.* Leiden: Brill, 1974.

Trotter, D. A. "The Influence of Bible Commentaries on Old French Bible Translations." *MÆ* 56 (1987): 257–75.

Tydeman, William. *The Theatre in the Middle Ages: Western European Stage Conditions, c.800–1576.* Cambridge: Cambridge UP, 1978, 1988.

Ullmann, Walter. "The Bible and Principles of Government in the Middle Ages." In Barblan, ed., 1962, pp. 181–227.

Vaughan, M. F. "Chaucer's Imaginative One-Day Flood." *PQ* 60 (1981): 117–23.

Vasta, Edward, and Zacharias P. Thundy, eds. *Chaucerian Problems and Perspectives: Essays Presented to Paul E. Beichner, C.S.C.* Notre Dame, Ind.: U of Notre Dame P, 1979.

Vernet, André, and Anne-Marie Genevois, eds. *La Bible au moyen age.* Paris: Éditions du C.N.R.S., 1989.

Vigoroux, F. G. "Glose." In *Dictionnaire de la Bible,* ed. F. G. Vigouroux and Louis Pirot, vol. 3, part 1 (1903), pp. 252–58. Paris: Letouzey, 1895–1912.

Vogels, Heinrich Jospeh. *St. Augustinus Schrift De consensu evangelistarum unter vornehmlicher Berücksichtigung ihrer Harmonistischen Anschauungen: Eine Biblische-Patristische Studie.* Biblische Studien 13/5. Freiburg im Breisgau: Herdersche Verlagshandlung, 1908.

Volk-Birke, Sabine. *Chaucer and Medieval Preaching: Rhetoric for Listeners in Sermons and Poetry.* ScriptOralia 34. Tübingen: Gunter Narr, 1991.

Wallace, David. *Chaucer and the Early Writings of Boccaccio.* Chaucer Studies 12. Woodbridge, Suffolk, Eng.: Boydell and Brewer, D. S. Brewer, 1985.

––––––. "'Whan She Translated Was': A Chaucerian Critique of the Petrarchan Academy." In Patterson, ed., 1990, pp. 156–215.

Walsh, Katherine, and Diana Wood, eds. *The Bible in the Medieval World: Essays in Memory of Beryl Smalley.* SCH, Subsidia 4. Oxford: Blackwell, 1985.

Walther, Hans, and Gerhardt Schmidt. *Proverbia sententiaeque latinitatis medii aevi: Lateinisch Sprichwörter und Sentenzen des Mittelalters in alphabetischer Anordnung.* 9 vols (vols. 7–9, ed. Schmidt). Carmina Medii Aevi Posterioris Latina II/5. Göttingen: Vandershoeck and Ruprecht, 1963–86.

Wasserman, Julian N., and Robert J. Blanch, eds. *Chaucer in the Eighties.* Syracuse, N.Y.: Syracuse UP, 1986

Wentersdorf, Karl P. "Theme and Structure in the *Merchant's Tale*: The Function of the Pluto Episode." *PMLA* 80 (1965): 522–27.

Wenzel, Siegfried. "The Source of Chaucer's Seven Deadly Sins." *Traditio* 30 (1974): 351–78.

———. "Chaucer and the Language of Contemporary Preaching." *SP* 73 (1976): 138–61.

———. "Notes on *The Parson's Tale.*" *ChauR* 16 (1981–82): 237–56.

———. Explanatory Notes to the *Parson's Tale.* In *Riverside Chaucer* (1987), pp. 954–65.

Wetherbee, Winthrop. "Constance and the World in Chaucer and Gower." In Yeager, ed., 1989, pp. 65–93.

White, Allon. *The Uses of Obscurity: The Fiction of Early Modernism.* London: Routledge and Kegan Paul, 1981.

Whiting, B[artlett]. J[ere]. "The Wife of Bath's Prologue." In Bryan and Dempster, eds., 1941, 1958, pp. 207–22.

Whiting, B. J., and Helen Wescott Whiting. *Proverbs, Sentences, and Proverbial Phrases, from English Writings Mainly before 1500.* Cambridge, Mass.: Harvard UP, 1968.

Whitlark, James S. "Chaucer and the Pagan Gods." *AnM* 18 (1977): 65–75.

Whitman, F. H. "Exegesis and Chaucer's Dream Visions." *ChauR* 3 (1969): 229–38.

Wilcockson, Colin. Introduction and Explanatory Notes to *The Book of the Duchess.* In *Riverside Chaucer* (1987), pp. 329–30, 966–76.

Wimsatt, James [I.] "The Apotheosis of Blanche in the *Book of the Duchess.*" *JEGP* 66 (1967): 26–44.

———. *Chaucer and the French Love Poets: The Literary Background of the "Book of the Duchess."* University of North Carolina Studies in Comparative Literature 43. Chapel Hill: U of North Carolina P, 1968.

———. "Chaucer and the Canticle of Canticles." In Mitchell and Provost, eds., 1973, pp. 66–90.

———. "*The Book of the Duchess*: Secular Elegy or Religious Vision?" In Hermann and Burke, eds., 1981, pp. 113–29.

Winnick, R. H. "Luke 12 and Chaucer's *Shipman's Tale.*" *ChauR* 30 (1995): 164–90.

Wood, Chauncey. *Chaucer and the Country of the Stars.* Princeton, N.J.: Princeton UP, 1970.

———. *The Elements of Chaucer's "Troilus."* Durham, N.C.: Duke UP, 1984.

Woolf, Rosemary. *The English Religious Lyric in the Middle Ages.* Oxford: Clarendon, 1968.

———. *The English Mystery Plays.* Berkeley and Los Angeles: U of California P, 1972.

———. "English Imitations of the *Homelia Origenis de Maria Magdalena.*" In Rowland, ed., 1974, 1975, pp. 384–91.

Wormald, Francis. "Bible Illustration in Medieval Manuscripts." In *Cambridge History of the Bible* 2:309–37.

———. *An Early Breton Gospel Book: A Ninth-Century Manuscript from the Collection of H. L. Bradfer-Lawrence, 1887–1965.* Ed. Jonathan Alexander. Cambridge: Roxburghe Club, 1977.

Wurtele, Douglas J. "The Predicament of Chaucer's Wife of Bath: St. Jerome on Virginity." *Florilegium* 5 (1983): 208–36.

———. "Chaucer's *Canterbury Tales* and Nicholas of Lyre's *Postillae litteralis et moralis super totam Bibliam.*" In Jeffrey, ed., 1984, pp. 89–107.

———. "The Anti-Lollardry of Chaucer's Parson." *Mediaevalia* 11 (1989, for 1985): 151–68.

Yeager, Robert F., ed. *John Gower: Recent Readings.* Studies in Medieval Culture 26. Kalamazoo: Western Michigan U, Medieval Institute, 1989.

Zink, Michel. "The Allegorical Poem as Interior Memoir." *YFS* 70 (1986): 100–126.

Index

Book of the Duchess, 33–34, 165–68, 174, 175, 207
Boren, James, 38
Burning bush story, 161

Cahn, Walter, 9
Caie, Graham D., 146
Cana, marriage feast at, 150
Canon's Yeoman's Tale, 35–36
Canterbury Tales, 10, 12, 148, 203, 204; General Prologue, 31, 40, 45–48, 58, 74, 100, 117, 161, 193; glosses of, 145, 146; linking of, to Bible, 205–207; Retraction, 40, 57–59, 193; structural connection to Bible, 192–93
Canticles (Song of Songs), 114, 123, 136, 137, 167, 177
Capellanus, Andreas, 133, 176
Cecilia, Saint, 62–63, 162
Celtic translation of the Gospels, 29
Charity, 41, 44, 180
Chastity, 106–108
Chaucer, Geoffrey: Bible, familiarity with, 195–96; Bibles and reference tools owned and used by, 12, 15, 198; as Father of English language, of English poetry, and of English prose, 201–202; glossing, distrust of, 156; major European writers, familiarity with, 17; modern criticism of, 198–200, 205–207, 209; pathos in poetry of, 24–25; and the Reformation, 6–7, 205
Christ, diction of, 46–49
Cleanness, 21
Clement of Llanthony, 12
Clerk's Tale, 15, 18, 25, 34, 116–17
Colloquialisms, 61–62, 65
Colossians, Epistle to the, 62, 74
Comestor, Peter, 105
Concordances, 8, 11, 12, 13
Corinthians, First Epistle to the, 62, 106–10, 154, 165, 188, 189
Corinthians, Second Epistle to the, 80, 140, 155, 173
Crane, Susan, 200
Creation story, 61–62, 186
Crucifixion (Towneley play), 22
Cupidity, 41, 43
Cursor mundi, 20, 21

Daniel, Book of, 63, 64, 65
Dante Alighieri, 16, 17–18, 46, 165, 169, 172, 173, 174
David, Alfred, 112
Death, 84, 86, 165–68, 188–91
De coniuge non ducenda, 133
Deguilleville, Guillaume, 73
De Maria Magdalena, 75, 76
Deuteronomy, 88, 89, 93, 176
Devotional literature, 23–24, 99, 197, 198
Distinctiones, 8, 12, 13, 76
Doublets, 81–82
Dronke, Peter, 175
Dryden, John, 206

Ecclesiastes, 30, 37, 82, 115, 125, 126, 128–35, 137, 156, 182, 185
Ecclesiasticus (Ben Sira; Sirach), 30, 72, 77, 78, 79, 82, 115, 116, 121, 124, 126, 127, 128, 172, 183, 190
Elijah, 122, 172
Ellesmere manuscript, 118, 145–46
English Bibles, 8, 196, 202–203; authority of, 201
English language, Chaucer's use of, 201–202
Enoch, 172
Ephesians, Epistle to the, 62, 121, 163
Esther, 34, 120–23, 167
"Eusebian Canons," 9
Exodus, 88, 89, 95, 96, 176, 192
Ezechiel, 169–70, 174

Fabula, 49
Fall, the, 84–87, 117, 125, 186
False Seeming, 30–32
Feminism, 112–13, 199, 200. See also Antifeminism
Ferster, Judith, 199
Figura, 6, 160–65, 187
Figural interpretation and texturing, 6, 19, 33, 41–42, 48, 53, 137, 138, 139, 160–64, 193; in Book of the Duchess, 165–68; in House of Fame, 168–74; in Legend of Good Women, 178–79; in Nun's Priest's Tale, 185–87; in Pardoner's Tale, 187–92; in Parliament of Fowls, 174–78
Fleming, John, 191–92
Flood, the, 88, 114–15